FIGHT YOUR TICKET

FOURTH EDITION

BY ATTORNEY DAVID W. BROWN

PLEASE READ THIS

IMPORTANT

Nolo Press is committed to keeping its books up-to-date. Each new printing, whether or not it is called a new edition, has been revised to reflect the latest law changes. This book was printed and updated on the last date indicated below. Before you rely on information in it, you might wish to call Nolo Press (415) 549-1976 to check whether a later printing or edition has been issued.

PRINTING HISTORY

New **Printing** means there have been some minor changes, but usually not enough so that people will need to trade in or discard an earlier printing of the same edition. Obviously, this is a judgment call and any change, no matter how minor, might affect you. New **Edition** means one or more major, or a number of minor, law changes since the previous edition.

First Edition	March 1982
Second Printing	January 1983
Second Edition	June 1984
Second Printing	May 1985
Third Printing	May 1986
Third Edition	September 1987
Second Printing	November 1988
Fourth Edition	April 1991
Production	Stephanie Harolde
	Terri Hearsh
Cover Design	Terri Hearsh
	Toni Ihara
Index	Sayre Van Young
Illustrations	Linda Allison
Printing	Delta Lithograph

Brown, David Wayne, 1949-
    Fight your ticket / by David W. Brown ; illustrated by Linda Allison.
      p.   cm.
      Includes index.
      ISBN 0-87337-132-1 : $17.95
      1. Traffic violations--California--Popular works. 2. Traffic courts--California- -Popular works.   I. Title.
KFC477.Z9876 1991
345.794'0247--dc20
[347.9405247]
                                        91-8772
                                        CIP

ACKNOWLEDGMENTS

This book could not have been published without the generous assistance of many people. Peggy Cuthrell, Richard Miller and Diane Van Schoten made numerous helpful suggestions and comments, nearly all of which were incorporated into the early drafts.

Many thanks to Elaine Cass, Lecturer in Law at the University of Santa Clara, Mervin Cherrin of that school's Law Clinic, Daniel F. Cook, and Kathy Galvin and Stephanie Harolde of Nolo Press for proofreading and editing the final drafts, as well as for their very helpful ideas. I'd especially like to gratefully acknowledge the major contributions of Ralph ("Jake") Warner and Peter Jan Honigsberg of Nolo Press, whose incisive editing and folksy phraseology have added readability, clarity, and brevity to this book.

Thanks, too, to Toni Ihara, Keija Kimura, Jane Fajardo, Barbara Hodovan, Amy Ihara, John O'Donnell, Carol Pladsen and Robyn Samuels. And finally, a big smile and an even bigger chuckle for Linda Allison, whose characteristically wonderful illustrations have actually succeeded in bringing a smile to the law.

A very special "Thank You" to Nolo editors Albin Renauer and Steve Elias. In the seven years since *Fight Your Ticket* was first published, my own repeated editings to incorporate new statutes and court decisions often felt like opening an already stuffed closet, throwing things in, and slamming the door quickly. Albin and Steve slaved diligently for many months to thoroughly reorganize the closet. Their dedication, energy and intelligence have greatly enhanced this book's enjoyability and usefulness.

ABOUT THE AUTHOR

DAVID W. BROWN practices law in the Monterey, California area. where he has defended numerous traffic cases in the California state and federal courts. For a short while, he was able to convince a Monterey County judge to declare the 55 mph speed limit unconstitutional. He teaches law at the Monterey College of Law and is the author of *The Landlord's Law Book, Vol. 1: Rights and Responsibilities,* and *Vol. 2: Evictions.* He is also the co-author of *How To Change Your Name* and *The Guardianship Book.*

UPDATE SERVICE

RECYCLE YOUR OUT-OF-DATE BOOKS AND GET 25% OFF YOUR NEXT PURCHASE!

It's important to have the most current legal information. Because laws and legal procedures change often, we update our books regularly. To help keep you up-to-date we are extending this special offer: Send or bring us the title portion of the cover of any old Nolo book and we'll give you a 25% discount off the retail price of any new Nolo book! You'll find current prices and an order form at the back of this book. Generally speaking, any book more than two years old is of questionable value. Books more than four or five years old are usually a menace. This offer is to individuals only.

OUT-OF-DATE = DANGEROUS

FYT 4/91

TABLE OF CONTENTS

1

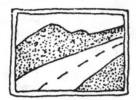

FIRST THINGS

A. A Typical Case

YOU'RE DRIVING HOME from your friend's place after a beautiful, romantic Friday evening. It's two-thirty in the morning. As you're reflecting on this, you suddenly realize you took a wrong turn some-place. You're now in the middle of a quiet residential district and realize you should turn around. You look for traffic coming from either direction and all you see is a car parked about three blocks away with its headlights on, so you make a U-turn.

Suddenly, in your rear view mirror you see a flashing red and blue light that seemingly grows out of the parked car. You begin to pull over to the right to let it pass. Instead, the car follows you to the curb. You realize you've just been pulled over by a police officer. As soon as your car stops, the officer has his

high-intensity spotlight pointed at you. Then, you hear his door slam, the sound of gravel under his boots, and finally you see a big, grim face just behind the flashlight pointed into your eyes.

Before you get a chance to ask him what's the problem, he says, "May I see your driver's license, please?" You fumble through your wallet, slowly and carefully, since he has his hand uncomfortably close to the butt of what looks to be a very big gun. Finally, hands shaking slightly, you hand him your license. (Don't you feel like a common criminal?)

The police officer returns to his car and uses the radio. A minute later he returns, hands you your license, and unemotionally says, "You made an unlawful U-turn in a residential district. Sign here, please," and he thrusts a three-part form in your face. You meekly sign the ticket (which he tells you is not an admission of guilt, but merely a promise to appear), and he hands you a copy. You gaze at the ticket, wondering how this could be happening to you. The officer spins out, off to catch another "criminal."

Your first thoughts might be: Should I just pay the ticket? (After all, didn't I break the law?) I wonder how much my insurance will go up. Will they revoke my license? If so, how will I get to work and support my family?

If you don't fight the ticket, you may very well end up:

- paying a fine you can barely afford;

- paying a higher insurance premium for the next three to five years; and

- starting or adding to a bad driving record with the DMV.

B. Should You Fight Your Ticket?

POLICE OFFICERS KNOW that very few people—perhaps one out of fifty—ever contest their tickets. Even those who do are often so unprepared and nervous that they have a tough time winning anyway. So police officers will occasionally cite motorists in situations where they know that the ticket probably wouldn't stand up in court if the motorist bothers to contest it.

Does it make sense for you to fight your ticket? The answer is that it depends. There are some people who almost always answer this question with a proud and forceful "yes!" unless they have done something incredibly stupid or dangerous, such as driving through a busy school zone at 50 mph. But there are others who don't believe in spending large amounts of time fighting cases where there is but a small chance of winning. It might be wise to try to separate the hopeless cases from those with a reasonable chance of success. (On the other hand, thousands of seemingly hopeless cases are won when police officers fail to show up in court to

testify.) A determined person can achieve great success in traffic court if he or she knows what to do.

In deciding whether or not to fight, you should first consider the consequences of giving up and paying the ticket. Will your insurance rates increase? Will you increase your chances of losing your license? Can you get your case dismissed by attending traffic school? Do you want to spend the time and effort it will take to fight your ticket effectively? This book will help you answer all these questions.

Once you understand the consequences of not fighting your ticket, you should try to determine your chances of winning, taking into account these tips:

1. The main way traffic tickets are beaten is to request a trial with the officer present and then get the ticket dismissed when the officer doesn't show up. There's a chance this might happen to you. You may want to try your luck. You've got nothing to lose but your time.

2. Even if the officer does show up, "guilt" (and "innocence") is often a matter of subjective interpretation. For example, under California law it's not illegal to drive 45 mph in a 35 mph zone if it is possible to show that your 45 mph speed was safe under the circumstances. (See Chapter 4, Section A(1), on speed violations.)

3. You might not be guilty of a particular violation, even if you think you are. When you read the Vehicle Code section, you will find that the offense you are accused of committing is more complex than you might have thought. It may be that you didn't do all the things that the prosecution must prove in order to convict you. We tell you in the next chapter how to read a Vehicle Code section with this in mind.

There are indeed the situations in which you were in fact scrupulously obeying the law and the policeman just plain got it wrong. The radar gun was used improperly, the police officer's visual perspective resulted in a mistake, you were accused of rolling through a stop sign when in fact you did come to a complete stop. When you get a ticket under these circumstances, and realize that you will have to undergo what can be a considerable hassle to fight it, you will most likely be torn between giving it a good fight and cutting your losses by paying your fine and getting on with your life.

What about the times when you were doing something wrong, but not wrong enough, in your opinion, to warrant intervention by a police officer? While most people manage to obey every traffic rule when they take their driving test, there are few—if any—drivers who continue to be the model of good driving once they get their license. Rather, the average driver tends to find an individual compromise between fanatical adherence to the law and unsafe behavior. Most people will commonly technically violate one or more traffic rules virtually every time they get in their car—but seldom, if ever, under circumstances that pose any danger to themselves or others. In fact, traveling a few miles over the speed limit on a clear and dry road will tend to put you among the snails rather than the grey-hounds.

When people are behaving badly or stupidly in their cars, they are inclined to welcome a ticket (after some initial grumbling) as a warning to get their act in order. The problem is, many tickets are given not for bad or stupid behavior but rather for insignif-icant violations of obscure rules in a book—things that are, in the classic sense, "mere technicalities." How many times have you seen cars run red lights with impunity, only to find the blue light flashing when you have rolled through a stop sign—however cautiously—at four o'clock in the morning at a deserted intersection? The problem is, when mere technical violations end up costing $80 in fines, adding points to your driving record and dollars to your insurance rates, they have a way of getting under your skin. You don't think you deserved the ticket. Why do the police waste time on you, when they could be doing serious work?

In this situation too, you may wish to fight your ticket, either for economic reasons or because you're just plain mad at being singled out for what most people do without getting caught. This book is for you, whether or not you're an innocent victim. However, you should understand that:

- Being singled out isn't normally a defense unless you can establish that the discrimination was for vindictive purposes (almost impossible to do).

- Being a little guilty still means you're guilty, although the judge may cut your fine.

- For the most part, the traffic-court system is inefficient and corrupt, packed with police-oriented judges who care more about feathering their own nests than about justice. (More on this in Chapter 18.)

In short, to win a traffic ticket fight, you must either obtain a dismissal or convince the judge you were innocent.

Parking tickets have their own logic. These tickets are given more to fill the city's coffers than to regulate parking. Nothing makes a harried driver more angry than to park in a truck zone out of desperation and come back to the car five minutes later to find a $25 ticket on the window.

C. How to Use This Book

THE MESSAGE OF THIS BOOK is a simple one. You can effectively fight your ticket—whether for parking or for a moving violation—if you're well-prepared and know your rights. To help you fight your ticket, we:

- instruct you on how to look up, read and understand the specific law you allegedly violated so you might discover a few technicalities of your own (Chapter 2);

- explain the various traffic laws that are most commonly violated (Chapters 4-8);

- tell you which violations go on your record and which ones are likely to raise your insurance rates (Chapter 3);

- explore the most common grounds for defending against a ticket issued under these laws (Chapters 4-8); and

- provide instructions on how to use these defenses to get your ticket dismissed (Chapters 4-8).

We also:

- help you decide whether to fight the ticket (Chapter 9);

- give you step-by-step guidance on the necessary procedures for fighting your ticket, suggest effective shortcuts and tactics where appropriate, and explain how the sentencing process works in case you lose (Chapters 10-14); and

- show you when and how to appeal a conviction, and how to fight a license suspension by the DMV, should the worst happen (Chapters 15-16).

Finally, in Chapter 17, you'll find tips on what to do the next time a police officer pulls you over. You'll learn how to be a good observer and look for things that will help you fight your ticket more effectively later on and in Chapter 18 we have a few suggestions for how the traffic enforcement system can be improved.

D. Overview Chart

THE FOLLOWING CHART shows the structure of the book in graphic form.

How to Use This Book

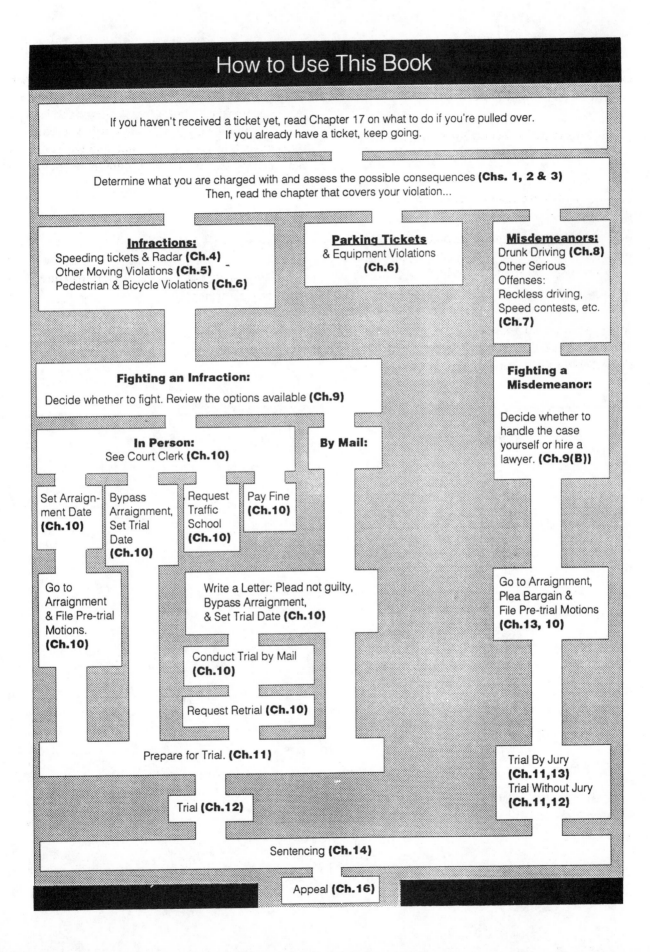

If you haven't received a ticket yet, read Chapter 17 on what to do if you're pulled over.
If you already have a ticket, keep going.

Determine what you are charged with and assess the possible consequences **(Chs. 1, 2 & 3)**
Then, read the chapter that covers your violation...

Infractions:
Speeding tickets & Radar **(Ch.4)**
Other Moving Violations **(Ch.5)**
Pedestrian & Bicycle Violations **(Ch.6)**

Parking Tickets
& Equipment Violations
(Ch.6)

Misdemeanors:
Drunk Driving **(Ch.8)**
Other Serious
Offenses:
Reckless driving,
Speed contests, etc.
(Ch.7)

Fighting an Infraction:
Decide whether to fight. Review the options available **(Ch.9)**

**Fighting a
Misdemeanor:**

Decide whether to
handle the case
yourself or hire a
lawyer. **(Ch.9(B))**

In Person:
See Court Clerk **(Ch.10)**

By Mail:

Set Arraign-
ment Date
(Ch.10)

Bypass
Arraignment,
Set Trial
Date
(Ch.10)

Request
Traffic
School
(Ch.10)

Pay Fine
(Ch.10)

Go to
Arraignment
& File Pre-trial
Motions.
(Ch.10)

Write a Letter: Plead not guilty,
Bypass Arraignment,
& Set Trial Date **(Ch.10)**

Go to Arraignment,
Plea Bargain &
File Pre-trial Motions
(Ch.13, 10)

Conduct Trial by Mail
(Ch.10)

Request Retrial **(Ch.10)**

Prepare for Trial. **(Ch.11)**

Trial By Jury
(Ch.11,13)
Trial Without Jury
(Ch.11,12)

Trial **(Ch.12)**

Sentencing **(Ch.14)**

Appeal **(Ch.16)**

2

HOW TO READ YOUR TICKET

The first step in fighting your ticket is learning how to use the information on it. Most important is the charge against you, which you need to know to prepare a defense. And you might even find that the officer used the wrong kind of ticket or made some other procedural error that might get your case dismissed. This chapter tells you how to read your ticket and use it to your advantage.

A. What Are You Charged With?

ALTHOUGH NOT ALL TICKETS are alike (we'll explore the differences in Section D of this chapter), every ticket contains the basic information you need to determine what you're charged with.

Near the middle of the ticket, usually under the heading "Violation(s)," the officer will have written a very short description of the law she says you violated. This consists of:

- Which "code" you violated. All laws passed by the legislature are collected in a set of books known as "codes." You will almost always be cited for a Vehicle Code violation.[1]

NOTICE TO APPEAR

[NAME OF AGENCY AND JURISDICTION]		
NOTICE TO APPEAR		NO. 0001

Date ___ 19 ___ Time ___ Day of Week ___

Name (First, Middle, Last) ___

Address ___

City ___ State ___ ZIP Code ___

Drivers License No. ___ State ___ Class ___ Birthdate ___ JUV. ☐

Sex ___ Hair ___ Eyes ___ Height ___ Weight ___ Other Des. ___

Vehicle License No. ___ State ___ Passengers M F ___

Year of Veh. ___ Make ___ Model ___ Body Style ___ Color ___

Registered Owner or Lessee ___ Same as above

Address of Owner or Lessee ___ Same as above

Items checked are cited in accordance with 40610(b) CVC – See reverse   ☐ Booking Required   Case No. ___

☐	Violation(s)	Code	Section	Description
☐				
☐				
☐				☐ Cont. Form Issued

Speed: Approx ___ PF/Max ___ Veh Lmt ___ Safe ___ Radar ___ City of Occur ___

Location of Violation(s) on ___

Comments: (Weather, Road & Traffic Conditions) ___

I certify under penalty of perjury that the foregoing is true and correct.

Executed on the date shown above at ___ , Calif.
Place ___

ISSUING OFFICER ___ Serial NO. ___

Division or Area | Detail or Beat | County Code | Dates Off ___

Without admitting guilt, I promise to appear at the time and place checked below

X Signature ___
Before a judge or a clerk of the municipal or justice court.

Telephone ___ Address ___

[ ] Juvenile Court, Traffic Division
☐ Date ___ 19 ___ Time ___ M ___ ☐ Within 15 days

☐ Or you may appear on the night(s) of ___ at ___ p.m.

Form approved by the Judicial Council of California
Rev 7-1-84 VC 40500 40513(b) 40522

SEE REVERSE SIDE

[1]Other codes are occasionally cited (e.g., the Penal Code, the Business & Professions Code for some alcohol-related violations, and the Health & Safety Code for narcotic substance violations). You might also be cited under a local ordinance for many types of parking violations and certain alcohol-related offenses.

The section number of the code that identifies the violation (VC for Vehicle Code, PC for Penal Code, B&P for Business & Professions Code, H&S for Health & Safety Code, etc.). In legal notation, the symbol "§" means "section number."

- A short description of the charge when moving violations are involved (e.g., "speed charge," "reckless driving"). For example:

CODE	SECTION	DESCRIPTION
VC	22350	basic speed law

NOTICE OF VIOLATION

NOTICE OF VIOLATION	NO. 00000
CITY OF	

IMPORTANT – READ CAREFULLY

This Notice of Violation DOES NOT constitute an arrest. It has been issued to you as a result of an accident in which you were involved. You are charged with committing the violation(s) described below. If you wish to respond to this Notice you MAY appear as provided below, but you are not required to do so (Veh. Code 40603). If you do not appear or deposit bail a verified complaint may be filed in your case, and an arrest warrant will then be issued (Veh. Code 40604).

DATE OF ACCIDENT ___ 19 ___ TIME OF ACCIDENT ___ M. ACCIDENT P.D. ☐ P.I. ☐

NAME (FIRST, MIDDLE, LAST) ___

RESIDENCE ADDRESS ___ CITY ___ ZIP ___

BUSINESS ADDRESS ___ CITY ___ ZIP ___

DRIVERS LICENSE NO. ___ STATE ___ CLASS ___ BIRTHDATE ___

SEX M F ___ HAIR ___ EYES ___ HEIGHT ___ WEIGHT ___ OTHER DES. ___

VEHICLE LICENSE NO. ___ STATE ___ PASSENGERS M F ___

YEAR OF VEH. ___ MAKE ___ MODEL ___ BODY STYLE ___ COLOR ___

REGISTERED OWNER OR LESSEE ___

ADDRESS OF OWNER OR LESSEE ___

VIOLATION(S) (INCLUDE CODE, SECTION & DESCRIPTION) ___

APPROX. SPEED ___ PF/MAX SPD. ___ VEH SPD LMT ___ SAFE SPD. ___ CITY OF OCCUR. ___

LOCATION OF VIOLATION(S) ON ___

COMMENTS: (WEATHER, ROAD & TRAFFIC CONDITIONS) ___

ISSUING OFFICER ___ SERIAL NO. ___

INVESTIGATING OFFICER – IF DIFFERENT FROM ABOVE ___ SERIAL NO. ___

IF YOU WISH YOU MAY APPEAR:

BEFORE A JUDGE OR A CLERK OF THE ___ COURT

(ADDRESS) ___

JUVENILE COURT, TRAFFIC DIVISION

DATE ___ 19 ___ TIME ___ M.

OR YOU MAY APPEAR ON THE NIGHT(S) OF ___ AT ___ P.M.

FORM APPROVED BY THE JUDICIAL COUNCIL OF CALIFORNIA, 11-10-69 V.C. 40600

SEE REVERSE SIDE

Grey areas indicate spaces subject to local or agency requirements.

In addition, on speeding tickets, you'll find the "approximate speed" at which the officer clocked your vehicle and the posted or "prima facie" (abbreviated "PF") speed limit (VC § 40503). The meanings of these legal terms are discussed in Chapter 4.

B. Are You Really Guilty?

Just because a police officer has written some code section on your ticket doesn't necessarily mean you violated it. Most laws are rather complex, so it's not uncommon to find that what you did was not, technically speaking, illegal. By finding the code and section number of the law you allegedly violated on your ticket, you can look up the law yourself to see if you really are guilty. This may sound elementary, but even lawyers often forget to do it.

You need the exact language of the law you're accused of violating. Chapters 4 through 8 of this book include the exact language of many of the most commonly violated Vehicle Code sections. If we don't include the statute you're cited for, you can find a current copy of the Vehicle Code (or other applicable code) in a law library. Every county has a law library open to the public,[2] and some law schools also allow public use of their law libraries. You can also purchase a copy of the latest Vehicle Code from your local DMV office (issued annually in mid-March) for $3 or from Nolo Press for $8-10. Make sure you're using the most recent version of the statute—that is, the section in the vehicle or other code that applies to your offense—you're charged with. [If you need help on how to do legal research, read Chapter 9, Section B(4).]

Once you've found the statute that is cited on your ticket, read it very carefully. Try to figure out which things the prosecution will have to prove

"beyond a reasonable doubt." Ask yourself, "What are the elements of the offense?"[3]

For example, our motorist in the first chapter was charged with making an illegal U-turn. The law prohibiting U-turns in residential districts, VC § 22103, states:

> No person in a residence district shall make a U-turn when any other vehicle is approaching from either direction within 200 feet, except at an intersection when the approaching vehicle is controlled by an official traffic control device.

U-Tern

At this point you should stop and read the statute again, more slowly. This time draw a line between each clause, and think about what it means. For example, this statute could be divided up as follows:

> No person/ in a residence district/ shall make a U-turn/ when any other vehicle/ is approaching/ from either direction/ within 200 feet,/ except at an intersection/ when the approaching vehicle/ is controlled/ by an official traffic control device.

To be found guilty of having committed this offense, the prosecution must prove all of the following "elements" of the offense beyond a reasonable doubt:

1. That you (a person) were driving in a "residence district";

---

[2]The county law library can usually be found near the Superior Court building, which is located in the city that is the "county seat." Some larger counties have branch law libraries in other cities as well. See Chapter 9, Section B(4), on basic legal research.

[3]An "element" is lawyer's lingo for a particular fact which must be proven by the prosecution in order to find you guilty of the offense. Some elements are central to the crime. Others are what non-lawyers might call "technicalities." Either way, every element must be proven against you in order for you to be found guilty.

2. That you drove your vehicle in a 180-degree or "U-turn";

3. That another vehicle was approaching within 200 feet or less from ahead or behind you; and

4. That you were not at an "intersection" controlled by an "official traffic control device."[4]

Thus, you will want to show that the area wasn't a "residence district,"[5] or that the vehicles the officer claims were approaching may have been over 200 feet away, or that you were at an intersection[6] controlled by an "official traffic control device."[7] If you can disprove any of these elements, you'll be found not guilty.

At this point you may be wondering, "Is a judge likely to follow such a technical reading of the law?" The answer is yes. This style of technical, word-by-word reading is one of the most important skills lawyers are taught in law school. Here's why. The American legal system under the Constitution and Bill of Rights provides the defendants in criminal cases a considerable number of "breaks" in order to give them a fighting chance in their battle against the all-powerful State. Although lawmakers have made many of these rights inapplicable to traffic court, the courts still must interpret traffic laws very technically or "narrowly," because the government must be able to point to a law that clearly prohibits what you did, before you can be found guilty. This means that you can't be found guilty unless the government proves beyond a reasonable doubt that you violated every "element" of the traffic offense you're charged with.

For all violations, it must also be true that you either intended to commit every element of the violation, or that you were careless in doing so. Penal Code § 20 says that "In every crime or public offense (including infractions) there must exist a union, or joint operation, of act and intent, or criminal negligence." In plain English, this means that to convict you of any offense, including all infractions (most of which are in the Vehicle Code[8]), the state must show that you:

• committed all the elements of the forbidden act described in the specific code section you're charged with; and

• had an intent to commit those acts, or were "criminally negligent" (careless) in committing them.

For example, you might be able to successfully maintain that you acted neither intentionally nor carelessly since the "No U-turn" sign at the intersection was not visible, the stop sign you accidentally ran was blocked from view by tree leaves, or even that your speedometer was reading too low. The key is showing you weren't reckless or even careless. Just saying you "didn't mean to" run the stop sign won't get you anywhere.

Finally, even if you really did commit every element of your violation, you still might not be guilty if you had a legal excuse for doing so. For example, if you were charged with driving too slowly in the left lane (VC § 21654), it is a legal defense (provided for in the statute) that you were planning to turn left. You're not denying that you were driving slowly in the left lane, but rather offering an additional fact that legally justifies your apparently unlawful action. However, it's up to you to introduce this fact at trial.

---

[4]You will notice that many of these terms, like "residence district" and "official traffic control device" are rather ambiguous. When you find words like this, you should immediately look for a definition of those terms somewhere else in the code you're working with. In the Vehicle Code, definitions are listed near the beginning of the book, starting with § 100.

[5]Defined as a quarter-mile stretch of road with at least 13 structures on one side or at least 16 on both sides. See VC § 515.

[6]This includes "T" as well as "x" intersections. See VC § 365.

[7]Stop signs, stoplights, etc. See VC § 440.

[8]Infractions are included in the category of "crimes and public offenses." PC § 16. The fact that most infractions are listed in the Vehicle Code, but procedural and technical aspects of general criminal law exist only in the Penal Code, makes no difference. The various codes are considered by the courts to be read together to make a coherent body of law. *People v. Ashley* (1971) 17 Cal.App.3d 1122, 95 Cal.Rptr. 509. (Information on the meaning of these funny hieroglyphics that come after case names—and which can help you find the case in a law library—is given in Chapter 9, Part B(4).)

C. Other Information on Your Ticket

AT THE TOP OF YOUR TICKET (in the case of moving or equipment violations), you'll find the information the officer has obtained from your driver's license—your name, address, license number, etc. There's also a place for the date, time and place of the alleged violation, the make, model and year of your vehicle, and the license plate number. If the officer has made enough mistakes in these entries, you may be able to challenge his powers of observation when you get to trial.

Occasionally, the officer will write his vacation dates on your ticket as a message to the court clerk indicating which dates he won't be able to appear at trial. As we'll see in Chapter 10, you may be able to use this information to your advantage by scheduling your trial to occur on one of those dates.

Finally, your ticket should indicate the name of the court in which you must appear to pay the fine or arrange for a court date, and the court's address. You will be cited to appear in the "Municipal Court" (or the "Justice Court" in some rural areas) nearest to where the offense supposedly occurred. Drivers under age 18 are cited to appear in "Juvenile Court," which, although a division of the Superior Court, usually has a juvenile traffic court department at the

local courthouse. The notice will also state how many days you have before you must appear. For juveniles, it may state "to be notified," or words to that effect. On parking tickets, there will be an address where you can mail your fine if you don't want to contest it.

D. Types of Tickets

There are basically four types of tickets: the Notice to Appear, Notice of Violation, Notice to Correct Violation, and Parking Ticket.

1. The Notice to Appear—Regular Ticket

If you were stopped for speeding, running a red light, or some other kind of moving violation, you should have received a "Notice to Appear." This kind of ticket was created to speed up and simplify the judicial process from arrest through trial. When the officer turns on the red light to pull you over, he technically places you under arrest.[9] While you are "under arrest," the officer fills out the ticket. Then, rather than placing you under actual arrest and taking you to jail,[10] he simply has you sign that part of the ticket that says you agree to appear in court. By signing the Notice to Appear, you are released from arrest and do not have to post bail. You are not admitting guilt, nor are you waiving any of your rights. If you refuse to sign the ticket, the officer is required to take you to jail [VC § 40302(b)]. When the officer files his copy of the ticket with the court, it is considered the equivalent of a "complaint," meaning, in the legal context, the formal charging

---

[9]*People v. Superior Court* (1972) 7 Cal.3d 186, 200, 101 Cal.Rptr. 837. See also VC §§ 40500, 40501. Note the "arrest" here described is not the kind of arrest that you have to report on job applications or other such questionnaires. Traffic stops are not "arrests" in the formal sense (i.e. taking you into custody, see PC § 834). And even if you are formally arrested (taken into custody), but are released before any formal accusatory pleading is filed with the court, the arrest does not appear on your record and is deemed a mere "detention." (See PC § 849.5.)

[10]This is known as a "custodial arrest." (See PC § 834.)

papers that formally begin the proceedings against you (VC § 40513).

The forms may vary some among police departments. Some forms include space for the number of passengers in the vehicle (in order to preclude your bringing a "witness" who wasn't really with you), the color of the vehicle (if the officer gets this wrong, you might be able to discredit his testimony since it reflects negatively on his ability to observe), and the weather, road and traffic conditions when a speed violation is involved. Sometimes the ticket will have a little intersection map for the officer to diagram the way various vehicles were positioned during the violation. This type of information is mostly to aid the officer in recounting the facts in court. Finally, there will be a place where the officer signs under penalty of perjury that everything he stated in the ticket is true. He can only fill this in if he actually observed the violation.

If you signed a Notice to Appear you have promised to appear at the court specified on the ticket, and failure to do so is a crime punishable by a fine of up to $1,000 (plus up to $1,600 more in "penalty assessments") and six months in jail. (See, generally, Chapter 7, Section B(3).) In Chapter 17, Section C, we explain that, before signing, you can (and should) demand that the officer specify the place to appear as the municipal court at the county seat, if your business or residence address is closer to the county seat than to the local court for the judicial district in which you're cited (VC § 40302(b)). We're assuming for now, however, that you've already received your ticket and you probably weren't aware of this.

2. The Notice of Violation—at Accidents

When an officer is called to the scene of an accident and believes you committed a violation (though he didn't see you do it), he cannot perform a formal "arrest," because he didn't observe the violation.[11] The officer therefore cannot insist you sign a Notice to Appear. Instead, if he issues you a ticket, it should be a "Notice of Violation" (VC § 40601). It looks very much like a Notice to Appear, but you do not sign it. Because you therefore do not promise to appear, you cannot be charged with the additional charge of failure to appear if you don't show. However, a warrant for your arrest on the original offense can be issued if you ignore both a first and a second certified-mail letter from the court, telling you to appear on the violation (VC § 40604).

Even though you don't sign a Notice of Violation, you still can (and should) demand that the officer specify the place to appear as the municipal court at the county seat, if your business or residence address is closer to the county seat than to the local court for the judicial district in which you're cited (VC § 40601). (See Chapter 17, Section C.)

The correct procedure for issuing a ticket at the scene of an accident is for an officer, trained in accident investigation, to come to the scene, investigate, and decide whether to issue a Notice of Violation on the spot. Instead, many police departments improperly decide later to issue a ticket and mail out the wrong form—a Notice to Appear. According to a California Attorney General opinion, this is illegal.[12] (Some court clerks don't notice you didn't sign the mailed notice and illegally charge you with failure to appear even though you never promised to appear!) If the wrong form is used, it is of no effect, and you should let the judge know at the arraignment. Even if the right form is used, the district attorney must file a formal "Verified Complaint" if you plead not guilty (VC § 40603). Without this, the court has no authority to proceed further. (See Chapter 10, Section D, for how to use this procedural mistake in fighting your ticket.)

---

[11]An exception to this rule allows an officer to physically arrest, at the scene of an accident, a person reasonably believed to have been driving under the influence (VC § 40300.5).

[12]59 Ops.Atty.Gen. 355 (1976).

One final word. In order to be authorized to issue a Notice of Violation at an accident, the officer is required to have successfully completed a course in accident investigation approved by the "Commission on Peace Officer Standards and Training" [VC § 40600(a)]. If you ever wind up in court on a Notice of Violation, you may be able to get the case dismissed if, upon cross-examining the officer, you find that he hasn't taken such a course.

3. The Notice to Correct Violation

You could be cited for an equipment violation (e.g., burnt-out tail light), or a minor license or registration violation other than an expired driver's license or vehicle registration (e.g., such as license or registration not in possession). If so, you may receive a "Notice to Correct Violation" or a Notice to Appear with a notation on the back stating the charge will be dismissed if you submit certified proof that the violation has been corrected. Both tickets have a place for you to sign, promising that you'll take care of the problem within a specified time period. If you ignore these tickets, the penalties can be severe.

Sometimes an officer issuing a parking ticket will notice an equipment violation and note it on the parking ticket. Since you don't sign a parking ticket, your failure to correct may not be punished as severely, but you will still be fined for the violation, and you should be able to get the charge dismissed if you show certified proof of correction. Read Chapter 6, Section B, for further information about equipment violations.

4. The Parking Ticket

Parking tickets are placed on your vehicle when you're not present. There's no place for you to sign so you can't be charged with a misdemeanor for ignoring the ticket. However, the DMV may refuse to renew your vehicle registration. We discuss this in greater detail in Chapter 6, Section A.

3

WHAT ARE THE CONSEQUENCES?
FINES, JAIL, YOUR "RECORD," AND INSURANCE

"Will it go on my record?"
"What's the maximum fine?"
"Is jail a possibility?"
"Will my insurance rates go up?"

If you're like most people, these are the first questions that go through your mind when you get a traffic ticket. It makes sense that you want to know what you're dealing with before making any decisions about whether to simply pay the ticket or invest the time and effort to fight it. With this information in hand, you'll be in a far better position to decide whether it is worth your while to fight. This chapter provides that information for the most commonly charged violations. Read Section A, then read only that portion of Section B that deals with your violation. If your ticket is from out-of-state, read Section C.

A. Generally

THE SEVERITY OF THE consequences of your ticket, and the difficulty of fighting it depend on whether it is an infraction, misdemeanor or felony, and whether it goes on your record. In Section 1, below, we tell you the maximum penalties provided for each type of offense. (In actuality, these maximums are rarely imposed.)

1. Types of Violations: Infractions, Misdemeanors and Felonies

Traffic offenses come in three types: infractions, misdemeanors and felonies. Most automobile-related violations are either infractions or misdemeanors.

Infractions include all parking and registration violations, and all but the most serious moving violations. If you're charged with an infraction, you can't demand a jury trial, and you are not entitled to a court-appointed lawyer regardless of your inability to afford one. On the other hand, jail cannot be imposed as the original penalty, but you can be fined up to $260 ($100 plus $160 in "penalty assessments") on most first-offense infractions—and even more for certain serious ones, such as driving over 100 mph. And, if you fail to pay the fine without sufficient justification, you can end up in jail. Most infractions can be fought through an abbreviated or more informal procedure. (See Chapter 10, Section B.)

Misdemeanors involve more serious offenses, such as drunk or reckless driving, drag racing, trying to outrun a cop, hit-and-run with property damage, failure to appear in court as promised (by signing a ticket), and failure to pay a fine. If you're charged with a misdemeanor, you're entitled to a jury trial and a court-appointed lawyer if you cannot afford one. Misdemeanors are punishable by up to a year in jail and fines up to $1,000 plus up to $1,500 in "penalty assessments." Fighting a misdemeanor charge is more formal, difficult and lengthy than fighting an infraction. To fight serious misdemeanors, like drunk driving, you will probably want to hire a lawyer.

Felonies are very serious crimes punishable by imprisonment in the state prison for more than a year. Obvious (non-traffic) felonies include murder, armed robbery and rape. Very few Vehicle Code offenses are felonies, the most notable being drunk driving or hit-and-run where someone was injured or killed in an accident.[1] This book is absolutely not intended for use in defending against a felony charge; anyone accused of a felony should definitely see a lawyer.

2. Your Record

The long-term consequences of your ticket primarily depend on whether the ticket goes on your "record." Your record is that infamous piece of computer-stored information listing most of your traffic convictions (including tickets you've paid). Exceptions are parking, registration and most equipment violations.[2] Your record is kept at the DMV in Sacramento, and is accessible by computer terminal from most DMV offices (VC § 1808). The information is not available to the general public, but is available to police agencies, courts, the driver herself and those whom the driver has given written authorization to inspect the record. Most violations are kept as part of your DMV record for at least three years.[3] If you commit another violation within that period, the record of your prior violations can result in stiffer penalties.

When you get auto insurance, your insurer will ask you to authorize them to view your driving record at any further date. Thus, a new offense on your record may result in an insurance rate increase. How your rates are affected by your driving record depends on your individual company. You may want to call your insurance company (without giving your name) to get a general idea of how much your rates would rise for the violation you're charged with.

Another function of your record is to keep track of "points." Most moving violations count as a single point on your record. Four points in a year, or six in two years, or eight in three years can result in your license being suspended. The license suspension process is discussed in detail in Chapter 15.

3. Fines and "Penalty Assessments"

In California, a traffic fine consists of a base fine plus various "penalty assessments," or taxes. Penalty assessments vary from county to county, and, believe it or not, can amount to 145% to 160% tacked onto the basic fine. Thus, a $100 fine becomes about $260, after adding the $160 "penalty assessments."

Suggested base fines for most traffic violations are listed in the Uniform Traffic Bail Schedule.[4] You

---

[1]VC §§ 20001, 23153.

[2]See VC § 1803.

[3]See VC §§ 1807, 12810, 12810.5; but convictions for driving under the influence or reckless driving are kept for at least seven years.

[4]Actually, the judges in each county get together and vote on their own county-wide bail schedules, but generally adopt the amounts listed in the Uniform Traffic Bail Schedule. However, Los Angeles County has adopted a schedule providing for higher fines for serious moving violations, including a $35 basic fine for not stopping at a red light or stop sign, driving on the wrong side of the road, following too closely, failing to yield to pedestrians, and illegal left or U-turns.

may wonder why it's called a "bail" schedule. Well, in the world of traffic tickets, fines aren't really "fines" at all. Before traffic enforcement was invented as a revenue-raising method, a fine could only be paid after a court appearance in which a judge sentenced a person who had pleaded or was found guilty. However, to make this system more efficient and speed up the traffic-revenue taxation system, a new meaning was placed on an old word—"bail."[5] In lieu of a court appearance, and instead of having to plead guilty before a judge as a prerequisite to paying a traffic fine, you can now pay the money directly to a court clerk.

Your total fine—that is your "bail"—is paid or "posted" with the clerk, supposedly in order to guarantee your appearance at a trial. When you don't show up (because you've already paid what is in reality a fine), your "bail" is forfeited.[6] The system then treats these bail forfeitures as convictions and the violations go on your record at the DMV in Sacramento.[7]

a. The Base Fine

The total fine or "bail" consists of what we call the "base fine" plus a 145-to-160% "penalty assessment." Currently, the Uniform Traffic Bail Schedule suggests a basic "bail" of:

- $10 for "infractions" committed by pedestrians;

- $20 for most moving violation infractions not involving speeding or alcohol;

- $30 for certain of such violations considered to be more serious (running a stop sign or stoplight, following too closely, and failure to yield right of way);

- $50 for alcohol-related violations (open container in vehicle, etc.), not including drunk driving; and

- for speeding tickets, $10 for the first 10 mph over the limit plus $10 for each additional 5 mph over that. (See chart in Section B.)

A second or third Vehicle Code offense within a year can cost you up to $200 or $250, respectively, plus "penalty assessments" (see below). Usually, however, the fines are less. For second or third infraction convictions within three years, the fine may be higher than that authorized by the Uniform Bail Schedule, plus penalty assessments. Some courts use computers to process each ticket by obtaining the driver's DMV record (often printed on a folder in which the original ticket is kept) and increasing the fine amount based on prior violations of the Vehicle Code.

Note: If you fight a ticket and lose, the judge isn't required to use the above formula. The judge can

---

[5]In other types of criminal proceedings, bail is a sum of money a defendant leaves with the court in order to insure that he will show up for trial or his next court appearance. If he doesn't show, the bail is forfeited and a warrant is issued for his arrest, demanding he appear in court.

[6]If all you want to do is pay the fine (the bail), don't set up a trial date. (See Chapter 10.) If you do, and then don't show up, you may find yourself facing a failure to appear charge, a serious offense. (See Chapter 7.) In practice, however, most judges won't bother to do this, and will simply declare your bail forfeited under VC §§ 40512 or 40512.5.

[7]VC §§ 40510-40512.5.

fine you less, or even more, based on prior offenses or aggravating factors. However, most judges will stick fairly close to the "bail" schedule in assessing fines; most of them don't want to be accused of routinely penalizing defendants who insist on asserting their right to trial.

b. Penalty Assessments

If there's one thing that shows the traffic enforcement system for what it really is—a source of revenue—it's the practice of adding "penalty assessments" to every fine. These assessments provide money for more police (to generate even more traffic fines), to train government employees and to modernize or build more courthouses and jails.[8] The money from these assessments goes into various state and county slush funds for modernizing courthouses and jails, and for "training" various types of government employees, depending on the power various special interest groups have in the Legislature. The "penalty assessments" are as follows:

PENALTY ASSESSMENTS FOR MOVING VIOLATIONS

(including misdemeanors, but not including registration, pedestrian and bicyclist violations—for which no penalty assessments are added)

$7 for each $10 (or fraction of $10) of fine: (Under PC § 1464, this money goes mostly to a "Peace Officers' Training Fund," a "Corrections Training Fund," and a "Driver Training Penalty Assessment Fund.")

+ **$2 (more) for each $10 (or fraction of $10) of fine:** (Under PC § 1465, this money goes to an "Emergency Medical Services Fund.")

+ **$2 (more) for each $10 (or fraction of $10) of fine:** (Under Government Code §76011, this money goes to each county's "Courthouse Temporary Construction Fund.")

+ **$2 (more) for each $10 (or fraction of $10) of fine:** (Under Government Code §76012, this money goes to each county's "County Criminal Justice Facilities (jail) Temporary Construction Fund.")

+ **50¢ (more) for each $10 of fine:** (Under Government Code § 76013, this money goes to each county's "Automatic Fingerprint Identification Fund.")

+ **Between $1 and $2.50 (more) per $10 of fine,** depending on the county and whether the County Board of Supervisors has approved additional "assessments" for jail and/or courthouse construction or other pet projects. (Government Code §§76020-76580.)

+ **a $1 flat "night court assessment"** [in areas where arraignments are held at night (trials never are)].

= **up to $16.00 total assessment added to each $10 of basic fine, plus $1. Outrageous!**

PENALTY ASSESSMENTS FOR PARKING VIOLATIONS

Two or three surcharges of $1.50 apiece on each parking fine (regardless of amount):
(for each county's jail and/or courthouse construction fund, and for additional pet projects, to the extent the County Board of Supervisors agrees).

= $3 or $4.50 total assessment added to each parking fine, depending on the County Board of Supervisors.

---

4. Insurance Consequences: Cancellations and Rate Increases

When you obtain auto insurance, your policy generally lasts for a fixed period of time, usually either six months or a year. During this time, an insurance company won't raise your rates or cancel your insurance unless you fail to pay your premium.

When it comes time to renew your policy, however, your insurance company might raise your rates or even refuse to continue insuring you if you've had more than a few violations, or at least one accident. You may qualify for regularly-priced insurance after a few years without further violations or accidents. It pays to shop around.

Many insurance companies raise rates at renewal time by taking away a "safe-driver discount." (This "discount" also tends to keep you from filing minor fenderbender claims.) Since the law requires insurance companies to give a "good driver" discount, this practice is likely to come into play where the driver has two or more moving violation infractions within a three-year period.

Some insurance companies raise rates by adding a "surcharge," and still others do this by refusing to insure you except through their own separate "indemnity" or "casualty" company, which specializes in "higher-risk" drivers—and charges a lot more. [This isn't the same as being on an "assigned-risk" plan; see Chapter 5, Section F(5).]

Most companies will definitely "cancel" (refuse to renew) your insurance or raise your rates dramatically if you have a very serious accident or are convicted of driving under the influence. Insurance companies must prominently list, on the front page of your policy or other documents, any grounds for non-renewal or cancellation of your policy.

Insurance companies obtain information about your driving record from their own files of claims made against your policy, random checks of DMV records (per your previously-obtained written authorization), or their own questionnaires and renewal applications. Omitting any information from these applications is a bad idea, since it may give the company an excuse to avoid paying off a large claim later on. The details of this practice vary so much among insurance companies that it is difficult to generalize.

The criterion for refusing to renew your insurance are usually less strict than for deciding initially whether to insure you. (See Chapter 5, Section F.) In other words, just because a particular company won't insure someone who has had three violations in three years doesn't necessarily mean they'll refuse to renew your insurance if you wind up with that many violations on your record later on. Some companies even guarantee never to refuse to renew your policy once you've been with them for a certain number of years—unless you manage to be convicted of drunk driving, hit-and-run, or some other very serious offense.

In June 1988, the voters enacted Proposition 103, a ballot initiative that promised to roll back auto insurance rates by 20%, then to regulate them and to forbid the setting of rates based on age, sex, marital status, geographical area and other factors. As of this writing, insurance companies, with the help of a few judges, are vigorously resisting all attempts at reform. The dust still hasn't settled, and it's still too early to tell how the law regulating insurance rates and practices will be affected by Proposition 103.

B. Overview of Specific Violations

NOW THAT YOU HAVE general information about the consequences of your ticket, we'll turn to an overview of the most commonly charged traffic violations. Read only the summary section that covers your violation, and skip the rest. Then go to the chapter (4, 5, 6, 7 or 8) that covers your violation in detail. For example, if you're charged with speeding, read only Section 1 and then move directly to Chapter 4.

Where to Find Your Violation

---

1. Speed Violations

2. Moving Violations Other Than Speeding

3. Illegal Parking

4. Pedestrian and Bicycle Violations

5. Defective Equipment

6. Registration and License Violations

7. Driving With Expired License

8. Driving While License Suspended

9. Driving Without Insurance

10. Serious Offenses (Reckless Driving, Hit-and-Run, etc.)

11. Drunk Driving

12. Minor Alcohol Related Offenses (Open Container, etc.)

13. Ignoring Tickets, Failing to Appear in Court, or Failing to Pay a Fine

1. Speed Violations

Most speeding violations are infractions (unless they involve something additional like reckless driving, in which case they are treated as misdemeanors). They always go on your record. They can make your insurance rates go up, or make it difficult to get insurance in the future. Because they are infractions, you can use many procedural shortcuts should you decide to fight (see Chapter 10, Section B). Since the law of speeding in California is complex and filled with technicalities, it is great for ticket-fighting. This is especially true where the speed limit you're accused of exceeding is 50 mph or less. You'll find numerous ways to fight a speeding ticket in Chapter 4. In sum, speeding tickets are often worth fighting, and by using the suggested defenses and procedural shortcuts provided in this book, you have a decent chance of winning. If all else fails, you can hope that the officer doesn't show up at trial and your case will be dismissed.

The basic fine or "bail" for speeding tickets depends on the speed limit and how much you're accused of having exceeded it. The fine may be higher if you drove a bus or tractor trailer.[9]

---

[9]Under VC § 42000.5, the maximum base fines for first- and second-offense speed violations are $200 and $300 (as opposed to $100 and $200) where the speed limit is exceeded by more than 10 mph and the vehicle is a bus or truck with three axles or more (the types of vehicles for which Class 1 and 2 licenses are required).

BASE FINES FOR SPEEDING VIOLATIONS
(Not including 145-160% penalty assessment)

Miles Per Hour Over Speed Limit	Speed Limit								
	15	20	25	30	35	40	45	50	55 & 65
1 to 5	$10	$10	$10	$10	$10	$10	$10	$10	$10
6 to 10	$10	$10	$10	$10	$10	$10	$10	$20	$20
11 to 15	$20	$20	$20	$20	$20	$20	$20	$30	$40
16 to 20	$30	$30	$30	$30	$30	$30	$30	$40	$50
21 to 25	$50	$50	$50	$50	$50	$50	$50	$60	$70
26 to 30	$60	$60	$60	$60	$60	$60	$60	$80	$100*
31 to 35	$80	$80	$80	$80	$80	$80	$80	$100*	$100*
more than 35	$100*	$100*	$100*	$100*	$100*	$100*	$100*	$100*	$100*

[* Mandatory court appearance required. Also, if speed is 100 mph or greater, the fine can be up to $500, plus up to $800 penalty assessment if a violation of VC § 22348(b) is charged.]

2. Moving Violations Other than Speeding

Moving violations appear on your record, so they may cause your insurance rates to rise. Moving violations not involving speeding, reckless driving or alcohol are infractions. Therefore, if you fight, you can use the procedural shortcuts discussed in Chapter 10. Your chances of success depend on the statute in question: Statutes that prohibit "unreasonable" actions (like unsafe lane changes or turns) are discussed based on subjective judgments, and thus you can argue that what you did was safe and reasonable. Violations like running red lights and stop signs can be fought by showing that the sign was blocked from sight or that the light changed so quickly that you could not have stopped in time. Chapter 5 contains specific information about how to argue defenses for these and other moving violations. Even if you don't have a good defense, you

penalty assessment) range from $50 to $75 for more serious violations (running a stop sign or stoplight, following too closely and failure to yield right of way).

3. Illegal Parking

Parking violations are infractions that do not go on your record. Therefore, your insurance rates will not go up. Parking tickets are usually based on local ordinances, and generally there will be some kind of informal procedure where you can either pay your parking ticket or set up a court date by mail. Although it is usually procedurally easier to fight parking tickets than moving violations, the minimal consequences often make it not worth the bother. Fines typically range from $15 to $40, but can be as high as $250 for multiple tickets. The fine is usually listed on the ticket. We say more about parking

4. Pedestrian and Bicycle Violations

Pedestrian and bicycle violations carry small fines (around $10) and do not appear on your record. They are infractions and are thus open to the procedural shortcuts listed in Chapter 10. However, the small fines and lack of insurance consequences generally make them not worth fighting. For further information, read Chapter 6, Section B.

5. Defective Equipment

All equipment violations are infractions. The procedure for dealing with most equipment violations is different than for other infractions. You are generally given an opportunity to correct the defect within a specified time period, have the correction "certified," present this certification to the court clerk or judge, and have the charge dismissed. Nothing goes on your record or affects your insurance rates. If you don't take care of the problem, however, the consequences can be severe, including a maximum fine of $500 and six months in jail.

If the equipment defect is causing an imminent traffic hazard or is the result of your "persistent neglect," you don't get a chance to correct it, and you'll be given a regular ticket that you'll have to fight or pay. But even if you get a regular ticket and are convicted or pay the bail, the violation will still not go on your record unless it is one of the following (listed by Vehicle Code section):

§ 24002   unsafe operating condition or illegally loaded;

§ 24004   unsafe operating condition after warning by police officer;

§ 24250   driving at night without proper lighting equipment;

§ 24409   improper use of high-beam headlights;

§ 24604   protruding load without safety lights or flag;

§ 24800   not having a lamp or flag on a projecting load;

§ 25103   driving with only parking lights lighted;

§ 26707   faulty windshield wipers;

§ 27151   modifying exhaust system to increase noise;

§ 27315   seatbelt violation;

§ 27360   child restraint law violation;

§ 27800   motorcycle improperly carrying passenger; or

§ 27801   too high seat or handlebars on motorcycle.

Total fines for equipment violations are usually about $50, if not dismissed following correction.

Equipment violations are covered in detail in Chapter 6, Section B.

6. Registration and License Violations

When you have a valid license or registration, but can't find it or don't have it with you when you're pulled over, you can be cited for a "correctable" violation that is treated in the same manner as correctable equipment violations above. They do not go on your record. See Chapter 6, Section B.

7. Driving with Expired License

Driving with an expired (or nonexistent) license is a misdemeanor theoretically punishable by a fine of up to $1,000 plus "penalty assessments." It isn't "correctable" by renewing your license, since you already committed the offense by driving without a current license. However, most judges will assess only a small total fine of $100 to $200 if you appear in court after having renewed your license and show it to the judge. See, generally, Chapter 7, Section B(4).

8. Driving While License Suspended

Driving with a suspended license is a misdemeanor. If charged with this, you have a right to a jury trial, which will give you leverage in plea bargaining. (See Chapter 13 and Chapter 8, Section E.) In some circumstances you can truthfully argue that you were unaware of the suspension and the charge should be dismissed. If you were aware of the suspension and drove anyway, you'll have more trouble fighting the charge. The penalties can be severe—fines up to $1,000 plus up to about $1,600 more in "penalty assessments" and six months in jail for a first offense. Convictions go on your record, although they have little effect on your insurance. License suspensions are covered in Chapter 7, Section B(4) and Chapter 15.

9. Driving Without Insurance

This offense has grown tougher over the years. You must show proof of insurance whenever you're stopped for a moving violation or investigated following an accident (even one on private property). If you don't have insurance, the penalties are stiff. Your license will be suspended until you can get insurance and present proof to the DMV. This can be a real "Catch-22" because it is difficult to get insurance without a valid driver's license, and you can't get a license without insurance. Also, you'll have to report your insurance status to the DMV for three years.[10]

Also, if you drive while uninsured and are involved in an accident with more than $500 in damages or if someone is injured, your license may be suspended for a year whether the accident is your fault or not. Read Chapter 5, Section F and Chapter 15, Section D(5).

10. Serious Offenses (Reckless Driving, Hit-and-Run, etc.)

Offenses such as reckless driving or "exhibitions of speed" (including squealing your tires) are misdemeanors that carry total fines of up to $2,600 and the possibility of license suspension and six months in jail. If someone is injured as a result of your reckless driving, you definitely could face a six month jail sentence. Failing to stop at an accident (commonly known as "hit-and-run") is also a misdemeanor. (It can be charged as a felony if someone is injured or killed.)

Convictions for these offenses always appear on your record and will definitely cause your insurance premiums to rise and possibly be cancelled. Since these offenses are misdemeanors, you have a right to request a jury trial and maybe gain some plea bargaining leverage. You must appear before a judge even if you simply want to plead guilty and pay a fine. You should probably consider hiring a lawyer to handle the plea bargaining and jury trial. For more information about these offenses and how to conduct a jury trial on your own, or how to get a lawyer, read Chapters 7, 9 (Section B), 10, 11 and 13.

---

[10]As of this writing, the Legislature has failed to pass a bill that would extend the mandatory proof-of-insurance law (VC § 16028) beyond its expiration date of January 1, 1991. However, we expect such a bill to pass in mid 1991. In any case, driving without insurance is still illegal and can result in a license suspension if you have an accident while uninsured.

11. Drunk Driving

Drunk driving is a serious offense. It is a misde-meanor that remains on your record for seven years. You should at least consult a lawyer with experience in drunk driving cases before trying to handle it yourself. On a fourth offense, or if someone is killed or injured because of your drunk driving, you can be charged with a felony, and should definitely be represented by a lawyer. There are ways of beating a drunk driving charge, and you may be able to plea bargain. Additional offenses within seven years are severely punished with maximum penalties up to three years in state prison (four years if someone is killed or injured), and mandatory license suspension or revocation. See Chapter 8 for details.

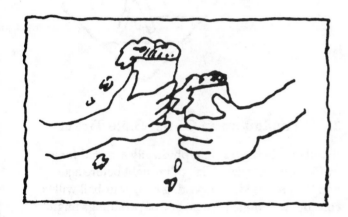

12. Minor Alcohol-Related Offenses (Open Container, etc.)

Having an open alcoholic beverage container in your car or on your person while driving is not as serious as driving while drunk. But it's still fairly serious. It goes on your record if the container was on your person, if the officer saw you actually drinking or you admit to doing so. It is an infraction, so you don't get a jury trial, but you can get a trial before a judge with the officer present. Total fines (including penalty assessments) range from about $100 to $200. A conviction for this charge will be reported to the DMV and may cause your insurance company to cancel your policy. For more information read Chapter 5, Section D, and Chapters 9, 10 and 11.

13. Ignoring a Ticket, Failing to Appear in Court or Failing to Pay a Fine

If you ignore a ticket that you've signed, fail to show up for a hearing you've scheduled or fail to pay a judge-imposed fine, watch out. A warrant will be issued for your arrest and your license will be held in abeyance. You will not only be forced to face the charge or pay the fine, but you'll face an additional misdemeanor conviction that could cost you a total fine of up to $2,500 and/or six months in jail. Also, if you ever happen to be arrested in the future, you'll have a much tougher time getting released before trial.

If you decide to challenge the charge (and you should, given its seriousness), you may be able to raise some procedural defenses and employ some plea bargaining strategy. You might get away with simply pleading guilty to the original charge, or paying the installments if you show that you can't afford to pay it all at once. Read Chapter 7, Section B(3), Chapters 9, 10, 11 and 12, and Chapter 15, Section F.

C. Out-of-State Tickets

"Can I be physically arrested for committing a minor traffic violation in another state?"

"What if I ignore a ticket I get in another state?"

"Will an out-of-state ticket go on my California driving record?"

1. Arrests for Out-of-State Violations

In a few states, out-of-state drivers accused of traffic violations are taken to jail, or before a judge (or justice of the peace), and aren't released until either bail is posted or a fine is paid.[11] This is done because the state has no way short of extradition (having the person arrested and sent back to the state in which the offense occurred) to guarantee the appearance or the payment of the fine of out-of-state residents. This practice is becoming less frequent, but still occurs in some localities. So, when doing extensive driving out of state, you might want to carry some additional cash (perhaps up to $200). Some nationally-known auto clubs have plans whereby members are guaranteed bail bonds of up to several hundred dollars.

2. Your Driving Record

Usually the trouble and expense of traveling back to another state to fight a ticket will outweigh the benefits of just paying the fine. Most people will therefore either plead guilty and pay the fine or arrange to "forfeit bail." If you do this, it might appear on your California driving record maintained by the DMV in Sacramento. More than half the states have a mutual agreement known as the "Driver's License Compact" under which each member state reports out-of-state residents' traffic violation convictions and bail forfeitures to the state that licensed the driver.[12] Member states are:[13]

Alabama	Iowa	New Mexico
Arizona	Kansas	New York
Arkansas	Louisiana	Oklahoma
California	Maine	Oregon
Colorado	Maryland	Tennessee
Delaware	Mississippi	Utah
District of Columbia	Missouri	Virginia
Florida	Montana	Washington
Hawaii	Nebraska	West Virginia
Illinois	Nevada	Wyoming
Indiana	New Jersey	

If the DMV receives the report of a conviction or bail forfeiture from a member state, the offense will appear on your record to the same extent as it would for a similar offense under California law.[14] Thus, speeding violations will appear, while parking infractions will not.

3. If You Ignore an Out-of-State Ticket

In a state where you were physically arrested for a traffic offense, taken to jail or brought before a judge, and then released after posting bail, your bail will be considered forfeited. Then, one of two things might happen. If you're lucky, the judge might choose to treat the matter as though you just paid the fine.

However, not all states allow this, and even in some states that do, it's left to the judge's discretion. It is thus possible that your bail could be declared forfeited plus a warrant would still be issued for your arrest whenever you drive through the state.[15] The state might also suspend your driving privileges within its own borders, in which case you'll also be charged with unlicensed driving.

---

[11]In California, a nonresident unable to supply a local address can be arrested for a traffic infraction, though this is rare in practice. (See VC § 40305.)

[12]VC § 15022.

[13]See VC, § 15000.

---

[14]See VC §§ 1803, 15023(b), (c).

[15]This will often occur where you were released on a signed promise to appear (instead of bail) and didn't show. You might be charged with a new violation of "failure-to-appear."

You will most likely not be arrested in California for ignoring a traffic ticket in another state. Police from other states have no jurisdiction to arrest you outside of that state, and it is unlikely that California law enforcement officers will spend their time and energy to detain you until you can be extradited to the other state to answer to a minor traffic charge.

Finally, since ignoring an out-of-state ticket doesn't result in a conviction or bail forfeiture—unless you actually posted bail—and since only convictions and bail forfeitures are reported by other states, ignoring that ticket won't affect your California driving record. Even if an out-of-state failure-to-appear charge were somehow reported to Sacramento, the DMV will not suspend or refuse to renew your license. The DMV will refuse, however, to renew it—and may suspend it—for a California failure-to-appear charge. (See Chapter 15, Section E.)

	Vehicle Code Section	Classification	Fines (add 145-160% for penalty assessments)/Jail
Speeding (Chapter 4)	§§ 22348-22413	Infraction	$10-100 for first offense, depending on how much over speed limit. (see Chapter 3, Section C)
Minor Moving Violations Other Than Speeding (Running stop lights, improper turns, right of way violations, etc...) (Chapter 5)	§§ 21000-23336	Infraction	$20-30 for most violations.
Reckless Driving, Exhibitions of Speed (Chapter 7)	§§ 23103-23109	Misdemeanor. Felony if hit-and-run and someone is injured	$145-1000 plus 90 days in jail plus license suspension. If injury: $220-1000 plus 6 months in jail.
Drunk Driving (Chapter 8)	§§ 23151-23229	Misdemeanor. Felony if person is injured or fourth offense	Severe. Multiple violations drastically increase penalties. Read Chapter 8, Part B.
Open Alcohol Containers or Marijuana in Your Car (Chapter 5)	§§ 23220-23240 §§ 13202-13202.5	(Alcohol) Infraction or (Marijuana) Misdemeanor if charged under Health & Safety Code	$50-100 (Alcohol) or $100 (Marijuana)
Parking Ticket (Chapter 6)	Local ordinance— varies from city to city	Infraction	$3-100
"Correctable" Equipment Violations (Chapter 6)	§§ 24000-28085	Infraction	No fine, if proof of correction is given to the court. If ignored, fines can be $1000 plus six months in jail. Chapter 6, Section B.
Registration/Expired License Violations (Chapter 6)	§§ 4000-9982	Infraction	Same as above
Driving While License is Suspended (Chapter 7)	§§ 12500-15028	Infraction or Misdemeanor [See Chapter 7, Section B(4)]	1st offense: $1000 plus six months in jail 2nd offense within 5 years: $2,000 plus 1 year in jail [See Chapter 7, Section B(4)]
Driving Without Insurance/Accident Reporting Requirements (Chapter 5)	§§ 16000-16560	Infraction—with stiff penalties. See (Chapter 5, Section E.)	$100. $240 if under influence of alcohol or drugs. $500 for producing false proof of insurance
Ignoring a Ticket/Failing to Show Up for a Court Date/Failing to Pay a Fine (Chapter 7)	§ 40508	Misdemeanor. Prosecutor may elect to treat as infraction. [See Chapter 7, Section B (3)]	Maximum: $500 and 6 months in jail. Likely: $50-100

Does It Go On Your Record?	License Suspension	Insurance Consequences	How to Fight It: (Procedure)
Yes	Rare for 1st or 2nd offenses. Maximum: 1st - 30 days 2nd—60 days 3rd in 3 years—6 months [Chapter 14, Section B(3)]	Rates may rise. Depends on the company. Cancellation is likely after many violations.	Chapter 9, Section A Chapter 10 Chapter 11 Chapter 12
Yes	No. But DMV may suspend license if 4 violations in 12 months, 6 in 24 months, or 8 in 36 months. (See Chapter 15, Section A)	Same as above	Chapter 9, Section A Chapter 10 Chapter 11 Chapter 12
Yes	Up to 6 months	Rates will rise. Policy may be canceled.	Chapter 9 Chapter 10-13
Yes. Remains on record for seven years	Up to 3 years	Same as above. Cancellation likely.	Chapter 8, Section D Chapter 9, Section B Shapter 13
(Alcohol) No, unless you were driving plus container was on your person. (Marijuana) Yes, even if you weren't in your care.	(Alcohol) No. (Marijuana) Yes, up to 3 years for a first offense.	Rates may rise, coverage may be canceled.	Chapter 9, Section B
No	DMV can refuse to renew auto registration for unpaid tickets	None	Chapter 6, Section A
No, except the following: §§ 24002, 24004, 24250, 24409, 24800, 25103, 26707, 27151, 27800, 27801 (See Chapter 3, Section B.)	No	Generally none	Chapter 6, Section B
No	No	Little effect, if any	Chapter 6, Section B
Yes	Will lengthen existing suspension	Few	Chapter 7, Section B(4) Chapter 9, 11-13 Chapter 15
Yes	3 year reporting requirement to keep license. 1 year suspension if in a $500 plus accident while uninsured.	Will be difficult to get insurance while license is suspended	Chapter 15, Section C(5)
Yes. May make it difficult to be released without bail in future cases	DMV will refuse to renew license until underlying offense and failure to appear charge is "adjudicated".	None	Chapter 7, Section B(3) Chapter 14, Section B Chapter 15, Section D

4

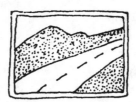

SPEED VIOLATIONS AND RADAR

BECAUSE MORE TICKETS are given for speed violations than for any other moving infraction, we're
devoting an entire chapter to the subject.[1] And since
many speeding tickets are based either on a cop's
use of radar or on aircraft sightings, we show you
how these law enforcement schemes work and the
common defenses you can employ when you are
victimized by them. We also explain how to fight
speeding tickets based on:

- an officer's pacing you (following you and comparing your speed to hers) by patrol car or aircraft;

- a speed trap involving the misuse of radar; and

- "photo-radar," where a combined radar unit and
  camera was used to generate a ticket which was
  mailed to you.

Note: If you weren't charged with speeding, you
can skip this chapter.

Another note: If you were going over 55 mph (or
65 on designated portions of federal interstate highways), skip Sections A, B, C and D, and begin
reading at Section E of this chapter. If you were
traveling less than 55, read on.

We begin with the good-and-bad news that
although California's speed laws are a little more
complicated than you might expect, this gives you
quite a bit more room within which to beat a ticket—
especially if radar was used.

A. The 'Basic Speed Law' (VC §§ 22350, 22351)

VC § 22350. No person shall drive a vehicle upon
a highway at a speed greater than is reasonable
or prudent having due regard for weather, visibility, the traffic on, and the surface and width of,
the highway, and in no event at a speed that
endangers the safety of persons or property.

---

[1] The more serious misdemeanors of "speed contest" and
"exhibition of speed" are covered in Chapter 7, Section B(2).

VC § 22351(a). The speed of any vehicle upon a
highway not in excess of the limits in § 22352 or
established as authorized by this code[2] is lawful
unless clearly proved to be in violation of the
Basic Speed Law.

(b) The speed of any vehicle on a
highway in excess of the prima facie speed limits
in § 22352 or established as authorized by this
code is prima facie unlawful unless the defendant
establishes by competent evidence that the
speed in excess of said limits did not constitute a
violation of the Basic Speed Law at the time,
place and under the conditions then existing.

1. The Elements of the Offense and the Burden of Proof

Violation of the Basic Speed Law—driving over the
speed limit, but less than 55 mph or 65 mph maximum speed limit on a highway or freeway—is an
offense for which most people have been ticketed at
one time or another. However, surprising as it may
seem, a person traveling over the speed limit—but
less than the usually-55 mph maximum speed
limit—isn't necessarily violating the law.[3] On the
other hand, in some rare circumstances, usually
during a heavy fog or a driving rainstorm, you can
actually be in violation of this law even though you
were driving below the speed limit. Why? Because
in these circumstances it may be imprudent and
unreasonable to drive faster than a crawl.

What you are really being charged with is
driving "at a speed greater than is reasonable or
prudent...." The posted or otherwise defined speed
limit is only *presumed* to be the "reasonable or prudent" speed. When you are ticketed for exceeding

---

[2] "[T]he limits in Section 22352 or established as authorized by
this code..." refers to the 25 mph speed limit in residence or
business districts and school zones and the 15 mph speed limit at
uncontrolled intersections and railroad crossings (VC § 22352) or
to properly posted speed limits (VC §§ 22354-22358.4).

[3] See VC §§ 22350, 22351 and *Ex parte Mosely/In re Johnson* (1935) 6
Cal.App.2d 654, 45 P.2d 241.

the posted speed, the officer is taking advantage of a legal "presumption" that anything above the posted speed is unsafe.

Now, let's look at the elements of Section 22350, the offense:

1. You must be driving a vehicle;

2. Upon a highway (defined as a "way or place of whatever nature, publicly maintained and open to the use of the public for purposes of vehicular travel")—including a "street" (VC § 360); and

3. Your speed either must be "greater than is reasonable or prudent" or must "endanger the safety of persons or property."

This last element is obviously the one most open to interpretation. Those readers who have recently moved to California may be unfamiliar with this concept, as opposed to the law in many other states that says that "if you were going over the limit, you're guilty, and that's it." In California, this is only true if you exceed 55 mph (or 65 on certain Interstate freeways), a different violation—see Section E of this chapter.

Section 22351 goes on to state that the law *presumes* that the reasonable or prudent speed is the one posted on the speed limit signs. This is called the "prima facie" speed limit.

If you were going over the posted speed limit, you have an opportunity to defeat the "presumption" that you were going over a reasonable and prudent speed. You might do this by proving that weather, visibility, road width, etc., did not make a higher speed unsafe. You should realize that even though you're presumed not guilty, you bear the burden of proving that a speed in excess of the posted limit was safe.[4] You are saying, essentially, "even if Your Honor finds that I was exceeding the speed limit, I'm still not guilty because my speed

was reasonable and prudent in light of the circumstances."

Note: It is entirely proper to advance inconsistent arguments, i.e. to argue that 1) you didn't exceed the speed limit, and 2) even if you did, it was still safe to do so.

B.   "Technical" Defenses to Basic Speed Law Charge

THERE ARE TWO BASIC TYPES of defenses to a speeding charge under the Basic Speed Law. One type—the technical defense—is that the police used impermissible methods to catch you. The other—the substantive defense—is that the police were wrong in their conclusions. We discuss the technical defenses first, in this part, because you normally raise them first in a trial, when the police officer testifies before you do. The substantive defenses are discussed next, in Section C.

1.   Illegal Use of Radar— "Speed Trap" Laws

There are certain rules restricting when a traffic officer may or may not use radar to detect violations of the Basic Speed Law. You'll soon discover that these rules don't make much logical sense. But they're great for fighting tickets. They contain lots of "technicalities" that can result in your ticket being dismissed.

Okay, now for the rules. On most streets, if the speed limit hasn't been "justified" within the past five years with an "engineering and traffic survey," the police may not use radar at that location. This is because state law defines the use of radar on streets with unjustifiably low speed limits as an illegal "speed trap." Vehicle Code Section 40802(b) defines a radar "speed trap" as:

---

[4]In lawyer's jargon, you need to "rebut" the presumption you were driving at an unsafe speed with evidence that establishes a "reasonable doubt" as to whether your actual speed was unsafe. See Evidence Code § 607.

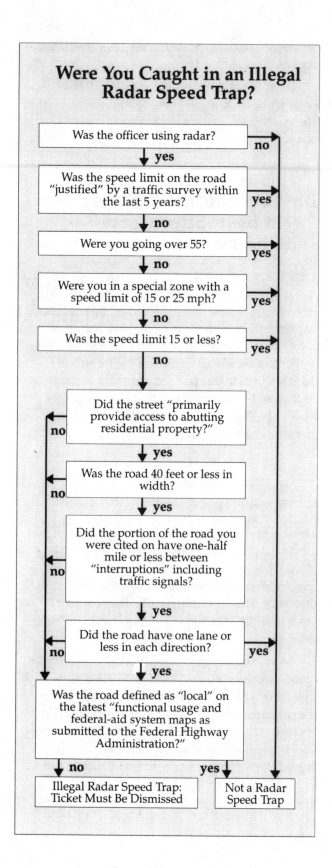

Were You Caught in an Illegal Radar Speed Trap?

Was the officer using radar? → **no**
↓ **yes**

Was the speed limit on the road "justified" by a traffic survey within the last 5 years? → **yes**
↓ **no**

Were you going over 55? → **yes**
↓ **no**

Were you in a special zone with a speed limit of 15 or 25 mph? → **yes**
↓ **no**

Was the speed limit 15 or less? → **yes**
↓ **no**

Did the street "primarily provide access to abutting residential property?" ← **no**
↓ **yes**

Was the road 40 feet or less in width? ← **no**
↓ **yes**

Did the portion of the road you were cited on have one-half mile or less between "interruptions" including traffic signals? ← **no**
↓ **yes**

Did the road have one lane or less in each direction? ← **no** / → **yes**
↓ **yes**

Was the road defined as "local" on the latest "functional usage and federal-aid system maps as submitted to the Federal Highway Administration?"
↓ **no**   **yes** ↓

Illegal Radar Speed Trap: Ticket Must Be Dismissed   Not a Radar Speed Trap

A particular section of a highway...where the speed limit is not justified by an *engineering and traffic survey conducted within five years prior to the date of the alleged violation* and where enforcement involves the use of radar or other electronic devices that measure the speed of moving objects.[5]

What this definition means is that wherever radar is used, some city, county or state agency should have, within the previous five years, examined traffic and road conditions, including prevailing speeds, accident records, potential hazards and visibility. According to the California Department of Transportation, the "justified" speed limit will be taken as the speed that is not exceeded by 85% of the traffic, though other factors, such as accident history, may be considered.[6] If the speed limit hasn't been justified by such a survey, the road is a "speed trap" and it is illegal for a traffic officer to use radar at all (VC § 40801). Cities and counties cannot enact local ordinances to evade the traffic-survey requirements.[7]

One appeals court has ruled that an officer's mere *statement* that such a traffic study was made is insufficient to prove that it actually was done—unless the officer personally participated in the study.[8] If the officer did not personally participate in the study, a "certified" (authenticated) copy of the study must be physically introduced into evidence by the prosecution (normally this will be the police officer, as very few prosecutors appear in traffic cases). In some courts, however, you may have to

---

[5]This is a fairly narrow definition of speed trap. Most folks think of a speed trap as a place where the speed limit is too low and the officer hides in wait for an unsuspecting speeder. However, this type of speed trap is perfectly legal, *unless* radar is used *and* the speed limit is not justified by an engineering and traffic survey.

[6]See also VC § 627 for the list of requirements for a valid survey. The Department of Transportation requirements for a valid traffic survey are found in a manual entitled: *Traffic Manual, State of California, Department of Transportation, Business and Transportation Agency*. For a copy, send a letter and $30 + sales tax by check or money order, payable to Caltrans, Attn: Headquarters Cashier, P.O. Box 942874, Sacramento, CA 94724-0001. Delivery takes one to two weeks.

[7]*People v. Stone* (1987) 190 Cal.App.3d Supp. 1, 236 Cal.Rptr. 140.

[8]*People v. Sterritt* (1976) 65 Cal.App.3d Supp.1, 135 Cal.Rptr. 552.

insist on this requirement rather than rely on the judge to require it on her own.[9] Unless proper evidence of such a traffic study has been admitted, the courts are legally forbidden to find anyone guilty of a speed violation detected by radar.[10]

---

[9]*People v. Halopoff* (1976) 60 Cal.App.3d Supp.1, 131 Cal.Rptr. 531. See also *People v. Abelson* (1980) 104 Cal.App.3d Supp.16, 164 Cal.Rptr. 369; *People v. DiFiore* (1987) 197 Cal.App.3d Supp.26, 243 Cal.Rptr. 359. The Los Angeles County Superior Court's Appellate Department has ruled a certified copy must be physically introduced into evidence, whether the defendant insists on it or not; the same court has also ruled that it isn't enough for the judge to simply refer to a survey filed with the court. (This is called taking "judicial notice.") *People v. Flaxman* (1977) 74 Cal.App.3d Supp.16, 141 Cal.Rptr. 799. However, Santa Clara County's Appellate Department ruled in *People v. Peterson* (1986) 181 Cal.App.3d Supp.7, 226 Cal.Rptr. 544 that the survey doesn't have to be introduced after the judge takes "judicial notice" of it, unless the defendant insists on its production. In either case, you have a right to insist on inspection of the survey or dismissal of the case. We discuss how this is done in Chapter 11, Section D(1), on trials in speeding cases.

[10]VC § 40805 absolutely forbids radar-based speed-trap convictions, even if illegal radar-based evidence is admitted.

Although the admission of such evidence is forbidden under VC §§ 40803(a) and 40804(a), Article I, § 28(d) of the California Constitution (added by ballot initiative in 1982), states, "relevant evidence shall not be excluded in any criminal proceeding." This may mean some judges will allow radar-based evidence to be admitted into the record even though such evidence is barred by statute. (But see *People v. Halopoff* (1976) 60 Cal.App.3d Supp.1, 7, 131 Cal.Rptr. 531 for the view that Sections 40803 and 40804 are more than mere rules of evidence.)

Nevertheless, even if one takes the view that Article I, § 28(d) does allow the admission of relevant but illegal evidence, it does not override the explicit language of VC § 40805, which plainly forbids convictions based on illegal radar-based evidence. The Alameda County Superior Court agreed that speed-trap convictions are prohibited despite Proposition 8, in an unreported decision, *People v. Wiegand*, Case No. 1869, April 21, 1986.

There are several exceptions to the above rule.[11] It does not apply to:

- roads where the speed limit is 55 mph or higher, including freeways;
- streets in school zones where the speed limit is 15 or 20 mph, in 25 mph school zones when children are present, near children's playgrounds while children are present, and 25 mph zones near senior centers where "SENIOR" sign is posted;
- most streets with 15 mph speed limits; *and*
- "local streets and roads," as defined by Section 40802(b).

For this last exception to apply, the officer must show that, either:

1. The local street or road is referred to as such on "the latest functional usage and federal-aid system maps as submitted to the Federal Highway Administration";

OR, *all* of the following:

2a. The street or road "primarily provides access to abutting residential property"; and

b. Is 40 feet or less in width; and

c. The portion of the street or road on which you were cited is one-half mile or less in length between "interruptions" including traffic signals; and

d. Has no more than *one lane* in each direction.

In practice, this last exception isn't too important. Very few places qualify as "local streets and roads" under either definition and still have enough

---

[11]The reason for all these exceptions is that a speed trap is defined on the basis that speed limits are set pursuant to VC §§ 22352(b)(1): 25 mph in business or residence district; 22354: state highway limits reduced from 55 mph; 22357: local limits increased from 25 mph, e.g., 30, 35, etc. mph in business or residence district; 22358: decrease of local limits in general; and 22358.3: decrease on narrow streets. Speed limits not included in the speed-trap definition include those in VC §§ 22352(a): 15 mph in certain areas; 22352(b)(2): school zones while children are present; 22352(b)(3): 25 mph zones where "SENIOR" signs are posted; 22357.1: 25 mph near park playgrounds when children are likely to be present; and 22358.4: 15 mph or 20 mph in school zones.

traffic to make radar enforcement worthwhile for the police.

To summarize, an officer who testifies that he used radar to nab you for speeding, must, in addition, prove that one of the following is true:

1. You were cited for going over the posted limit on a road where the speed limit was 55 or greater (a violation of the *maximum* speed law, actually, rather than of the Basic Speed Law); or

2. You were cited for exceeding the 15 or 20 mph speed limit in a school zone; or

3. You were cited for exceeding a 25 mph speed limit in a school zone where children were present; or

4. You were cited for exceeding a 25 mph limit near a park playground where children were present or likely to be present; or

5. You were cited for exceeding a 25 mph limit in a "SENIOR" zone; or

6. You were cited for exceeding any other 15 mph limit; or

7. The "local street or road" on which you were driving is defined as such on a map of the city or county submitted to the Federal Highway Administration; or

8. The road on which you were driving was in a residential zone, was 40 feet or less in width, had no more than one lane in either direction, and had a half mile or less between "interruptions"; or

9. An engineering and traffic survey justifying the speed limit was conducted within five years prior to the date of the violation.

> **Example:** You were cited for doing 35 mph on a four-lane road near no schools. The city council (due to pressure from local residents) set the speed limit at a ridiculously-low 25 mph. Since an impartial engineering and traffic survey recommends a 30 mph limit, the speed limit isn't "justified" by the survey. Neither is the road considered "local," because it has four lanes and is 50 feet wide. Use of radar on this road, to enforce the Basic Speed Law, is forbidden as a speed trap.

When a police officer testifies that she used radar, but neither she nor anyone else mentions anything about an engineering and traffic survey, the "local streets" exception, or any of the other exceptions listed above, the judge must find you not guilty. (Be warned, however, that some judges think that *you* have to raise this point during the trial in order to have it apply. To be on the safe side, it is best to raise an objection to any radar evidence at the moment the officer tries to introduce it at trial. We show you how to do this in Chapter 11.)

2. "Photo-Radar"—Radar Unit With Cameras

In 1988, the city of Pasadena began using a "Zelleweger-Ulster Photographic Doppler Unit" (a fancy name for an unmanned radar unit linked to a camera) to detect speeders. Not happy with the fact that live police officers may legally hide in the bushes with radar guns, Pasadena figured on raising revenue without having to pay police officers. Typically, a radar unit is placed in an unmarked parked car and set to activate a camera when it detects a vehicle traveling at a pre-set speed. The unit registers the vehicle's speed and takes a picture of the front of the vehicle, including the front license plate and driver. A notice to appear in court is mailed to the vehicle's registered owner. Several cities have since followed Pasadena's lead, and now do this also.

Unfortunately, no law prevents the use of such Big Brother technology, and other cities are considering using these devices. However, all the speed trap laws apply whenever radar is used—whether used by a live police officer or not. That means when photo-radar is used, the prosecution must still prove the road isn't an illegal speed trap, as discussed above.

If you receive a notice to appear in court on a photo-radar speeding charge, there will be no police officer to 1) identify you or 2) testify to the road, weather and traffic condition. However, the local police department will have obtained a driver's license photograph of the person to whom the vehicle was registered, to compare with the photo that the photo-radar unit took.

There is no legal rule that says the owner of a speeding vehicle was necessarily the person who drove it and committed the offense.[12] Also, you have a Fifth Amendment right to refuse to admit you were the driver. This means that the photo taken must clearly identify you in the driver's seat. If glare, darkness, tinted windows or other factors prevent a clear photo of the driver, the case should be dismissed without your having to testify.[13] That being so, you should exercise your right to insist on seeing the photographs *before* you appear before the judge. The police department is required to let you see the photographs first. Also, as we'll see in Section C(2) of this chapter, your testimony that you were driving safely under the circumstances may get

you an acquittal. And, in photo-radar cases, there will be no officer to testify otherwise.

Note: More about radar—how it works and how it is used—is found in Section F of this chapter.

3. Other "Speed Trap" Defenses

There's one other Vehicle Code definition of speed trap that's not of much importance, but which you should keep in the back of your mind. Before radar came into widespread use, speeds were often determined by "clocking" the time it took a vehicle to drive over a marked road distance. Sometimes an actual hand-held stopwatch was used, and a frustrated or dishonest officer could fudge a little and get a higher speed by starting the stopwatch a little later or stopping it a little sooner as the vehicle passed by the appropriate point on the road. This method of apprehending speeders is outlawed by VC § 40802(a), which also defines a speed trap as:

> A particular section of a highway measured as to distance and with boundaries marked, designated, or otherwise determined in order that the speed of a vehicle may be calculated by securing the time it takes the vehicle to travel the known distance.

This prevents police agencies from using not only the stopwatch method, but also "Prather" devices. These involve two rubber tubings (something like the kind you drive across at gas stations to alert the attendant) stretched across a lane and spaced about a car length apart. A built-in timer is turned on and off as the vehicle drives across the first and second hoses. (Whenever you see these devices, they are used for traffic-survey, not law enforcement, purposes.)

Also outlawed by VC § 40802(a) is a certain use of "VASCAR," which is an acronym ("Visual Average Speed Computer and Recorder") for a glorified electronic stopwatch connected to a simple distance/time computer. (VASCAR has absolutely nothing to do with radar, and does not emit electronic signals.) Simply stated, the officer travels a measured distance between two points on a road and this distance

---

[12]See *People v. Forbath* (1935) 5 Cal.App.2d Supp. 767, where the court ruled that even in parking cases, the law won't automatically presume the owner committed the offense by illegally parking the car. This rule applies to non-parking violations as well.

[13]If you choose to be represented by a lawyer, and don't appear yourself (allowed per VC § 40507), your lawyer can point out that even a *clear* photo of *someone* driving a car registered to you is not enough to convict you, absent evidence of what you look like! This argument may work well if your driver's license photo does not closely match the photo that the radar unit took.

is fed into the computer. While parked out of sight, he then operates the timer controls based on his visual perception of when your car passes through those points, in the same manner as the buttons on old stopwatches were pushed.[14]

However, for legal hair splitting and exotic reasons beyond the scope of this book (and beyond reason), VASCAR can legally be used by a *moving* police vehicle. (The difference has to do with the idea that a moving police car does not use any one "particular" stretch of road to measure your speed.[15]) Nevertheless, in view of the abandonment of VASCAR by most police departments in favor of low-priced hand-held radar guns, cases involving the illegality of VASCAR as a speed trap rarely occur.

C. Substantive Defenses to Basic Speed Law Charge

The fact that the speed limit on a particular stretch of road has not been justified by an engineering and traffic survey (see Section B, above) does *not* mean that the speed limit is unenforceable. It just means that *radar* can't be used to enforce it. The police are free to use other methods of estimating the speed of a fast moving vehicle, including "pacing" or following it while observing the patrol car's own "calibrated" (certified as accurate) speedometer. When faced with this type of law enforcement, you will need to prove that the officer's estimate of your

---

[14]This type of arrangement was held to be an illegal "speed trap" in *People v. Johnson* (1972) 29 Cal.App.3d Supp.1, 105 Cal.Rptr. 212.

[15]A 1969 Attorney General's opinion (52 Ops. Atty. Gen.231) says that since VASCAR can be used along *any* distance measured by the patrol car's odometer, and not just a "particular" section of a highway, its use in moving vehicles is not prohibited under the law prohibiting speed traps. And while there are no appeals court cases on whether moving police *cars* can use VASCAR, it has been held that *aircraft* patrols can use measured distances on the road to calibrate their own speed and then pace the automobile's speed because no particular section of the road is used to calculate the car's speed. See *People v. Darby* (1979) 95 Cal.App.3d 707, 157 Cal.Rptr. 300 and *People v. Echols* (1975) 46 Cal.App.3d Supp.1, 120 Cal.Rptr. 375.

speed was mistaken. In Section 1, below, we explain how you can do this.

We'll also show you, in Section 2, that even if you can't prove the officer incorrectly estimated your speed, you can still argue that the speed you were allegedly going was reasonable under the circumstances, so no laws were broken and your ticket should be dismissed.

Note: Of course, in cases where radar was legally used, you can try to challenge the accuracy of the radar measurements, but these arguments are tough to make and require some technical knowledge of how radar works. Accordingly, that subject is covered separately in Section F of this chapter.

rush hour

1. Pacing

Many tickets for violation of the Basic Speed Law result from the police officer following the suspected speeder and using his own speedometer to clock the suspect's speed. This technique is known as pacing. Contrary to popular belief, there is no law stating that an officer must follow a vehicle a given distance, say one-eighth or one-fourth mile, before ticketing the driver. In practice, a cop will try to follow you for some reasonable distance if he can, to increase the effectiveness of his testimony should you contest the ticket. But cops who are out to fill their quotas sometimes present "evidence" based on tailing a speeding car less than a block, or even by guessing at the approximate speed. One Oakland judge convicted a supposed speeder on the officer's testimony that the driver's car "sounded like it was being driven at an excessive speed."

If you know an officer was behind you for only a short distance, your best tactic is to cross-examine the officer as to the distance he tailed you. If he admits it was, say, only one-eighth mile (between one and two city blocks), it will help to testify (if true) that while you were driving (at the speed limit) you noticed in your rear view mirror that the officer was closing the gap between your car and his very quickly, having the effect of giving him a high speedometer reading. This can be represented graphically as follows:

When the officer starts following (and clocking) you:

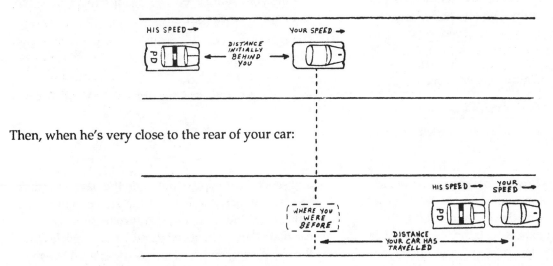

Then, when he's very close to the rear of your car:

You can see from this diagram that the faster police car bearing down on you will cover more distance in the same amount of time. The mathematical relationship between the two speeds (the officer's and yours), the distance the officer initially was behind you, and the distance your car traveled since the officer began following you can be expressed by the formula:[16]

---

[16]This formula is derived as follows: First, let "t" be the time it takes you going at speed "vyou" and the officer, going at speed "vcop," to travel the respective distances "dyou" and "dcop." This time "t" will equal both (dyou/vyou) and (dcop/vcop), which are equal to each other, both being equal to time "t." Therefore, (dcop/vcop) = (dyou/vyou). It's also true that if the officer drove faster to gain on you, then dcop = dyou + the distance the officer was originally behind you (we call this dcop behind). Also, from rearranging (dcop/vcop) = (dyou/vyou), we get dcop = (dyou x vcop)/vyou. These last two "dcop" equations are equal to each other, so, dyou + dcop was behind you = (dyou and vcop)/vyou. Rearranging this last equation gives: vyou = (dyou x vcop)/(dyou + dcop behind). Dividing both numerator and denominator by dyou, we get: vyou = vcop/ [1 + (dcop behind /dyou)].

$$\text{Your speed} = \frac{\text{Officer's speed}}{1 + \dfrac{\text{Distance the officer was initially behind you}}{\text{Distance your car travelled until he was on your bumper}}}$$

Here's an example of how this formula works. If the officer was going 65 mph on the freeway (they do it all the time) starting out one-quarter mile behind you and tailed you for one and one-half miles,

finally bearing down on your rear bumper, he will say that since his speed was 65 mph and he was following you, your speed was 65 mph too. However, your speed works out to:

$$\frac{65 \text{ mph (officer's speed)}}{1 + \dfrac{1/4 \text{ mile initially behind you}}{1\text{-}1/2 \text{ miles you drove as he followed you}}} = \frac{65 \text{ mph}}{1 + 1/6} = 55 \text{ mph}$$

If the officer testifies, on cross-examination, to speeds and distances which, when put into the formula, show you were driving under the speed limit, your case is almost won. If the officer testifies to distances that won't calculate in your favor, you might be able to truthfully testify to ones that will. When your turn comes to testify, emphasize (if true) how you initially saw the patrol car some distance back in your rearview mirror, then saw it bear down on you so fast that you thought it was going to rear-end your car.

You should also testify (if true) that you were periodically glancing at your speedometer, that it indicated a certain speed, and that you held steadily to this speed—without slowing down—before and after you saw the patrol car.

A certified speedometer calibration can be obtainable from a speedometer shop (look under "speedometers" in your yellow pages). This is excellent proof that your own speedometer was accurate, but it's fairly expensive. You can also check your speedometer's accuracy on the freeway by using a stopwatch while going exactly "55 mph," according to the speedometer, between mile markers. These are white strips about a foot wide

and several feet long, painted on the paved shoulder of the road, perpendicular to the direction of travel. Officers in slow-flying aircraft use these markers to calculate their own speed as they pace vehicles from the air. When you travel at exactly 55 mph between mile intervals, your speed is 80.67 feet per second, and you travel the 5280 feet (or one mile) in exactly 65.5 seconds. If the number of seconds between mile markers at "55 mph" is something *other* than 65.5 seconds, use the following chart to calculate the true speed:

Seconds elapsed between mile markers	Your true speed (MPH)
50 seconds	72.0 mph
55 seconds	65.5 mph
60 seconds	60.0 mph
65 seconds	55.4 mph
70 seconds	51.4 mph
75 seconds	48.0 mph

You can also use the following formula to calculate your true speed:

$$\text{Speed, mph} = \frac{3,600}{\text{seconds between mile markers}}$$

A speedometer inaccuracy that makes yours read too high will help you. If, for example, your speedometer reads 55, but your watch says that 75 seconds passed, you were really going 48 mph. Your speedometer reads 8 mph lower (at 55) than it should.[17] Your testimony to this effect would indicate that you were going *slower* than you thought you were when you looked at your speedometer.

If, on the other hand, your speedometer read 55, but your stopwatch indicated that only 55 seconds had passed, you were really doing 65.5 mph. So here your speedometer reads *lower* than it should, fooling you into believing you're doing 55 when you're actually doing 65. If you testified to this, it would be almost an admission you were going over the speed limit. But, this too is a legal defense *if* you had no reason to believe your speedometer was in error.[18] (If you'd noticed that the pace of traffic had seemed to be unusually slow whenever you drove, that might give you reason to believe your speedometer reading was too low. Of course, you have no obligation to volunteer information about your speedometer's accuracy.)

2. Proving an Over-the-Limit Speed Safe

As we saw earlier, you can defend against a charge of violating the Basic Speed Law not only by showing you weren't exceeding the speed limit, but also by establishing that even if you were over the limit, your speed was nevertheless "safe" under the circumstances.

Example: You were clocked by radar going 43 mph on a street where 35 mph signs are properly posted. The law presumes that you were driving faster than was reasonable or prudent. To fight this ticket you might advance two arguments (depending, of course, on the facts):

1. the police officer misused the radar and his clocking was therefore inaccurate (discussed later in this chapter); and

2. the weather was perfect, the road was dry and unobstructed, the traffic was very light—or if it was heavy, that you had to drive over the posted speed limit in order to keep up with traffic.

If you establish the first point to the judge's satisfaction, you will win. But even if you lose on this point, you may be able to establish that the speed you were driving was safe under the Basic Speed Law—assuming you get an open-minded and fair judge.

The important things to remember when fighting the presumption created by the posted speed limit under the Basic Speed Law are:

1. the prosecutor or police officer has the burden of proving what the speed limit was, and that you were driving at a certain speed over that; and

2. you have the burden of proving that such a speed was nevertheless safe (in addition, of course, to any evidence you can truthfully present to show that you weren't going over the limit.)

Proving your case becomes more difficult, of course, as your speed increases. For example, proving that 38 mph in a 35 mph zone was safe may not be very difficult. Indeed, it's precisely for this

---

[17]Just because it reads 8 mph lower when you're going 55 mph does not mean it reads 8 mph lower at 35, i.e., 28 mph. Speedometer calibration inaccuracies are never the same at each speed.

[18]Some judges think you're guilty of going over the speed limit even if you had an honest but mistaken belief you were doing less than that. This is incorrect; as a few judges do understand, the "mistake of fact" defense applies in *all* criminal cases, since infractions are "public offenses" [PC § 16(3)] and criminal intent or negligence is an element of all public offenses (PC § 20). See also PC § 19.7. You may have to point this out to the judge, who otherwise might be inclined simply to find you guilty and give you a break on the fine only.

reason that some judges automatically dismiss tickets—and few officers bother giving them—for driving five mph or less over the speed limit.

"Proving" that it was perfectly safe to drive over the speed limit depends solely on testimony given by you and possibly others who were in the car with you. Remember to address the following facts:

- **Weather:** It will count in your favor if you were driving during the *daytime* and there was no fog or rain, nor a cloud in the sky.

- **Visibility:** If you were driving on a straight stretch of road with very few or no visual blocks such as trees, parked cars and curves, you can use these facts to help establish that it was safe for you to go over the posted speed limit.

- **Neighborhood:** It helps if there were no side streets from which cars might have suddenly appeared or residential areas where children could have run out into the street.

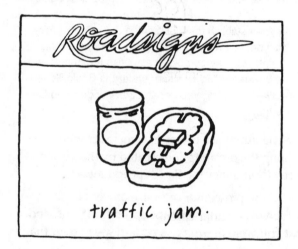

- **Traffic:** This is one that might work in your favor either way. If there was a lot of traffic and everyone was going about the same speed (and over the speed limit), you could argue that you might have endangered yourself and others by slowing down the flow of traffic. In fact, you might be able to argue that, had you had driven more

slowly, you would have been illegally impeding traffic. [See Chapter 5, Section C(2).][19] Also, if there was a lot of traffic, and radar was used, you may be able to successfully argue that the officer's radar unit was focused on another vehicle instead of yours. (See Section F.) If there was little or no traffic on the road, and the posted speed limit was designed with average traffic flow in mind, you might be able to justify going 5 to 10 mph over the limit.

- **Road Width:** There are some roads designed for safe driving at 35 to 45 mph, but on which for some reason (usually pressure on local city councils from nearby residents), the speed limit is a ridiculous 25 or 30 mph. When you've been caught for speeding on such roads, there are two things working in your favor: First, your testimony as to the very large road width, along with other testimony regarding weather, visibility and traffic, may convince a judge that you were driving safely, even though over the posted limit. Second, as discussed in Section B(1), above, if radar was used, it may have been used illegally.

D. Speeding on Bridges, Tunnels and Overpasses (VC § 22405)

VC § 22405(a). No person shall drive a vehicle on any bridge, elevated structure, tube, or tunnel constituting a part of a highway, at a speed which is greater than the maximum speed that can be maintained with safety to such structure.

(b). Upon the trial of any person charged with a violation of this section...proof of the determination of the maximum speed by the Department of Transportation or local authority and the erection and maintenance of the speed

---

[19]As discussed in Chapter 5, this defense would be particularly effective if traffic was too heavy to allow you to get into the slow lane, or if you were on a two-lane road with a line of cars behind you and no place to turn out.

signs shall constitute prima facie evidence of the maximum speed that can be maintained with safety to the bridge, elevated structure, tube, or tunnel.

ONCE IN A WHILE, a ticket will be given for driving over the speed limit posted on a bridge, freeway overpass or tunnel. This violation is similar to the Basic Speed Law in that it forbids driving faster than a "speed that can be maintained with safety." Again, the posted speed limit isn't absolute; any speed over it is only *presumed* to be unsafe, and this presumption can be rebutted. Therefore, everything we said about arguing that your speed was safe under the circumstances with respect to the Basic Speed Law (Section C(2), above) applies here too. However, the police may use radar even though an engineering and traffic survey hasn't been made, though they almost never do—it's too dangerous to use while parked on bridges, tunnels and overpasses.

E. Exceeding the 55/65 mph Speed Limit— (VC §§ 22349/22356)

VC § 22349(a). Except as provided in Section 22356, which allows the California Department of Transportation to raise the speed limit to 65 on some rural portions of freeways, no person shall drive a vehicle upon a highway at a speed greater than 55 mph.[20]

1. Basic Speed Law Defenses Are Not Available

Under this statute, the prosecution need only prove you were going faster than 55 mph, or 65 mph if posted on certain highways in rural areas. The relative safety of your speed under the circumstances is beside the point and the Basic Speed Law defense covered in Section C, above, cannot be used.

The 65 mph speed limit applies mostly on some rural portions of certain Interstate-system freeways (ones designated with a red, white and blue marker):

on a few state highways:

and some U.S. system highways that cross state lines:

Common radar defenses will often be of no use under the maximum speed law, for two reasons. First, the "radar speed trap" defense may not apply to violations of this statute.[21] Second, "over 55/65"

---

[20]It is theoretically possible for a person to simultaneously violate *both* this code section *and* the Basic Speed Law, for example, by doing 58 mph in a 35 mph zone. But police officers almost never cite for two speed violations arising out of the same offense, and the constitutional prohibition against double jeopardy (as well as PC § 654) prevents double punishment for two offenses simultaneously committed in the same "act."

[21]The speed trap laws set out in VC §§ 40802-40805 seem to apply only to violations of the Basic Speed Law (VC § 22350) under some circumstances, and not to the maximum-speed law (VC § 22349). Even so, the cases of *People v. Flaxman* (1977) 74 Cal.App.3d Supp.16 and *People v. DiFiore* (1987) 197 Cal.App.3d Supp.26 say the speed trap rules do apply *if you are charged with violating the Basic Speed Law* (VC § 22350)—even if your speed was over 55. However, these cases are binding only in Los Angeles County.

tickets commonly are given by the highway patrol, and the highway patrol does not use radar unless it is so equipped by the local county government.[22]

Don't think that you cannot fight the ticket, however. Several means are still available: The officer may not show up for trial [see Chapter 12, Section C(2)], or you may be able to establish enough doubt about your speed because the officer was measuring it while gaining on you from behind. [See Section C(1).]

2. Defense against Aircraft Patrol Sighting

If your ticket was based on a reading from an aircraft patrol, there are several ways you may be able to challenge it. Increasingly, drivers on California highways are receiving their tickets from a CHP unit that has been alerted to your speed by radio reports from airplanes. The aircraft is supposed to pace the car and measure the speed according to the time it takes the aircraft to pass between two markers on the highway set a mile apart. However, sometimes the aircraft measures the speed by the time it takes the car to pass between these markers. Either way, if a car is found to be speeding, a waiting ground patrol car is radioed. It, in turn, will either independently check your speed by pacing you, or will pull you over solely on the basis of the aircraft report.

If the ground patrol car did not independently verify your speed, your chances of successfully fighting this ticket are greatly increased. Why? Both the aircraft officer and ground officer will have to be present—the aircraft officer to testify about your speed, *and* the ground officer to testify that you were

the driver.[23] If either officer fails to appear, you can ask the court to dismiss the case. If you are asked to allow an absent officer's police report or other written record into court in place of live testimony, you have a right under the hearsay rule to refuse and insist that the case be dismissed if the officer is not personally present.

Even if both officers show up, it is possible for you to win. First, ask the judge to exclude one officer from the courtroom while the other is testifying. This will help prevent them from taking cues from each other. The aircraft officer will usually be the first to take the stand. He or she will testify that the car's speed was computed either from the speed of the aircraft passing through the marks, or from the speed of the car passing through the marks. In the first case, there is plenty of room for error (e.g., angle of flight, shortcut straight flight path along curving highway, inconsistent distance while pacing, inaccuracy in ascertaining reference points from the air, etc.). In the second situation, they have used a "speed trap," illegal under VC § 40802(a).[24]

---

[22]As of this writing (March 1991), radar has been supplied to the highway patrol for local use by the following 25 counties: Los Angeles, San Diego, Santa Clara, Alameda, Orange, Ventura, Sacramento, Fresno, Santa Barbara, San Bernardino, Santa Cruz, Contra Costa, Marin, Monterey, Riverside, San Joaquin, Sonoma, Kern, Kings, Placer, Nevada, Mono, El Dorado, Mendocino and Inyo. Still, radar is not used entirely throughout these counties, but only in certain areas where county supervisors are concerned about safety.

---

[23]If the ground officer fails to show, the prosecution cannot prove its case because the state must prove you were the driver independent of your own statement—and you have a Fifth Amendment right not to be forced to admit that.

[24]See *People v. Darby* (1979) 95 Cal.App.3d 707, 157 Cal.Rptr. 300.

After testifying about how the speed was computed, the aircraft officer will next tell about radioing the ground unit. Here it is possible that he got the wrong car. License plate numbers are too small for the airborne officer to see, and many modern cars tend to look alike from above. If the ground-unit officer is excluded from the courtroom, and takes with him the copy of the ticket—which he, not the aircraft officer, issued—the aircraft officer won't be able to use the ticket to "refresh his memory" while testifying. In this situation, it isn't difficult to get the aircraft officer to admit, on cross-examination, that he can't remember details of particular cars he observed from the air.

If the ground officer testifies that he independently checked your speed, you can argue that he was prejudiced by the radio report and too eagerly bore down on you at a high speed—hence *his* high speedometer reading.

F. All About Radar

The majority of moving violations are given for speed violations. Since many involve the use of radar, it makes sense to examine how radar works, how it is used, how it malfunctions, and even how dishonest cops can put false readings on radar equipment.

It can be an uphill battle trying to convince judges (and most other people with little or no scientific training) that sophisticated electronic gadgetry is *not* infallible and *not* always superior to human observation. Nevertheless, after you've read this section, you'll know more about radar than most police officers and judges, and may be able to use that advantage in court. Tickets based on radar readings can be beaten.

1. How It Works

The word "radar" is an acronym for "radio detection and ranging." In simple terms, radar uses the rate at which radio waves are reflected off a moving object to determine its speed. With police radar, that moving object is your car. In more specific terms, radar units have a "transmitter" to generate radio waves and a receiver to amplify the reflected waves (make them stronger) and analyze them. The analysis is then reflected in a speed readout device.

Radar uses waves similar to those involved in AM and FM radio transmissions, but with a higher frequency (i.e., more waves within a given period of time). Although it may seem mind-boggling, the frequency of the radio waves you pick up on an AM radio is about one million per second. FM involves 100 million cycles a second. UHF television waves use frequencies of approximately one billion cycles per second. By comparison, radar uses frequencies up to twenty-four billion per second.

Why so high? Because the higher the frequency, the straighter the beam and the truer the reflection. Ordinary radio frequencies can't be used for radar, and only such higher frequencies give radar its accuracy. As we discuss below, the primary defenses to speeding tickets based on radar involve attacking this accuracy.

To best understand radar it will be helpful for you to journey back to your childhood and imagine yourself with a new peashooter. You are standing behind a motionless car with a regular peashooter. You can't shoot a few billion peas per second, but you can shoot one every second without much trouble. If you bounce the peas off the back window at the rate of one each second, they will come bouncing back to you (if you blow hard enough), one at a time, at the same rate of one every second. It will take each pea a little time to make the trip from your peashooter to the car and back to you, and assuming you blow with the same force each time, it will take the same amount of time for each pea. This will allow you to say to yourself, for reasons you'll better understand in a minute, "Since there's no difference between the rate at which the peas are leaving the peashooter and the rate at which they're coming back—the car is standing still."

Now, let's say the car is moving forward at a very slow 2 mph (about 3 feet per second). That means that before the second pea hits, the car will have moved forward about 3 feet from the spot where the first one hit. So the second pea will have to travel 3 more feet to the car than did the first pea, *plus* 3 feet on the rebound. That's 6 feet altogether. If the peas are travelling at, say 12 feet per second, it will take that second pea an extra half second to travel that extra 6 feet. What this means is that instead of the second pea coming back to you 1 second after the first pea, it will come back 1-1/2 seconds later. Assuming the car continued to move slowly forward, the third pea will come back 1-1/2 seconds later than the second pea, and so on, even though you're still shooting one each second. Similarly, if the car were doing 4 mph instead of 2 mph, the peas would come back every 2 seconds, even though you were shooting one every second. If you didn't know how fast the car was going, you could calculate it by comparing the time it took for each pea to come back (1-1/2 seconds for 2 mph, 2 seconds for 4 mph) with the time it took to shoot each one (one second). In this example, the car's speed in miles per hour would equal four times the difference between the number of seconds between peas coming back and the number of seconds between peas being shot.

What does all of this have to do with police radar? Think of a police radar transmitter as an extremely fast repeating peashooter sending out tiny balls of energy (instead of peas) at the rate of several billion per second.

A modern radar device is composed of 1) a transmitter whose frequency is set at 10.525 ("X-band") or 24.150 ("K-band") billion cycles (or little bouncing balls of energy) per second, 2) an antenna to both transmit the impulse and receive the reflected impulses, and 3) a special receiver.

The receiver measures the transmitter frequency and the very-slightly-different frequency of the bounced waves reflected back from the target vehicle. It then electronically subtracts the second from the first to get the difference in frequencies. An electric current representing this frequency differ-

ence is converted into miles per hour and appears on a meter or digital readout. The greater the difference between the transmitted and reflected waves, the greater the relative speed or *difference* of speed between the target vehicle and the police car. Since the police car is not moving[25] while clocking you, your speed is obtained by multiplying the difference in frequencies by a number dependent upon whether the X-band or K-band is used. The X-band frequency difference is 31.4 cycles per second for every mile per hour of speed, and the K-band difference is 72 cycles per second for each mile per hour.[26]

One final point. Although radar signals can be bounced off stationary or moving objects, they cannot be bent over hills or around curves. In order for a cop to clock your speed with radar, the radar signals must travel in a straight line from her car to yours and back, or, in other words, you must be in her "line-of-sight." This doesn't necessarily mean you will always be able to see the radar unit ahead of you in time to slow down, however. Either the radar-equipped police vehicle will be hidden behind roadside shrubbery through which radar beams can easily pass, behind a parked car with just the radar sticking out, or, by the time you do see the radar unit, the officer will already have clocked your speed.

Many people are so awe-inspired by any sort of electronic wizardry that when they see a "Speed Checked by Radar" sign they tend to imagine something out of *Star Wars*. Some people even

[25]Some sophisticated radar sets can be used while the police car is moving, but most cannot. Moving radar sets present a whole new set of technical problems, not the least of which is that of calibration of *both* the *relative* speed detector (the one used on the target vehicle) and the *absolute* speed detector (which tells the officer what *his* speed is). Your speed is either the sum or the difference of the relative and absolute speeds, depending on whether your car and the officer's are moving in the same or opposite directions.

[26]If you like formulas, try: Difference in frequency (cycles per second) = 3 x car speed (mph) x radar frequency (billions of cycles per second). This works out to 31.4 cycles per second difference for the X-band at 10.525 billion cycles per second for each mph of speed, and 72 cycles per second difference for the K-band at 24.150 billion cycles per second, for each mph of speed.

believe that somehow they are under constant police surveillance from some central control panel similar to that in an air traffic control tower.[27] This is not possible. Radar beams travel in straight lines, and in police radar, that straight line has to be more or less in the same direction as you travel. Thus police radar can only clock the speed of a vehicle at which the antenna is pointed.

2. Types of Equipment

The use of radar for determining automobile speed started in the early 1950s with huge, but delicate and awkward, vacuum tube circuitry operable only by skilled technicians. The radar unit was so bulky and unstable, in fact, that there had to be a separate chase vehicle to pull the speeder over. With the advent of transistors in the late 50s and early 60s, integrated circuits in the late 60s, and compact microchips in the 70s and 80s, radar units became highly compact, durable and even relatively inexpensive. But they are not necessarily any more accurate than the early models. Modern technology hasn't changed the basic problem with police radar—the radar beams unavoidably diverge (spread out) with distance and can track objects other than those at which they're aimed.

Although dozens of types of radar units can be purchased with your tax dollars, with prices ranging from $300 to $3,000 per unit, there are essentially three types of units in common use: car-mounted stationary radar, hand-held stationary radar "guns" and car-mounted "moving" radar.

---

[27]In military or air traffic control radar, a rotating disk antenna pointing upward sweeps the sky in a full 360-degree circle. When the beam hits an aircraft, part of it is reflected back down to the ground, showing up as a "blip" at a particular angle on the sweep of the screen. The location, direction and speed can be determined from watching the position of the blip change with each sweep. Police radar works at about the same radar frequency, but there the resemblance ends. The only information given by the officer's instrument is the speed; he already knows the direction to be that fixed by his antenna, and only his power of visual observation tells him it's you.

a. Car-Mounted Stationary Radar

This type of radar device is currently the most common type used in patrol cars. The radar antenna is shaped something like a side-mounted spotlight without the glass reflector on the front. If you're really sharp-eyed and know what to look for, you can see it sticking out a little from a line of parked cars; it's usually mounted on the rear left window of the police car and faces toward the rear. Often an officer finds a nice tight parking spot in front of another vehicle, and sticks the antenna out past that vehicle in order to track the speed of moving traffic.

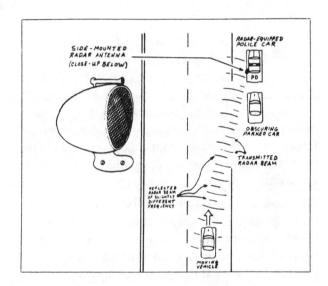

Sometimes the radar antenna will be placed inside the police car so that the beam travels through the rear window. But this has the disadvantage of not allowing the officer to park in front of a vehicle that hides his car, as the rear window must face the traffic flow without obstruction by stationary vehicles.

Once an officer gets set up and clocks your speed, he reads that speed on a little console about the size of a CB radio, which is either mounted under the dashboard or resting on top. On older models, the console has a meter that indicates the speed of the vehicle. This type of unit is equipped with a "hold" switch to keep the needle at the highest-read speed during the pass.

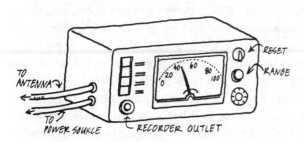

Later console units have a digital readout that will display the highest speed read during the second or two the target vehicle passes through the beam. This means that once your speed is recorded, slowing down does no good at all, and hitting the brakes only lights your stoplights and causes the front of your car to dip (front brakes grab hold better than rear brakes), so as to tell the officer that you knew darn well you were speeding.

These units also have a "speed set" switch that is set to the speed at which the officer has decided a ticket is appropriate. This allows the officer to direct his attention elsewhere while your car travels through the beam. If the speed reading exceeds the "speed set" value, a sound alarm goes off. The officer looks at the readout, then at your car, and takes off after you.

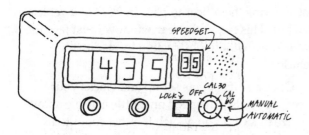

A Typical Radar Gun

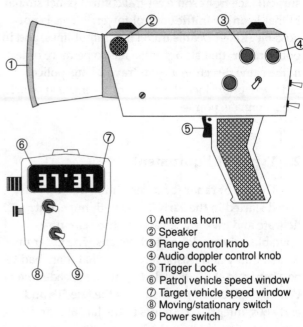

① Antenna horn
② Speaker
③ Range control knob
④ Audio doppler control knob
⑤ Trigger Lock
⑥ Patrol vehicle speed window
⑦ Target vehicle speed window
⑧ Moving/stationary switch
⑨ Power switch

b. Hand-held Radar

Hand-held "radar guns" are rapidly gaining in popularity, particularly among motorcycle officers. A "radar gun" is simply a gun-shaped plastic molding in which the transmitter, receiver and antenna are all mounted. The antenna is mounted at the front of the gun, and a digital speed readout, as well as the controls, are mounted on the back. The designers even included a trigger switch so as to activate the radar beam only when needed, namely when the officer sees a car that appears to be traveling fast enough to spark his interest.

Note: The intermittent operation afforded by the trigger also tends to foil radar detectors and mini-mizes radar officers' worries about possible health hazards involved in the repeated day-to-day operation at close range.[28]

---

[28]There is some legitimate concern that *prolonged* exposure to very high intensity radar beams may cause health hazards, including cataracts. Radar officers suffer far more exposure due to frequent operation than any motorist, shielded in a steel vehicle, suffers from occasional beams attenuated over the distances involved. There is absolutely no evidence that police radar constitutes any kind of health hazard to drivers.

Radar guns generally have a cable of wires leading either directly to the police vehicle's 12-volt power supply, or possibly even into the car's cigarette lighter outlet.

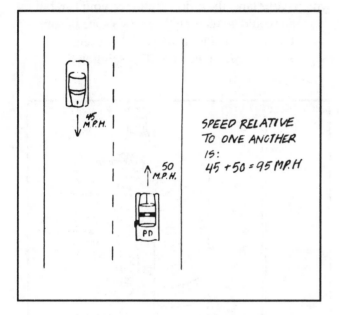

SPEED RELATIVE TO ONE ANOTHER IS:
45 + 50 = 95 M.P.H

c. Moving Radar

"Moving radar" works in the same way as stationary radar, with one extra sophistication: the speed of the moving patrol car or motorcycle is taken into account to determine your vehicle's speed from the "relative" speed. The relative speed is the difference between your car's speed and the officer's. This is what the radar unit actually measures. This kind of radar measures the speed of traffic coming from the opposite direction or going in the same direction.

Example 1: Two cars are going in opposite directions on a two-lane road—one is a police car going North at 50 mph, and the other is going South at 45 mph. The relative speed is 95 mph because the two speeds are added to get the relative speed. This means that a radar unit in the 50-mph patrol car with its beam pointed at the 45 mph car, will receive a reflected radar signal indicating a 95 mph relative speed. After the police

vehicles' 50 mph speed is subtracted from this relative speed, your *actual* speed of 45 mph is obtained.

Example 2: Just ahead of the 50 mph radar-equipped patrol car is a truck doing 70 mph. The relative speed between the two vehicles is 20 mph, which the radar unit detects and adds to the patrol car's 50 mph speed. The result is a reading showing that the truck ahead is doing 70 mph.

Moving radar is not in as wide a use in California as it is in many other states. Proper calibration during operation is somewhat more difficult. One further note—some hand-held radar guns have the moving radar option, but almost all of them are operated from a fixed or stationary position.

3. Qualifications for Radar Use

Unlike the old days when police radar units had to be operated by skilled technicians, today's units can be operated by nearly anyone. Officers using radar do not have to hold any kind of certificate or license, but the agency employing them has to be licensed by the Federal Communications Commission. The license will specify the number of units in operation and the authorized frequencies. Most law enforcement agencies are licensed, but often they'll buy more units than authorized without updating their license. In addition, sometimes they'll only be licensed for the older X-band, but buy new K-band equipment. Even so, this sort of violation of federal regulations does not affect the validity of any speed law prosecutions in which the offending equipment was used.

Although the officer doesn't have to be licensed, it may look bad in court if he says he's never had any instruction in the use of radar equipment. If asked, an officer will usually testify that he had a given number of hours of instruction and completed some obscure course. The course is often only a short pep talk given by a sales representative of the company selling the radar equipment. Sometimes the officer will receive a fancy certificate for satisfactory completion of this so-called "course."

4. Malfunctions and Inaccuracies

Contrary to police department propaganda, the latest technology has *not* completely ironed out problems known to cause malfunctions and interferences on radar units. Most malfunctions result from the radar's operation in "real world" conditions, which are less than ideal. As you will see, you'll need a clear recollection of the traffic and weather conditions existing at the time you were stopped to successfully argue that the radar might have malfunctioned in your case.

While it's certainly true that radar units of the 50s and 60s suffered from more calibration and accuracy problems than do the units of today, there is absolutely no way, technologically or otherwise, to remove all sources of interference and inaccuracy in order to get the "perfect" radar unit. The necessity of human interaction with such a device also leaves plenty of room for error. Modern computers may be nearly infallible, but the people who program and feed data to them are not. The same goes for the police officer operating the radar unit. Following is a description of common malfunctions and sources of inaccurate readings.

a. More Than One Target

Police radar transmitters do not transmit a tight, narrow, laser-like beam that can be precisely aimed at a particular vehicle. Instead, radar beams are much like flashlight beams—the further the beam travels, the more it diverges—or spreads out. The more it diverges, the more likely it will hit more than one moving object, such as a vehicle in an adjacent lane. The typical beam angle or spread is 12 to 16 degrees, or about 1/25th of a full circle.

The result is that the beam will have a width of one foot for every four feet of distance from the radar antenna. The beam width will be two lanes wide (about 40 feet), only 160 feet distant from the radar antenna. Thus, if you're in one lane and a faster vehicle is in another, the other vehicle will contribute to a high reading on the officer's radar unit, yet he may mistakenly attribute it to you. The mistaken reading of another vehicle (and attributing

its speed to you) is especially likely to occur if the other vehicle is larger than yours. In fact, the vehicle contributing to the officer's high radar reading needn't even be in another lane; if a larger vehicle, such as a truck, is rapidly coming up from behind you in your lane, the officer could see your car, but his radar could be reading the truck's speed. Inability of the equipment to distinguish between two separate objects is called lack of "resolution."

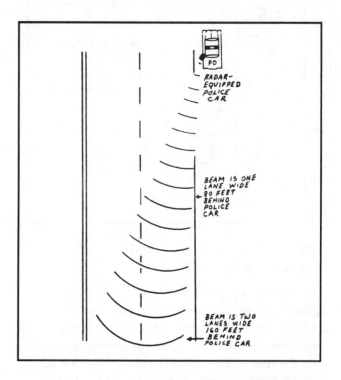

At a distance of a mere 1/8th mile, the radar beam will be four lanes wide, which means that the officer may well be reading the speed of cars on the other side of the road while trying to read yours as you're coming up behind him. In a situation where the officer merely puts the radar unit on automatic and waits for a buzzer to sound, and hasn't aimed at a specific vehicle, this inaccuracy in resolution can be very important.

b. Wind, Rain and Storms

Although metal surfaces reflect radar beams better than most surfaces, pretty much anything will reflect radar waves, at least to some extent. On windy days, windblown dust or tree leaves can be "read." These spurious readings can be attributed to you. You may have read the newspaper story about the state legislator who pointed a hand-held radar gun at a tree and "clocked" it at 70 mph!

Windblown rain will even reflect enough energy so as to give false signals, particularly if the wind is strong enough to blow the rain at a substantial angle to the ground. The more rain or wind blowing it, the more likely an erroneous radar reading.

It may also be possible for pre-thunderstorm atmospheric electrical charges to interfere with a radar unit. Electrically-charged storm clouds are great radar reflectors and can reflect a signal back to the radar unit even though the storm clouds are high up in the sky. This is possible because the beam increases in width farther away from the radar unit's antenna. (It gets larger vertically as well as horizontally.) If such a storm cloud is being blown by the wind at sufficient speed, a false radar reading may result. One New Mexico justice court speeding case was dismissed when testimony showed that a high radar speed reading was obtained immediately prior to a thunderstorm.

If you're serious about trying to point out all the perils and pitfalls of radar readings when you get to trial, you may want to subpoena the instruction manual that comes with the radar unit that was used to clock your speed. (See Chapter 11, Section A.) The manufacturer will usually include a page or two on inaccurate readings and how to avoid them. This gives you a chance to point to this page and say, "Look Your Honor, even the manufacturer, who is no doubt optimistic about his product, states that radar readings can be wrong in cases similar to this one." Police departments have been known to tear this page out before sending a subpoenaed manual, so be warned.

c. Calibration Problems

Every scientific instrument used for measuring a physical quantity needs to be "calibrated" to check its accuracy. Radar equipment is no exception. This means that the radar equipment must be checked for accuracy against an object traveling at a known (not radar-determined) speed. If the speed on the radar equipment matches the known speed, the unit is properly calibrated. In practice, radar officers use a tuning fork as their moving object. While this may seem a far cry from a moving car, the use of a tuning fork is scientifically sound; tuning forks, when struck against a hard object, vibrate at a certain frequency (which we hear as an audible tone). Each fork has not only a unique frequency, but also a unique back-and-forth speed of vibration, this speed corresponding to a particular radar-determined speed.

Tuning forks are supplied by the manufacturer of the radar equipment and "certified" to correspond to the speed printed on the fork. According to most operations manuals, the radar unit should be calibrated with the tuning forks before each and every working shift and also before and after each violation. Ideally, several tuning forks of different speeds should be used to check the radar unit's accuracy over a given range.

Note: Tuning forks can easily become inaccurate unless they're kept in a little box and protected from mechanical damage; a good scratch or drop of a few feet can render one inaccurate.

As you might have figured, it's probably too much trouble for most officers to repeatedly open the boxes, remove the metal forks, strike them, hold them in front of the radar unit, and then return them to their boxes before and after each of the many violations they process every day. Most officers therefore do not calibrate their units with any regularity.

But if you go watch a few traffic court trials, you'll notice that quite a few officers swear they calibrated the radar unit immediately prior to and after the violation. Here's the catch. While often not an outright lie, this small oath usually means that the officer flicked on a "calibrate" or "test" switch built into the radar unit itself, read the proper calibrate reading, and switched it back to regular operation. It almost never means that the officer used a tuning fork. There's a big difference and it may be important to you.

The calibrate or test switch merely causes an internal frequency-setting device (called a "crystal") to generate a signal. The crystal's pulses are counted according to a preset ratio of pulses counted to pulses generated. The number of pulses counted in a certain period is indicated on the readout, and this number is supposed to correlate with a certain predetermined speed. But here's the problem with this sort of testing. There is a frequency circuit as well as a counting circuit, and only the counting circuit is tested in the so-called "calibrate" mode. This means that if the counting circuit is okay but the frequency circuit is off, the unit will be inaccurate, but this defect will not be detected by the officer. In other words, the accuracy of the unit will be affected, since frequency differences are indicative of a certain speed.

The fact that this limited test is mislabeled a "calibrate" test by most manufacturers misleads many officers into thinking that it's a substitute for a test with a certified tuning fork.[29] It isn't—and thus it's extremely important in any traffic trial involving the use of radar to cross-examine the officer and see whether he really did use a tuning fork. Don't dwell on this, just in case he claims he did. If he says he didn't, then it's time to belabor the point. If you were able to ask the officer some of the questions listed in Chapter 17, Section C, when he stopped you on the road, you will be better prepared for trial.

d. Electrical Interference

This type of interference is pretty rare, but it's worth mentioning. Occasionally a passing motorist's CB transmitter will generate "harmonics" that interfere with the radar unit and cause a false reading. A harmonic is a numerical multiple of a basic signal frequency at which a transmitter is transmitting.

CB rigs utilize basic radio frequencies of about 27 million cycles per second. The second harmonic has a frequency of 54 million cycles, the third a fre-

quency of 81 million cycles, and so forth. Although each successive harmonic frequency signal gets progressively weaker the higher the harmonic, poorly electrically-filtered CB rigs are capable of generating 400th and higher harmonics to interfere with X-band, and 900th and higher harmonics to interfere with K-band radar. But this requires an unusual set of conditions—namely a poorly electrically-filtered CB transmitter and a poorly filtered radar receiver unit. The more recent car-mounted radar units are fairly well-filtered. Radar guns are not as well-filtered and are therefore slightly more susceptible to such interference.

It also requires that the passing vehicle's CB rig be transmitting (not merely receiving) while passing near the radar unit. The kind of reading such interference would cause is hard to say. It could either be higher or lower, depending on the harmonic frequency of the interference.

e. False "Ground Speed" Reading in Moving Radar

As we said earlier, a radar unit used while the patrol car is moving must take into account both 1) the speed of an oncoming vehicle *relative* to the patrol car, and 2) the speed of the patrol car *relative* to the ground. If the patrol car's speed is 50 mph, the speed of an oncoming 45 mph car relative to the patrol car is 50 + 45, or 95 mph. In the radar unit, this value gets converted back to the 45 mph reading by electronically subtracting the patrol car's 50 mph speed. This means that the moving radar unit can incorrectly attribute an erroneously high speed to the oncoming vehicle either 1) by measuring too high a relative speed for the oncoming car, or 2) by measuring too low a speed for the patrol car. This latter speed is determined by a patrol car-mounted radar unit pointed at the ground. Once in a while, however, the portion of the radar unit that is supposed to measure the speed or the ground whizzing by will instead measure the speed of a passing truck.

Example: If a patrol car is doing 53 mph in the right-hand lane of a four-lane divided highway, and a truck is slowly passing it in the left lane,

---

[29]The Connecticut case of *State v. Tomanelli* (1965) 216 A.2d 625 indicates that *certified* tuning forks are the only scientifically acceptable method of calibration.

doing 55 mph, the ground reading unit that improperly locks onto the truck will read a difference or relative speed of 2 mph. The electronics of the radar unit will then subtract this incorrectly low value for the reading for the relative speed (105 mph) of an *oncoming* car (it's own 55 mph plus the patrol car's 50 mph, for a total of 105 mph) so that its speed will be read as 105 – 2, or 103 mph, when it's only doing 55.

Given the scarcity of moving radar units in California and the rarity of incorrectly-read ground speed, this error seldom occurs. Still, if you're ever tagged by moving radar aimed from the other side of the highway, and there was a lot of traffic in the officer's direction, you might be able to raise a reasonable doubt about the accuracy of the reading.

f. Aiming Angle of the Beam

Unless the officer is directly in front of or behind you, there is no way he can avoid aiming his radar beam at some angle to your direction of travel. He will then be reading, depending on the angle, some "component" or fraction of your speed. For a 45-degree angle between the beam and your vehicle, he will read only 71% of your actual speed.[30]

Unfortunately, this error can only work against you. Since the radar unit's reading will be lower than your actual speed, exposing this error will only tend to prove that you were really going faster than the radar reading.

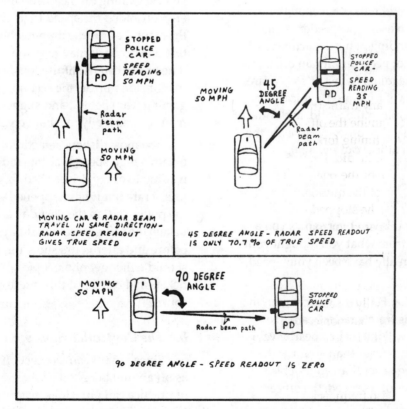

---

[30] A 10-degree angle will give a reading equal to 98% of your speed; a 30-degree angle 87%, a 45-degree angle 71%, and a 60-degree angle 50%. A 90-degree angle should give a zero reading and is, of course, never used. This source of error is known as the "cosine angle factor" because the percentage of the speed that is read is equal to your actual speed multiplied by a "trigonometric" mathematical quantity called the "cosine" of the angle.

5. Police Cheating

People go over speed limits often enough for a determined cop to catch as many speeders as he wants to bolster his standing in his department's ticket race. Thus, it is not necessary for an officer to produce a false radar reading. In fact, it's very rare. However, there are lots of frustrated, cynical, lazy and even dishonest people in the world, and some of them just happen to be police officers. Here are the most common ways an officer can put a false reading on his radar unit.

a. Someone Else's Speed

If the officer who pulls you over shows you a reading very different from what you thought your speed was, it may not really have been your speed, but someone else's.

As we saw in Section F(4)(a) of this chapter, the farther away your car is from a radar beam, the more likely that beam will intercept a nearby vehicle, especially one that is larger than yours. If this larger vehicle is moving faster than your vehicle, you might well be cited for its speed, the officer being unaware of the error.

On streets where traffic naturally flows at a speed over the limit, some especially zealous officers will take a reading on a "lead" vehicle and then pull over not only that vehicle, but also one or two others following behind. (Officers can, and do, single-handedly pull over several cars at once.) Then he'll use the reading for the lead vehicle as the speed for everyone else. He may even be up front about it, saying that he saw the vehicles behind following at the same speed (with no change in bumper-to-bumper distances), or that when the second and/or third cars passed, there was no change in the reading. This is all pretty shaky evidence. The officer would have had to note the lead car's reading while very carefully looking at the other cars. If the driver of the second car can truthfully testify as to how the lead car was going faster and increasing the distance, it should help in court.

Conversely, an officer might have inadvertently locked onto a higher reading of a second or third vehicle gaining on the one(s) in front and improperly attributed the speed to those in front. The larger the second or third gaining vehicles, the more likely this will occur. It may help the driver of the lead car if he or she can truthfully testify to seeing (in the rear or side mirror) the second vehicle quickly gaining from behind and suggest that the radar reading was really for that vehicle.

The most dishonest tactic, of course, is simply to obtain a high speed reading and show that same reading to every driver cited. If you suspect this (it's pretty rare but it has happened), you should go to the police station the next day and ask to see all the tickets the officer wrote that day. If all the tickets before and after yours show the same speed, you should either get photocopies or subpoena the tickets and bring out this interesting coincidence in court.

b. The Controlled Sweep

Since radar beams reflect off the ground as well as off automobiles, a dishonest cop who's had a bit of practice can put a false reading on a radar unit by "sweeping" the antenna (or the hand-held gun) in an arc along the ground. This tells the unit that the ground is advancing or receding at a certain speed relative to the radar unit. Experienced officers can vary the speed and angle of the sweeping motion to get almost any reading they want.

c. Calibration

If the officer is really dishonest, he may simply turn the selector switch on his radar unit to the calibrate mode. As we learned in Section B(4)(d), this will cause a preset reading to appear on the readout. Common calibrate readings include multiples of 5 (30, 35, 40, 45, etc.), and 32, 54, 67 and 72. If the officer goes to the trouble to enter a false reading on his unit, it's usually to show you the reading as the "infallible" electronic proof of your speed. Therefore, you are likely to get a chance to see the radar set. If he has set the unit on a calibrate mode, there should be a switch on the unit set to "CAL," "CALIBRATE" or something similar. Also, on units which have a decimal point and readout to the tenth of a mile per hour, a zero for that fraction may indicate that the unit is in a calibrate mode.

6. Radar Detectors

No chapter on radar would be complete without a few words on the technological ways of beating it, primarily with a radar detector. Usually this is a little black box you clip to your sun visor or put on your dashboard and plug into your cigarette lighter outlet. It is nothing more than a very sensitive radio receiver for signals in the radar frequency range. Instead of powering a loudspeaker, though, this type of radio circuit trips a little relay when a radar signal is received. The relay then activates a buzzer or light to warn that your speed is being monitored. Many of the commercially available detectors have a sensitivity control that can be adjusted to give the best compromise between detecting faint, far-away signals and rejecting interfering off-frequency signals that come from sources other than police radar.

a. They're Legal

Radar detectors are perfectly legal. Although a few places, most notably Virginia and the District of Columbia, have experimented with laws making it illegal to drive a radar detector-equipped vehicle, California has no such law. Several cities, most notably Los Angeles, do have laws making it illegal to use a vehicle-mounted radio receiver for receiving official police frequencies, but these laws (most of which were enacted before the use of police radar) were primarily intended to prevent mobile monitoring of verbal police radio communications by would-be criminals. These types of laws are rarely successful in banning the use of radar detectors because the courts frown on attempts to extend such laws beyond their original purpose.

Therefore, you needn't worry about trying to hide your radar detector. In fact, with the exception of the specially-designed "remote" units whose sensor is mounted under the hood, you should not hide it because the placement of a radar detector anywhere other than near the front windshield will shield it from incoming signals.

b. Problems

Folks who equip their cars with radar detectors are often lulled into believing they will never be caught for speeding. But radar detectors are not foolproof. Some will fail to give warning, and others will not give it in time. Here are a few reasons why:

- Many police radar units, and all hand-held radar guns, have push-button switches that allow the radar beam to be switched on and off at will. So instead of transmitting a steady, constant beam that can be picked up by a detector, the officer simply waits for an obviously speeding car, then activates the beam. A good radar detector will then warn the driver, but it will be too late to slow down before the officer takes his reading.

- Some radar detectors are not sensitive to all police radar frequencies. As mentioned earlier, police radar utilizes both the X-band and the newer K-band, but some of the cheaper or older "single-channel" detectors will only detect X-band signals. The newer "dual channel" (also called "stereodyne" or "heterodyne") and the scanning-type detectors—which scan back and forth between the X and K bands—are sensitive to both frequencies.

- The more sensitive detectors, particularly the scanning-type units, even though tuned or containing electronic filters, can give "false alarms" due to nearby strong signals from airport radar, telephone microwave links and TV transmitters. As with "the boy who called wolf," enough false alarms will result in ignoring a real alarm.

- It is possible (though a violation of federal law) for police technicians to use a radar unit so that it operates off-frequency and goes undetected by properly-tuned detectors. The practice has apparently become frequent enough for the Federal Communications Commission to issue a public warning noting the practice is illegal and could "cause interference to other licensed and important users of the [radio frequency] spectrum." (FCC Public Notice No. 1517, 1/15/87.) The scanning-type detectors, however, will still detect tampered radar units.

- Some of the cheaper units have a limited range. This means that by the time you're close enough to a radar unit for the light or buzzer to come on, you may be within the officer's range and your speed already determined. If there's another vehicle ahead of you, you're probably safe. But if your car is the "lead" car, you may get cited. The better radar detectors, of course, have a range

such that they "see" the radar beam before the beam "sees" the car they're in. But even with these, an officer's cunning use of road features, such as bends in the road and crests of hills, may prevent detection of her beam until it's too late.

c. Other Devices

Finally, a few words about the supposed methods of beating radar. First and foremost, the long-held belief that you can "jam" police radar by putting balls of tin foil in your hubcaps or "chaff" in or on other places of your car is quite simply a myth. The only way to jam police radar is to utilize your own radar transmitter to broadcast signals of specific frequencies strong enough to override the reflected signal the officer reads, so as to produce a false reading on his equipment. This is expensive, impractical, technologically tricky and illegal.

It would be nice if your car simply absorbed the officer's radar waves and reflected nothing back. A few people have actually spent hundreds of dollars to have their cars painted with an effective, but expensive, radar-absorbing paint called "Echo-sorb." Unfortunately, all metal surfaces—chrome, bumper and grill included—have to be covered to be completely effective. This, of course, is not likely to win any beauty awards for your car.

5

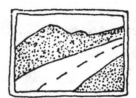

OTHER MOVING VIOLATIONS

WHILE MORE CITATIONS are given for speeding than for any other single moving violation, a large number of tickets are given for non-speeding violations. Like speeding violations, convictions for these other "moving" violations will wind up on your driving record. This chapter deals with the elements for each of the most common moving violations besides speeding.

Although space limitations don't allow us to list all moving violations here, we cover the most common ones for which people are cited. (Speeding is covered in Chapter 4.)

A. Not Stopping

THIS SECTION COVERS FAILING to stop at stop signs and stoplights.

1. Going Through a Stop Sign (VC § 22450)

A common violation involves stop signs (Oh, those rolling stops!). Cops love to give tickets for this at quota time. The law simply says:

> VC § 22450. The driver of any vehicle approaching a stop sign at the entrance to, or within, an intersection, or railroad grade crossing shall stop at a limit line, if marked, otherwise before entering the crosswalk on the near side of

the intersection. If there is no limit line or crosswalk, the driver shall stop at the entrance to the intersecting roadway or railroad grade crossing.

The elements of this offense are *all* of the following:

1. You must drive a vehicle and approach a stop sign.

2. The stop sign must be at the entrance to or within an intersection or railroad grade crossing.

3. You must fail to come to a *complete stop* at:

- a limit line (a white stripe painted halfway across the street from the stop sign), if marked; or

- a crosswalk, if any; or

- the entrance to the intersection or railroad grade crossing if there was no marked limit line or crosswalk.

Occasionally, an officer will park on a cross street so that all she sees is the stop sign and limit line, and maybe a few feet of road in front of the line or sign. A conscientious driver might well come to a complete stop a few feet behind the line where the officer can't see; then, having already stopped as required, drive ahead into the intersection. If this happens to you, you should try to find out where the officer was parked. Later you can take pictures from that location to show just how limited the officer's view was.

It may happen that local conditions made the stop sign invisible—e.g., leaves from adjacent trees covered or obscured your view of the sign until it was too late to stop. This too can be shown with photographic evidence, and establishes the defense that you were neither willful nor criminally negligent in driving through it.

One other good (if rare) defense applies to newly-installed stop signs. It's all too easy to miss seeing a recently-installed stop sign on a familiar road. In one case, a Monterey driver beat a ticket by admitting that he didn't see the stop sign but defending on the basis that it had been installed during his absence from the area for several months. The judge understood and found him not guilty.

Since, as we stated in Chapter 4, Section C, willfulness or carelessness is an implied essential element of every violation, a judge should find you not guilty if the stop sign wasn't visible until too late, or you didn't realize it had just been put there after being used to its absence.

People sometimes get a ticket because they stopped in front of the limit line or crosswalk, rather than behind. If this happens to you, perhaps you can truthfully testify that it hasn't been repainted for so long that it was unnoticeable. Here again, a picture is truly better than a thousand words.

2. Going Through a Stoplight (VC § 21453)

This is almost like going through a stop sign. The very similar law on stoplights reads:

VC § 21453(a). A driver facing a steady circular red signal alone shall stop at a marked limit line, but if none, before entering the crosswalk on the near side of the intersection or, if none, then before entering the intersection, and shall remain stopped until an indication to proceed is shown.

Although the elements of this offense are pretty much the same as those for driving through a stop sign, more needs to be said about this one because stoplights have a nasty habit of changing from green to yellow to red before you know it.

It is not illegal to deliberately drive through a *yellow* light. Vehicle Code § 21452(a) says that a yellow light means only that traffic facing the light is "warned" that a red light will soon follow. As long as the front of your vehicle *entered the intersection* or passed the crosswalk or limit line before the light turned red, you haven't broken the law.[1] And unless the officer is sitting right at the intersection on the cross street and has a view unobstructed by other waiting vehicles, you're in a better position than he is to judge that.

Reminder: Never tell the officer who stops you that it was a really short yellow light. That comes pretty close to admitting that you did indeed enter the intersection when the light was red.

B. Improper Turning (VC §§ 22100-22106)

SINCE TICKETS ARE LESS frequently handed out for unsafe turning and related offenses, we'll briefly cover the possible infractions and offer a few pointers.

Note: As you read these sections remember that the term "highway," as used throughout the Vehicle Code, means *any* public road or street (VC § 360).

---

[1] Laws preventing a driver from pulling into and blocking an intersection are covered in Chapter 6, Section C(4), which discusses the "Anti-Gridlock Act."

1. The Turn Itself

You can be cited for failing to make a proper turning movement, as the following (sub)sections describe.

a. Staying to the Right or Left Edge of the Road (VC § 22100)

This violation consists of failing to keep as close *as practicable* to the right or left edge of the road when respectively turning right or left, except at certain intersections when you're initially on a one-way street.

VC § 22100. Except as provided in Section 22100.5 or 22101, the driver of a vehicle intending to turn upon a highway shall do so as follows:

(a) Right Turns. Both the approach for a right-hand turn and a right-hand turn shall be made as close as practicable to the right-hand curb or edge of the roadway...[except at certain unusual intersections].

(b) Left Turns. The approach for a left turn shall be made as close as practicable to the left-hand edge of the extreme left-hand lane or portion of the roadway lawfully available to traffic moving in the direction of travel of such vehicle, and, when turning at an intersection, the left turn shall not be made before entering the intersection. After entering the intersection, the left turn shall be made so as to leave the intersection in a lane lawfully available to traffic moving in such direction upon the roadway being entered...[except at other unusual intersections].

Though you should read the entire code section if you're cited for this, a key element is usually the phrase "as close as practicable." Local conditions at the time (such as bike riders several feet out from the curb) may make "as practicable" pretty far away from the curb.

b. Turns Prohibited by Signs or Marked Lanes (VC § 22101)

VC § 22101(a). The Department of Transportation or local authorities, in respect to highways under their respective jurisdictions, may cause official traffic control devices to be placed or erected within or adjacent to intersections to regulate or prohibit turning movements at such intersections.

Roadsigns
right tern

(b). When turning movements are required at an intersection, notice of such requirement shall be given by erection of a sign, unless an additional clearly-marked traffic lane is provided for the approach to the turning movement, in which event notice as applicable to such additional traffic lane shall be given by any official traffic control device.

(c). When right- or left-hand turns are prohibited at an intersection, notice of such prohibition shall be given by erection of a sign.

(d). When official traffic control devices are placed as required in subdivisions (b) or (c), it shall be unlawful for any driver of a vehicle to disobey the directions of such official traffic control devices.

This law forbids prohibited right, left or other specified turns when "notice" of special turning requirements is given by either 1) a sign, or 2) a *clearly-marked* traffic lane *plus* a traffic signal (i.e., red or green arrows on a stoplight), which requires or forbids a certain type of turn. If you got a ticket at a particularly bad intersection where the sign or signal was difficult to see (for example, the sign was obscured by a pole or was not visible during darkness), then "notice" had not been given. The same is true if a right- or left-turn traffic lane is not "clearly marked." Photographs may help convince a judge.

2. Prohibited U-Turns (VC §§ 22100.5, 22102-22105)

There are three types of illegal U-turns. Let's look at each.

a. U-turn in Business District (VC § 22102)

VC § 22102. No person in a business district shall make a U-turn, except at an intersection, or on a divided highway where an opening has been provided...

You can always make a U-turn at an intersection or opening in a divided highway unless a *visible* sign prohibits it. A "business district" is defined as a place where over 50% of the property fronting the street is "in use for business" along 300 feet of the highway—or 600 feet if the business area is only on one side (VC § 235). At intersections with stoplights, any U-turn must be made from the far-left lane (VC § 22100.5).

b. U-Turn in Residence District (VC § 22103)

VC § 22103. No person in a residence district shall make a U-turn when any other vehicle is approaching from either direction within 200 feet, except at an intersection when the approaching vehicle is controlled by an official traffic control device.

As we saw back in Chapter 2, the elements of this one are all of the following:

1. You were driving in a "residence district." This is where there are "dwelling houses" and "business structures" numbering at least 13 on one side of the road or 16 on both sides, over a quarter of a mile (VC § 515).

2. You made a full 180-degree or U-turn.

3. Another vehicle was *approaching* (not merely *stopped*) within 200 feet or less in front of or behind you.

4. You were not at an intersection controlled by an "official traffic control device" (sign or signal).

As stated earlier, you need only show *one* missing element to beat this one. The best way to do this is to raise doubt about whether another vehicle was *approaching* within the 200 feet or, if applicable, whether the area was a "residence district."

c. U-Turns in Nonresidential, Nonbusiness Districts (VC § 22105)

VC § 22105. No person shall make a U-turn upon any highway where the driver of such vehicle does not have an unobstructed view for 200 feet in both directions along the highway...

This refers to areas of "highway" (i.e., any street or road) which are neither residence nor business districts. You can make a legal U-turn across a double yellow line, provided you have 200 feet of unobstructed view (VC § 21460). It doesn't matter whether other vehicles are approaching within 200 feet, so long as you have an unobstructed[2] view for that distance. However, you can't cross two pairs of double yellow lines two or more feet apart or a highway divider strip.

---

[2]If the officer claims the view was obstructed, it's up to him to prove that in court with either very precise testimony or with pictures. The burden of proof is on him, not you.

3. Unsafe Turns and Lane Changes

Two Vehicle Code sections deal with making unsafe turns or lane changes.

a. Pulling Onto a Road and Backing Up (VC§ 22106)

> VC § 22106. No person shall start a vehicle stopped, standing, or parked on a highway, nor shall any person back a vehicle on a highway until such movement can be made with *reasonable safety*...

Unless your violation of this section caused an accident, this one is almost always worth fighting. Your own testimony as to the precautions you took prior to starting from a complete stop should raise a reasonable doubt that you proceeded without "reasonable safety."

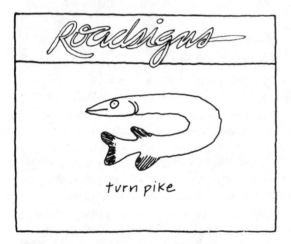

turn pike

b. Other Turns (VC § 22107)

> VC § 22107. No person shall turn a vehicle from a direct course or move right or left upon a roadway until such movement can be made with reasonable safety and then only after the giving of an appropriate signal in the manner provided in this chapter in the event any other vehicle may be affected by the movement.

The same sort of fuzzy and subjective aspects of "reasonable safety" mentioned just above apply here too. And remember that it's up to the officer or prosecutor to prove you proceeded *without* reasonable safety, not for you to disprove it. You do have the responsibility to rebut the officer's testimony on this point. (See Chapter 11 on preparing for trial.)

4. Signaling a Turn (VC §§ 22107, 22108, 22110)

> VC § 22108. Any signal of intention to turn right or left shall be given continuously during the last 100 feet traveled by the vehicle before turning.

> VC § 22109. No person shall stop or suddenly decrease the speed of a vehicle on a highway without first giving an appropriate signal in the manner provided in this chapter to the driver of any vehicle immediately to the rear when there is opportunity to give the signal.

> VC § 22110. The signals required by this chapter shall be given either by means of the hand and arm or by a signal lamp, but when the body or load on any vehicle or combination of vehicles projects 24 inches or more to the left of the center of the steering wheel so that a hand and arm signal would not be visible both to the front and rear of such vehicle or combination of vehicles, or under any condition when a hand and arm signal would not be visible both to the front and rear of the vehicle or vehicles, then the vehicle or vehicles shall be equipped with, and signals shall be given by, a signal lamp, except that implements of husbandry need not be equipped with signal lamps, but drivers of implements of husbandry shall give a hand and arm signal when required by this chapter.

Without going into too much detail, these jumbled sections taken together say you have to give the proper turn signal "continuously during the last 100 feet traveled by the vehicle before turning." To violate one or more of these code sections, all of the following must be true:

1. You either "turned your vehicle" from a direct course; or moved the vehicle right or left.(This includes changing lanes and even making a U-turn.)

2. You did this on a "roadway" (same as a highway—any road or street).

3. You failed to give an electrical or hand turn signal continuously during the last 100 feet of the turn, and there was another vehicle nearby that *may* have been affected by the (turning) movement.

When changing lanes, a signal is required if there is anyone behind you in any lane in your direction.

Most officers are not likely to give tickets for failing to signal unless you cut someone off or caused an actual or near-accident. At trial, the issue will usually be whether or not there was:

- another vehicle near where you turned, which
- may have been affected by your turn.

> **Example:** You're making a right turn from the right-hand lane at an intersection. Usually the only other vehicle that could be affected by your failure to signal would be the one on the opposite side of the intersection if the driver were planning to turn left onto the same street in the same direction as you.

Other possible defense strategies might include that you never really turned the vehicle, you were not on a "roadway" (perhaps on a private lot in a shopping center) or you were in an emergency situation in which you didn't have time to signal.

If your turn signals aren't working and you're aware of it, you should use hand signals. They're just as legal as electric signals. If you're not aware of a burnt-out turn signal and you get stopped for this, the officer will usually merely cite you for a correctable equipment violation (VC § 40610). This will not result in a violation on your record provided you correct the problem within the specified time and get the item "checked off." (More about this in Chapter 6.)

Dashboard turn signal indicators may still blink even though a front or rear signal lamp is burned out.[3] If that's the case, you should suggest to the officer that you did signal and *maybe* the light's burnt out. It is obviously unwise from a strategic point of view to admit that you were aware of a defect. If you say you didn't signal because your turn signals aren't working, you'll be told something like, "You should have signaled by hand then." Also, the officer may cite you for an equipment violation as well as failure to signal. As we'll see in Chapter 6, you can probably get the court to dismiss the equipment violation once you've replaced the signal lamp.

If your turn-signal lamp was burnt out and you are cited for a moving violation, you should contest the ticket. Give as your basis VC § 40610, under which you should have been cited for the equipment violation instead, and provide proof that you've since replaced the burnt-out lamp.

C. Being Rude (Miscellaneous Violations)

A FEW CONSCIENTIOUS OFFICERS write tickets only when they honestly feel a driver is endangering life or property, *or* is being outright rude to other drivers. "Being rude" includes offenses such as failure to yield the right-of-way to other drivers or pedestrians, improper passing, tailgating, driving so slowly as to obstruct traffic and changing lanes abruptly in front of someone else. Let's look at some of these violations.

1. Failure to Yield Right-of-Way

Numerous Vehicle Code sections punish different types of failures to yield the right-of-way.

---

[3]On many cars, however, a burnt-out turn signal light will cause the indicator to blink either faster, slower or not at all.

tender bender

a. Traffic Accidents

Several Vehicle Code sections say when and where you should yield to a pedestrian or another vehicle. A large number of tickets for right-of-way violations are written by officers called to the scene of an accident.[4] If the officers have not witnessed either the accident or the alleged violation, all they have to go on are the positions of the collided vehicles, other people's statements to them and *your* admissions. Your own admissions, of course, can be used against you by the officer later on in court. Obviously, then, it's unwise to admit fault. If you are unsure of what to say, it's perfectly proper and legal to tell the officer you simply don't wish to talk about it.

But what about the statements of bystanders or others involved in the accident? Even if you remain silent, can't these be repeated in court by the officer? No. They are inadmissible "hearsay" evidence. The people who actually made the statement would have to personally testify against you. Such people, even when subpoenaed, will often fail to show up to testify. Therefore, tickets for right-of-way violations are almost always worth fighting when the officer bases her information on an accident she hasn't seen.

---

[4]See Chapter 2, Section D, for the legal requirements to issue and prosecute this type of ticket.

b. Yielding to Other Vehicles, Generally

The following is a brief rundown on the most common violations for failing to yield to other vehicles:

VC §§ 21451, 21453 (right-of-way in intersections): Before you lawfully go through a green light or turn on a green arrow, you must give the right-of-way to vehicles already in the intersection. However, you don't have to wait until the intersection is completely clear before entering it, so long as you don't deliberately crowd the other vehicles. This is a matter of subjective interpretation.

> **Example:** You entered the intersection fairly cautiously, anticipating that a vehicle already legally there would be moving on. But its driver couldn't seem to figure out which way to turn. You had no way of knowing this would happen.

VC § 21800 (uncontrolled four-way-stop sign intersections): This applies only at intersections that have:

1. no traffic signal, stop sign or yield-right-of-way sign (the dangerous sort of intersection where accidents are likely to occur);

2. four stop signs, one for each street and in each direction; or

3. stoplights that are inoperative because of a power or other failure.

At any of these types of four-way uncontrolled intersections, whoever gets to the intersection first has the right-of-way, and if two cars get there at the same time from cross streets, the one on the other's *right* has the right-of-way. At intersections with four-way stop signs or with inoperative stoplights, each vehicle must come to a complete stop first.

The elements include all of the following:

- You were driving a "vehicle approaching a four-way intersection."

- The intersection had four stop signs, one for each street in each direction *or* had no yield sign, stop sign or operative traffic light on *any* street approach.

- Another vehicle also entered the intersection from "a different highway" (i.e., not directly across from you, but usually to your right or left).

- The other vehicle either entered the intersection first or, if you both entered at the same instant, the other vehicle entered from the street or road to your right.

- You failed to yield to the other vehicle.

This particular violation is the one officers most often cite after they're called to an accident they didn't see. If you *admit* that the other car was there first or admit that the other one came in from your right when you both entered at the same time, you're through. The obvious defense, then, is to contend (if true) that *you entered the intersection first*.

At three-way or "T" uncontrolled intersections, the rules are different. The driver on the road that dead-ends must *always* yield to the other driver (the one crossing the "T"), no matter who got to the intersection first.

VC § 21801(a) (left turn or U-turn):

VC § 21801(a). The driver of a vehicle intending to turn to the left or to complete a U-turn at an intersection, or to turn left into public or private property, or an alley, shall yield the right-of-way to all vehicles approaching from the opposite direction that are close enough to constitute a hazard at any time during the turning movement, and shall continue to yield the right-of-way to the approaching vehicles until the left turn or U-turn can be made with reasonable safety.

This one is also pretty subjective. It states that when you're turning left or making a U-turn at an intersection (and not in a special left-turn lane controlled by a green arrow signal), you have to yield to traffic coming straight ahead from the opposite direction until your left turn can be made "with reasonable safety." All of these elements must be met:

- You "intended" to turn to the left or make a U-turn at an intersection or onto a driveway or alley from the street.

- One or more vehicles approached from the opposite direction.

- Such approaching traffic was "so close as to constitute a hazard" at any time during the turning movement. (If the traffic moved fairly slowly or was some distance away, or even if you drove fairly fast, this won't be true.)

- You made the left turn anyway, and it wasn't done "with reasonable safety." (Unless the other car had to suddenly brake or swerve to avoid collision—or you had a collision—you should be able to raise "reasonable doubt" on this one.)

Once you start a U-turn at an intersection, Section 21801(b) says you have the right-of-way to complete it.

VC §§ 21802, 21803 (stop signs and yield signs):

Even though you may have stopped as required at a stop sign, you still might have failed to yield the right-of-way to another driver when you should have. The elements are:

- You either entered an intersection where a stop sign required you to stop, or encountered a yield-right-of-way sign;

- One or more other vehicles approached on an intersecting street or road;

- Such approaching traffic constituted "an immediate hazard" (it probably didn't unless you had an actual or near-collision); and

- You went through anyway.

Example: After signaling your intention to turn right, you stop at a stop sign. If you rush into that right turn and a car approaching from the left on the cross street has to suddenly slow down to avoid rear-ending you, you're probably guilty. On the other hand, if because of obstructions (such as hills or bends) you couldn't see the traffic from your left, or the other driver was driving too fast, you may have been in the right.

c. *Yielding to Pedestrians*

Here are the most common violations for failing to yield to pedestrians:

VC § 21950(a) (pedestrian in a crosswalk):

VC § 21950(a). The driver of a vehicle shall yield the right-of-way to a pedestrian crossing the roadway within any marked crosswalk or within any unmarked crosswalk at an intersection...

This section requires you to yield to a pedestrian crossing the road not only at a crosswalk but at an "unmarked crosswalk" and is the source of California's somewhat undeserved reputation for going to extremes to protect pedestrians. An unmarked crosswalk at an intersection is defined as "that portion of a roadway" defined by the "prolongation" of sidewalk boundaries across roads meeting at right angles [VC § 275(a)]. This means that whenever two streets or roads (but not including alleys) cross each other at an intersection, imaginary "unmarked crosswalks" connecting sidewalks on opposite sides of a street are deemed to exist. So it doesn't help you to maintain that you were at an intersection without a marked crosswalk.

The elements of this one are:

- You drove a vehicle;
- You approached either a *marked* crosswalk anywhere, or an *unmarked* crosswalk at an *intersection*;
- There was a pedestrian actually crossing or trying to cross (there's plenty of room for doubt as to whether he was just standing there waiting or leisurely thinking about crossing); and
- You failed to yield to the pedestrian by either refusing to stop (even though there's no stop sign or traffic light) or coming very close to running the pedestrian down. There may be some room for doubt here, too.

Example: If a pedestrian walks from your right to your left across the street, you may continue to drive along at a slow speed, since she will have already passed in front of your car's path. This is not a "failure to yield" to the pedestrian, even though she may still be in one part of the crosswalk while you drive across another part. Contrary to what many think, it's not necessarily illegal, as it is in some states, for you to drive in one part of a crosswalk when another part of it is occupied by a pedestrian. It's enough that you yield to the pedestrian to allow her to cross safely.

VC § 21951 (passing vehicle stopped at crosswalk):

VC § 21951. Whenever any vehicle has stopped at a marked crosswalk or at any unmarked crosswalk at an intersection to permit a pedestrian to cross the roadway, the driver of any other vehicle approaching from the rear shall not overtake and pass the stopped vehicle.

This means you cannot pass another vehicle already stopped at either a marked or an unmarked crosswalk (at an intersection) while a pedestrian is crossing. In this situation, you must wait for the pedestrian to pass and the other car to proceed. You can't breeze past the adjacent stopped vehicle just because the pedestrian isn't in front of your car yet.

VC § 21952 (pedestrians on sidewalks near driveways):

VC § 21952. The driver of any motor vehicle, prior to driving over or upon any sidewalk, shall yield the right-of-way to any pedestrian approaching thereon.

This means it's illegal for you to:

- drive over any part of a sidewalk (e.g., to enter a driveway), while
- failing to yield to a pedestrian "approaching" that portion of the sidewalk.

2. Driving Too Slowly

There are several ways a person can illegally slow or impede traffic by driving too slowly or failing to yield to a long line of vehicles behind.

a. *Driving Too Slowly in Left Lane (VC § 21654)*

VC § 21654 (a). Notwithstanding the prima facie speed limits, any vehicle proceeding upon a highway at a speed less than the normal speed of traffic moving in the same direction at such time shall be driven in the right-hand lane for traffic or as close as practicable to the right-hand edge or curb, except when overtaking and passing another vehicle proceeding in the same direction or when preparing for a left turn at an intersection or into a private road or driveway.

> (b) If a vehicle is being driven at a speed less than the normal speed of traffic moving in the same direction at such time, and is not being driven in the right-hand lane for traffic or as close as practicable to the right-hand edge or curb, it shall constitute prima facie evidence that the driver is operating the vehicle in violation of subdivision (a) of this section.

You are not permitted to drive in any lane other than the far-right one (unless you're preparing to turn left) if you're driving at a speed "less than the normal speed of traffic moving in the same direction." The elements are:

- You drove at a speed "less than the normal speed of traffic"; and

- You didn't drive "as close *as practicable* [5] to the right-hand edge or curb." This usually means in the right-hand lane, unless there are unusual circumstances (like a farm tractor was going 15 mph in the far right lane).

Note: Don't think that you're safe from being cited for this if you're sticking steadfastly to the posted speed limit while in the left lane. Unless the speed limit is 55 mph (65 on parts of some Interstate freeways), you have a duty to drive the same speed as other traffic *even if you have to go slightly over the speed limit*. Still, your speed has to be "safe" so that you don't violate the Basic Speed Law. However, this does not mean that you can exceed a maximum 55 (or 65) mph. However, the fact that you were planning to *turn left* from the street on which you

---

[5]The fact that the law therefore requires someone in the left lane to drive faster than the posted speed limit (but under 55) so as not to obstruct traffic may help you if you're charged with violation of the Basic Speed Law.

supposedly drove too slowly in the left lane can be used as a defense. This defense is particularly effective if the officer observed you for a few blocks or less.

> **Example:** It's a damp, drizzly day, and you're doing 35 mph. The speed limit is 35 mph. You want to turn left after a few blocks, and you move over into the left lane in preparation. Rip Snorter, the village idiot and drag racer, comes roaring up behind you, followed by his two buddies, horns blaring. A nearby officer ignores Rip and cites you for not keeping up with traffic. While perhaps you might have driven a little faster on another day, anything over 35 mph during bad weather conditions would be unsafe. Also, the fact that you were going to turn left justifies your being in the left lane.

Remember, this is a defense, which means *you* must raise it at trial. Once the officer shows that you were driving slowly in the left lane, she's satisfied her burden of proof. It's up to you to show a legal excuse for your action.

b. Impeding Traffic [VC § 22400(a)]

> VC § 22400(a). No person shall drive upon a highway at such a slow speed as to impede or block the normal and reasonable movement of traffic, except when reduced speed is necessary for safe operation, because of a grade, or compliance with the law.

The code section makes it illegal to drive "at such a slow speed as to impede or block the normal and reasonable movement of traffic." This is subjective. An officer trying to make this one stick should testify that there was a long line of frustrated, finger-gesturing drivers behind you trying to pass on a narrow road and that your speed was less than the legal speed limit. The section excuses slow driving if either you were traveling at the posted speed limit or that your lower speed was "necessary for safe operation." Be prepared to testify as to poor weather or visibility and road conditions, or steepness of the road, which might have rendered a higher speed unsafe or impossible. Also, a fragile load you're carrying might make your slow speed "necessary for safe operation."

> **Example:** Jake was cited for this offense, but defended on the basis that a fragile load of china he was carrying to his grandmother's house rendered the low speed "necessary for safe operation." In view of his having kept as far as possible to the right at all times, he was found not guilty.

Vehicle Code Section 22400(b) allows the Department of Transportation to post minimum speed limits (e.g., "Minimum Speed 45 mph"), but this is pretty rare. Even so, slower driving is still allowed "when necessary for safe operation."

c. *Failing to Use Turnouts (VC § 21656)*

VC § 21656. On a two-lane highway where passing is unsafe because of traffic in the opposite direction or other conditions, a slow-moving vehicle, including a passenger vehicle, behind which five or more vehicles are formed in line, shall turn off the roadway at the nearest place designated as a turnout by signs erected by the authority having jurisdiction over the highway, or wherever sufficient area for a safe turnout exists, in order to permit the vehicles following it to proceed. As used in this section, a slow-moving vehicle is one that is proceeding at a rate of speed less than the normal flow of traffic at the particular time and place.

This section requires you to pull over into a "turnout" when driving a slow-moving vehicle that's slowing down a line of at least five other vehicles behind. In order to be guilty of this, all of the following must be true:

- You were driving a "slow-moving vehicle," meaning one that is going slower "than the normal flow of traffic" at the time.

- You were on a highway with two lanes, one in each direction.

- There were at least five other vehicles in a line behind yours, all slowed down because of you.

- You failed to pull over at a "turnout" marked as such by a road sign or other widened area to the right where you could safely pull over.

With this violation, it's no defense that you had to drive slowly in order to do so safely. Only your inability to pull over safely is a defense, and the law assumes you can do so at a specially-marked turnout.

3. Tailgating (VC § 21703)

VC § 21703. The driver of a motor vehicle shall not follow another vehicle more closely than is reasonable and prudent, having due regard for the speed of such vehicle and the traffic upon, and the condition of, the roadway.

This code section makes it illegal to follow too closely, taking into account the speed, traffic and road conditions. If you were following at a distance closer than one car length (15 feet)—the *very* minimum for each 10 mph of speed, particularly on the freeway—you were not reasonable.[6] Even so, an officer's determination of what was "reasonable and prudent" may be different from the judge's. Also, the officer may have observed the short distance between your car and another that was only a temporary situation—such as when another car pulls in front of you, and you have to adjust to it by slowing

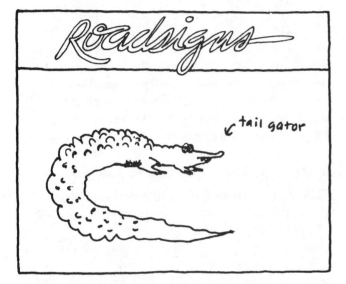

Roadsigns

tail gator

to increase the distance. Where a ticket for this is given following an accident in which the driver rear-ended the vehicle in front, the officer cannot testify to the violation unless he saw the accident happen. You should always contest the violation in this situation. [See Chapter 2, Section D(2), on citations given at accidents.] The other driver may not have noticed you in his rearview mirror, and the fact that an accident occurred doesn't necessarily prove you weren't driving safely, just that all your prudence didn't help.

---

[6]At least one-and-one-half car lengths for each 10 mph is recommended—and at speeds over 50, even this may not be enough space.

4. Unsafe Lane Changes [VC § 21658(a)]

VC § 21658. Whenever any roadway has been divided into two or more clearly marked lanes for traffic in one direction, the following rule applies:

(a) A vehicle shall be driven as nearly as practicable entirely within a single lane and shall not be moved from the lane until such movement can be made with reasonable safety.

Whenever the road is divided into two or more lanes, you shouldn't move from the lane until you can do so with *reasonable safety*. Even if you signal beforehand, you may still be making an unsafe lane change. CHP quota-hounds love this one and often pounce when a freeway driver moves quickly into an adjacent lane in traffic. To establish that the lane change wasn't made with reasonable safety, the officer will have to testify that she saw the other car's brake lights flash as it slowed down to accommodate your lane change.

The necessary elements are:

• The road had two or more lanes for traffic in the same direction.

• Lane boundaries were clearly marked.

• You either failed to drive "as nearly as practicable" within the lane, or changed lanes without regard for "reasonable safety."

Example: You're doing 55 mph on the freeway in the right-hand lane. To avoid cars entering from an upcoming on-ramp, you decide to move into the center lane. Preparing to change lanes, you flick on your left turn signal and look in your rear and sideview mirrors. You see another car in the middle lane, but it's about eight car lengths back, so you change lanes. You did your part by signaling and checking your mirror. If the other car has to slow down, it's because it's going over the 55 mph speed limit, and any unsafe conditions are due to the other driver's high speed, not your lane change.

5. Crossing into a High-Occupancy Vehicle Lane (VC §§ 21655.5-21655.8)

It is an infraction to drive on a highway or freeway "high-occupancy vehicle" lane in violation of posted restrictions limiting the use of the lane to vehicles having a minimum number of occupants. For example, the far left lane of portions of some freeways is marked with diamonds painted on the road surface every few hundred yards, with signs on the median indicating the "diamond lane" is to be used only by vehicles with a minimum of two or three occupants during posted days and hours. The lane must be marked by "signs and other official traffic control devices to designate the exclusive or preferential lanes, to advise motorists of the applicable vehicle occupancy levels" and "to advise motorists of high-occupancy vehicle usage" (VC § 21655.5).

Where such a lane is separated from other rightward lanes by a double solid line, it is also against the law to enter or exit the lane across those solid double lines, even if your vehicle is eligible to be in the high-occupancy vehicle lane. So, once you're in such a lane, you must stay there until the double lines end (VC § 21655.8).

A first conviction of either of the above offenses is punishable by a fine of $100 to $150 plus a penalty assessment. For a second offense within one year, or a third or subsequent offense within two years, the fines are $150 to $200 and $250 to $500, respectively (plus the usual 100%+ penalty assessment).[7]

---

[7]VC § 42001.11.

6. Improper Passing

Five Vehicle Code sections basically define three unlawful ways of passing unsafely.

a. Endangering Those You Pass (VC §§ 21750, 21751)

You are forbidden from "interfering with the safe operation" of any vehicle you pass, and any vehicle coming from the opposite direction on a two-lane highway. Unless you cause an actual or near-accident—either by forcing the car you pass to veer to the right toward the road shoulder, or by causing a vehicle approaching from the other direction to slow down or pull off safely to the right—you should probably fight this ticket. Your obvious defense would be that you simply didn't interfere with the other vehicle's safe operation.

b. Unsafe "Blind" Passing (VC § 21752)

This section forbids you to drive on the left side of the road (while passing) when approaching the top of a hill or a curve, so as to "create a hazard" to vehicles that *might* approach from the other side. Though this, too, is somewhat subjective. It doesn't matter that there were no other vehicles approaching; it's enough if there *might* have been, creating the possibility of a head-on collision. The section further prohibits passing within 100 feet of a bridge, tunnel or railroad crossing, but the officer's estimate of your distance from such places may be uncertain. (Remember, the *officer* has the burden of proving that the distance was less than 100 feet.)

c. Passing on the Right (VC §§ 21754, 21755)

You are prohibited from passing on the *right* unless one of the following applies:

- The passed vehicle is about to turn left (note that you can't drive onto the unpaved shoulder of the road);

- The street or road is wide enough to accommodate two lanes of traffic (that need not be marked off in a business or residence district), not counting widening of the paved area at intersections; or

- You're on a one-way street or a divided highway.

Even if passing on the right is allowed under one of the above exceptions, you must do so "under conditions permitting such movement in safety."

D. Minor Alcohol-Related Offenses

THE SERIOUS OFFENSES OF driving under the influence of liquor and drugs are covered in Chapter 8. However, there are also some so-called minor offenses having to do with alcohol. These can be nasty since the violations are considered minor—so you can't have a jury trial or court-appointed attorney—but the fines are often at or near the maximum $100 (plus up to $145 more in "penalty assessments") for the first offense, and may be even higher for repeaters. Moreover, some insurance companies will cancel your insurance, or at least raise your rates for violations involving a driver drinking or having an open container, which are reported to the DMV. (See Sections 1 and 3, below.) Thus, you will have a real incentive to fight these tickets.

1. Open Container on Person of Driver [VC § 23222(a)]

VC § 23222(a). No person shall have in his or her possession on his or her person, while driving a motor vehicle upon a highway, any bottle, can or other receptacle, containing any alcoholic beverage that has been opened, or a seal broken, or the contents of which have been partially removed.

This is the most common "minor" alcohol-related offense. Convictions for this offense *are* reported to the DMV.

The elements of this violation are all of the following:

- You drove a motor vehicle.

- You drove the vehicle "upon a highway"—any public road, but private roads or parking lots don't count.

- You kept a container, such as a bottle, can or glass *on your person* (i.e., you held it in your hand or kept it in a pocket or purse).

- The container held *any* amount of an alcoholic beverage when the officer found it.

- The seal, if any, on the bottle was *broken, or* the container's contents were "partially removed."

This offense requires that the open container be "connected to the person" cited.[8] If there are "unclaimed" open containers in the vehicle, but not on anyone's *person*, the driver of the vehicle should be cited only for keeping an open container in the vehicle, an offense for which convictions are *not* reported to the DMV. (See Section 2, below.)

Police frequently cite a vehicle's *driver* when a *passenger* has the open container on his or her person. This can be the basis of a good defense, as a bottle held by a passenger as his own is not "on the person" of the driver, so the passenger, not the driver, should be ticketed under VC § 23226. (See Section 4, below.) If the legislature had intended to hold the driver responsible for a passenger's drinking, the law would have forbidden the driver to "allow" a passenger to drink or have an open container.

Example: You and your friends are on the way to the beach with a few unopened six-packs of beer. Unbeknownst to you, one of your friends in the back seat can't wait, and opens a can of beer before you get there. When an officer pulls you over for an expired registration, he notices the open beer can in the back and tickets *you*, the driver. Your defense is that you didn't have the open container on your person, and the officer should have cited your passenger instead.

---

[8]*People v. Squadere* (1978) 88 Cal.App.3d Supp.1, 151 Cal.Rptr. 616; *People v. McCloskey* ((1990) __ Cal.App.3d __, 277 Cal.Rptr.509.

2. Open Container Kept in Vehicle by Driver or Owner (VC § 23225)

> VC § 23225. It is unlawful for the registered owner of any motor vehicle, or the driver if the registered owner is not then present in the vehicle, to keep in a motor vehicle when the vehicle is upon any highway, any bottle, can or other receptacle containing any alcoholic beverage that has been opened, or a seal broken, or the contents of which have been partially removed, unless the container is kept in the trunk of the vehicle, or kept in some other area of the vehicle not normally occupied by the driver or passengers if the vehicle is not equipped with a trunk. A utility compartment or glove compartment shall be deemed to be within the area occupied by the driver and passengers.
>
> This section shall not apply to the living quarters of a house-car or camper.

This second most common "minor" alcohol-related offense differs from the first in that the container need not be "on the person" of the driver. This section prohibits a driver or a passenger from keeping an open alcoholic beverage container (or one with a broken seal) in a place other than the trunk—while the vehicle is "upon any highway." Also, an owner who isn't driving but is in the car—perhaps when parked on the road or letting someone else drive—can be cited. Convictions for this offense are *not* reported to the DMV.[9]

The elements of this offense are all of the following:

- You were a driver or owner of a vehicle.
- You were in the vehicle.
- The vehicle was "upon any highway," but the vehicle doesn't have to be driven for the owner to be cited.

---

[9]VC § 1803(b)(8). Since this offense isn't reported to the DMV, a person appearing in traffic court on a violation of VC § 23222(a) might be able to persuade a judge inclined to convict, to find him guilty of violating VC § 23225 instead. The same argument might be made to a police officer about to issue a ticket.

- You kept a container, such as a bottle, can or glass somewhere in the vehicle *other than the trunk.* (For vehicles without trunks—such as pickups and liftbacks—the container must be kept "in some area of the vehicle not normally occupied by the driver or passengers," but *not* in the glove compartment.)
- The container held *some* amount of an alcoholic beverage when the officer found it.
- The seal, if any, on the bottle, etc. was *broken, or* its contents were "partially removed."
- The container was not in the "living quarters of a house-car or camper."

3. Driver Drinking in Vehicle (VC § 23220)

This law forbids drinking "any alcoholic beverage while driving a motor vehicle upon any highway." The elements of this one are pretty obvious; however, the citing officer must testify that he actually *saw* you raise the bottle or can to your mouth and drink from it. Even if your breath smells of alcohol, *that alone* is no proof you drank while *driving* the vehicle, even if you are carrying an open container.

This offense *is* reported to the DMV on conviction.

4. Alcohol Violations Involving Driver or Owner (VC §§ 23223, 23226, 23221)

The three laws mentioned above [VC §§ 23223(a), 23225 and 23220] apply to an owner or driver who has an open container in the vehicle. However, persons other than the owner or driver may be cited under other sections of the Vehicle Code. Sections 23223 and 23226, respectively, forbid *any* person (whether or not he or she is an owner or driver) to have "on his or her person" or to "keep" an open container in a "motor vehicle upon a highway." Vehicle Code Section 23221 prohibits drinking "any alcoholic beverage while in a motor vehicle upon a highway." Since these offenses don't include driving or ownership of a vehicle as an element, they apply to passengers, as well as to situations where no driving is involved—such as when the vehicle is parked on a public street. They do not apply to passengers in taxis, limousines or buses, however (VC § 23229). With these exceptions, the elements of violation under these sections are essentially the same as those covered above [VC § 23222(a)—open container on person, VC § 23225—open container "kept" in vehicle and VC § 23220—drinking in vehicle].

These offenses are *not* reported to the DMV.[10]

5. People Under 21 (VC §§ 23224 and 23140)

If a person under age 21 is convicted of *any* offense involving drugs or alcohol (including VC §§ 23222-23226), the court is required to suspend his license for a year. On written request, the court can issue a restricted license—for example, to allow driving to school or work.[11] This mandatory license suspension also applies to nondriving offenses, such as mere possession of alcohol by a person under 21 (B & P Code § 25662), being drunk in public [PC § 647(f)] or possession of marijuana or other illegal drugs. It also applies to vandalism by graffiti (PC § 594).

6. People Under 18 (VC § 23140)

Besides being subject to a one-year license suspension for any alcohol-related offense committed by anyone under 21, a person under age 18 can be punished for "almost-drunk" driving—having a blood alcohol level of 0.05% or higher while driving. (For adults, it's illegal to drive at 0.08% and above.) In addition to the fine for an infraction, the juvenile must attend an alcohol education program (VC §§ 23141-23144). Failure to complete the program will result in the one-year suspension under VC § 13202.5.

E. Marijuana in Your Car [VC § 23222(b)]

Driving with one ounce or less of marijuana in your car is a misdemeanor. You're entitled to a jury trial, but the offense is punishable only by a fine of up to $100 plus "penalty assessments." Even so, a judge may suspend your license for up to three years for this offense, and *must* suspend it for a year if you're under age 21.[12]

Ordinary possession of marijuana is a violation of H & S § 11357. Convictions are reported to the DMV. Because a three-year license suspension for this offense is mandatory if a motor vehicle was "incidental" to the offense, you're better off if charged under VC § 23222(a), in which case such a suspension is not mandatory.[13]

---

[10] VC § 1803(b)(8).
[11] VC § 1803(b)(8).

[12] VC § 1803(b)(8).
[13] VC §§ 1803(a), 13202(b).

F. Insurance Law Violations

Police officers issuing citations for moving violations must ask drivers to prove that the vehicle is insured.

Under new VC § 16028, you can be cited with the additional violation of not having insurance whenever you get a ticket for a moving violation. Let's look at how the law works.[14]

1. Proof of Insurance

When an officer stops you for a moving violation, she may ask you for proof of insurance. You must provide the name of your insurance company and your policy number. This can be done either orally or in writing. The officer will write the information on the same ticket she issues for the moving violation.

The best way to comply with the law is to stop whatever you're doing right now and write your insurance company and policy number on your vehicle registration card and carry it with you whenever you drive. By law, insurance companies must issue special cards providing the necessary information, but not all companies do.

2. Penalties

If you can provide the appropriate information to the citing officer, you will only be ticketed for the moving violation. If you are uninsured or don't know the name of your insurer and the policy number, the officer can charge you with a second violation (on the same Notice to Appear) of VC § 16028, failing to provide proof of insurance.

If you are insured but weren't able to prove it when you were stopped, you can get the insurance violation dismissed by presenting either a copy of your current insurance policy, or a policy card (issued by your insurance company) to the court clerk.

If you weren't insured when you were stopped, or for any other reason cannot prove insurance coverage, you have a big problem. First, you will face a fine of $100 ($240 in the event the ticket was for driving under the influence of alcohol or drugs) plus a penalty assessment. In addition, you will be required to post proof of adequate insurance for the following three years as a condition of retaining your driver's license (VC § 16034). (See Chapter 15.)

If you are an employee driving your employer's vehicle and are unable to provide the necessary insurance information, you sign for the Notice to Appear on behalf of your employer, who must then establish that the vehicle was insured when you were driving it [VC § 16028(e)]. This won't work if you're just driving the car of a friend or acquaintance and are asked to prove insurance. You have the responsibility to prove you're insured to drive your friend's car, either through your own or your friend's policy.

What's to prevent you from simply providing a fake insurance company and policy number to the officer? Giving wrong information about insurance (or the lack of it) is a misdemeanor punishable by a fine of up to $500 (plus penalty assessment), imprisonment of up to 30 days, and a one-year driver's license suspension or restriction limiting you to drive to, from and in your work (VC § 16029). This, too, is followed by a three-year subsequent insurance requirement.

How will a court know if you give phony insurance information? The courts are required to conduct 1% random sample verifications of the information written on the tickets (VC § 16030). This method of enforcement probably will not deter everyone from providing the wrong information (after all, people cheat on their income tax despite

---

[14]As of this writing, the Legislature has failed to pass a bill that would extend the mandatory proof-of-insurance law (VC § 16028) beyond January 1, 1991. However, we expect such a bill to pass by mid 1991. In any case, driving without insurance is still illegal and can result in a license suspension if you have an accident while uninsured.

the possibility of an audit). Still, most will probably prefer not to take the chance.

3. Mandatory Reporting of Certain Accidents

Vehicle Code § 16075 provides that if an accident involves personal injuries or property damage in excess of $500, all drivers must file an accident report giving their side of the event and providing evidence of financial responsibility. Failure to be covered by insurance in this circumstance (as opposed to being stopped for a moving violation) will result in a one-year license suspension by the DMV. Failure to file a report of this kind of accident with the DMV will result in a suspension of your license (assuming the accident is reported to the DMV by someone else), until you do submit a report. [See Chapter 15, Section D(5).]

A person who is driving someone else's vehicle, and who becomes involved in a reportable accident, may face a suspension if he doesn't show proof of the owner's insurance. To prompt owners to cooperate, the law makes it an infraction for an owner to fail to provide insurance information under these circumstances (VC § 16050.5).

4. A Few Words About Getting Insurance

As long as you have a driver's license, you can always get auto insurance. The trick is to get it at a rate you can afford. Most companies won't insure you at the normal rates if you've had three or more moving violations plus accidents over the past three years, an accident or violation in the past year, or if you've had any drunk or reckless driving convictions within the past five years. Also, if you've recently had your license suspended, been refused insurance by another company or had your policy cancelled, many companies will refuse to insure you at their regular rates.

If you can't get regular-rate insurance, you'll have to apply for what's called the "assigned risk plan." This is an arrangement by which a "high risk" driver with too many accidents or violations is assigned to a particular company. Each insurance company is assigned a number of assigned-risk drivers in proportion to how much regular business it does in the state. The company is required to sell liability insurance (but not collision, fire or theft insurance) to drivers assigned to it at rates regulated by the California Department of Insurance. These rates are very high, on the order of $1,000 per year, just for minimum liability insurance. After paying this for several years without getting any more violations or accidents on your record, you should be able to get the rates reduced.

As you can see, the system can really grind you under if you don't have automobile insurance. Imagine becoming the victim of a vicious cycle in which 1) your insurance rates are raised because of traffic violations on your record, and 2) you can't afford insurance any more, so you do without. Then 3) you're involved in an accident in which you're not at fault. Since fault doesn't matter, you 4) lose your license for being uninsured during an accident, and 5) find that in light of your violations, accident, and license suspension, no one will insure you—even after the year suspension—for less than $1,000 per year. Still, you 6) have to drive in order to get to work (you can't afford to move closer to work and there's no decent mass transit), so you 7) drive without a license, 8) get caught, 9) go to jail, and 10) lose your job while you're there. This means you 11) can't make your rent and 12) lose your home, and 13) your mate leaves you and takes the kids. Your life is ruined—all because of those tickets you sheepishly paid off without a fight. Is this an exaggeration? Sure. But many folks have experienced at least some parts of this vicious cycle.

6

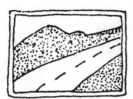

TICKETS THAT DON'T APPEAR ON YOUR RECORD

PARKING, PEDESTRIAN, BICYCLE and most equipment violations will not affect your driving record, as long as you take care of them. But if you ignore them, these minor violations can balloon into a difficult and costly situation. In fact, if you ignore them long enough, you may even lose your driver's license or car registration.

A. Parking Tickets

ENFORCING PARKING LAWS is a lucrative business that has very little to do with public convenience or safety—and local officials know it. Like any other business, the cities are trying to raise the maximum money at the minimum expense. Although this may anger you when you think about it, it can often work in your favor.

As we all know, most parking tickets are issued by "meter maids" or "parking enforcement officers." Police officers will also issue them—especially in bus and other red zones in the evening. If you contest the ticket, the person who wrote the ticket must come to court and prove the case against you. In addition to showing the vehicle was illegally parked, the officer or employee must also prove it belonged to or was parked by you. Since each enforcement officer issues hundreds of parking tickets each day, it's unlikely that an officer can honestly testify to the circumstances under which a particular ticket was written. Moreover, the people who issued these tickets usually will not appear in court to testify against you, as that would take valuable time from their revenue-raising duties. So parking tickets are fairly easy to beat. Nevertheless, since the fine for routine parking tickets is usually only $5 to $20 and no report of a conviction or fine payment is sent to the DMV, you may not want to bother.

It is important to understand that a person who owns a vehicle is not guilty of a parking offense just because someone else illegally parked the vehicle, even with the owner's permission.[1]

1. What Happens If You Ignore Them?

Unlike tickets for moving violations, parking tickets have no place for you to sign.[2] Thus, if you ignore a parking ticket, you can't be charged with the misdemeanor offense of failing to appear. But eventually (as we'll see in more detail in Chapter 15, Section D), the court will notify the DMV, which will refuse to let you renew your vehicle registration until you pay an increased fine plus an "administrative" fee as high as $20 or $30. Also, if you ignore five or more parking tickets issued over a five-day period, or if your car has no valid license plates, your car can be immobilized or towed and stored by the authorities until you pay up [VC §§ 22651(i) and (j), 22651.7]. (The car can be immobilized by the fastening of a locked "Denver Boot" around one of the front wheels, which prevents it from being driven away without severe damage.)

2. Procedures for Contesting Parking Tickets

Since parking offenses are very minor violations and they're normally not reported to the DMV—except to temporarily put a hold on the registration of a vehicle whose owner has ignored a parking ticket—procedures for contesting parking tickets are usually

---

[1] *People v. Forbath* (1935) 5 Cal.App.2d Supp.767, 42 P.2d 108. The *driver*, not the owner, commits the offense. Under VC § 41102(a), the law presumed the owner was the driver, but only when the prosecution shows proof of ownership. Even then, you can "rebut" this presumption with testimony to the effect you were not the driver. We discuss this more later in the chapter.

[2] According to VC § 40202, a parking ticket is legally a "Notice of Parking Violation," though some parking tickets are incorrectly labelled "Notice of Violation," "Parking Violation Summons" or even "Notice to Appear." A true Notice to Appear (which includes a promise to appear signed by the person cited) can be issued for a parking violation only where the officer observes the driver in or near the vehicle [VC § 40200(b)]. A parking ticket issued in the driver's absence and placed on a vehicle does not have the effect of a Notice to Appear, even if it is improperly that label. See Chapter 2 (D).

more informal than for contesting moving violations. Also, in many places, parking fine payments are collected, and court appearances initially set up, by counties, cities or even private companies that contract with a city or county (VC §§ 40200.1-40200.6). Here's how it works:

a. Step One—Setting a "Trial Date"

A parking ticket should include (in addition to the date, time, type of violation, and description—including color—of the vehicle), a "place for appearance" to answer the notice of parking violation (VC § 40202). The address might be that of a county or city office, or even a private business, instead of the local traffic court. Some tickets list only a post-office box or telephone number; although a "place to appear" is legally required, this at least allows you to set up a court appearance by telephone or by mail.

If you appear at the place indicated and indicate a desire to contest the ticket, the office must "set a trial date" and "file a complaint" in court [VC §§ 40215(a)(2), 40206.5(d)]. Before you insist on a court date, you might want to attempt to explain any extenuating circumstances to the clerk, who is authorized to dismiss a parking violation if "satisfied that the violation did not occur" [VC § 40215(a)(1)]. (This won't work for court clerks as to moving violations; see Chapter 10.) If the clerk won't dismiss the ticket or refuses to listen to your explanation, you can insist on a trial date.

Or, you can request a trial by mailing in the fine (as true bail to guarantee your appearance) with a letter indicating a not-guilty plea and requesting a trial [VC § 40519(b)]. You simply mail the fine (by personal check or money order, do not send cash)—as bail to guarantee your appearance—with a letter insisting the clerk set the matter for arraignment and trial with the officer present on the same date. Vehicle Code Section 40519 requires the clerk to notify you of your trial date. [This procedure is explained in more detail in Chapter 10, Section B(4), with regard to moving violations.] If you live more than 100 miles from the court, you have the right to present your case by written statement without going to court at all [VC § 40902(b)]. [This procedure is explained in Chapter 10, Section A(3)(c), for moving violations.]

A person who has not responded to a parking ticket in the time allowed will receive a mailed notice demanding that the parking fine be paid. This is called a "Notice of Delinquent Parking Violation," which will also threaten a DMV "hold" on your vehicle registration. If the original parking ticket has either blown off the vehicle or been stolen,[3] this will be your first notice of the ticket. If your only objection is that you didn't receive the ticket, wouldn't have ignored it if you'd received it and don't think you should have to pay an increased fine for that reason, relax. The law allows you to pay the original fine if you do it within 10 days of the mailing date of the Notice of Delinquent Parking Violation (VC § 40207). Also, you're entitled to a photocopy of the original ticket on request, or to its dismissal if the clerk can't provide you with one (VC § 40206.5).

If you're contesting a ticket that has since been reported to the DMV and is now being used to put a "hold" on your vehicle registration, you should still be able to contest the ticket without any problem. Before filing the complaint in court, as required

---

[3]Some people will steal a parking ticket from someone else's car and put it on their own, hoping to mislead a parking enforcement officer into thinking their vehicle has already been ticketed.

when you insist on contesting the ticket, the agency must recall the DMV hold based on that ticket.[4]

b. Step Two—Appearing in Court

When you finally appear in court, the person who issued the ticket might not be present. Although VC § 40215(a)(2) requires that this appearance be a "trial date" at which the officer should appear, many courts won't subpoena the officer for this appearance. Instead, they often treat the appearance like an arraignment, where most people either plead guilty with an explanation or not guilty. In another common variation, the judge may tell you the appearance is simply to plead guilty or not guilty, and to either plead guilty with an explanation or come back another day for trial. In this situation, you may just want to give your explanation in the hope that the judge may reduce or "suspend" the fine. Though this is a guilty plea to an offense, there's really no harm, since parking violations don't go on your driving record.

In any case, if the complaint required by VC §§ 40215(a)(2), 40206.5(d) and 40230(a) hasn't been filed within 15 days after the date you requested a court hearing, you can insist the court is without jurisdiction to hear the case. However, if you had previously ignored the ticket, and a "Notice of Delinquent Parking Violation" was mailed to you, a copy of that, filed with the court, constitutes an equivalent of a complaint [VC § 40230(b)].

If you want to seriously contest the ticket, though, and the officer shows up to testify, he probably won't remember having issued your particular ticket. In addition, that person must prove that you —the person accused—own the vehicle, by showing a DMV record to this effect [VC § 41102(a)]. You have the right to refuse to testify and be found not guilty if he fails to produce the DMV record.

"Instant Hearings" Note: In some cities, including San Francisco and Berkeley, you can opt for an

"instant hearing" procedure in which you waive the officer's presence but get to see a traffic judge the same day. Since parking convictions aren't reported to the DMV anyway, you might want to give up your right to the officer's presence in exchange for getting the matter over with the same day. But if you encounter a judge who fines harshly in the cases that precede yours, tell her, when your case is called, that you want to insist on a regular trial at which the officer is present.

3. Fines

As we saw in Chapter 3, the maximum possible fine for infractions is $100 for a first offense, $200 for a second offense, and $250 for a third offense within 12 months—plus penalty assessments.[5] You might think this means you'll be fined more for a second or third parking ticket. While such elevated fines are possible in theory, they're extremely unlikely. First, most judges don't take such maximum fines seriously. Second, even if they did, a judge hearing only a parking matter usually doesn't have your driving record before him and therefore does not know how many prior convictions you've had.

One word of caution, though. Some people like to save up their tickets and then pay them all at once. This really isn't a good idea. If you have too many tickets, you might be required to appear before the judge, who may decide to "teach you a lesson" and fine you the maximum $250 on the third ticket.

The best strategy when you have a lot of parking tickets is to deal with them a few at a time. Bring a couple to the clerk on different days. You'll then only be charged the regular fine[6] plus any penalties for lateness. If you intend to fight the tickets—and

---

[4]VC § 40221. This procedure does not apply to moving violations used to put a similar DMV "hold" or suspension on your driver's license.

[5]Parking in a handicapped zone, however, carries a mandatory $100 fine for a first offense.

[6]For parking tickets only, you can also simply mail in the fine to the appropriate court. But *you're* held responsible even if through no fault of your own the mailed fine doesn't reach the court or some clerk misplaces it (VC § 40309). Remember, you should not send cash. Instead, send a personal check.

you can do so, regardless of how long ago the ticket was issued—space them further apart by bringing two or three in every few weeks and request regular trials with the officer present.

B. Equipment, License and Registration Violations

TICKETS FOR CORRECTABLE equipment violations or for not having your license or registration with you (provided they were valid and up-to-date when you were driving) must be dismissed when you show a timely "proof of correction" to the judge or court clerk. A "correctable violation" is any equipment violation which:

- is not the result of "persistent neglect" (bald tires, for example, would be);

- doesn't show "fraud" (i.e., a forged license or registration); and

- doesn't present an "immediate safety hazard" (a broken windshield or no headlights would be considered such a hazard). (See VC § 40610.)

1. Regular Tickets—the Notice to Appear

When an officer cites you for equipment, registration or license violations on a regular ticket or Notice to Appear (on which he usually also cites you for a *moving* violation), the ticket will usually indicate on the back that the charge can be dismissed by showing "proof of correction" to the appropriate court. If you're unlucky enough to get slapped with a mechanical violation ticket while driving someone else's car, though, you may have trouble if the owner fails to correct the defect. *You*, not the owner, must deal with the ticket.[7] (Of course, you have nothing to lose by fighting the ticket and pointing out this unfairness to the judge, who might dismiss the charge.)

The procedure for getting equipment violations corrected is straightforward. Any type of violation can be certified as corrected by the Highway Patrol or by *any* sheriff or police department. It doesn't have to be the same agency that issued the Notice to Appear (VC §§ 40303.5, 40522, 40610). But don't stop a Highway Patrol or other officer on the freeway; it's dangerous and they don't appreciate it. Instead, call the nearest Highway Patrol office or police or sheriff's department, and ask them when it's convenient to obtain a certification.

Note: The Highway Patrol, police and sheriff's department will often refuse to certify corrections of misaligned headlights, bad brakes, faulty mufflers and other defects where special equipment or training is necessary. You'll have to go to an authorized gas station or auto repair shop, which may charge you between $50 and $100.

For a license or registration violation, you can also have a DMV employee certify that you have a valid driver's license or registration. There is a space at the bottom of the reverse side of the Notice to Appear for the police officer or DMV employee to certify that the equipment, license or registration violation has been corrected.

---

[7]Unfair as this may be, VC § 24002 makes it illegal to operate a vehicle with an illegal mechanical defect—no matter who owns the vehicle.

When you show this "Certificate of Correction" (or a valid driver's license or registration) to the court clerk or judge, she will dismiss the violation.

The law forbids imposition of a fine where "proof of correction has been timely and properly secured" (VC § 40522).

DRIVER'S LICENSE AND VEHICLE REGISTRATION VIOLATIONS:

You must bring a valid license or registration certificate at the time of your appearance if you have one or can lawfully obtain one, or have the correction certified below.

MECHANICAL DEFECTS:

If you are cited for a mechanical defect, you are directed to make the proper corrections and have the correction certified below or obtain other satisfactory evidence of correction. You may be required to explain to the judge any failure to make necessary corrections.

CERTIFICATE OF CORRECTION

Section Violated	Signature of person certifying correction	Badge No.	Agency	Date

---

2. The "Notice to Correct Violation"

An officer who stops you and is convinced that an equipment, license or registration violation (other than failure to renew registration on time) isn't the result of "persistent neglect" or fraud, and isn't an immediate safety hazard, can issue you a Notice to Correct Violation, instead of listing a Vehicle Code violation on a regular Notice to Appear ticket (VC §§ 40303.5, 40522, 40610). By signing it you don't promise to make a court appearance, but only to correct the violation within the amount of time the officer specifies on the notice. Thus, you don't have to deal with the court.

After you get the violation certified as corrected, deliver or mail it to the police agency that issued it. If you don't, you may find yourself facing both the equipment, license or registration violation— charged as a regular infraction—plus a misdemeanor charge of failure-to-correct as promised. (See Section 3, below.)[8] Make a copy of the correctable certification and note when and where you mailed or delivered it, in case it gets lost. If you mail it, use certified mail with a return receipt. If you ever wind up in court, remind the judge that the law forbids imposition of a fine where "proof of correction has been timely and properly secured" [VC §§ 40522, 40610(e)].

3. Ignoring Correctable Violations

If you ignore a Notice to Appear, on which you signed a promise to appear in court or offer proof of correction, you'll face a failure-to-appear charge,

---

[8]Because this possible double penalty may be unconstitutional "double jeopardy," the CHP no longer issues such notices, but instead issues regular Notices to Appear on which to list correctable violations. Local police agencies, however, may still be using the Notice to Correct Violation.

punishable by a maximum fine of $1,000 and six months in jail. Also, the judge will probably not dismiss the charges even if you've corrected the problem, and you'll have to pay the fine for that violation too.

If you ignore a Notice to Correct Violation, on which you promised the police you'd correct the violation, the police agency will complain to the court. The court will then formally charge you with the violation *and* with the offense of failing to correct a violation as promised. The maximum penalty for this one is also a $1,000 fine and six months in jail (VC § 40616).

Also, if you ignore a Notice to Appear, a warrant may be issued for your arrest or the DMV will be notified and you will be prevented from renewing your driver's license.

4. Noncorrectable Violations

If the officer fails to list a particular equipment, license or registration violation (except driving with a suspended or revoked license) as correctable, you should get the violation corrected and fight the ticket. Judges often dismiss the violation if you've corrected the problem. If the judge is hesitant to dismiss, you should present evidence showing that you met all three conditions which required the officer to give you a chance to correct it, namely that:

- the violation isn't the result of "persistent neglect" (bald tires, for example, would be);
- there was no "fraud" involved (i.e., a forged license or registration); and
- the violation doesn't present an "immediate safety hazard" (a broken windshield or no headlights would be considered such a hazard).

> **Example**: You are stopped and cited for having a burnt-out tail light. Unlike having burnt-out headlights or bad brakes, this isn't really an "immediate safety hazard." Your testimony that you didn't know about the faulty tail light until the officer told you about it will establish that you weren't guilty of "persistent neglect." Then, if you show the judge that you fixed the tail light promptly after the officer told you about it, the charge will most likely be dismissed.

5. Equipment or Registration Violations Written on Parking Tickets

When an officer who issues a notice of parking violation also sees a vehicle-registration or equipment violation on the parked vehicle, he may also list the violation on the parking citation. This type of ticket must be initially processed by the agency that handles parking tickets (VC § 40225). The law is unclear

---

City of

NOTICE TO CORRECT VIOLATION   NO. 0001

Date		Time		Day of Week
	19		M	

Name (First, Middle, Last)

Residence Address   City

Business Address   City

Drivers License No.	State		Class	Birthdate

Sex M F	Hair	Eyes	Height	Weight	Other Des.

Vehicle License No.	State		Passengers M F

Year of Veh.	Make	Model	Body Style	Color

Registered Owner or Lessee

Address of Owner or Lessee

Violation(s)	Code	Section	Description

Location of Violation(s)
on
Judicial District

Name of Issuing Officer	ID Badge No.

I promise to correct the above violation(s) and to give proof of correction within _____ days from the date shown above to the citing agency as directed.

X _____
Signature

(Return Proof of Correction to:)

Form Approved by the Judicial Council of California
7-1-79 V.C. 40610(d) 40618   SEE REVERSE SIDE

☐ Grey areas indicate spaces subject to local or agency requirements   [C200]

whether a county, city or private contractor handling parking matters must dismiss such violations on a showing of proof of correction, just like a court would, but it is anticipated that procedures of this sort will be developed. However, if this becomes a problem, simply arrange to contest the ticket in the same way a parking ticket is contested. [See Section A(2) of this chapter.] The matter will then be turned over to the court. A verified complaint must be filed by the agency and a trial date set. When you get to court, show your proof of correction to the judge and the matter should be dismissed. If necessary, remind the judge that VC § 40522 requires dismissal of a license or equipment violation "for which proof of correction has been timely and properly secured."

C. Other Non-Moving Violations

THIS SECTION COVERS miscellaneous Vehicle Code violations that are not reported to the DMV.

1. Violations by Pedestrians

Violations committed by pedestrians are not reported to the DMV. Neither are they subject to the laws that increase the fines for repeated violations, add penalty assessments, or possibly charge you with a misdemeanor on the fourth offense in 12 months (VC §§ 40000.28, 42001, 42006). They are, in effect, less serious than parking tickets; the fines are approximately $10 to $20.

Still, if you're one who wants to fight, keep in mind that all the pedestrian violations are listed in the Vehicle Code. This means that you can demand the officer specify the place to appear as the municipal court at the county seat. (See Chapter 17, Section C.) If the officer has nothing better to do than bust pedestrians, make him drive a few miles to make the charges stick!

Here are a few of the violations for which pedestrians are most commonly cited.

VC § 21955 (jaywalking):

VC § 21955. Between adjacent intersections controlled by traffic control signal devices or by police officers, pedestrians shall not cross the roadway at any place except in a crosswalk.

The elements are:

- The pedestrian walked across a roadway *between* (not *at*) two intersections;

- The area walked over was not within a marked crosswalk; and

- *Both* intersections were controlled by traffic signals (not just stop signs) or police officers. (Neither need have had a painted crosswalk.) Just one stoplight-controlled intersection is not enough.

VC §§ 21950(b), 21953, 21954 ("immediate hazard"/unnecessarily stopping traffic):

These sections make it unlawful for a pedestrian to dart out into a roadway, to "unnecessarily stop or delay traffic" even while in a crosswalk, or when not in a crosswalk to fail to yield to an oncoming vehicle when the oncoming traffic is "so near as to constitute an immediate hazard." It may be easy to raise a reasonable doubt as to whether there was an immediate hazard or whether the stop or delay of traffic was unnecessary.

Example: You are cited for darting out into a street between two intersections controlled by stop signs. Only if the officer establishes that you caused a vehicle to suddenly swerve or come to a screeching halt should the judge find you guilty.

2. Violations by Bicyclists

Violations committed by bicyclists—even though classified as moving violations—are not supposed to be reported to the DMV [VC § 1803(b)(6)], nor are any penalty assessments supposed to be added to the base fine.[9]

Violations by bicyclists can, however, count as prior offenses for the purpose of increasing a fine for a subsequent Vehicle Code violation within a year or for elevating a fourth infraction in a year to a misdemeanor. But if bicycle violations aren't reported to the DMV, they won't be on your record, so the judge shouldn't know about them unless you bring them up.

---

[9]VC § 42006, PC §§ 1464 and 1465, Gov. Code §§ 76011-76580.

Example: You just got your second ticket within six months for bicycling through one of those ridiculous four-way stop signs at a deserted intersection in a residential neighborhood. Also, some quota-anxious rookie officers busted you a little less than a year ago for jaywalking, and you paid the fine. Although the present ticket means it's your third infraction in less than a year, you don't have to worry about an increased fine. Previous jaywalking tickets don't count toward increasing the maximum fine. And although your prior bicycle stop sign-running ticket theoretically *does* count toward raising the possible fine on your present offense, it won't be on your DMV record. So the judge won't know about it unless you admit to it. Thus, the maximum fine won't be more than the first-offense maximum of $100, and will probably be less. Finally, no penalty assessment will be tacked onto the fine, and the violation won't be reported to the DMV.

a. Specific Violations

Vehicle Code Section 21200 makes all traffic laws that apply to motor vehicles applicable to bicycles. However, VC § 21202 requires a bicyclist moving at a speed "less than the normal speed of traffic moving in the same direction" to "drive as close as practicable to the right-hand curb or edge of the roadway" except when passing or turning left, or when essential to avoid a collision.

Vehicle Code Sections 21650 and 21650.1 also permit bicyclists to ride on the shoulder of the road, if there is one, as long as they ride in the same direction as the traffic.

Speed laws apply to bicyclists.[10] So do laws requiring stops at red lights or stop signs. Demoralizing as it is for a cruising bicyclist to have to stop and restart at a deserted 4-way intersection, bicyclists are frequently cited for running stop signs. Bicycling while drunk is also against the law. (See Chapter 8.)

---

[10]Speed limits of 25 mph or less can be easily broken without realizing it. On the other hand, you can argue that exceeding the speed limit with a bicycle was safe under the circumstances, even if doing so in a car might not have been.

3. Seatbelt and Child Restraint Violations

Seatbelt and child-restraint violations are reported to the DMV, but they have no "point value" and therefore can't be used as a basis for suspending your license as a "negligent operator" (VC § 12810.2). (See Chapter 15, Section A.)

a. Seatbelt Violations

Anyone who drives an automobile in which he, or any passenger of age four or older, doesn't have his or her seatbelt fastened can be charged with a violation of VC § 27315. Any passenger over 16 who rides without a seatbelt can similarly be charged. Exceptions to this law include emergency vehicle operators, newspaper or postal carriers making deliveries and anyone who has been excused by a doctor because of a medical condition or disability.

An auto owner who doesn't keep every seatbelt originally sold with the vehicle "maintained" can also be cited, even if no passengers are in the vehicle to be endangered by this fact. This includes tucking the seatbelts under the seat where they can't easily be reached.

The total fine per individual ticketed is $20 for a first offense and $50 for a second or subsequent offense, plus penalty assessments. The law also provides that an officer:

- may not stop you solely for a seatbelt violation she happens to observe; and

- may only cite you for such a violation if she stopped you for some other legitimate reason. (Unfortunately, this aspect of the law may encourage officers to actually cite for moving violations where they might otherwise have given only a warning.)

b. Child Restraint Violations

Vehicle Code Section 27360 requires that all child passengers under four or weighing less than 40 pounds be restrained in special child-restraint safety seats that contain a sort of harness and fit onto a passenger seat. The law applies to any parent or guardian of such a child, who is present in the vehi-cle, either as a driver or passenger. A first violation is a correctable one that must be dismissed by a court on showing proof (a receipt) that such a seat was purchased or that a class on its use was attended.

If the child's parent or guardian is not in the car at all, seatbelts are sufficient restraints for the child. But if seatbelts aren't used, the parent or guardian passenger can be cited. If no parent or guardian is in the car, the driver can be cited. This violation is not correctable.

congestion

4. The "Anti-Gridlock Act"

You may not "enter an intersection" unless there is "sufficient space on the other side" to pull into without "obstructing the through passage of vehicles from either side." This is called the "Anti-Gridlock Act of 1987." Simply put, in crowded traffic, you have to make sure there will be space for your car to fit into so that you don't block the intersection. A wrong guess is punishable by fines of $50 to $100 on a first offense, $100 to $200 on a second offense, and $250 to $500 on a third—plus the up-to-145% penalty assessments.[11] However, in terms of your record, it's treated as a nonreported parking violation. (We

---

[11]These enhanced penalties only apply where signs about the law are posted at the intersection by local authorities (VC 42001.1).

wonder, then, how the judge will know if you've committed prior violations of this law.)

D. Federal Government Tickets

DESPITE THE ABSENCE of state authorities from federal lands, such as national parks and military bases, you can be cited by federal authorities for violating state traffic laws or federal traffic regulations on federal land.

1. Traffic Laws on Federal Lands

The United States government issues traffic and parking tickets for violations that occur in national parks and on military bases and other federal property. In national parks, you can be ticketed for disobeying specific national park traffic regulations, including disobeying the speed limit and driving under the influence.[12] On other property owned and operated by the federal government in California, including military bases, you can get a ticket for violating California law.[13] These tickets are issued by federal civilian or military police, and must be contested in federal court.

Even when California traffic laws apply on federal property in the state, the procedures involved in the issuing of the ticket and in fighting it, are governed only by federal law. For example, the law may be different on what the federal police can do when they first stop you (like radioing for warrant checks) and on getting a ticket dismissed because you did not properly comply with the law.

---

[12]See Title 36, Code of Federal Regulations, § 4.

[13]The Assimilative Crimes Act, 18 U.S.C. § 13, makes all criminal laws of a state in which a federal government facility is located applicable on the facility. State crimes tried as federal crimes are "subject to a like punishment," i.e., punishment similar to what would have been given in state court. For example, a violation of a state's speed laws is punishable as a federal "petty offense" when committed on federal property inside the state. *U.S. v. Dreos* (U.S.D.C. Md., 1957) 156 F.Supp. 200.

(See Chapter 10.) Also, since federal tickets are tried in federal court rather than in a California municipal or justice court, you cannot demand the county seat. (See Chapter 17, Section C.) In fact, most counties don't have a federal court, and you might find yourself traveling a great distance to fight the ticket.[14]

There is no law saying that federal violations have to be reported by the federal courts to the California DMV. However, some federal magistrates will do so anyway. Therefore, whether a conviction or bail forfeiture will go on your driving record will depend on the particular court.

2. Arraignment and Trial

To contest a federal ticket of any kind, you must make at least two court appearances. First, you must go to the arraignment on the day, time and place listed on the ticket and plead not guilty. Then, you must return for the trial.

In federal court, "misdemeanors" are those offenses punishable by up to a year in jail, in which case the defendant has a right to a jury trial. "Petty offenses," on the other hand, are those punishable by up to six months in jail, and there is no right to a jury trial. Where you are charged with a state offense, the punishment imposed by the federal court can be no greater than the maximum penalty under state law. Since under California law, ordinary moving violations, being infractions, are punishable by a fine only and no jail, they are classified as "petty offenses" and there is no right to a jury trail. In fact, most Vehicle Code misdemeanors are punishable by six months in jail at most, rather than a year. In federal court, these are "petty offenses" and there is no right to a jury trial. Therefore, first-offense drunk driving charges do not entitle you to a jury trial, because the maximum penalty is "only" six months in jail.

---

[14]Federal Courts hold regular sessions in Los Angeles, San Francisco, San Diego, Sacramento, San Jose and Fresno, and occasional sessions in other cities.

The inside of a federal courtroom looks pretty much like the inside of a courtroom in municipal court, except the furnishings are fancier and there's no California flag—just an American flag. (See Chapter 12, Section B.) Often there is a podium facing the judge, at which you must stand while addressing the court. The judge (called a "magistrate")[15] sits on the same type of high wooden box-throne and wears the well-known dreary black robe, and a court clerk and bailiff (deputy U.S. marshal) are present.

Although a little more formal, procedures at arraignment and the actual conduct of the trial are pretty much the same as in California courts. (See Chapter 10, but ignore anything having to do with pretrial. Also see Chapters 11 and 12.) The case will always be prosecuted by an attorney or law student who works for the local U.S. Attorney's Office.[16] Also, the sentencing procedures mentioned in Chapter 14 do not apply to federal courts.

There are other important differences between California and federal court procedures if the trial is for a speed violation in a national park. If you are charged with a speed violation in a national park, you cannot use the defense that your speed, though above the posted speed limit, was safe, because national park regulations flatly prohibit driving over the speed limit.

In speeding cases where federal police used radar, the prosecution might claim it doesn't have to show that an engineering and traffic survey was made on the road, as it must in California state courts. (See Chapter 4, Section B.) It depends upon whether this requirement is considered "procedural" or whether it relates directly to the violation. You should argue the latter, saying that California's VC § 40803(b) specifically makes this requirement an element of the offense in radar cases.[17]

3. Fines

The federal statute that "assimilates" all of the states' criminal law into federal criminal law provides for "like punishment" as under state law. This means that the maximum fine for infractions under California law cannot exceed $100, $200 or $250 for respective first, second or third Vehicle Code offenses. As we'll see in Chapter 14, Section B(1), a prior offense can't be used to raise your fine unless the prosecutor initially alleges the offenses in a complaint—seldom done in federal courts, or you admit to having committed the prior offense—which you should take care not to do. So, the maximum permissible fee will almost always be $100 and the actual fine will usually be less. Also, a federal court can't add state penalty assessments to the fine, since these are state-imposed taxes on the fine, not part of the "punishment" itself.

Finally, federal courts cannot suspend your driver's license under *any* circumstances.[18]

---

[15]A magistrate is a sort of assistant judge who can preside over your arraignment but not your trial, unless you sign a form allowing this. Unless the magistrate appears to be biased or rude, it's a good idea to sign this form, which you'll be given at your arraignment. If you refuse, your case will be rescheduled before a regular judge, who probably won't be thrilled about hearing such a "minor" case. Also, your case may be transferred to the main court, usually further away.

[16]Law students who work for the local Office of the Federal Public Defender also may be present in some courts. They may be available to defend people accused of traffic violations—for the trial experience—free of charge. You might ask the magistrate about this at arraignment. Of course, you always have the right to represent yourself.

---

[17]Vehicle Code Section 40803(b) requires the prosecution to introduce a survey (or "prove the road a local street") "as part of its prima facie case" in radar cases, thus making such evidence a substantive element of the offense. Federal prosecutors often neglect to introduce surveys into evidence, if they exist at all. (Radar is covered in detail in Chapter 4.)

[18]See *U.S. v. Best* (9th Circ., 1978) 573 F.2d 1095. The appeals court suggests that a federal court should perhaps notify the DMV of traffic violations, especially drunk driving convictions. But in practice, federal courts often don't report convictions to state agencies such as the DMV.

7

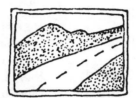

THE SERIOUS OFFENSES (MISDEMEANORS)

A. Generally

WHILE MOST VEHICLE CODE offenses are classified as infractions, a few are considered to be more serious "misdemeanors."[1] This chapter deals with the most common misdemeanor violations. The most serious one—driving under the influence, or "drunk driving"—is covered in Chapter 8.

sports car

---

[1] Very serious crimes punishable by imprisonment in state prison are classified as felonies. [See Chapter 3, Section A(1).]

1. Arrests and Notices to Appear

You can be physically arrested and taken to jail for most misdemeanors.[2] However, the normal procedure is to release you upon your promise to appear at a later time in court to answer the charge. (We cover Notices to Appear in Chapter 2.)

The Vehicle Code *allows* an officer to physically arrest you for reckless driving, property damage hit-and-run, speed contests ("drag racing") or "exhibitions," trying to evade arrest (i.e., outrun the patrol car or motorcycle), driving with a suspended or revoked license, trying to evade an officer, or other misdemeanors not listed in the Vehicle Code.

Police officers are *required* to take you to jail if you are arrested for the misdemeanor of driving under the influence of alcohol or drugs or for any felony.[3] Should you be taken to jail, the police have the right to search the entire passenger compartment

of your car and open any unlocked containers they find inside, such as suitcases and paper bags. (They do not have the right to open locked containers in a trunk, however.) Any incriminating evidence can be seized and used against you.[4]

Marijuana Note: You can't be physically arrested for possession of one ounce or less of marijuana, even though the offense is a misdemeanor.[5] However, the officer can arrest you if he has probable cause to believe you are driving under the influence of marijuana. When you're charged with any misdemeanor,.you have the right to a jury trial and, if you're indigent, to a court-appointed lawyer.[6]

2. Misdemeanor Trials

The main aspect of trials for misdemeanor violations (as opposed to trials for infractions), is that you have the right to a jury trial. We believe you should almost always assert this right. Why? Because judges are often a lot more cynical and "case-hardened" than people who serve on juries. To state the matter as straightforwardly as possible, you have a better chance with twelve jurors than with one judge, since if even only one juror agrees with you, you can't be convicted.

Whether or not you opt for a jury trial, your misdemeanor trial will be more formal than if you were charged with an infraction. A prosecuting attorney will represent the state,. and procedural requirements, such as rules of evidence, will be strongly adhered to. Unless you're an unusual person who is experienced in conducting yourself in courtrooms, you are probably best advised to hire an attorney, or to ask the court to appoint a lawyer for you if you can't afford one. (See Chapter 9, Section B.) When first confronted by the rules of conducting a case in a court of law, it's all too easy for an inexperienced

---

[2]This is not true if you commit an infraction, unless you fail to show identification or refuse to sign the ticket. (See Chapter 2, Section D(1).)

[3]Although you are taken to jail for these violations, you will be released pending trial, or other disposition of the charge, as long as you post bail or satisfy the court's requirements for release on your own recognizance. If later on you are convicted, you may at that time be sentenced to serve some jail time.

---

[4]*New York v. Belton* (1981) 453 U.S. 454.

[5]See H & Code § 11357(b).

[6]This is even true when the misdemeanor is possession of one ounce or less of marijuana, for which the only penalty is a $100 fine. *Tracy v. Municipal Court*(1978) 22 Cal.3d 760, 150 Cal.Rptr. 785.

person—even with an excellent case—to feel like a toddler trying to cross a freeway.[7]

3. Fines and Jail Sentences

Most Vehicle Code misdemeanors carry the threat of a jail term for up to six months and a fine of up to $1,000 plus penalty assessments (VC § 42002). A few misdemeanors prescribe different maximum penalties. For example, second-offense driving with a suspended license carries a maximum fine of $2,000 (plus "penalty assessments"),[8] while first-offense exhibition of speed carries a maximum jail sentence of 90 days.[9] There is also the possibility that your license will be suspended. (Punishments for the more common misdemeanors are listed in Section B of this chapter.)

While rare, a judge can order a person sentenced to pay a fine to work off the fine at the rate of $30 per day spent in jail (VC § 42003(b)). This used to be popular among judges until higher courts ruled that you can't be imprisoned for nonpayment of a fine you can't afford.[10]

4. Sealing Your Record

Most employment and other types of applications expect you to list misdemeanor offenses but not "minor traffic violations." Misdemeanors may keep you from getting a particular job. However, you can get some misdemeanors legally purged from your record. Then you can truthfully say on employment applications that you have not been convicted of the offense.

The procedure works like this. You file a form requesting to have the record of a misdemeanor conviction or guilty plea retroactively changed on the court records to look like you pleaded not guilty and the charges were dismissed. If you were granted probation, you must wait until the probationary period expires and you have fulfilled all the terms of probation. If no probation was given, you must wait a year from the date you were sentenced before you can make the request (PC §§ 1203.4, 1203.4a).[11]

Unfortunately, the procedure does not erase the conviction from your driving record, and the DMV can still consider it for the purpose of suspending your license (VC § 13555). Also, for misdemeanors carrying a heavier penalty on a second or third offense, the erased conviction can still be used as a prior offense to raise the penalty in a subsequent legal procedure.

B. Common Vehicle Code Misdemeanors

ASIDE FROM DRIVING under the influence (which is covered in Chapter 8), the following are the most commonly charged Vehicle Code misdemeanors.

1. Reckless Driving (VC §§ 23103, 23104)

The most serious of these driving-related misdemeanors is reckless driving.

a. The Violation

§ 23103(a). Any person who drives any vehicle... in willful or wanton disregard for the safety of persons or property is guilty of reckless driving.

---

[7]Normally, judges do not give much help to people representing themselves, on the theory that this would make the judge a participant and be unfair to the prosecutor. If you represent yourself, you will need to understand how a trial works, how to introduce evidence, how to question witnesses and how to make opening and closing statements to the jury. For help in addressing these and other issues, we provide a procedural outline of the process and a list of resources that are available in most law libraries. (See Chapter 13.)

[8]VC § 14601. [See Section B(4) of this chapter.]

[9]VC § 23109. [See Section B(2) of this chapter.]

[10]*In re Anzano* (1970) 3 Cal.3d 100, 89 Cal.Rptr. 255.

---

[11]For more information and step-by-step instructions on purging criminal records, see *The Criminal Records Book*, by attorney Warren Siegel (Nolo Press).

This law applies to driving on "a highway"—which includes any public road or street—and an "offstreet parking facility"—which includes most public and private parking lots [VC § 12500(c)]. It does not apply to private roads.

Reckless driving is covered in one of the most vaguely-worded statutes in the Vehicle Code. Court decisions over the years have interpreted "willful or wanton disregard for the safety of persons or property" to mean that:

- you were driving so dangerously as to be in danger of causing an accident; *and*

- you were, or should have been, aware that you were driving dangerously.

Thus, you can be found guilty even if you didn't know you were driving dangerously (i.e., you lacked "willfulness"). The test is whether a "reasonable and prudent person" in your situation (driving your car, having your knowledge of the road conditions, etc.) *should have known* that driving the way you did was dangerous.

Examples of reckless driving include rounding corners at excessive speeds, weaving in and out of slower-moving traffic, driving through a school zone on a weekday at 50 mph, or driving when you know you can't stay awake. It's one of those things that is difficult to define exactly, but most people know it when they see it.

Reckless driving is a "discretionary arrest" misdemeanor, meaning that the officer can either give you a ticket or place you under physical arrest and take you to jail. Clearly then, if you're ever stopped for reckless driving, your attitude should be civil, without making admissions, and you should tell the officer that you'd be happy to sign the Notice to Appear.[12]

---

[12]Reckless driving often occurs because the driver is angry to begin with and is expressing it while driving. If you are in an angry state when stopped by an officer, you are well advised to instantly become as meek as a lamb. Otherwise, you greatly increase the risk of being taken to jail and additionally being charged with resisting an officer if you lose control when being taken into custody (PC § 148).

b. Penalties

Reckless driving is punishable by:

- a fine of $145 to $1,000 (plus penalty assessments), and/or

- a jail sentence of up to 90 days.

As with speeding violations, the court can order a license suspension of up to one, two or six months respectively for the first, second and third offenses committed within the time the DMV keeps them on your record (VC § 13200). For this purpose, ordinary speeding violations count as prior offenses, so that a person convicted of reckless driving after having previously been convicted of speeding face a two-month suspension.

If someone other than you was injured as a result of your reckless driving, the penalty increases to:

- a mandatory license suspension for up to one year (VC § 13350); and

- a fine between $220 and $1,000, plus penalty assessments; and

- a jail sentence of up to six months (VC § 23104).

If the injury is very serious and you were previously convicted of reckless or drunk driving or engaging in a speed contest or exhibition, you can be charged with and convicted of a felony.

2. Speed "Contests" and "Exhibitions" (VC § 23109)

VC § 23109(a). No person shall engage in any motor vehicle speed contest on a highway.

        (c) No person shall engage in any motor vehicle exhibition of speed on a highway.

This code section is primarily aimed at people who drag race and show off—for example, by screeching their tires.

a. Speed Contests

Vehicle Code Section 23109(a) prohibits any "motor vehicle speed contests," such as racing with another vehicle on a highway, or even against a clock. (It does not include legitimate auto rallies where the course is 20 miles or more and posted speed limits are not exceeded.)

To convict you, the prosecution must prove that you:

- were driving a motor vehicle on a "highway" (including a public—but not private—street or road);
- were driving at a high rate of speed in relation to the applicable speed limit, or were at least accelerating very quickly; and
- intended either to pass, or avoid being passed by, one or more other vehicles or to beat a clock or other timing device, so as to demonstrate that your vehicle is capable of a higher speed or acceleration.

A "speed contest" does not have to be pre-arranged or formal. Two drivers who meet, dart daggers at each other at a stoplight, rev their engines and zoom off are just as engaged in a speed contest as are those who arrange their race a week in advance.

It's not necessary for the officer to nab more than one "drag racer" to make a case. Even though a "contest" seems to require that there be more than one driver, testimony by an officer or bystander that there was someone else involved is sufficient to establish that element. Also, a race against a timing device is considered a speed contest.

It is illegal under this section to "aid or abet in" a speed contest. This includes people who came to watch an illegal, pre-arranged drag race, since the presence of spectators is deemed to encourage the actual participants. It is also illegal to help place a barricade or obstruction in the highway as part of organizing a speed contest or exhibition of speed [VC § 23109(d)].

b. Exhibition of Speed

Even if you aren't found guilty of engaging in a speed contest, you may still be convicted for an "exhibition of speed" under Subdivision (c) of VC § 23109(c). The elements of this misdemeanor are all of the following:

- You were driving a motor vehicle on a "highway" (or any public road or street).
- You were either driving very fast or accelerating very quickly, usually causing a screeching of tires.
- You thought someone else would probably be watching or hearing and you were showing off for their benefit, or even to irritate them.
- The spectators do not have to be anyone you know.

While the violation is called an "exhibition of *speed*," courts have ruled that sudden acceleration (getting up to a high speed from a standstill in a very short time) "so rapid as to break the traction between a vehicle's tires and the pavement" is an exhibition of speed even though the car does not continue at a high speed.[13] Thus, tire screeching done as part of showing off how fast the car can accelerate or take corners, is covered by this statute. Unfortunately, many police will cite people who accidentally screech their tires; a ticket in this situation should be vigorously contested because only intentional conduct of this sort violates the law.

---

[13]*People v. Grier* (1964) 226 Cal.App.2d 360, 38 Cal.Rptr. 11; *In re F.E.* (1977) 67 Cal.App.3d 222, 136 Cal.Rptr. 547.

Since exhibition of speed is a fairly serious offense, many people try to plea bargain down to a regular speed violation.[14] If you fail to have the charge reduced and you go to trial, you should argue that although you might have been speeding (without actually admitting that you were), you didn't intend to screech your tires for someone else's benefit. For example, if it was a very hot day, you may be able to argue that the stickier road surface made it harder for your tires to hold traction—hence the screeching was accidental.[15] Or, if you were driving someone else's car, you may be able to successfully claim that you were unfamiliar with its acceleration characteristics.

c. Penalties

The maximum penalty for taking part in a *speed contest* is:

- a $1,000 fine;
- 90 days in jail;
- a six-month license suspension; and
- having your car impounded for 30 days.

On a second offense, the maximum jail sentence is six months (with a 48-hour minimum), and a six-month license suspension or restriction is required [VC § 13352(a)(8), (9)].

The maximum sentence for exhibition of speed is:

- a $500 fine, plus penalty assessments;
- a jail sentence of 90 days, or both; and
- a license suspension for up to 30, 60 or 90 days, depending on whether it's your first, second, or third conviction, taking *all* prior speed violations or reckless driving convictions into account (VC § 13200).

While it's rare for a court to suspend someone's license for occasional speeding infractions, judges commonly do it for drag racing and "showing off your wheels."

3. Ignoring Tickets and Not Paying Fines (VC § 40508)

You should never ignore a ticket you signed promising to appear in court. Nor should you "forget" to show up for a court appearance. Dealing with the fallout from the original violation is bad enough without going through the harassment and indignities involved in having a warrant issued for your arrest.[16]

If you can't make a scheduled court appearance because you're unavoidably delayed (stuck in traffic) or because of an illness or emergency, phone the traffic division of the court. The phone number is in the county listings of the phone book under Municipal Court or Justice Court. Make a note of the time you called, to whom you spoke and what was said.

Finally, be sure to pay any fine on a charge you fought and lost.

---

[14]You'll have more bargaining power if you insist on a trial by jury, since prosecutors often don't want to bother with a jury trial.

[15]This happens because a very thin semi-liquid layer of hot asphalt on top acts as a sort of imperfect lubricant between the tires and road surface.

---

[16]Having a "failure to appear" on your record can come back to haunt you years later. If you are ever arrested and try to convince the judge to release you on your own recognizance or lower your bail, your record may be used to indicate your untrustworthiness and thus seriously hinder your efforts to obtain freedom.

If you violate a written promise to appear in court (which you sign on a Notice to Appear before the officer lets you go) or neglect to pay a fine, a warrant can be issued for your arrest, your license may be suspended and you will be charged with a misdemeanor—even if the ticket you ignored or fine you didn't pay arose out of an infraction. This means that you then face the prospect of a $1,000 fine plus penalty assessments and the theoretical possibility of going to jail for six months. Now let's look at the specific violations.

a. Failure to Appear as Promised

VC § 40508(a). Any person willfully violating his written promise to appear or a lawfully granted continuance of his promise to appear in court or before a person authorized to receive a deposit of bail is guilty of a misdemeanor, regardless of the disposition of the charge upon which he was originally arrested.

Most non-felony Vehicle Code moving violations begin with a Notice to Appear, the standard "ticket" which the officer asks you to sign. By signing, you promise to appear at the court listed on the ticket, either to forfeit bail or set up a court date.[17]

The language of VC § 40508(a) says that "any person *willfully* violating his written promise to appear" is guilty of a misdemeanor. However, failure to appear can also be charged as an infraction punishable only by a fine of up to $100, plus penalty assessment, unless at arraignment you object and insist it be charged as a misdemeanor.[18] [See Chapter 10, Section C(2)(b).]

Willfully violating "a lawfully granted continuance" is also a misdemeanor. This means that you violate VC § 40508(a) by failing to show up in court

not just the first time you must appear to deal with your ticket, but also for any subsequent appearance required. For example, if you go to the court clerk to set up a future court date, that later date is legally regarded as a "continuance" or postponement of the case. Also, if you appear before a judge at an arraignment, but then don't show up for the trial, you may be charged with failure to appear, even though technically you didn't promise in writing to show up at the trial.

The elements of "failure to appear" are both of the following:

- You signed a written promise to appear, whether on a Notice to Appear given to you as part of the ticket or on a form supplied by the court clerk when you set a court date.

- You *willfully* failed to show up at the court, either at the clerk's window (to pay the ticket or set a court date), or in court before a judge as lawfully directed on a later date.

"Willfully" sounds as if you must have *intended* not to show up. Perhaps, then, you might think you're not guilty if you just forgot. While forgetting to appear might be technically true, it probably won't work as a defense. You will have a hard time convincing a judge or jury that you were so preoccupied with other things that you were not a willful violator. Your excuse for forgetting will have to be a very good one—like a major earthquake or the death of a close relative.

The excuse of having lost the ticket will probably not work. You still have a duty to follow the matter up with the personnel at the courthouse. If you've ever walked into a busy court clerk's office without your ticket and tried to get them to look it up for you, you may have learned just how slow and unhelpful some traffic clerks are. Nevertheless, the burden is on you to try. If you try to have them locate your file and are unsuccessful, you may be able to convince a judge or jury your failure wasn't willful. Be prepared to testify in detail about whom you spoke to and the dates.

---

[17]Types of tickets are covered in Chapter 2, Section D. A failure to appear does not apply to parking tickets, since you don't sign any promise to appear. (See Chapter 6, Section A.) However, a warrant can still be issued for the owner's arrest on an unpaid parking violation. Furthermore, the fine can be increased, and a "hold" can be put on the car's registration by the DMV. (See Chapter 15, Section E.)

[18]PC §§ 17(d) and 19.8.

If you mailed a fine to the court in lieu of a personal appearance, and the fine got lost in the mail or by a court clerk, that *is* a valid defense. Your failure to come to court wasn't willful because you understood you didn't have to appear, since you mailed in the fine, if that's what a "courtesy notice" said, or a clerk told you so over the phone.

Some Strategy

Unfortunately, most folks who get pulled in on a failure to appear charge sheepishly plead guilty and pay fines—sometimes totaling several hundred dollars on both violations—without realizing the consequences. It's not just an increased fine on the original violation; you now have a misdemeanor on your record. In most cases (except when the DMV refuses to renew an about-to-expire license until the case is concluded[19]), you should plead not guilty on both the underlying charge and the failure to appear and demand a jury trial on the misdemeanor failure to appear charge and on any original charges that are misdemeanors.

There are a couple of reasons for this. First, a jury is more likely than a judge to acquit you. Judges have heard hundreds of lame excuses for failures to appear, and often don't believe them.[20] Second, jury trials require a lot more time, work and energy on the part of judges and prosecutors. As a result, the prosecution is much more likely to be willing to plea bargain. For example, you might be offered the chance to plead guilty to the original traffic violation (which will then appear on your record) in return for a dismissal on the failure to appear charge. Or, if you think another moving violation will jack up your insurance rates or result in a license suspension (see Chapter 15, Section A), you might instead want to plead guilty to the failure to appear charge (which will go on your record, but it's not a *moving* violation and has no "point" value), and have the traffic charge dropped, provided it's understood in

advance that there will be no jail sentence.[21] If failure to appear was originally charged against you as an infraction, and you didn't object, jail isn't a possibility. [See PC §§ 17(d), 19.8.]

Of course, having several failure to appear convictions can hurt you in the future, if you're ever arrested for a serious offense, such as drunk or reckless driving. A judge who might otherwise release you from jail without your having to post bail, may be inclined to insist you pay a very high bail if she sees a lot of failures to appear on your record.

Finally, if you're charged with failure to appear, you may have a reasonably good chance of having the ticket for the original offense dismissed. Chances are that a lot of time has passed, perhaps a year or two, since the officer issued the ticket on the original traffic charge. Sometimes, because of storage limitations, police agencies only keep records of tickets issued (including the officer's notes) for a certain length of time, often 18 months, after which they're destroyed—sometimes without regard to whether or not the charges are still pending. Without such notes to refresh the officer's memory, he's not likely to remember the circumstances surrounding his long-ago encounter with you. Moreover, it's possible that the officer may not even be with that particular police agency any more, and they might not even know how to contact him. Nevertheless, even if you're found not guilty on the underlying offense, you still can be found guilty on the failure to appear charge.

b. *Failure to Pay a Fine [VC § 40508(b)]*

VC § 40508(b). Any person willfully failing to pay a lawfully-imposed fine for a violation of any provision of this code or a local ordinance adopted pursuant to this code within the time authorized by the court and without lawful excuse having

---

[19]Unfortunately, people often plead guilty in such cases, rather than go to trial, because they need their licenses.

[20]One of the most commonly-heard excuses is, "I got held up in traffic," which many judges refuse to believe, even if true.

[21]No matter what they tell you, the judge *does* have the power to promise this beforehand. If you plead guilty and the judge goes back on her word on your deal with the prosecutor, you can have the guilty plea set aside.

been presented to the court on or before the date the fine is due is guilty of a misdemeanor regardless of the full payment of the fine after such time.

A "fine" is the amount the judge orders you to pay *after* you plead guilty or are found guilty in court. "Bail" is what you pay if you don't fight the ticket. [See Chapter 3, Section A(3).] The offense of willfully failing to pay a lawfully-imposed fine consists of all of the following:

- You appeared before a judge on a Vehicle Code or local ordinance violation.

- You pleaded or were found guilty.

- The judge "lawfully" ordered (sentenced) you to pay a fine.

- You willfully failed to pay the fine.

The most important element of this violation is whether your failure to pay was "willful."

Willful Nonpayment

If you are sentenced to pay a traffic fine and cannot afford to pay it because doing so would seriously jeopardize your ability to support yourself or your family, you are not acting "willfully."[22] Explain your circumstances to the judge and, if you can, offer to pay it in installments. If even that would be a hardship, ask the judge to hold a hearing on your ability to pay the fine, taking your income, expenses and other factors into account. (We'll go over this in more detail in Chapter 15.)

The judge may fail to give an immediate ruling in the hearing on your ticket, and instead will "take the matter under submission" (or "advisement").[23] If this happens, you will be notified of the verdict by mail and told the amount of the fine, if any. Natu-

rally, until you receive this notice,[24] or otherwise learn of the result and fine, your failure to pay is not willful. Since the courts don't send such notices by mail providing for a return receipt, they have no way of knowing if you received the notice. Unfortunately, they will assume the worst of you and charge you with failure to pay, and it will be up to you to convince a judge or jury otherwise.

Again, if you mailed in the fine in time for it to be received in the court's mail before any deadline is imposed, the court's failure to receive it does not make your conduct willful. If a judge tells you differently, insist on a jury trial!

c. Penalties

The possible penalties for ignoring a ticket (other than a parking ticket) and failing to pay a fine include an additional fine, and even jail if the offense is charged as a misdemeanor. Your driver's license can also be suspended by the DMV until you resolve the matter.

---

[22]A "willful" act is done consciously, knowingly, and with "stubborn purpose." *Helme v. Great Western Milling Co.* (1919), 43 Cal.App.416.

[23]They can't do this unless you agree. You have a right to make the judge tell you her finding immediately. *People v. Kriss* (1979) 96 Cal.App.3d 913, 158 Cal.Rptr. 420. [See Chapter 12, Section C(11).]

[24]Sometimes the clerks also delay in sending out these notices. Unfortunately, this may work to deprive you of your right to appeal, which expires within 30 days after judgment.

Fines and Jail

The maximum fine for the failure to appear or failure to pay a fine is $1,000, plus penalty assessments. The longest possible jail term is six months. In most situations, though, jail sentences are extremely rare, and fines vary from $50 to $150.

Your Driver's License

If you ignore a ticket (other than a parking ticket) or neglect to pay a fine, the law allows the DMV to refuse to renew, or sometimes to suspend, your license, and sometimes allows a judge to "impound" your license. If you fail to appear, the court reports that fact to the DMV. The DMV may then refuse to renew your license until you "adjudicate"—or resolve—both the traffic offense for which you were originally cited and the failure to appear charge [VC §§ 12808(a), 40509(a)]. (See Chapter 15, Section E.)

If you fight a traffic infraction charge and are found guilty, but don't pay the fine, the judge can "impound" your license for up to 30 days—regardless of whether your failure to pay is willful or whether you can afford the fine [VC § 40508(c)]. Also, this failure to pay is reported to the DMV [VC § 40509(b)]. The DMV will not only refuse to renew your license, but can even suspend it right away upon receiving notification of your failure to appear or pay a fine (VC § 13365).

4. Driving While Your License Is Suspended (VC §§ 14601-14601.2)

Of course it's illegal to drive if your license has been suspended. The seriousness of this offense depends on the reason for the original suspension.

a. The Offense

What happens if you get caught driving while your license is suspended or revoked? It's not a defense that your livelihood depends on getting to and from work in the face of an inadequate or nonexistent mass-transit system.

The elements of this offense are simply:

- You drove a motor vehicle.
- Your license was suspended or revoked (but not "impounded") at that time, either by a court or the DMV.
- You knew about the suspension or revocation.

This last element requires a little explanation. To convict you of driving with a suspended or revoked license, the prosecution must prove that you knew your right to drive had been taken away. This is pretty easy to prove if your license was suspended by a judge when you appeared in court. But if the DMV suspended or revoked your license, the prosecution must prove that the DMV mailed or otherwise sent you a notice of that fact. Then you have the burden of proving to a jury (if true) that you never received the notice. *Never* waive the right to a jury trial on this one.

b. Penalties

The potential penalties for driving while your license is suspended are severe:

The *maximum* penalty for a first offense is a $1,000 fine, plus penalty assessments and/or jail for six months. For a second offense within five years, the maximum penalty is a $2,000 fine plus up to one year in jail.

The *minimum* fine for a first offense is $300, plus penalty assessments. For a second offense in five years, it is $500. It is rare to receive a jail sentence for a first offense, but in some cases, a judge is required to impose one.

Sometimes the severity of the sentence depends on why your license was suspended in the first place.

ORIGINAL REASON FOR LICENSE SUSPENSION	PENALTY IF YOU DRIVE WHILE LICENSE SUSPENDED
Reckless driving or for having too many violations on your record.	Mandatory t10 days in jail if you're caught driving with a suspended license for a *second* time within five years.[25]
Driving under the influence.	A first offense of driving while under suspension must be punished by at least 10 days in jail. A second offense within five years carries a mandatory minimum jail term of 30 days.[26]
Too many violations or for drunk driving.	If your driving during the suspension resulted in a "point count" [see Chapter 15, Section A(1)] of three or more over a possible 12-month period, you can be prosecuted as a "habitual traffic offender." As such you will face a possible $1,000 fine and 30-day jail sentence for a first offense. A second such offense in seven years is punishable by a fine of up to $2,000 fine and a jail sentence of up to two months.[27]

If your license was originally suspended because of an earlier ticket you ignored—a failure to appear—the judge or the district attorney may reduce the charge to an infraction punishable by a fine of up to $250 plus penalty assessment (VC § 14601.1). You don't have to agree to this, however, and may insist it be treated as a misdemeanor with a right to a jury trial.[28]

---

[25]VC § 14601.2. This penalty also applies to the offense of violating a "restriction" on driving (i.e., only to and from work) imposed by a judge following a conviction for driving under the influence. (See Chapter 8.)

[26]VC § 14601.2. This penalty also applies to the offense of violating a "restriction" on driving (i.e., only to and from work) imposed by a judge following a conviction for driving under the influence. (See Chapter 8.)

[27]VC § 14601.2. This penalty also applies to the offense of violating a "restriction" on driving (i.e., only to and from work) imposed by a judge following a conviction for driving under the influence. (See Chapter 8.)

[28]VC § 14601.1; see PC §§ 17(d), 19.8.

5. Fourth Offense Within a Year (VC § 40000.28)

VC § 40000.28. Any offense which would otherwise be an infraction is a misdemeanor if a defendant has been convicted of three or more violations of this code or any local ordinance adopted pursuant to this code within the 12-month period immediately preceding the commission of the offense and such prior convictions are admitted by the defendant or alleged in the accusatory pleading. For this purpose, a bail forfeiture shall be deemed to be a conviction of the offense charged. This section shall have no application to violations by pedestrians.

a. An Infraction Can Be a Misdemeanor

If you were convicted of three or more violations within 12 months prior to another alleged violation, that fourth offense can be charged as a misdemeanor, even if it's an infraction.

The three prior Vehicle Code or local-ordinance violations need not be moving violations of the type reported to the DMV, though pedestrian violations don't count. If you were convicted of three *parking* violations (or merely forfeited bail by paying off parking tickets) within a 12-month period, a fourth violation of any kind (even just another parking offense) could at least in theory be treated as a misdemeanor.

b. Prosecution as a Misdemeanor

In practice, fourth offenses classified as infractions are almost never prosecuted as misdemeanors. It is just too much of a bureaucratic nightmare for prosecutors to deal with. They are too busy to spend their time on what is still basically a minor offense. Besides, even if the charge remains an infraction, you can still be fined $250, plus penalty assessments.

c. Insisting on a Misdemeanor Jury Trial

You may have noticed that VC § 40000.28 says a fourth offense infraction is a misdemeanor when the three "prior convictions are admitted by the defendant." Does this mean that if you had three convictions or bail forfeitures within the 12 months before you were cited for a fourth offense that you could insist on being charged with a misdemeanor and demand a jury trial? Amazingly, yes, as long as you have the records.[29] But subjecting yourself to a maximum $1,000 fine, plus penalty assessment, and a six-month jail sentence is a very high price to pay for getting a jury trial. And if the jury finds you guilty, the judge may be disposed to give you a rough time. While judges are not supposed to penalize you for asserting your right to a jury trial, the fact that you have used a lot of court time over a minor offense won't count in your favor.

---

[29]*People v. Shults* (1978) 87 Cal.App.3d 101, 150 Cal.Rptr. 747.

8

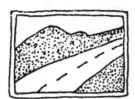

DRUNK DRIVING

ONE OF THE MOST serious driving offenses is that which we call "drunk driving." Because this charge is so serious, and because factual and legal issues in such cases can be very complicated, we don't intend here to tell you how to conduct your own drunk-driving defense—that would take a book in its own right.[1] Here we simply give you the basic information you will need to understand your options and to deal intelligently with your lawyer, if you decide to hire one.

"Drunk driving" under California law includes not only driving while "under the influence" of alcohol and/or drugs (legal or illegal), but also includes driving with a blood-alcohol level of 0.08% or greater—whether you were feeling any "influence" of the alcohol or not. Both offenses are treated equally severely. They are the most serious, as well as the most frequently charged, Vehicle Code misdemeanors.

Though much of this book is designed to help you handle your own traffic court case, you should decide to be more cautious about doing a drunk-driving case, since the stakes are very high. Even a first conviction will result in a large fine, *plus* at least two days in jail or a 90-day driver's license restriction that forbids you from driving other than to and from work. A second conviction within seven years means you will definitely serve at least 10 days in jail (probably more) and have your license restricted for at least a year and a half. And those are the

minimum penalties—which judges frequently exceed, especially in sentencing repeat offenders.

The *maximum* penalties for a first offense include a $1,000 fine—*plus* about $1,600 in penalty assessments—and six months in jail. For a second offense you can be put in jail for a year. In addition, a first offense will result in your license being suspended for at least four months by the DMV. It may also result in your insurance being cancelled, or at least the rates drastically increased. And a drunk-driving charge stays on your driving record for *seven years*. (Minimum and maximum penalties for first and repeat offenses are listed in detail in Section B of this chapter.)

Before you read further, we wish to emphasize general rules that you should understand when dealing with the subject of drunk driving:

1. You will almost always be better off taking the chemical test when it is offered by the police.

2. Your chances of beating a drunk-driving charge are exceedingly slim if the chemical test result is substantially over the limit (0.08% or greater).

Read the rest of this chapter with these two points firmly in mind.

[**Editor's Note:** *The subject of drunk driving stimulates much passion in those who wish to stamp it out. In fact, we have previously been accused by these people of abetting drunk driving by explaining the different ways to defend against this offense. We believe that every criminal defendant is presumed innocent until convicted and should have the benefit of the information we provide here. Our job, as we see it, is to disseminate information about*

---

[1]The best book on the subject is *Defense of Drunk-Driving Cases*, by Richard Erwin (Matthew-Bender, San Francisco). Written mostly for lawyers, it is sometimes very technical, but this three-volume set is extremely thorough.

the law in a form that can be understood and utilized by non-lawyers. We leave it to others to implement the law and change it if they believe it doesn't go far enough.]

A. The Offenses

IN THIS SECTION, we explain the elements of several different types of drunk-driving offenses. (For less serious alcohol-related offenses, such as "open-container" violations, see Chapter 5, Section D.)

1. Driving Under the Influence

VC § 23152(a). It is unlawful for any person who is under the influence of an alcoholic beverage or any drug, or under the combined influence of an alcoholic beverage and any drug, to drive a vehicle.

The elements of this misdemeanor offense are:

- You drove a vehicle—i.e., steered and controlled it while it was moving; and

- At the same time, you were "under the influence" in that your ability to drive safely was affected to an appreciable degree by an alcoholic beverage you drank, a drug that you took, or the combination of the two.

a. Driving

The first element—"you drove the vehicle"—is usually not in dispute. Even when it is, it can be proved in court by "circumstantial" or indirect evidence. In one case, for example, a person accused of drunk driving had been discovered passed out in a car with its engine running. The jury was allowed to infer from the running engine that he had been driving.

Sometimes a drunk driver and a sober (or, at least, less drunk) passenger will try to switch places in their seats just before the officer approaches the car. This tactic usually fails to fool the officers, and can often make the situation worse if the officer later testifies in court as to all the "furtive movements" occasioned by this awkward and desperate ploy.

In sum, the defense that you weren't driving (or that no one saw you drive) can sometimes be a fairly difficult one. You should definitely talk to an attorney experienced in drunk-driving defense if you think you might be able to use it.

b. Simultaneous Driving and Intoxication

Though it may sound obvious, both the driving and the under-the-influence elements must occur at the same time for a person to be guilty. For example, if you gulped down a double martini just before you started to drive and drove only a few minutes before being stopped and arrested, you might have been sober enough while driving. However, by the time a blood sample is taken a half hour later, it may show a substantial alcohol content.[2] A more unusual, yet similar, situation occurs when a driver who has had nothing to drink gets into an accident, and then walks into a nearby bar to get a drink and calm his nerves. When the police arrive to investigate the accident, they smell alcohol on his breath and arrest him. By the time he gives a sample of his blood, breath or urine, the alcohol will have worked its way through his body and he will be erroneously charged with having driven under the influence.

It is important to understand that the delay between the time a person was driving and the time he gave a blood, breath or urine sample can be used to his advantage. Once you stop drinking, your blood alcohol level decreases as time passes. This means that it was higher when you were driving than when the blood, breath or urine sample was taken. And although the police and prosecution know how to take this into account, the calculation is not a precise one, and you may be able to raise a reasonable doubt in the jury's mind. We'll learn more about this in Sections C and D of this chapter.

---

[2]As we discuss below, the rate at which ingested alcohol enters your blood stream and passes out of it (your absorption rate) can sometimes be used to show that your blood alcohol content was different when you were driving than it was when you were tested.

c. Being "Under the Influence"

You don't have to be falling-down drunk to be "under the influence." (In a sense, the phrase "drunk driving" is a misnomer.) The issue is only whether your ability to drive was "impaired" so that you weren't as cautious or alert as a sober person would have been in similar circumstances.

A 1970 court decision still applicable today defined the state of being "under the influence" as follows:

> A person is under the influence of intoxicating liquor when as a result of drinking such liquor his physical and mental abilities are impaired so that he no longer has the ability to drive a vehicle with the caution characteristic of a sober person of ordinary prudence under the same or similar circumstances.[3]

How is this determined? Well, the arresting officer will testify about your allegedly unsafe driving that led him to stop your car, your "symptoms" (slurred speech, red eyes, dilated pupils, flushed face, strong alcoholic beverage odor on breath, unsteadiness on feet after getting out of car, etc.), and your supposed inability to pass the roadside "coordination" test. The coordination test may involve rapidly saying the alphabet, closing your eyes and touching one index finger to the other or to your nose, balancing on one foot, picking up a dropped coin, and the well-known walking a straight line (usually a sidewalk cement line), etc.

Finally, "scientific" evidence—the concentration of alcohol in your blood shortly after you were arrested—allows the judge or jury to infer, perhaps after hearing the testimony of a physician or other "expert witness," that you were under the influence while driving. However, this kind of evidence isn't absolutely necessary to convict you. Many people who have refused to submit to blood, breath or urine tests for alcohol have been convicted of driving under the influence solely on the basis of the testi-mony of police officers that they flunked coordination tests.

d. Blood Alcohol Levels

As we'll see in Section D, the law requires a person arrested for driving under the influence to give a blood, breath or urine sample to be tested for alcohol content—when asked. Your refusal to do so will result in a minimum one-year license suspension by the DMV (see Chapter 15, Section C)—even if you're eventually found innocent of the charge. Because of this, most people submit to one of these three "chemical tests." As a result, the prosecution is usually armed with "scientific" evidence of a defendant's supposed intoxication. The more alcohol in your blood, the more likely it will be presumed that you were under the influence.[4]

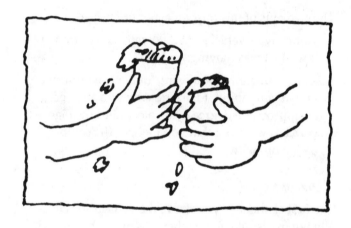

To make it easier for a jury to decide whether you were "under the influence," the Legislature has come up with a set of "presumptions" which are

---

[3]*People v. Schoonover* (1970) 5 Cal.App.3d 101, 85 Cal.Rptr. 69.

[4]It's important to realize that you can be convicted of driving under the influence even though your blood alcohol level is fairly low—particularly if your drove erratically, slurred when you spoke, staggered around, etc. As we'll see in Section C, some people are more intoxicated at a given blood alcohol level than are others.

based on the amount of alcohol the jury determines to have been in your blood while you were driving. The jurors do this by considering the chemical test evidence.

If your blood alcohol is found by a jury to have been *less* than 0.05%, the law "presumes" that you were *not* under the influence. This means that unless there's other strong evidence against you (such as testimony that you were erratically weaving all over the road), you should be acquitted. Prosecutors will almost always drop the charge when the blood alcohol results come out this low.

If your blood alcohol is found to have been between 0.05% and 0.08%, the law says that there's no presumption either way. [5] In this range, most prosecutors are willing to plea-bargain down to a lesser charge, such as reckless driving.[6] An attorney can be of assistance here, but if you know what you're up against, you may be able to do it yourself. Indeed, many over-burdened prosecutors may also be willing to plea bargain the charge down to reckless driving if your blood alcohol level is only slightly over 0.08%.[7]

Finally, the jury is told that if they determine your blood alcohol level, while driving, to have been 0.08% or more, they must presume you were under the influence. This means that the jury must find you guilty unless you raise a "reasonable doubt" as to whether you really were under the influence. But even if you win this way, you still can be found guilty of the separate offense of driving with a blood alcohol of 0.08% or more, as we'll see shortly in Section 2.

e. Drugs: Legal or Illegal

Vehicle Code Section 23152(a) also makes it illegal to drive under the influence of a drug, or under the combined influence of alcohol and a drug. Subdivision (c) of this same law makes it illegal to drive while addicted to a drug—other than methadone for treating heroin addiction—even though not under the influence at the time.

Most folks are surprised to learn that the "drug" doesn't even have to be an illegal one.[8] You can be arrested and convicted for driving under the influence of legally-prescribed tranquilizers, or even over-the-counter nonprescription drugs, like antihistamines or other decongestants, if they adversely affect your ability to drive.

2. Driving While Blood Alcohol Is 0.08% or Higher

The law flatly prohibits anyone with a blood alcohol concentration of 0.08% (eight one-hundredths of one percent[9]) or more from driving, whether or not any driving is impaired.[10]

> VC § 23152(b). It is unlawful for any person who has *0.08% or more*, by weight, *of alcohol* in his or her blood *to drive a vehicle.*
>
> In any prosecution under this subdivision, it is a rebuttable presumption that the person had 0.08% or more, by weight, of alcohol in his or her blood at the time of driving the vehicle *if the*

---

[5]VC § 23155.

[6]However, your plea of guilty to a reckless driving charge will go on your record as having been plea bargained down from drunk driving. Then, if you're charged with drunk driving again within seven years, you will face the same increased penalty you'd face on a second drunk-driving charge (VC § 23103.5). See Section B of this chapter. (This is not the way plea bargaining works for other kinds of offenses.)

[7]This was especially true before 1982. Now, however, merely having a 0.08% blood alcohol level while driving is illegal in itself—whether or not a person can be considered "under the influence" in light of other factors. So, prosecutors' cases are easier than before, and prosecutors today are less likely than in earlier years to plea bargain, even at fairly low blood alcohol levels like 0.10% or 0.11%.

[8]VC § 23201.

[9]Eight one-hundredths of one percent is equal to eight tenths (0.8) of a milligram of alcohol in each cubic centimeter of blood. For those unfamiliar with the metric system, a cubic centimeter is the volume of a cube measuring one centimeter (about 3/8ths of an inch) on each side—about the size of a small sugar cube. A pinhead weighs about 3 milligrams.

[10]The constitutionality of a law that forbids driving at a fixed blood-alcohol content, regardless of sobriety, was upheld by the California Supreme Court in *Burg v. Municipal Court* (1983) 35 Cal.3d 257.

person had 0.08% or more, by weight, of alcohol in his or her blood at the time of the performance of a chemical test within three hours after the driving.

The elements of this offense are:

- You drove a vehicle; and

- Alcohol was present in your blood at a concentration of 0.08% or greater *while you were driving.*

The latter is legally "presumed" if a blood test taken within three hours of the driving showed your blood alcohol to be 0.08% or more, but the presumption can be rebutted. This is done with evidence relating to the time and amount of drinking, or your condition and behavior at the time of driving, which suggests that your blood alcohol level might have been lower while driving than when taking the chemical test. For example, you took a stiff drink just before driving, but its alcohol didn't work its way into your blood stream until after you were arrested and took the chemical test. (See Section C of this chapter.) Or, your friend who was with you before you drove testifies to your lack of slurred speech or staggering—so as to suggest a high-result blood test to be in error.

What this law means is that regardless of whether you have been "driving under the influence," you can still be found guilty of the offense of "driving with an over-0.08% alcohol level." In many cases, the jury will be given a choice of finding a defendant guilty of either driving under the influence [VC § 23152(a)] *or* driving with a blood alcohol level of 0.08% or higher [VC § 23152(b)], or both. So, even if you and your witnesses could convince a jury that your ability to drive was superb and that you were just as cautious and conservative a driver as a person who'd had nothing to drink, the jury can still find you guilty of what we call "drunk driving" if it believes your blood alcohol was 0.08% or more while you were driving.

Example: Tom Tippler, just out of a late business meeting, was driving down the freeway at 9:00 p.m. Although he'd had two stiff Mai Tais at Pete's Plateau, his reflexes and muscular coordination were close to normal because, quite frankly, he drank like that every day and his system was used to it. When he leaned over to light a cigarette, his car swerved just a bit inside his lane. A zealous CHP officer pulled him over, smelled the alcohol on his breath, and asked him what he'd had to drink. Tom replied truthfully and the officer arrested him. A blood sample he gave showed an alcohol concentration of 0.09%. Even if the jury believes Tom's business associates when they testify to his apparent total sobriety when he left them, it will still convict Tom under § 23152(b)—driving with a blood alcohol level of 0.08% or more—if the jurors believe Tom's blood alcohol level was 0.09%, or even 0.08%, while driving.

Note: Occasionally, the prosecution may try to narrow down the issues in trial by charging a defendant only with a violation under subdivision (b) of § 23152. Since being "under the influence" isn't part of this offense, you might not be allowed to present any evidence as to how sober you were. A judge might consider such evidence irrelevant to the simple question of whether your blood alcohol level was 0.08% or higher.[11]

Example: Bill Blotto walked out of Jake's Bar and got into his car after having drunk only two bottles of beer. While scratching a flea bite, his car weaved just a little bit and an officer stopped him, smelled the beer on his breath, and arrested him. Bill consented to a blood test. Because of a blood sample mix-up unbeknownst to anyone, Bill's blood alcohol was found to be an amazing 0.31%. At this level, Bill should have been in a near coma.

---

[11]If the judge does allow such evidence, the jury will have to consider it only for the purpose of shedding doubt on the accuracy of the blood alcohol test results. For example, believable testimony that a driver (whose blood alcohol was "measured" at a very high level) acted totally sober may lead jurors to disbelieve the chemical test results. The jurors shouldn't consider this testimony for the purpose of determining whether the person was "under the influence," since that is not part of the offense under subdivision (b). However, it is not unheard of for jurors to ignore a judge's instructions and acquit for the wrong reason (namely that the defendant wasn't under the influence)—but it's rare. This is why defense lawyers will try to introduce "sobriety" testimony, using the guise of attacking the test results. Whether a defendant will have a right to use the "he-looked-sober-to-me" variety of testimony when only subdivision (b) is charged is one of the details the appeals courts will have to work out.

He was charged under § 23152(b)—driving with a blood alcohol level of 0.08% or more. Bill's friends at Joe's (including Joe) will testify that Bill had only two beers (which cannot lead to that high a blood alcohol level). Also, they'll want to testify that he acted totally sober. If the judge allows this, he or she will tell the jury to consider this testimony only for the purpose of shedding doubt on the accuracy of the blood test results, and not to use it to acquit Bill because he wasn't under the influence.

In cases where blood, breath or urine testing shows an alcohol concentration much greater than 0.08%, prosecutors will charge only under subdivision (b) (driving with a blood alcohol level of 0.08% or higher), and thus simplify the trials. If the concentration is equal to or only slightly above 0.08%, prosecutors will charge under both (a) and (b) to give the jury a choice. For blood alcohol levels under 0.08% or when the driver refuses to take a blood, breath or urine test, prosecutors will just charge driving under the influence.

> **Example 2:** Tess Teetotaler was also at the business meeting with Tom Tippler. She only had two glasses of wine. But unlike Tom, she doesn't drink very often. The wine took its toll on her coordination, and a city police officer caught her weaving in and out of her lane. Her blood alcohol level was only 0.06%, but if the jury believes that her driving ability was impaired, it can convict her under § 23152(a)—driving under the influence.

3. "Attempted" Drunk Driving

You probably know that attempted murder, burglary, etc., are crimes. This is because PC § 664 makes it a crime to attempt to commit a crime. Recently, an appeals court ruled that this rule applies to driving under the influence as well.[12] The offense can occur when a person under the influence merely attempts to start or drive a vehicle. There are no minimum penalties and the maximum penalties are half those for driving under the influence (three

months in jail, $500 fine, plus penalty assessments, for first offense).

4. Felony Drunk Driving

If you *kill* or *injure* anyone as the result of driving while you are under the influence of alcohol, *or* while your blood alcohol is 0.08% or more, you can be found guilty of a felony[13] and could go to state prison for over a year, and possibly for up to five years, depending on whether it's your first, second or third offense.[14] The jury (and sometimes the judges) will have the option of reducing a first or second offense to a misdemeanor, but even in such cases, the person convicted could spend up to a year in the county jail. Also, a person faced with a fourth drunk-driving charge over a seven-year period may be charged with a felony, even where no one was injured as a result of the offense.[15]

This is all we'll say about felony drunk driving. Needless to say, no one should ever attempt to handle a felony trial without a lawyer, and anyone accused of felony-under-the influence or over-0.08% driving should use this book only as an introductory resource.

---

[12]*People v. Garcia* (1989) 214 Cal.App.3d Supp.1, 262 Cal.Rptr. 915.

[13]VC §§ 23153, 23180, 23185, 23190.

[14]Prior convictions of misdemeanor under-the-influence or over-0.08% driving count as prior offenses for the purpose of increasing the prison sentence. So do prior convictions of alcohol-related reckless driving (VC §§ 23185, 23190).

[15]VC § 23175.

B. Penalties

THIS PART OF THE chapter lists the state-imposed penalties for drunk-driving convictions. There's no need to read this section word-for-word. (It's pretty boring if you do.) Use it as a reference, reading only that part that pertains to your offense. However, you may want to skim these pages to get an overall view of how drunk drivers are treated in California. Keep in mind that in addition to these penalties, your insurance company may cancel your policy or increase your rates dramatically.[16]

[**Editor's Note:** *These penalties are subject to frequent change by the Legislature, almost always in the direction of greater severity. While we do our best to keep this book completely up-to-date, penalties for drunk driving is the one area where we may occasionally fall behind.*]

1. Drunk Driving Not Involving Bodily Injury or Death

The range of penalties for drunk driving depends largely upon whether it's your first, second, or third offense. Note also that the range of penalties are the same regardless of whether you were driving while dead drunk or were merely driving while alert but with a blood alcohol level of 0.08% or higher. (Of course, within the permitted range of sentences, judges can and do sentence those who were very drunk more harshly than those with borderline blood alcohol levels.)

The provision for fines, jail sentences and other penalties are as follows:

a. First Conviction

The *maximum* penalties for a misdemeanor first conviction of a violation of VC § 23152 (driving under the influence *or* with an over-0.08% blood alcohol level (VC §§ 23160, 23161)) are as follows:

- a $1,000 fine *plus* about $1,600 in penalty assessments; in addition to other penalty assessments [see Chapter 3, Section A(3)(b)], an extra $50 penalty assessment is added in all drunk-driving cases (VC § 23196);

- six months in the county jail;

- six month's license suspension by the DMV—if the judge orders it, or doesn't grant probation [VC § 13352(a)(1)];[17] and

- having your car "impounded" (stored at your expense) for 30 days (VC § 23195).

While total fines (plus penalty assessments) as high as $1,000 are common, jail sentences of several months for first offenses are not. But shorter jail sentences of two, five or even ten days are meted out by some judges.

The *minimum* penalties are as follows:

- a $390 fine (*plus* about $700 in penalty assessments) *plus* one of the following (VC § 23160):

  ~ Ninety-six hours in jail (48 of which must be served consecutively) if probation is not granted;

  ~ If probation is granted, attendance at drug or alcohol abuse classes, *plus* either 48 hours in jail or a 90-day restriction (to be noted on your license) whereby you can drive only to, from, and in your employment, and to and from drug or alcohol abuse classes (VC § 23161).

The last sentencing alternative above involves your agreeing to accept "terms of probation" which you must abide by. (If you don't—e.g., by failing to finish traffic school, failing to pay the fine imposed or getting in trouble again over the next three-to-five-year period of probation—you could wind up before the same judge, facing a jail term after he "revokes" your probation.) The judge must require terms of probation at least as strict as those above,

---

[16]As we discuss in Chapter 5, Section F, and Chapter 15, Section D(5), if you lose your insurance (or can't afford it) you will not be able to drive until you obtain it again.

[17]However, the suspension is mandatory if the offense occurred while driving a semi rig or bus ("Class 1" or "Class 2" driver's license required), and the individual may be allowed only to drive automobiles and light trucks under a "Class 3" license.

and may impose even stricter terms, like a 180-day driving restriction and five days in jail.

After your license suspension or restriction is lifted, you will be required periodically to supply proof of insurance to the DMV for the next three years.

b. Second Offense in Seven Years

The penalties for a second conviction of driving under the influence (or with a blood alcohol of 0.08% or more) within seven years are more severe.

Convictions of the following offenses count as prior offenses (or "priors") for the purpose of determining whether your current offense is a second offense:

- prior misdemeanor violations of the same offense (VC § 23152);
- prior misdemeanor or felony under-the-influence or over-0.08% convictions involving injury or death (VC § 23153);
- a prior guilty plea to reckless driving that was plea bargained down from a drunk-driving charge (VC § 23103.5).

The *maximum* penalties for a misdemeanor second conviction within a seven year period are as follows (VC § 23165):

- a $1,000 fine *plus* up to about $1,600 in penalty assessments;
- one year in the county jail;
- having your car impounded for 30 days (VC § 23195); and
- an 18-month license suspension by the DMV (which can be avoided only by being granted probation, which requires participation in an 18-month alcohol abuse treatment program and having to apply to the DMV for a "restricted" license that allows driving only to, from, and in your work)—see Chapter 15, Section D [VC §§ 13352(a)(3), 13352.5(a)].

The *minimum* penalties the judge must impose include (VC § 23165):

- a $390 fine (*plus* up to about $700 in penalty assessments) *plus* one of the following:
  - ~ Ninety days in jail if probation is not granted;
  - ~ If probation is granted, then a) 10 days in jail plus an 18-month license suspension, or b) 48 hours in jail, participation in an 18-month alcohol treatment program and restriction of your driving (for the 18 months) to trips between home and work and to and from the alcohol treatment program (VC § 23166).

At a minimum, violation of any term of probation will result in either your going back to jail for at least 30 days or the suspension of your driver's license (VC § 23167).

c. Third or Fourth Conviction in Seven Years

The penalties for a third or fourth conviction in seven years are very severe. Prior offenses for the purpose of determining whether you've had two or three earlier offenses include those discussed in (b) above. The maximum penalties are the same as for a second offense, except that the DMV *must* revoke your license, for at least three years.[18] (Even after the revocation period, you still cannot get a driver's license until you've completed an 18-month alcohol treatment program.) A fourth offense can also be prosecuted as a felony, punishable by 16 months, two years, or three years in a state prison (VC § 23175). The court can also order an owner-driver's vehicle sold, with the proceeds going to the state (VC § 23198).

The minimum conditions of probation a judge must impose include a jail sentence of 120 days (third offense) or 180 days (fourth offense) and a $390 fine (plus penalty assessments), *plus* participation in an 18-month alcohol treatment program if you haven't done so previously (VC §§ 23171, 23176). Unlike for a second offense, participation in such a program will not keep the DMV from taking your license, but is a requirement for ever getting it back. (Also, a failure to complete the program would

---

[18]VC §§ 23170, 23175, and 13352(a)(5) and (7).

constitute a violation of a term of probation and would likely result in the serving of even more jail time.)

2. Additional Penalties

In addition to the penalties listed above, the court must impose additional jail time if there was a passenger under age 14 in the vehicle at the time it was being driven by the defendant. This additional jail time is 2, 10, 30 and 90 additional days in jail on a first, second, third and fourth offense, respectively.[19]

Similarly, the court must impose 60 days additional jail time if it finds that, while driving under the influence (or with a blood alcohol level of 0.08% or more), the defendant drove in a "willful and wanton" manner and at least 20 mph over the posted speed limit (30 mph on freeways).[20]

3. Drunk Driving Involving Death or Bodily Injury

Although this book is not intended for use by people accused of driving under the influence where death or bodily injury resulted (an offense punishable as a felony), we're listing the minimum and maximum possible punishments here because misdemeanor drunk-driving convictions—where no death or bodily injury resulted—will count as prior offenses for any future felony charges. In other words, a person accused of drunk driving involving bodily injury faces much more serious penalties as a result of any prior misdemeanor convictions of drunk driving or alcohol-related reckless driving.

a. First Offense

The maximum penalties are:[21]

- a $1,000 fine *plus* up to about $700 in penalty assessments;
- one year in the county jail (if punished as a misdemeanor) or three years in state prison (if punished as a felony);
- one year's license suspension by the DMV; and
- having your car impounded for 30 days.

The minimum penalty includes a $390 fine (*plus* penalty assessments) *plus* five days in jail (VC § 23181) *and* a one-year license suspension by the DMV.

b. Second Offense in Seven Years

A second offense in seven years—involving death or injury—is punished more severely regardless of whether injury occurred as a result of the first offense. Prior convictions, for the purpose of determining whether an offense is your second, include all those mentioned in Section 1(b) of this part.

The *maximum* penalties are:[22]

- a $5,000 fine;
- one year in the county jail (misdemeanor) or three years in state prison (felony);
- three years' license revocation by the DMV; and
- having your car confiscated (that's right, they keep it, forever—VC § 23196).

The *minimum* penalties that the judge must impose (VC § 23186) include a $390 fine *plus* either:

---

[19]VC § 23194.
[20]VC § 23208.

[21]VC §§ 23180, 13352(a)(2).
[22]VC §§ 23185, 13352(a)(4), 13352.5(b).

- 120 days in jail (followed by an automatic license revocation by the DMV); or

- as a condition of probation, 30 days in jail *plus* a one-year license suspension followed by a two-year restriction whereby you can drive only to, from, and in your work, *plus* participation in a one-year alcohol treatment program.

c. *Third Offense in Seven Years*

A third offense—where death or injury results—is always punished as a felony. (Neither the judge nor the jury may reduce it to a misdemeanor.)

The *maximum* penalties are:[23]

- a $5,000 fine;

- four years in state prison;

- a five-year driver's license revocation;

- having your car confiscated.

The *minimum* penalties[24] include

- a five-year license revocation

plus either:

- two years in state prison and a $1,015 fine *plus* up to about $1,700 in penalty assessments; *or*

- as a condition of probation, one year in the county jail *plus* payment of a $390 fine (plus penalty assessments) *plus* one year's participation in an alcohol treatment program, *plus* a requirement to repay the injured victims (restitution).

4. Other Offenses

In certain situations, a drunk driver involved in an accident in which someone is killed may also be charged with felony manslaughter or even second-degree murder. Defense against charges of this sort is obviously beyond the scope of this book.

---

[23]VC §§ 23190, 13352(a)(6).
[24]VC § 23190.

C. How Alcohol Interacts with Your Body

JUST AS THE AMOUNT of gasoline in your fuel tank depends on how often you fill it and how much you burn off as you drive, the amount of alcohol in your blood stream is determined by a balance between how fast beverage alcohol is absorbed into your blood and how fast it's eliminated from it. Elimination occurs when most of the alcohol is "burned" or "oxidized" in your body, while the rest of the alcohol is excreted in breath, urine and perspiration. Since alcohol is eliminated from the blood stream at a fairly steady rate, the degree of intoxication depends almost entirely on the rate of absorption. If alcohol is absorbed rapidly into the bloodstream, the blood alcohol level will get high fast—and so will you. If it is absorbed slowly enough to be eliminated before it builds up, you won't feel very high.

1. Absorption into the Blood Stream

When you take a drink, the alcohol is absorbed into the blood through the mucous lining of the entire gastrointestinal tract: the mouth, the esophagus, the stomach, and the small intestine. The rate of absorption increases as the drink moves down the tract. Absorption from the stomach into the blood stream (by way of blood-carrying capillaries in the stomach lining) is faster than from the esophagus or mouth. The street wisdom that says that drinking on an empty stomach will get you higher, faster is true because there is nothing else in your stomach to compete with the alcohol in terms of getting absorbed. The fastest rate of absorption is from the upper end of the small intestine.

For an "average individual," about 60% of the alcohol consumed at a given time will have been absorbed into the blood stream a half-hour later. About 90% will have been absorbed in an hour, and all of it will have been absorbed in an hour and a half. However, this is just for an "average" individual with an "average" stomach food load, drinking "average" drinks.[25] In fact, the rate of alcohol absorption depends on all sorts of things— the quantity of alcohol ingested, the concentration of alcohol in the drink, the rate of drinking, and the nature and amount of diluting material already in the stomach.

2. Elimination from the Body

Alcohol is eliminated from the body in two ways. Ninety to ninety-five percent of it is oxidized, mostly in the liver, to form water and carbon dioxide (a gas that dissolves in the blood, goes to your lungs and is exhaled). The rate of its oxidation is pretty much the same over time, but varies, depending on how well a person's liver functions. People who drink regularly burn alcohol faster than casual drinkers. Chronic alcoholics burn it even faster. The remaining 5 to 10% of the alcohol is eliminated unchanged by perspiration, in urine by way of the kidneys and bladder, and in the breath by way of the blood as it reaches the lungs.

3. Calculating Approximate Blood Alcohol Levels

Since driving while your blood contains at least 0.08% of alcohol is illegal, it can be helpful for you to be able to estimate your own blood alcohol at any given time, based on the number of drinks you had and the time you had them. Although a person's exact blood alcohol level depends on a number of factors, there's a simple, reasonably accurate way you can figure what your highest possible blood alcohol level could be (for example, if you drank very fast on an empty stomach).

If you divide the number 3.8 by your body weight in pounds, you should obtain a number between 0.015 and 0.040. Call this your own personal "blood-alcohol-maximum-per-drink" number. This is the maximum percentage alcohol that will be added to your blood with each "drink" you take. For the purposes of this calculation, a "drink" is a 12-ounce, 4%-alcohol, bottle of beer, or a 4-ounce glass (a small wine glass) of 12%-alcohol wine, or a one-ounce shot glass of 100 proof liquor (most bars' mixed drinks have this amount of alcohol). (Malt liquor, *pint* bottles of beer, large (6 oz.) wine glasses, 20%-alcohol ("fortified") wines, and very stiff or large mixed drinks (such as Mai Tais) should be counted as "1-1/2" drinks.) For each such "drink," your blood alcohol concentration will be increased by about the following percentages.

MAXIMUM BLOOD ALCOHOL LEVEL (%)[26]

Your Weight in Pounds	Drinks Consumed in One Hour				
	1	2	3	4	5
100	0.038	0.076	0.114	0.152	0.190
120	0.032	0.064	0.096	0.128	0.160
140	0.027	0.054	0.081	0.108	0.135
160	0.024	0.048	0.072	0.096	0.120
180	0.021	0.042	0.063	0.084	0.105
200	0.019	0.038	0.057	0.076	0.095
220	0.017	0.034	0.051	0.068	0.085
240	0.016	0.032	0.048	0.064	0.080

Shaded Section: over .05%; subject to prosecution for driving under influence

Black Section: over .08%; guilty of misdemeanor if you drive a vehicle

---

[25]The fact that an "average" is just that—and that a lot of situations are not "average"—can be used by a skilled lawyer to try to raise the all-elusive reasonable doubt in jurors' minds.

[26]Obtained by dividing the number 3.8 by the body weight in pounds. This factor takes into account various English-to-metric and other conversion factors, the body's typical weight-percentage of blood (per pound of body weight) in which the alcohol will be mixed, and the proportion of alcohol that will wind up in the blood.

Example: Linda Light, weighing a petite 100 pounds, could possibly have had a blood alcohol level of up to 0.038% from just one drink and up to 0.072% from two drinks. Three drinks could put her over the 0.08% blood alcohol level, especially if she drank them quickly on an empty stomach.

Hans Heavy, on the other hand, weighs in at 240 pounds, and his maximum blood alcohol increase per drink is only 0.016%. He's barely feeling the effects of the first one. To get past 0.08% blood alcohol, he'd have to down at least six drinks in an hour.

Now let's look at how long the alcohol elimination process takes. *After* 40 minutes have passed, your body will begin eliminating alcohol from the bloodstream at the rate of about 0.01% for each *additional* 40 minutes. So, once you multiply the number of drinks you've had by your blood alcohol maximum per drink, subtract 0.01% from that number for each 40 minutes that have passed since you began drinking—but don't count the first 40 minutes.

For those of you who like mathematical shorthand:

$$\text{APPROX. BLOOD ALCOHOL LEVEL (\%) OVER TIME} = \frac{3.8 \times \#\ \text{OF DRINKS}}{\text{BODY WEIGHT}} - \frac{0.01 \times \#\ \text{OF MINUTES} - 40}{40}$$

Example: 100-pound Linda Light's blood alcohol level after two drinks gulped down rather quickly could be as high as 0.076%. But if she drank them over a period of an hour and 20 minutes (or 40 minutes beyond the first 40 minutes) her blood alcohol would be about 0.010% less, or 0.066%. Forty minutes later, it would be down to about

0.056% and so on. (Keep in mind that these are only approximate calculations.)

Finally, for those of you who prefer bar graphs over numbers and formulas, here's a reproduction of a set of graphs printed by the Department of Motor Vehicles:

NEW .08% DUI* CHARTS
DRINKING UNDER 21 YEARS OF AGE IS ILLEGAL

Prepared by DMV in cooperation with the CHP, Office of Traffic Safety, Department of Alcohol and Drug Programs and Department of Justice.

There is no safe way to drive after drinking. Even one drink can make you an unsafe driver. Drinking affects your **BLOOD ALCOHOL CONCENTRATION (BAC).** **Starting in 1990,** it is illegal to drive with a **BAC** of .08%. Even a **BAC** below .08% does not mean that it is safe or legal to drive. The charts show the **BAC** zones for various numbers of drinks and time periods.

HOW TO USE THESE CHARTS: Find the chart that includes your weight. Look at the total number of drinks you have had and compare that to the time shown. You can quickly tell if you are at risk of being arrested.* If your **BAC** level is in the grey zone, your chances of having an accident are 5 times higher than if you had no drinks, and 25 times higher if your **BAC** level falls into the black zone.
*VC 23152, VC 23153, VC 23140 DUI/Driving under the influence of alcohol and/or drugs.

REMEMBER: "One drink" is a 12-ounce beer, or a 4-ounce glass of wine, or a 1¼-ounce shot of 80-proof liquor (even if it's mixed with non-alcoholic drinks). If you have larger or stronger drinks, or drink on an empty stomach, you can be **UNSAFE WITH FEWER DRINKS.** Also you can be unsafe with fewer drinks if you are tired, sick, upset, or have taken medicines or drugs.

TECHNICAL NOTE: These charts are intended to be guides and are not legal evidence of the actual blood alcohol concentration. Although it is possible for anyone to exceed the designated limits, the charts have been constructed so that fewer than 5 persons in 100 will exceed these limits when drinking the stated amounts on an empty stomach. Actual values can vary by bodytype, sex, health status, and other factors.

BAC Zones:	90 to 109 lbs.	110 to 129 lbs.	130 to 149 lbs.	150 to 169 lbs.	170 to 189 lbs.	190 to 209 lbs.	210 lbs. & Up
TIME FROM 1st DRINK	TOTAL DRINKS	TOTAL DRINKS	TOTAL DRINKS	TOTAL DRINKS	TOTAL DRINKS	TOTAL DRINKS	TOTAL DRINKS
	1 2 3 4 5 6 7 8	1 2 3 4 5 6 7 8	1 2 3 4 5 6 7 8	1 2 3 4 5 6 7 8	1 2 3 4 5 6 7 8	1 2 3 4 5 6 7 8	1 2 3 4 5 6 7 8
1 hr							
2 hrs							
3 hrs							
4 hrs							

SHADINGS IN THE CHARTS ABOVE MEAN:
☐ (.01%-.04%) **May be DUI**   ▨ (.05%-.07%) **Likely DUI—*DEFINITELY DUI IF UNDER 18 YRS. OLD***   ■ (.08% Up) **Definitely DUI**

DL 606 (REV. 10/89)

4. Effects of Alcohol

Alcohol affects you because of its presence in the brain cells. It reaches your brain within seconds after it has been absorbed into your bloodstream.

The three serious types of impairment resulting from the "depressant" effects of alcohol on the brain are:

- Less efficient vision and hearing;

- Lack of muscular coordination (clumsiness);

- Deterioration of judgment and self-control (euphoria and loss of inhibitions).

EFFECTS OF BLOOD ALCOHOL

% Blood Alcohol	State	Symptoms
0.01 - 0.05	relaxation	mild feeling of relaxation, very little effect
.05 - .12	mild euphoria	slower reflexes, less coordination, lowered inhibitions and increased self-confidence
08 - .25	impairment	memory and muscular coordination greatly reduced
.15 - .30	great impairment	dizziness, disorientation, confusion
.27 - .40	drunken stupor	inability to stand or walk; vomiting likely
.35 - .50	coma/near death	body temperature falls and death from respiratory paralysis may result

Again, the extent of impairment will vary from person to person, and the above figures represent only a range of averages. Some people, particularly regular drinkers, will have a sort of built-up immunity to alcohol. At the other extreme, people who normally abstain from alcohol begin to suffer slight impairment at a blood alcohol level as low as 0.02%! Moderate drinkers begin to show mild symptoms at 0.04 to 0.07%, while some heavy drinkers require 0.07 to 0.09% to suffer any impairment at all. Some

persons, who over long periods of time consume large amounts of alcohol on a daily basis, can never be seriously affected in terms of muscular coordination—although alcohol can still cloud their judgment. (Of course, claiming that your 0.27% blood alcohol had no effect on your driving because you've been an alcoholic for years is not a recommended line of defense, since you must be found guilty if the jury (or judge in a nonjury trial) believes your blood alcohol was 0.08% or more while you were driving.

What does "under the influence" really mean? Do you wonder why the exact figure of 0.08% blood alcohol is used to define an offense under VC § 23152(b)? Is it because everyone is drunk at that level, or is it just a nice convenient round figure having little to do with reality? The truth lies somewhere in between. Here's the story.

In 1939, the American Medical Association had a "Committee to Study Problems of Motor Vehicle Accidents" look into the blood alcohol level at which a person is "under the influence" as far as driving is concerned. As a result of the study, the AMA and the National Safety Council concluded that:

- A person whose blood alcohol was 0.05% or less is definitely not under the influence;

- A person whose blood alcohol was between 0.05% and 0.15% might be under the influence, depending on the individual and the circumstances;

- A person with over 0.15% blood alcohol was definitely under the influence.

California uses only the first of the above conclusions in the form of a presumption that a person with less than 0.05% blood alcohol is not under the influence [VC § 23155(a)(1)]. But the range of alcohol levels between which a person legally may or may not be under the influence, is conservatively set at 0.05% to 0.08% [VC § 23155(a)(2)] rather than at the range suggested by the AMA study, namely 0.05% to 0.15%. For years, the law defined 0.10% and above as under the influence, even though many experts believe that this cutoff level should be 0.15%.

However, in more recent years, special interest groups and politicians anxious to cater to them and "do something" about the drunk-driving problem have lowered the 0.10% cutoff to 0.08%.

The truth is that some people really are poor drivers at a particular blood alcohol level, but many others are not. Nevertheless, the Legislature in 1969, after intense lobbying by district attorneys, police officers' associations, insurance companies and other special interest groups, adopted the 0.10% standard as the level at which a driver would be presumed to be "under the influence." After more intense lobbying by these same groups in 1981, the Legislature took away even the right to prove one's innocence—when a blood alcohol level of 0.10% or more is involved. What this means is that some sober—and "innocent"—drivers may be unjustly convicted. And, once again in 1989, these same special interest groups got the level lowered from 0.10% to 0.08%.

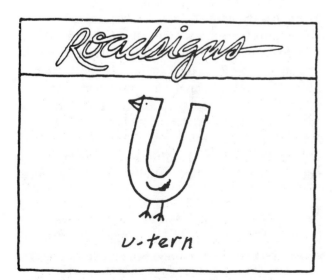

v-tern

D. Blood, Breath and Urine Tests for Alcohol

MOST DRUNK-DRIVING arrests result in the arrested person taking a "chemical test" for the presence of alcohol in his blood, breath or urine. This section briefly explains the law that requires this, as well as the tests themselves.

1. The "Implied Consent" Law

California's "implied consent" law requires any person lawfully[27] arrested for driving under the influence to give a blood, breath or urine sample when taken down to the jail or police station.[28] If you refuse, your driver's license will be suspended by the DMV for a year,[29] or more if you've previously suffered a "drunk-driving" conviction or previously received a similar suspension. This is true even if you're eventually found not guilty of the current drunk-driving charge.[30] If you have been convicted of drunk driving (or plea-bargained reckless driving), or have suffered a similar suspension within seven years prior to your refusal to take the test, your license suspension is for two years. If you've suffered two such convictions and/or suspensions, you lose your license for three years. Also, if you are convicted of drunk driving after a refusal, the judge *must* sentence you to 48 consecutive hours

---

[27]This means the officer had a "reasonable suspicion" to pull you over. An officer has a reasonable suspicion to stop you if he saw you commit a violation or drive erratically. If after he pulls you over he notices the obvious symptoms of intoxication, he will then have "probable cause" to physically arrest you and charge you with driving under the influence.

[28]An arrested person who has "need for medical treatment" and is taken to a "medical facility" must choose among those tests available. This will mean a choice between a blood or urine test, since breath-alcohol analyzers aren't generally available at medical facilities. [See VC § 23157(a)(3).]

[29]See also Chapter 15, Section C.

[30]VC §§ 13353, 23157. Although this may look like a violation of your constitutional right not to incriminate yourself, as well as to not be punished without a trial, the appeals courts have said otherwise. See *Hernandez v. DMV* (1981) 30 Cal.3d 70; *Finley v. Orr* (1968) 262 Cal.App.2d 656, 69 Cal.Rptr. 137.

in jail on a first offense and add 96 hours to your jail sentence on a second offense.

a. Your Right to a Choice of Tests

Even though you must submit to some kind of test, *you have the right to choose* among a blood, breath or urine test (VC § 23159) (unless you are in a medical facility where some of the tests are not available) and the police are supposed to inform you of your right to choose. Sometimes they'll try to pressure you into taking the blood or breath test if you insist on the less accurate urine test, but stand your ground.

[**Editor's Note**: *Be aware that "standing your ground" can sometimes result in more trouble than it's worth, especially if you are a little drunk. So, be firm, but not abusive; be polite, and, whatever you do, don't physically resist the officer.*]

Which test should you choose? It depends on the circumstances. If you had only one beer, glass of wine or mild drink, your blood alcohol will be under .05%, a level so low that no sane prosecutor would try the case. Since results from a breath test (unlike those from urine or blood tests) can be directly displayed on the measuring device right away [see Section D(2)(c)], it will become clear that you're sober and the police might therefore let you go. (However, if you choose the breath test, and it gives a low or zero alcohol reading, and if the police still have a "reasonable belief" that you're under the influence of *drugs*, they can insist, again under penalty of losing your license if you refuse, that you take a blood or urine test.)

If you've had more than one drink, you should probably insist on a urine test. [See Section D(2)(b)]. Why? Because this test is the least accurate and

therefore more subject to attack at trial than those of breath or blood tests.

You should avoid giving a blood sample if you've had three or more drinks. Blood tests are more accurate than urine or breath tests [see Section D(2)(a)], and the results are therefore less vulnerable to attack at trial. Also, any drugs you've taken will show up in a blood sample. As with a urine sample, a chemist analyzing a blood sample will look for drugs if little or no alcohol is found.

Despite the requirement that the police offer you a choice of tests, the courts have refused to enforce this provision. In one case,[31] the police refused to give the suspected drunk driver a choice and insisted on a blood test. The court refused to exclude evidence based on a coerced blood test, thereby gutting the law allowing such a choice of any enforcement mechanism.[32] The general trend is that the courts will wink at police misconduct in this respect, for anything short of forced stomach-pumping. Of course, if the police didn't offer you a choice of tests, your driver's license can't be suspended because of your insistence on a test you weren't offered. However, the evidence from the test can still be used against you at your drunk-driving trial.

b. Other Rights

The rule is that you do not have the right to have your attorney present for the test [VC § 23157(a)(4)]. You do have the right to an additional blood, breath or urine test performed by an independent doctor, nurse, clinical lab technologist, bioanalyst or any other person of your choosing. You have the right to have this person come down to where you're being held to collect your blood, breath or urine sample at your expense. Still, this is difficult to arrange, and is not usually useful, unless your own test results are

---

[31]*People v. Pucinelli* (1976) 63 Cal.App.3d 742, 135 Cal.Rptr. 34.

[32]See also *In re Garinger* (1987) 188 Cal.App.3d 1149; *Carleton v. Superior Court* (1985) 170 Cal.App.3d 1182 (six police officers allowed to hold down refusing driver and extract blood), *People v. Ryan* (1981) 116 Cal.App.3d 168, *People vs. Fite* (1968) 267 Cal.App.2d 685, and *Schmerber v. California* (1966) 384 U.S. 757, 86 S.Ct. 1826.

much lower than the police test—a rarity unless the sample taken by the police got mixed up with someone else's—and can be expensive if you want to use the results at trial, since you need to pay witnesses to testify. This test is not, however, a substitute for the test done by the police, and you cannot delay the test until the person you call comes. You must submit to the police-administered test of your choosing when they ask you to do so. If your independent test results come out much lower than the results of the one the police made you take, the police tests will appear more questionable to a jury. If they don't, your lawyer doesn't have to use the results.[33]

Finally, after the results are in on your blood, breath or urine test, you have the right to "full information concerning the test" [VC § 23158(c)]. This means you're entitled to a copy of the results, *plus* a written explanation of the manner by which the analysis was performed. You or your attorney should request this information by letter within a week or two of your arrest. Also, if a blood or urine test was taken, you have the right to have part of the preserved sample collected by the police tested by an independent laboratory.[34] If the police administer a breath test, they must advise you of your right to give an extra "back-up" sample for this sort of retesting, since a breath sample can't be saved easily. Unfortunately, the failure of the police to do this cannot be used to keep the breath test results from being used as evidence (VC § 23157.5).

2. The Chemical Tests: How They Work, How They Fail

In this section, we introduce you to how the different tests work, and some of the ways they go wrong.

---

[33]VC § 23158(b). If you have an independent test taken, make sure the results are communicated only to your lawyer, not to you. That way, if the test results don't help your case, you can truthfully say on cross-examination that you don't know what they were.

[34]*People v. Hitch* (1974) 12 Cal.3d 641.

a. Blood Tests

Other than directly measuring the alcohol content of your brain cells (which can be dangerous), the most accurate test to determine the possibility of alcohol affecting your driving is the blood sample test. Challenging the accuracy of this test is not as easy as challenging the accuracy of the breath or urine tests. Also, a blood sample is a very good indicator of whether you had taken any drugs. So, unless you're really clean, you should choose one of the other tests.

However, if you have submitted to (or were coerced into taking) a blood test, there are several ways you may be able to challenge its accuracy.

The most common modern method for analyzing alcohol in a blood sample utilizes a "gas chromatograph," a device that vaporizes a liquid sample and passes the vapor through a "column" of dry chemicals that separate the vapor. Different vapors come out of the other end of the column at different times, and when the alcohol vapor comes off, its amount is measured by a detector whose output is displayed on a graph or digital readout. This method also relies on the use of standard solutions containing known amounts of alcohol to "calibrate" the gas chromatograph. Still other tests involve reaction of the alcohol with an enzyme.

An older procedure for the chemical analyses of blood samples for alcohol involve distilling the alcohol out of the blood and reacting it with a chemical called an "oxidizing agent." The more alcohol there is, the more oxidizing agent is used, allowing the analyst to calculate the alcohol from the amount of chemical required to oxidize all the alcohol. This oxidizing agent is really a solution of potassium dichromate ($K_2Cr_2O_7$) in distilled water. Its concentration has to be known with great precision in order for the result to be accurate.

In challenging any type of chemical analysis, a good defense lawyer should know how to cross-examine the analysts to shed doubt on the accuracy of the result. Did the analyst prepare the "standard" solution herself, or just take someone else's word for its content? Does the analyst periodically check the solution concentration to make sure it hasn't changed? Are tests periodically performed on samples of known alcohol concentration?

Also, most laboratories that analyze blood samples run numerous samples every day, making some errors on some samples (maybe yours!)—more probable than if an analyst were carefully concentrating on just one. Proper record keeping and laboratory organization are necessary to guard against sample mix-ups, as different parts of the analyses are carried out in different bottles and beakers. You may be able to cast some doubt on the test readings by raising questions about their recordkeeping.

Finally, blood samples that aren't properly preserved and sit around a long time before being analyzed have a tendency to either coagulate or decompose. If the sample coagulates, so that the red blood cells separate out from the liquid blood portion, the alcohol is further concentrated in the remaining liquid portion—contributing to a false high reading. If the sample decomposes, a false high reading will also be obtained because one of the chemical products of this decomposition is alcohol. Therefore, it is important that the analysis be done shortly after the sample is taken, and that the sample be properly preserved to minimize decomposition.

These are only remote possibilities, however. More than likely, the analysis of a blood sample will be correct, and a very good indicator of the blood alcohol in your system, at least at the time the sample was taken. Also, the prosecution's science-trained "expert witness" will almost always favorably impress a jury.

b. Urine Tests

Because of its inaccurate measurement of blood alcohol, the urine test is the best test to take if you've had quite a bit to drink. (Like the blood test, however, it is a pretty good indicator of whether drugs are in your system, though some drugs won't show up in urine.) The urine alcohol level has to be "correlated" to an "equivalent" blood alcohol level. An "average" 1.33-to-1 ratio of urine alcohol to blood alcohol is generally used. However, studies have

shown that some people have alcohol levels only 40% as high in their urine as in their blood, while others have twice the alcohol content in their urine as in their blood. This means that the blood alcohol level the prosecution infers from a urine alcohol analysis might be incorrect in some cases.

Example: The prosecutor assumes your urine alcohol to be an "average" 1.33 multiple of your blood alcohol. If a sample of your urine is found to contain, say, 0.133% alcohol, the prosecutor would divide this value by 1.33 to calculate a blood alcohol value of 0.10%. But if your kidneys actually pump out urine with an alcohol content *twice* that of your blood, a 0.133% urine alcohol content, divided by two, corresponds only to a 0.066% blood alcohol value. Thus the prosecutor would try to "prove" your blood alcohol level was 0.10%, when in fact, it was under 0.07%.

Also, a specimen of bladder urine only represents a composite of a continuously-changing blood alcohol content. The pool of urine in the bladder at any given time is an accumulation of secreted urine since the last emptying of the bladder. It therefore tells much less about a person's blood alcohol at a particular moment than does a blood sample. This can work for or against you. If you had a lot to drink several hours beforehand and hadn't urinated since that time, the urine test result may be misleadingly high. If your drinking was relatively recent, though, say within an hour of the time you gave the sample, and especially if you'd had any nonalcoholic liquids before that, the urine test would give a misleadingly low result. Because of this, the only way to properly test a person's urine is to have him or her void the bladder and then produce a second urine sample. The police know this, and will insist that you also produce a second sample 20 minutes later. If you can't, you'll have to take the more accurate blood test, or the breath test, or the DMV will suspend your license for six months, or for two years if you have a prior conviction.[35] You might ask for a drink of water, preferably right after they take off your handcuffs at the station and before you tell them you're opting for a urine test.

Urine samples are analyzed for alcohol in almost the same way as blood samples. The results are therefore also subject to some of the same laboratory errors. (See above.)

The police will, of course, want you to convict yourself by giving them the most reliable sample—a blood sample. A request for a urine test will sometimes be met by police intimidation to force you to change your mind and give a blood sample, such as illegal threats to hold you longer in a jail. So stand firm, assuming you're able to produce at least an initial urine sample at the time it is requested.

If you do choose the urine test, the police are required to give you "such privacy in the taking of the urine specimen as will insure the *accuracy of the specimen*, and at the same time, maintain the *dignity of the individual* involved" [VC § 23158(e)]. In other words, you have the right to some privacy, but you can't insist on going alone into a bathroom where you might be able to secretly dilute the sample with tap, or toilet, water. At the very least, though, they have to exclude all persons of the opposite sex from the room in which you give the sample. If they will not provide you with at least some privacy after

you've insisted on a urine test, you can refuse to take *any* test. You will, however, have to convincingly explain your refusal to a DMV hearing officer who has the power to suspend your driver's license if he or she doesn't believe you.

c. Breath Tests

Usually, you should only take the breath test if you're unable to give a urine sample. However, if you've had very little to drink, you may want to opt for the breath test. With this test, the police will know your approximate blood alcohol level immediately, and if the reading indicates less than 0.05% blood alcohol, they may release you right away. But don't count on it. They may simply charge you with reckless driving and keep you in custody until someone bails you out. Also, after seeing the low alcohol reading, and still being convinced your driving ability truly was impaired, they may think you're on drugs instead, and insist on a blood or urine sample after that.

Like an analysis of urine, an analysis of breath gas gives only an indirectly-determined value for blood alcohol. A breath test determines how much alcohol is in some portion of exhaled air, not how much alcohol is in the blood. To calculate content of blood alcohol from those of exhaled air, the content of alcohol in the air is normally multiplied by the number 2100. This number, known as a "partition coefficient" or "partition ratio," is used because the lung air exhaled by an "average" person usually has 1/2100th the amount of alcohol of an equal volume of blood. Using this "average" figure amounts to little more than scientific guesswork. For example, one study showed some people have lung-air alcohol concentrations 1500 times smaller than their blood alcohol values, while other people have lung-air alcohol concentrations 3000 times smaller. Also, the value varies for the same person over time and depends on body temperature and even respiration rate. As with results from a urine alcohol analysis, the calculated blood alcohol level (already printed or displayed on a readout on the machine) may be erroneous.

---

[35]See *Miles v. Alexis* (1981) 118 Cal.App.3d 555.

Example: Based on an "average" for all persons studied, the prosecutor assumes your blood alcohol content to be 2100 times the content of alcohol in your breath. (Actually, this calculation is already done inside the breath-analyzing device.) So, if your breath contains 0.00004% alcohol, this number multiplied by the "partition coefficient" of 2100 will give a calculated percentage of 0.08. But if your own "blood-to-breath" ratio is really 1500 to 1, the 0.00004% breath alcohol content really means a blood alcohol level of 0.06%. Thus, the results should "prove" your blood alcohol was an illegal 0.08%, when in fact it was less than that.

Formerly, a person with a "borderline" breath alcohol level was allowed to use the "erroneous partition coefficient" defense to show a breath test inaccurate.[36] However, VC §§ 23152 and 23153 now define the offense in terms of grams of alcohol per 210 liters of breath (a value consistent with a 2100:1 partition coefficient), as well as milligrams of alcohol per 100 milliliters of blood. Thus, any evidence tending to show a partition coefficient other than 2100:1 will have no bearing on the concentration of alcohol in the breath gas itself, and will probably be disallowed by most courts.

Alcohol-containing substances in your *mouth* can also produce falsely high readings, since the amount of alcohol vapor given off by anything in your mouth is much greater than any amount you exhale from your lungs. This includes stomach fluid vomited or regurgitated up within 20 minutes of taking the test, some toothache medicines, mouthwashes and breath fresheners. Even a burp just before or while you blow into the breathalyzer tube may cause a falsely high reading. For this reason, the person administering the test is supposed to watch you for at least 20 minutes prior to taking the test to make sure you don't burp, belch, regurgitate, vomit or put anything into your mouth.

There is also the possibility of a malfunction in the breath-testing devices. To assure accuracy, the device must be calibrated with air containing known amounts of alcohol vapor every 100 tests or 10 days, whichever is more frequent. The police department's records should indicate how often the device has been calibrated, serviced and used. A lapse in record keeping and/or police memory as to calibration and preparation of sample solutions can help your attorney establish reasonable doubt about the accuracy of the instrument. Other errors may result from the particular type of breath gas analyzer used.

Finally, because breath gas analysis is often inaccurate, you may be asked to take the tests two, or even three, times to produce a consistent result. Your failure to give them all the breath samples they want will result in your license being suspended by the DMV.[37]

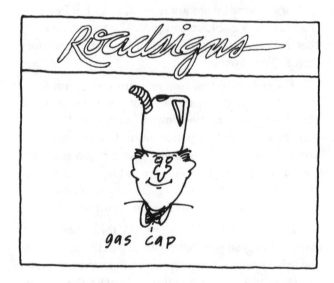

Breath Gas Analyzers: Another device uses a "gas chromatography" detector in which the components of breath gas are separated by passing

---

[36]See *People v. McDonald* (1988) 206 Cal.App.3d 877 and *People v. LePine* (1989) 215 Cal.App.3d 91, 263 Cal.Rptr. 543.

[37]In *Hasiwar v. Sillas* (1981) 118 Cal.App.3d 295, the police measured 0.10% alcohol on the first try, then 0.15% on the second. They then insisted on a third breath test, which was refused. The DMV suspended his driver's license for failing to "complete" the test, and the court rubber-stamped the suspension.

the sample through a chemical packed into a glass column. An electronic detector figures out the percentage of alcohol. The most common device uses a beam from an infrared heat source. When the beam encounters alcohol vapor, some of its energy is absorbed by the alcohol molecules. The more infrared energy absorbed, the higher the blood alcohol.

A few police departments use an older device that works differently. When you blow into a tube-like mouthpiece, a piston and cylinder arrangement collects the final ten percent of your exhaled breath (the part most likely to be in "equilibrium" with the alcohol coming into your lungs' air sacs from the bloodstream). The piston then pushes the gas sample to bubble it through a yellow solution of sulfuric acid and potassium dichromate (the same chemicals used in some laboratory analyses of alcohol in blood and urine samples). The alcohol uses up some of the potassium dichromate, changing the solutions' color to a lighter yellow. This color change is detected with a photocell (or "electronic eye") connected to a meter or digital readout. The more alcohol in your breath, the more pale the yellow dichromate solution becomes, and the higher the breath gas alcohol reading. This reading is displayed in terms of blood alcohol percentage, the manufacturer having used the "average" 1-to-2100 breath-to-blood alcohol ratio to convert breath alcohol to blood alcohol.

Aside from the problems already mentioned, one of the major weaknesses of the breathalyzer is that its chemicals may also react with other "organic" (or carbon and hydrogen-containing) materials to produce a falsely high reading. Such substances include:

- acetone from the breath of diabetics;

- tiny blood particles, from blood in the mouth because of an accident, fight, beating by the police, or acute gingivitis (bleeding of the gums);

- small amounts of vapors given off by denture adhesives or lip ointment;

- residual industrial vapors such as methyl (wood) alcohol, toluene, chlorinated hydrocarbons,

gasoline, solvents, to which the person was exposed earlier;

- grease, oil or other organic material on the hands of the breathanalyzer operator as she opens the glass "ampoule" containing the yellow dichromate solution or inserts a glass "bubbler tube" into it.

The first two methods measure alcohol to the exclusion of other organic materials better than some older devices, but are easily subject to the same interferences from alcohol-containing substances in your mouth. Also, the measuring devices have to be periodically maintained and standardized.

In sum, then, most chemical analyses of your breath, blood or urine will give an accurate indication of your actual blood alcohol level. However, the tests are not infallible, and an experienced criminal defense attorney may be able to cast enough doubt on the test results to convince a jury that you might not be guilty.

E.   License Suspension Procedures

YEARS AGO, A PERSON convicted of driving under the influence did not necessarily face a driver's license suspension for one conviction of driving under the influence. The DMV would suspend a person's driver's license only if the person's driving record showed other violations as well.

Then, in response to changing attitudes toward drunk driving, license suspensions became automatic for a first offense unless the person was granted probation and was required to attend an alcohol treatment program. Such license suspensions were imposed by the court, or by the DMV, after the person had violated probation. Naturally, this occurred *after* the person was convicted.

Now, however, your license is suspended *before* any conviction, and your suspension notice is handed to you by a police officer. Suspension is then automatic, unless you request a hearing from the

DMV. If you can't convince the DMV to overturn your suspension within 45 days, your license is suspended—even if the court dismisses or reduces the charges. Here is how this works:

After arresting you for driving under the influence, a police officer will take away your driver's license and present you with 1) a notice that your license is suspended effective 45 days later, and 2) a temporary license to allow you to drive within that 45-day period.

The request for hearing must be made to the DMV within 10 days, or the suspension will go into effect, even if the charges in court are later reduced or dismissed. For that reason, every person arrested for driving under the influence should request a hearing, in the event that they later prevail in court. The request for a hearing does not stop the suspension, until and unless you appear at the DMV hearing.[38] For further information on how to request a DMV hearing when you receive a notice of suspension, see Chapter 15.

Whether you default or show up at the hearing and lose, your driver's license will be suspended for a period of time that depends on a number of factors, including:

- whether you refused a chemical test;
- the total number of prior convictions of driving under the influence (or plea bargained reckless driving);

---

[38]VC § 13358.

- suspensions you have received for driving under the influence on any separate occasions; and
- previous suspensions for refusing blood, breath or urine tests within the previous seven years.[39]

Prior DUI convictions (or suspensions) plus suspensions for refusal.	0	1	2 or more
Suspension for driving with blood alcohol over 0.08%	4 months	1 year	1 year
Suspension for refusal of chemical test	1 year	2 years	3 years
Consecutive suspensions for blood alcohol over 0.08% and refusal	16 months	3 years	4 years

Persons who receive suspensions for driving with blood alcohol levels over 0.08% (but not for refusing a chemical test) may receive a restricted driving privilege to drive to and from work and to and from an alcohol treatment problem, if they enroll in such a program.[40]

F.   Dealing With a "Drunk-Driving" Charge

THE FOLLOWING IS ONLY a very brief summary of what you need to consider if faced with a drunk-driving charge.

1.   Evaluating Your Case

After you've been arrested for driving under the influence, and have been released from jail, you should try to objectively evaluate your case. Your alternatives include:

---

[39]VC §§ 13353-13354.
[40]VC § 13353.7.

- simply pleading guilty as charged;

- trying to plea bargain down to a reduced charge [like reckless driving, see Section D(3)];

- asking for a trial before a judge; or

- demanding a jury trial.

The general rule is that if you choose to fight the charge, you should always demand a *jury* trial—you'll have a better chance than with a case-worn and possibly cynical judge who has seen a lot of guilty people.[41] As with any jury trial in a criminal case, the prosecutor must convince *all twelve* jurors of your guilt, as opposed to just one judge in a non-jury trial.[42]

Still, even jury trial conviction rates for driving under the influence are high, though they vary in different parts of the state. (Sadly, this is partly because special interest groups have, over the years, fostered a public attitude to the effect that eradicating the drunk-driving problem is more important than having fair trials.) Part of the money you're paying your lawyer is for the value of her experience in knowing what a local jury is likely to do in a given situation.

Generally, the more a jury is likely to find you guilty of driving under the influence (or with an over-0.08% blood alcohol), the more you will want to plea bargain, or negotiate a settlement, with the prosecutor. Since drunk-driving juries unfortunately put a lot of faith in the blood test results (and the prosecutor's scientific mumbo-jumbo that goes along with it), it is these results that are most likely to affect your choice of options.

As a general rule, a person whose blood alcohol test results are higher than 0.12% (whether blood alcohol is measured directly, or by urine or breath analysis) will have a very low chance of winning at trial. This is especially true today, now that an over-0.08% blood alcohol level is sufficient to convict you—whether you were drunk or not [VC § 23152(b)]. The only way you can be acquitted of such a charge is to shed doubt on the validity of the test results so that either the jury entirely disbelieves them, or thinks that after adjusting for possible analytic errors in your favor, your blood alcohol *might* have been less than 0.08%. It is very difficult for even a trained and experienced lawyer to do this. Therefore, a confident prosecutor is not likely to enter into a plea bargain where you agree to plead guilty to a reduced charge like reckless driving.

If your blood alcohol tested out at between 0.08 and 0.11%, your chances of winning in a trial are slightly better, but not much. You still have to convince a jury that the test results are at least inaccurate enough to raise a reasonable doubt as to whether your blood alcohol was 0.08% or higher. And, if the prosecutor charges you "in the alternative" with driving under the influence [VC § 23152(a)], you'll also have to establish that you weren't "under the influence" at whatever blood alcohol level you had.

Whether you have a decent chance of convincing a jury you weren't under the influence will depend largely on the type of testimony your lawyer can elicit from anyone who was with you either before or while you were driving. The types of witnesses who can testify as to your sobriety may range from local "pillars of the community" the jurors might believe to barroom buddies who were also enjoying plenty of sauce (good luck!).

Example 1: Irwin spent an entire evening in a bar—9 p.m. to closing time at 2 a.m. He drove home alone, was pulled over, and admitted to the mythical "two beers," though he probably had a lot more. Although his drinking buddies at the bar, as well as the bartender, would say Irwin wasn't under the influence, none of them saw him take the "field sobriety" or coordination tests. The

---

[41]The only exception to this general rule is when your defense is fairly unusual or technical. For example, if you staggered out of a bar and into your car, and fell asleep—but you didn't *drive*—a judge might be more receptive to your defense than a jury.

[42]The U.S. Supreme Court has ruled that a person accused of drunk driving punishable by up to six months in jail isn't entitled, under the U.S. Constitution, to a jury trial. *Blanton v. City of North Los Vegas* (1989) _U.S. _ , _ 109 S.Ct. 1289, 103 L.Ed.2d 550 However, under California's own state constitution, the right to trial by jury exists for any offense punishable by any imprisonment whatsoever. *Mitchell v. Superior Court* (1989) 49 Cal.3d 1230, 1242-1243, 265 Cal.Rptr. 144.

results of his blood test showed a 0.13% alcohol level. When interpreted ("extrapolated") back to the time he was driving, his blood alcohol worked out to about 0.15%.

In this situation, Irwin (if he represents himself) or his lawyer should probably try to get the best possible deal for a guilty plea—perhaps a minimum fine, or a 90-day license restriction in lieu of a jail term. If the prosecutor refuses to bargain[43] Irwin may not have much to lose by going to trial, except a higher lawyer's fee—which may not seem so large when compared to the extra costs he'll incur over the next few years should he be convicted. And who knows? He might get lucky.

Example 2: Suppose instead that Irwin had just left a "business lunch" where more than one person who *hadn't* been drinking could testify they saw Irwin with his wits about him. Or suppose Irwin drove back to work with at least one other person who saw him perform the sobriety test successfully. In these situations, he should see what the prosecutor will offer in a plea bargain. It may be just a slap on the wrist, though Irwin would then have a "prior"—even if he pleaded guilty to only reckless driving [see Section D(4)(d)]. If no favorable plea bargain is forthcoming, Irwin should seriously consider getting a lawyer and fighting his case.

If your blood alcohol was measured at less than 0.08%, your chances of beating a drunk-driving charge are better. First, you won't be convicted of having a blood alcohol of 0.08% or more,[44] and the prosecutor will have to establish that you were under the influence at the below-0.08% level. A skilled attorney should be able to properly cross-examine the prosecutor's expert witnesses to show

that the likelihood of one's driving ability being affected at a blood alcohol level of less than 0.08% is small. Naturally, the farther below 0.08% your blood alcohol was, the better your chances are of being acquitted and the more likely the prosecutor will be willing to plea bargain.

What if you refused to submit to a blood, breath or urine test? Your chances of beating the drunk-driving charge at trial will be slightly better than if you have submitted to the test and the results showed a very high blood alcohol level. (However, your refusal to take the test can be used against you, and jurors may consider this to be a damning admission on your part.) The prosecutor may be unable to convict you for having a blood alcohol level of 0.08% or more, but she still may be able to convict you of having been under the influence. This will depend almost entirely on how much weight the jury gives to the testimony of the police officer [see Section D(5), below] and prosecution witnesses compared to how much the jurors will believe any testimony you can present (VC § 23159). And, of course, your refusal to take the test will result in an automatic license suspension for at least a year. If you've had one or two prior alcohol-related reckless driving and/or drunk-driving convictions within five years, the suspension will last for two years or three years respectively (VC § 13353).

2. Getting a Lawyer

As mentioned earlier, defending yourself against a drunk-driving charge in a jury trial is not recommended. Once you've been released from jail and have had a chance to evaluate your case, you should think about getting an attorney to represent you (see Chapter 9, Section B), in addition to putting in an automatic hearing request to the DMV. (See Section E.) If you're unable to afford an attorney, you should ask the judge to appoint a lawyer for you when you first appear in court. Even if your case looks hope

---

[43]The prosecutor isn't the only one who can bargain. Many judges engage in what is called "sentence bargaining." The judge simply tells you (or your lawyer) what kind of sentence you can expect if you plead guilty to the charge. So you might be able to bargain with the judge for a minimum sentence (see Section B) even if the prosecutor refused to deal.

[44]However, if your blood alcohol level were found to be slightly under 0.08%, say 0.06% or 0.07%, measured about an hour after you were driving, the prosecutor would then claim that it was

higher, namely 0.08%, when you were driving and fell below that level before the blood, breath gas or urine sample was taken.

Roadsigns

back seat driving

less because of a sky-high blood alcohol level, you have nothing to lose by taking advantage of free legal representation. If you aren't poor enough to qualify for a court-appointed lawyer, and believe that your case falls in the narrow range where you may be able to win a jury trial, begin by making an appointment with an attorney experienced in criminal defense work. Even though you may be unable to afford to pay her to defend you in a jury trial (the fee for this could be as high as several thousand dollars), you should be able to afford the fee for one or two office visits. At the very least, you can hire her for the limited purpose of fully explaining your options to you, or perhaps to try to work out a plea bargain with the prosecutor. Defense attorneys' statistics show that the chances of beating a drunk-driving charge by going to trial are low. If your case is rife with hopeless circumstances (e.g., blood alcohol over 0.15%, dismal failure on coordination tests, etc.), you should be wary of an overly-optimistic lawyer who tells you your chances are excellent while demanding more and more money as the case drags on.

3. Plea Bargaining

Plea bargaining (sometimes also referred to as "sentence bargaining") is a process where a criminal defendant (or his or her lawyer) and the prosecutor

reach a compromise, then the defendant enters a guilty plea to a reduced charge or, sometimes, in exchange for the promise of a reduced fine or jail sentence. Plea bargaining generally takes place over the phone or at the prosecutor's office, and often at a "pretrial conference" in the judge's chambers before trial. As part of the process, the judge informally tells you—or your lawyer—the sentence that he or she will impose if you plead guilty.

The "bargain" of a plea bargain is that the prosecutor avoids having to try a questionable case, but still gets to rack up a conviction, while the person accused of drunk driving receives the minimum sentence or, perhaps, only a mildly serious conviction for reckless driving (for example)—for which the DMV may not suspend a driver's license. (See Chapter 15.)

Plea bargains in drunk-driving cases, however, are no longer as common as they once were. A major overhaul in California's drunk-driving laws in 1982 has made it less attractive for both sides to enter into a plea bargain.[45] Now that driving with a blood alcohol level of over 0.08% or more is illegal—regardless of whether the driver is under the influence—it is easier for prosecutors to obtain convictions in the formerly borderline cases (0.08 to 0.15% alcohol levels). And from the accused's perspective, the incentive to plead guilty to reckless driving is far less under the new law, since the law now requires that a statement be placed on your record that alcohol was involved in the offense (VC § 23103.5), and since your license will be suspended by the DMV even in the face of such a conviction. (See Section E of this chapter.) Also, your insurance company may treat records of such guilty pleas as drunk-driving convictions and cancel your policy anyway. Also, if you're charged with drunk driving again within the next seven years (after having plea

---

[45]PC § 1192.7, added by Proposition 8 ("Victims' Bill of Rights" initiative) in June 1982 theoretically forbids plea bargaining in drunk-driving cases, but has numerous loopholes, and appears to apply only to felony, not misdemeanor, cases. Also, prosecutors in some cases must, under VC § 23212, file with the court a document which explains, in detail, why the plea bargain was allowed.

bargained a previous drunk-driving charge down to reckless), the earlier plea will be used against you for the purpose of increasing both the minimum and maximum penalties if you're convicted—just as if you had been convicted of drunk driving the first time.

> **Example:** The first time Bill Blotto was accused of driving under the influence, he faced a minimum penalty of a $390 fine (*plus* penalty assessments) *plus* either two days in jail or a 90-day license restriction whereby he would have been allowed to drive only to, and from, and in work. Instead, Bill was allowed to plead guilty to reckless driving and pay a smaller fine. Two years later, Bill was charged with drunk driving again. Although it will be his first drunk-driving conviction, if he pleads or is found guilty, he will face the same penalty as would a second-offense drunk driver—mandatory minimum penalties of two days in jail (probably more), and an 18-month alcoholism treatment program and license restriction. (See Section B of this chapter.)

Despite the attempts of "law-and-order" types to forbid plea bargaining, it will always be with us. Without it, defense attorneys would have nothing to lose by pleading each and every one of their clients not guilty and demanding a jury trial all the time. When you consider that only about 20 percent of all serious criminal cases ever go to trial, and that nearly all the remaining cases are plea bargained, an end to plea bargaining would increase five-fold the number of trials in the criminal courts. This would require more courts, judges, court personnel, and taxes.

Although more will be said in Chapter 13, Section C, about conducting your own plea bargaining negotiations, you may wish to hire a lawyer to do it for you. A prosecutor may not be as willing to enter into a plea bargain with an inexperienced defendant who might well do a poor job of representing herself. Also, an experienced lawyer who regularly handles drunk-driving cases will be more familiar with local practices, prosecutors and judges than you can ever hope to be. Nevertheless, many defendants who have taken the time to educate

themselves both as to the law and to the nuances of bargaining have done every bit as well as, and sometimes better than, lawyers and have saved themselves a big fee.

4. Pretrial Court Proceedings

Pretrial court procedures for offenses other than drunk driving are covered in detail in Chapter 10. However, since drunk-driving cases are more complex and should generally be handled by an attorney, this section is designed to give you information you'll need to intelligently participate in your attorney's defense of your drunk-driving case.

a. Arraignment

Some time after you're arrested, you will appear before a judge for arraignment (Chapter 13, Section B). You will be asked to plead to the charge, either guilty or not guilty. Arrangements will also be made regarding your right to counsel and bail. If you tell the judge you can't afford to hire a lawyer, she will probably ask you to fill out a financial disclosure form and refer you to the Public Defender's office. In smaller counties, the judge may appoint a private defense lawyer to represent you (Chapter 9, Section B). Most defendants charged with misdemeanors who have not already posted bail are released on their own recognizance at arraignment. Having an attorney represent you at arraignment is normally unnecessary. At this stage, you are only entering a plea, and you can plead not guilty and demand a jury trial. You can always change your plea to guilty or nolo contendere [see Chapter 10, Section A(2)], or drop the demand for a jury trial later.[46] If you're also charged with having prior under-the-influence convictions ("priors"—see below), you should deny

---

[46]Contrary to the belief of some, there is absolutely no shame or penalty involved in pleading not guilty even when you believe you are. All the not-guilty plea does is give you time to calmly assess your situation and decide where to take your case from there. If later on you plead guilty, the judge will not fault you for having pled not guilty earlier. Also, consider your not-guilty plea as a just response to a rotten and corrupt system whose beneficiaries are district attorneys, judges and other politicians.

them so that you or your attorney can challenge their validity later. At arraignment, the case will also be set for a "pretrial conference" [discussed below in Section 4(e)].

SOMETIMES I THINK THE BEST THING ABOUT BEING A JUDGE IS THE COSTUME.

b. Getting the Best Judge

If you hire an experienced attorney to defend you against a drunk-driving charge, he will generally know which judges to avoid because they usually favor the prosecution or sentence harshly. Lawyers can use various procedures (such as changing pleas, dropping the demand for a jury trial, asking for continuances) to minimize the chance that such a judge will hear your case. If all else fails, the attorney can use one "peremptory challenge" to disqualify a judge, indicating that she or he "believes" the judge to be prejudiced. True , you could do this yourself [see Chapter 10, Section A(3)(e)], but an attorney experienced in drunk-driving trials will be more likely to know which judge, if any, to challenge.

c. Motions to Suppress Evidence

If the police illegally arrested you and/or obtained any evidence against you in an illegal manner, your attorney can schedule a special pretrial hearing to suppress certain evidence.[47] The prosecution is then prevented from using it at trial. For example, if you consented to give a blood sample only after the police beat you into submission, your attorney may want to make a "motion to suppress" the test results, thereby keeping them from being introduced into evidence at trial.

A motion to suppress is heard several weeks (sometimes months) before the trial actually takes place. It is only heard before a judge, perhaps one who will not be presiding at your trial. This type of motion is fairly technical and complicated, and will probably involve cross-examining the officer who arrested you. You're advised not to try to handle it yourself.

d. Motions to "Strike a Prior"

As we saw in Section B of this chapter, a person who pleads guilty to, or is convicted of, a second or third offense of driving under the influence can suffer a far heavier penalty than a first offender. In order to obtain the heavier penalty—a mandatory jail sentence and license suspension—the prosecution must "charge" the prior conviction against you. When you initially plead "not guilty" to the offense, *never* admit any priors charged against you.[48] Simply "deny" them. This is perfectly legal. If you "admit" them, you destroy any chance of challenging their validity on technical grounds.[49]

---

[47]PC § 1538.5.

[48]A court cannot require that you discuss uncharged prior convictions if and when you plead guilty. *Municipal Court v. Superior Court* (1988) 199 Cal.App.3d 19, 244 Cal.Rptr. 519.

[49]If your attorney is unable to successfully challenge the validity of the priors you denied, the prosecution gets to introduce them into evidence. Although the judge is supposed to warn the jury that the evidence of a prior is admitted only for the purpose of increasing your sentence if found guilty of the current charge, the jury is likely to use this information as an indication that you probably also committed the current offense. For this reason, if your attorney is unable to get the priors stricken before trial, it may be best to ask for a "bifurcated" (two-part) trial where the jury considers your priors only if, and after, it finds you guilty of the offense. [See *People v. Bracamonte* (1981) 119 Cal.App.3d 644, 174 Cal.Rptr. 191.] Another approach is to admit them just before trial (out of hearing of the jurors). This renders the prosecution's evidence of your priors irrelevant and inadmissible.

By having a prior conviction "stricken," you face a less severe penalty if convicted on the current charge. The procedure to strike a prior is based on whether you were properly informed of and/or intelligently waived (gave up) certain rights at any hearings related to the prior offenses. Again, this type of motion is extremely technical and better left to your attorney.

e. The Pretrial Conference

In most counties, a "pretrial conference" is scheduled some time before a jury trial. The pretrial conference usually occurs inside a judge's chambers, and is where most plea bargaining (and sentence bargaining) occurs. (See Chapter 13, Section C.) The prosecutor usually begins by emphasizing the blood alcohol test results and summarizing what the police officer and any other witnesses will testify to. This is to establish that he or she has a very strong case, implying that the defendant might as well plead guilty, or at least accept any offer of a plea bargain. To sweeten this prospect, the prosecutor might also offer to recommend a minimum sentence to the judge in exchange for a guilty plea. The judge might indicate whether or not he or she will accept such a recommendation; if the judge says he'll accept it, this will tell you or your lawyer what your sentence will be if you plead guilty to the original or a reduced charge.

If the prosecutor refuses to consider offering you the prospect of pleading guilty to a lesser charge and/or recommends more than the minimum sentence (see Section B) if you plead guilty, this is the time for you or your lawyer to briefly summarize your defense to the judge and prosecutor. You should emphasize the proposed testimony of any witnesses you may have regarding how sober you were just before you were driving. Also, if the blood alcohol test results are not much above 0.08%, indicate that you're prepared to cross-examine the chemist or breath gas analyzer operator regarding the scientific validity of the results. (This is especially important where a urine or breath test is involved.)

Then, depending on the judge's personality, she may try to convince you, your lawyer or the prosecutor, to compromise. (Some judges are very forceful in this regard and even take pride in insisting on compromise, so as not to have to do as many jury trials.) If a compromise is worked out, a time will be scheduled (possibly right then and there) for you to plead guilty to the original or a reduced charge in the courtroom. If not, a trial date will be set if one hasn't been already.

5. The Trial

The trial of drunk-driving cases is similar to the trial of any other misdemeanor offense. (Misdemeanor jury trial procedure is explained in Chapter 13.) The selection of jury members is very important, however, and a lawyer should try to exclude all nondrivers, all nondrinkers and all MADD-sympathizers from the jury. Lawyers can do this by using peremptory challenges, where no reason need be given for excusing a juror.

SHOULD YOU FIGHT YOUR TICKET/
SHOULD YOU GET A LAWYER?

NOW THAT YOU'VE read all about the type of ticket you received, you probably want to jump into your trusty old steed, drive (slowly, of course) down to traffic court and demand your right to contest it. Unfortunately, the procedure isn't that simple. As the following chapters will explain, before you can have a trial, you need to contact the court clerks, possibly post bail, decide whether you want an arraignment, and determine whether you need to make any pretrial motions.

So, the first thing you should do is go home, pour yourself a glass of wine (or bowl of chicken soup, if you prefer), curl up in a chair, and think things over. Above all, relax; anger won't help you to think clearly and you won't be able to do anything about the ticket for several days after you get it anyway.

Note: If you're facing a misdemeanor charge (see Chapters 7 and 8) you should definitely contest it, or at least try to plea bargain, and should seriously consider getting a lawyer to assist you. Section B offers advice on how to find a good lawyer to represent you.

A. Things to Consider

BEFORE DECIDING WHETHER or not to contest your ticket, you should consider whether you are, in fact, guilty, what's involved in contesting it, the chances of successfully doing so, and the possible consequences.

1. Are You Really Guilty?

In deciding whether to fight, you should begin by determining whether you really are guilty. Examine the ticket for the code section the officer says you violated. (See Chapter 2.) Then, study the exact language of that code section, set out in the appropriate chapter of this book (Chapter 4 for speeding violations, Chapter 5 for other moving violations, etc.). If we don't reprint the code section that you were cited for, look it up in the Vehicle Code that you got from the DMV, or go to your local law library. (See Chapter 2.)

Carefully read and reread each "element" of the offense, as we instruct in Chapter 2. If you are not guilty of each and every element, you are not guilty of the offense. Also, don't overlook the possibility of arguing that you lacked willfulness or criminal negligence.

Pay particular attention to elements that require a subjective judgment on the part of the officer. For example, reckless driving involves driving "in *willful* or *wanton* disregard for the safety of persons or property." What seems like willfulness or wantonness to one person may appear to be the height of caution to another. Another example: The "Basic Speed Law" requires that you not be driving "at a speed greater than is *reasonable* or *prudent....* " What seemed like a lack of prudence to the police officer may in fact have been the height of prudence from your viewpoint (and hopefully the viewpoint of any witnesses to the event).

On the other hand, violations that require only objective observations by the cop, like going over the 55 mph speed limit or running a stop sign, will turn solely on which version of the facts the court believes—yours or the cop's. (Good luck!) These kinds of arguments are rarely successful, but you might get lucky.

Finally, pay close attention to any defenses you might be able to raise to legally justify your action. In Chapter 5 for example, we noted that driving slowly in the left lane is legally justified if you were planning to make a left turn. These kinds of defenses are generally more successful because they raise some additional fact or legal point that precludes a conviction, rather than simply contradicting what the officer saw.

2. Will the Officer Show At Trial?

Whether you are guilty or not, you should consider whether it is likely the officer will appear at trial. If he or she does not, the case probably will be dismissed. The great majority of tickets that are beaten are done so on this basis.

If you asked for a trial at the county seat (see Chapter 17, Section C), there is a good chance that the officer won't show. Also, in some places, such as San Francisco, which encourage people to agree to "informal" hearings without the officer present [see Chapter 10, Section A (3)(c)], officers aren't used to showing up for trial—and might not do so, even if you opt for a regular trial. Also, for some reason, city police officers and county sheriff's deputies have a higher no-show rate than do Highway Patrol officers.

Finally, the more serious the violation the more likely it is the officer will show up in court. An officer will be more inclined to appear in court to testify against someone who zipped through a school zone at 45 mph than against someone she cited for doing 42 mph in a 35 mph zone. (This writer once noticed that a CHP officer failed to show for a trial where he wrote someone up—at quota time on the last day of the month—for the heinous crime of doing 60 mph on the 55-mph-limit freeway.)

3. Will Your Insurance Rates Rise?

You should also consider whether your insurance will rise as a result of this ticket should you be convicted or pay the fine. [See Chapter 3, Section A(4).] Given Proposition 103's requirement for a "good driver discount," this is more likely now than in years past for a second moving-violation infraction in three years. If not, would it rise if you got a second ticket (which wouldn't be a second ticket if you fought this one and won)? You may want to call your insurance agent to ask if another conviction would affect your insurance premium.

4. Were You in an Accident?

If you were cited for a moving violation at the scene of an accident in which you were involved, you should *never* plead guilty. A guilty plea can be used against you later in a civil lawsuit by anyone else involved in the accident. But the guilty plea must be before a judge; merely paying off the ticket by forfeiting bail to a clerk is not considered pleading guilty for this purpose. Nor is pleading nolo contendere a guilty plea. A not-guilty plea, of course, cannot be used against you in a civil action, and neither can a conviction following a not-guilty plea (VC § 40834).

5. How Much Time and Effort Will It Take to Fight?

The time and effort it will take to fight your ticket depends on (1) the kind of violation you're charged with, (2) the extent to which you want to fight it, and (3) other factors, like the distance between the court and your home.

a. Parking Violations

Parking violations are handled by a unique procedure that involves relatively little hassle. In many cases, you can handle the entire matter by mail. (Parking ticket procedure is fully described in Chapter 6.) Since the violation does not go on your driving record, you may want to look at the matter simply in terms of balancing your time lost from work versus the fine.

b. Infractions

Infractions (other than parking tickets and equipment violations) allow for numerous fighting options. These options are summarized here from the most ambitious to the least ambitious. You may want to refer to the flowchart at the end of Chapter 1 to get an overview of how these options fit together.

Infraction Option #1: Fight Your Ticket to the Hilt. If you want to pull out all the stops, you can insist upon every procedural formality to which you're entitled. The idea is to make the state give up before you do.

This tactic gives you the most chances for success, but also requires the most amount of time and energy. You must appear at an *arraignment*. (See Chapter 10, Section C.) You may need to type up your procedural requests (called "*motions*") and argue them before a judge. (Read Chapter 10, Section D, to find the kind of requests you can make. Do any apply to your situation?) If your requests are granted your case might be dismissed at this stage, but the chances are rather slim.

If your requests are denied, you must prepare for trial. At trial, you hope the officer doesn't show. If he doesn't, you win. If he does, you try to cast a reasonable doubt on his version of the events through your cross-examination, which you've prepared for in advance. (See Chapter 11, Section D.) You also must prepare to make specific legal "objections" to the officer's testimony, to get certain evidence excluded [like radar evidence for example— see Chapter 4, Section A, and Chapter 11, Section D(1)]. Finally, you present your own side of the story through your own testimony and that of witnesses you've arranged to be there. This too requires advance preparation to be done effectively.

This option is best suited for those who have a valid legal excuse or who qualify for a procedural dismissal of their ticket. Note, however, that by pleading not guilty, you give up your right to attend traffic school and have the charges dismissed. (See Option #4.) If traffic school is not an option for your violation, or not available in your county, you might as well fight.

Infraction Option #2: Bypass Arraignment and Go to Trial. If you don't want to take the time to request every pretrial procedural formality at arraignment, but still want to have a trial with the officer present, you can bypass the arraignment and proceed directly to trial. Most court clerks won't tell you about this option.

There are two ways to bypass arraignment. You can go to the court clerk and say that you're pleading "not guilty" and that you want your next appearance to be a formal trial with the officer present. [See Chapter 10, Section B(3).] If you don't want to go to the courthouse and wait in line, you can plead not guilty by mail, and state in your letter that you'd like to have a formal trial with the officer present. [See Chapter 10, Section B(4).]

In a few counties (or in any county if you live at least 100 miles from the courthouse), you can also conduct your trial by mail, through a procedure called a "trial by declaration" [see Chapter 10, Section A(3)], in which you lay out your side of the story in a carefully drafted letter to the court. If you lose this trial by mail, you still get another shot at winning at an in-person trial with the officer present.

Bypassing the arraignment is a sensible option for those who want to fight, but who want to minimize the number of court appearances they have to make. But remember, once you've pleaded not guilty, you have forfeited your opportunity to attend traffic school.

Infraction Option #3: An "Informal Hearing." Many people who don't want the hassle of a formal trial elect to settle for an "informal hearing" before the judge at arraignment. [See Chapter 10, Sections A(3) and C.]

Beware. This is not always a wise move. At an informal hearing, you give up many of your most important rights—like your right to have the police officer appear at your hearing. Furthermore, your chances of talking your way out of a conviction at an informal hearing are generally slim at best.

Many people end up pleading "guilty with an explanation" in hopes of getting a lower fine. They may get the lower fine, but they still end up with a conviction on their driving record, which can result in higher insurance rates and stiffer penalties next time they get a ticket.

The only time this option makes sense is when you're charged with an offense that does *not* go on your record, and you simply want to argue for a lower fine.

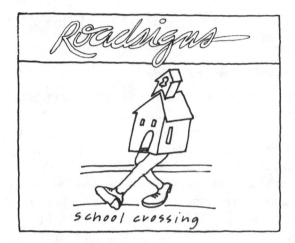

Infraction Option #4: Traffic School. For minor moving violations not involving alcohol, you can go to the court clerk (in most counties) and request traffic school instead of admitting guilt or paying any fine. After you complete traffic school, the case is dismissed and no conviction record is sent to the DMV. (All that results on your DMV record is a notation that you went to traffic school—information disclosed to courts only, and not insurance companies.) In some counties you have to go to an arraignment to request traffic school.

Traffic school is a reasonable option for people charged with an infraction that would appear on their record but who either don't want to take the time to fight, or know that they're guilty. The time it takes to attend traffic school—a Saturday or two— may not be much more (or even less) time than it takes to fight your ticket to the hilt. And with traffic school, your chances of keeping the violation off your driving record are very good (100%, in fact), while your chances of beating a ticket by contesting

it are uncertain, at best, if the officer shows at trial. Traffic school cannot be chosen as an option more than once in a 12 month period. And some individual counties have extended this period by a year or two.

There's some hassle involved in opting for traffic school. You have to attend it—usually on a weekend—and in some counties you may have to make an extra trip down to the courthouse for arraignment to request it. On the other hand, since traffic schools are often privately run (for profit), they also are frequently more interesting than any government bureaucrat could make them. Thus, in some counties, like San Francisco and Alameda, "comedy" traffic school (still traffic school, but taught by comedians), is available.

Warning: If you decide to fight (by pleading not guilty), you usually forfeit the option of having your case dismissed in exchange for attending traffic school. [See Chapter 10, Section A(2)(e).]

Infraction Option #5: Pay the Fine (Don't Fight). You can always simply pay the fine and suffer the consequences. This of course involves the least amount of hassle. The system makes it as easy as possible. You can even pay by mail in most cases. But think carefully about the effects of "giving up" before you finally decide. Especially consider the long-term consequences of having a conviction on your record: higher insurance rates, points on your record and stiffer penalties on future tickets.

In sum, then, you have lots of choices when it comes to fighting an infraction. Read the selections cross-referenced in the above summaries to get a better idea of what each option entails.

c. *Equipment Violations*

Equipment violations, as we saw in Chapter 6, are dealt with by a unique procedure. You really have no choice but to have the defect cured and show certification of the correction to the court within a specified time. Failure to do so can result in a misdemeanor charge against you. If you feel the equipment wasn't defective in the first place, getting certification of that fact shouldn't be difficult.

d. *Misdemeanors*

Misdemeanor defendants have different options. You must appear at arraignment even if you simply want to plead guilty. If you want to fight, you have the choice of either a jury trial or a trial before a judge. Conducting a jury trial is almost always the best choice, but it is very difficult to conduct one successfully on your own. Plea bargaining is also an important part of handling a misdemeanor charge. You should seriously consider hiring a lawyer skilled in such matters if you're charged with a misdemeanor. (Read Section B, below.)

6. The Big Picture

If you're still undecided, you may want to consider this: only a vigilant and aggressive attitude by the motoring public will ever take the profit out of the ticket business. If everyone fought unjustified tickets, the police establishment would be too busy testifying in court to continue raising revenue for politicians. At the very least, if a traffic cop knew he'd have to back up every citation with a court appearance, before a fair and honest judge, ticketing activities would be limited to serious violations, as they should be. (See Chapter 18.)

B. Do You Need a Lawyer?

WITHIN THE PAST DECADE, people have become more sophisticated in dealing with legal problems. Many people present their own cases in court. If you face a fairly minor infraction punishable by no more than a $50 fine, it might not make sense for you to get a lawyer.

When serious offenses are involved, such as driving under the influence, reckless driving, driving while your license is suspended, or other misdemeanors punishable by time in the county jail, you should consider hiring a lawyer, or, if you can't afford one, getting the public defender to represent you. Even if you previously represented yourself in a civil proceeding, such as a divorce, name change or simple lawsuit, and know something about criminal law, it often isn't wise to represent yourself when you're charged with a misdemeanor punishable by jail.

1. What Lawyers Can Do for You

There are three basic ways a lawyer can help you when you're charged with a traffic violation.

a. Consultation and Advice

The lawyer can listen to the details of your situation, analyze it for you, and advise you on your position and best plan of action. Ideally, she will give you more than just conclusions—she can educate you about your whole situation and tell you all the alternatives available from which you can make your own choices. This kind of service is the least expensive since it only involves an office call and a little time. A charge of more than $50 to $75 for a half-hour consultation might be considered excessive. Find out the fee before you go in.

b. Negotiation

When you're charged with serious violations, the lawyer can use her special talents, knowledge and experience to help you negotiate with the prosecuting agency (the district or city attorney's office) to your best advantage. Often she will be able to do this more successfully than you could. If the lawyer specializes in criminal law, she may even have a good working relationship with several prosecuting attorneys. Without spending much of her own time, she can sometimes accomplish a lot through even a letter or phone call.

c. Represent You in Court or Before the DMV

If you're charged with a serious offense such as driving under the influence, or if you face loss of your driver's license, a lawyer can present your defense in court, or perhaps represent you in a DMV driver's license suspension hearing. When you're faced with a heavy sentence if you lose, you're under a lot of pressure to present your case, and that alone can cause you to do it poorly. You'd be surprised at how many people can come across like Perry Mason while fighting a $10 parking ticket on principle but will stutter, stammer and fall into quiet, disorganized desperation when they're charged with drunk or reckless driving. But a person not facing those consequences, particularly one with some experience in criminal defense work, can do a fairly good job. This is probably the reason all modern cultures—and many ancient ones—have invented lawyers in the first place.

2. Types of Lawyers

Now let's look at the various kinds of lawyers and lawyer services that are available.

a. Private Attorneys

Not every lawyer in private practice is adequately equipped to defend you against a misdemeanor or even an infraction traffic charge. Like physicians, many lawyers specialize, and you don't want a lawyer who mostly handles divorces defending you in a criminal case (all traffic tickets are handled criminally) any more than you'd want a plastic surgeon prescribing something for your stomach upsets. Since no lawyers specialize in traffic ticket defenses (it just doesn't pay enough), the next best thing might be a competent criminal defense lawyer, provided you can afford it. Use the same sorts of common-sense techniques that you use to find quality services in other areas. Start by asking a lawyer you know, a friend, or a business associate for a referral

to a good criminal defense lawyer who practices locally. You will want to seek out a person who spends at least a third of his or her time on criminal cases because a "full-time" criminal lawyer is more likely to know all the subtleties of the most recent criminal cases. If you're charged with driving under the influence, you should try to find a lawyer who has tried at least several "drunk driving" cases and who knows when and when not to "plea bargain" a case. (See Chapter 8.) You should also try to find a local lawyer because he will be in a position to know the idiosyncrasies of the judges and prosecutors who will handle your case and who have great discretion in disposing of it.

Note: We generally do not recommend referral panels set up by local bar associations. Lawyers are given only minimal screening as to their expertise in traffic cases in order to be listed on these panels. For the most part, the attorneys listed there are either new to the practice of law or don't have enough business. If you try an attorney referred by one of these panels, be sure to ask the attorney a lot of questions about her qualifications. (How many cases like yours have they done? Are there any former clients you could contact? And so on.)

Once you have the name of a lawyer or, preferably, several lawyers, who handle criminal cases, you will want to meet them and see if you feel comfortable with their approach. Remember, it's your case—not the lawyer's—and you want to be sure to hire a person whom you respect and who will respect you enough to explain fully what is going on at all times. If a lawyer is not open and frank with you at the first interview, it is unlikely his communication skills will improve later. Remember, the Latin root of the word client is "to hear, to obey." (The word was invented with the idea that the one who *has* the client is supposed to hear and obey the *client*, not vice versa.) It is easy to find a lawyer who encourages that kind of relationship, but if you want some say in your own case, you will have to be a bit more choosey.

Probably the best way to approach payment with a lawyer you don't know is to agree on a price for an initial consultation. Some lawyers will briefly discuss your case for free, or for as little as $20 for a half hour. For a more detailed discussion of the facts of an average misdemeanor case and the lawyer's suggestions about a defense strategy, something in the range of $50 to $100 would seem fair. If you don't like the lawyer, you haven't wasted much money. One way to judge whether a lawyer will satisfy you in the long run is to pay attention to how straightforward he is willing to be at the beginning.

b. Group Legal Practices and Prepaid Legal Services

A new but rapidly growing aspect of California law practice is the group legal practice program. Many groups, including unions, employers and consumer action groups, are offering plans to their members whereby they can get legal assistance for rates that are substantially lower than offered by most private practitioners. Some of these plans are good, some mediocre, and a few are not worth much, but most are better than nothing. It is unclear whether legal clinics such as Jacoby & Myers in the L.A. and San Francisco area, or Hyatt Legal Services are any better than a solo practitioner. It really depends on whether you end up with an attorney with any expertise in handling traffic cases. Because the group practice area of the law is changing so rapidly, we can't give you a state-wide list of group legal plans.

If you contact one of the above groups, however, they may be able to help you find a good group practice plan in your area.

c. The Public Defender

If you're charged with a misdemeanor and cannot afford the hundreds of dollars for a criminal defense attorney, you can request a court-appointed lawyer, usually a deputy public defender, to represent you. In most counties, you fill out a financial declaration in court, and the judge then refers you to a public defender. In other counties, you make an appointment with the Public Defender's office to discuss both your case and financial situation. In smaller counties, a judge may appoint a private attorney to represent you, payment being made by the county.

The legal determination of whether or not you can afford a lawyer depends upon the requirements specified by the particular county. If you have a relatively low-paying job, or no job, if your family is living on a tight budget, and if you do not have a savings account large enough to pay a lawyer to represent you, most judges will allow the public defender to represent you or authorize a private attorney to do so.

Even if you do have some financial resources but not thousands of dollars, the county will often provide you a lawyer if you insist you can't afford one. The county does not want to risk having to prosecute your case a second time if appellate judges determine later that you could not afford a lawyer and were thus deprived of your constitutional right to counsel at your first trial. However, the county can require you to pay back the cost of your legal services after your trial, using a fee schedule based on your income.

When you're charged with a misdemeanor, trying to qualify as an "indigent" so that a court-appointed lawyer can represent you is often a sensible way to proceed. Although there are a few (very few) incompetent public defenders with little training in criminal law, the public defender system is better than you might think. Many public defenders chose their careers because they genuinely want to help people. As a result of handling so many criminal cases, they are generally both experienced and competent. Indeed, you have a far greater chance of finding a lawyer mediocre at criminal defense by looking blindly through the Yellow Pages, than you do by consulting a public defender. Even if you don't qualify for free representation, the public defender's office may refer you to a relatively inexpensive but competent private criminal defense lawyer if you ask.

Perhaps the biggest drawback of being unable to afford a criminal defense attorney is that you risk getting an appointed lawyer to represent you with little experience or interest in criminal law. Another less serious disadvantage of having public representation is that public defenders are almost always overworked and may not give your case—especially if it is a minor one—the attention that you feel it deserves. If you think that your case is not getting enough attention or that it is not being handled with sufficient care, ask the lawyer to explain to you exactly what is being done. If his explanation doesn't satisfy you, try to get another lawyer.

Note: You do not have a right to a lawyer paid by the county if you are charged only with an "infraction."[1] For example, if you are cited for doing 95 mph on the freeway, punishable only by a $100 fine (plus penalty assessments), the county is not required to provide you with a lawyer.

3. Getting the Most out of Your Lawyer

Once a lawyer agrees to represent you, she has a duty to represent you to the best of her ability,

whether or not you are guilty. Indeed, except under the most unusual circumstances, a criminal defense lawyer has a moral responsibility to continue to defend you, even if you say that you have committed the act with which you are charged. Because your lawyer is not the judge or the jury, she cannot rely on her "opinion" of your guilt, or even on your own "opinion" of whether you are guilty. Unless you want to plead guilty, the attorney's job is to provide you with the best possible defense, short of allowing you to lie under oath.

It is important to emphasize that if you want to participate in your defense, you should make this agreement with your lawyer before she begins to represent you. If you are a participating type, you should try to find a lawyer who feels comfortable explaining to you the legal aspects of your case and consulting with you about your case. There are some decisions, such as whether to object to evidence or how to cross-examine a witness, which are appropriate for the lawyer to make. There are other choices, such as whether to plead guilty or accept a plea bargain, that should be yours. As a general rule, tactical decisions about procedure should be explained to you, but you should be willing to pay close attention to your lawyer's advice. Think of it this way: if you hire a carpenter to build a bookshelf, you will want to go over the plans carefully, but you will probably rely on the carpenter's experience when it comes to choosing and placing the nails.

There is no substitute for finding a lawyer whom you can honestly trust. Honesty is important because to defend you against the state's prosecution, your lawyer must know the whole truth about your activities. If you cannot be completely honest and forthright with your lawyer, then find another one. Finding another lawyer is easy if you can afford to hire one, but if the judge has appointed you a lawyer, then you must convince her to appoint a different one. To persuade a judge to do this, you will have to give very specific good reasons why you do not want to work with the lawyer. The fact that she is not spending enough time on your case is a good reason.

---

[1]PC § 19.6.

4. Legal Research

Much of what lawyers know about law they didn't learn in law school. Instead, they researched it. Legal research isn't all that difficult. You sure don't need a law degree to do it. In fact, many basic techniques of legal research can be learned in several hours. An excellent resource for helping you find your way around the law library is *Legal Research: How to Find and Understand the Law*, by Steve Elias (Nolo Press). This section will very briefly note some of the techniques discussed in that book.

The tattered Vehicle Code you bought from the DMV a year or two earlier is a good starting point, but while it lists all the "statutes" (laws passed by the Legislature), it doesn't list any of the appeals court decisions that determine what those laws mean. Sometimes these case decisions can make a big difference. [For example, decisions by California appeals courts have established that the misdemeanor offense of "exhibition of speed" can be committed not only by speeding, but also by deliberately accelerating so rapidly as to screech a car's tires—see Chapter 7, Section B(2).]

The best way to find written court decisions that interpret a particular law is to look in an "annotated code." An annotated code is a set of volumes of a particular code (Vehicle Code, Penal Code, Health & Safety Code, etc.) that list below the text of each law, (also called "code section"), and brief summaries of the court decisions which have interpreted the meaning of that law. These annotated codes—published by West Publishing Company (West's Annotated California Codes—blue volumes) and by Bancroft-Whitney (Deering's California Codes—brown volumes)—can be found in any law school library in the state. They have comprehensive

indexes by topic, and are kept up-to-date each year with paperback supplements ("pocket parts") located in a pocket in the back cover of each volume. (Don't forget to look through these pocket parts for the latest law change or case decision since the hardcover volume was printed.)

The brief summaries of the court decisions are followed by the title of the case, the year of the decision and the "citation," so that you can find the case and read it. The "citation" is a sort of shorthand identification of the page, volume and series of volumes where the case can be found. The "official" volumes of cases are published by the appeals courts as *Official Reports of the California Supreme Court* (abbreviated "Cal.," "Cal.2d," or "Cal.3d," respectively representing the first, second and third "series" of volumes) and as *Official Reports of the California Courts of Appeal*[2] (similarly abbreviated "Cal.App.," "Cal.App.2d" and "Cal.App.3d"). The cases are also published in "unofficial" volumes by the West Publishing Company. These are *California Reporter* (abbreviated "Cal.Rptr.") and *Pacific Reporter* (abbreviated "P" or "P.2d," respectively for the first and second series). The case is the same whether you read it in the "official" or "unofficial" reporter.

This information should take some of the mystery out of legal research. If, in the course of your research, you still have questions, don't hesitate to ask a law librarian for assistance. As long as you don't appear to be asking for legal advice, and you look like you have some idea of what you're looking for, most law librarians will go out of their way to help you.[3]

---

[2]The Courts of Appeal are California's "intermediate" level appeals courts, on a lower legal level than the California Supreme Court, but "higher" than the superior, municipal and justice courts of the counties. There are six appellate districts in the state, with courts in San Francisco, Los Angeles, Sacramento, San Diego, Fresno and San Jose. (The California Supreme Court resides in San Francisco, not Sacramento, with only branch offices in Sacramento and Los Angeles.)

[3]Be sure to also ask the librarian whether other legal source books like encyclopedias, treatises, digests and law reviews may help you understand the areas of law you are researching and, if so, how you can find these sources.

Here are some examples of case citations:

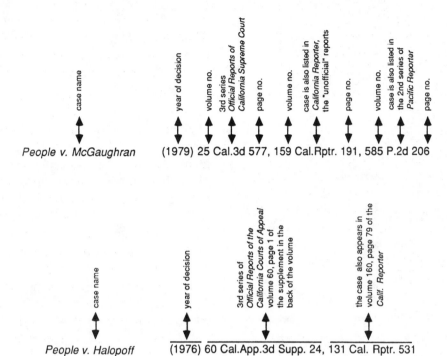

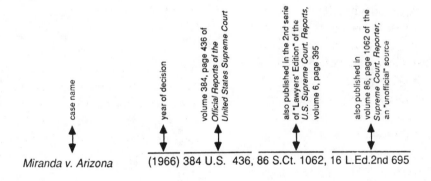

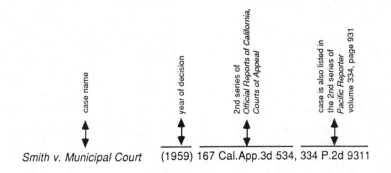

10

FIGHTING AN INFRACTION CITATION

THIS CHAPTER COVERS the initial steps of fighting an infraction charge. If you're charged with a misdemeanor, skip this chapter and go directly to Chapter 13. If you're charged with an infraction, read Section A of this chapter carefully before deciding how you want to fight.

A.   Preliminary Steps for Fighting an Infraction

THERE ARE NUMEROUS procedures you must follow before you can ever get to trial. For some people, however, most of these steps may be unnecessary. In this chapter, you learn how these procedures work, and how to bypass the ones you don't need, so you can save yourself a few wasted hours of waiting in line.

Note: As mentioned before, parking tickets are handled by a simpler procedure, which is fully described in Chapter 6. If you have a parking ticket, you probably don't need the information in this half of the book. The same is true for "correctable" equipment violations. (See Chapter 6, Section B.)

1.   Phoning the Court for Information

You probably have noticed the little notation on the bottom of your ticket telling you to appear at a certain date, time and place "before a judge of the Municipal Court at..." This doesn't necessarily mean that any trial, or even a scheduled court appearance before a judge, will occur on that date. All it means is that if you don't see the court clerk before that

date about paying the ticket or scheduling a court appearance, the system will start treating you as if you were a very small stone caught in a very large grinder. [See Chapter 7, Section B(3).]

But before you take that trip down to the courthouse to see the clerk, you should phone the clerk's office and ask some questions about the county's procedure. By asking a few questions in advance, you can save yourself a lot of time once you actually begin to fight. If your ticket doesn't list the court's phone number, look it up in the telephone book under the listings for the county in which the court is located, under "courts," "municipal court" or "justice court." Unfortunately, more and more traffic courts are shifting to recorded phone-message systems (the kind where you hear an announcement but can't leave a message) and give no specific information over the phone, so as to require a trip to the courthouse and a long wait in line to get any information. Even in courts where clerks still answer the phone, you can probably expect to be put on "hold." Persist.

When you finally do get through to a live person on the telephone or after you have trekked down to the courthouse in person, be ready to ask some fairly simple questions. You might say something like this:

• "I received a moving violation citation on [Month, Day, Year], and I would like to know whether I can arrange today for a court appearance to contest the violation, or do I have to wait until I receive a 'courtesy notice' in the mail?" (A courtesy notice is a computer-printed reminder to do something about your ticket. See below.)

- "Does the court permit trial by written declaration for traffic infractions under § 40902 of the Vehicle Code?" (As we'll see in Section 3, below, this is where you write out your testimony and swear to it under penalty of perjury; if you're found guilty, you still have the right to a regular trial with the officer present.)

- You may also want to ask the clerk whether the county has a traffic school program. [See Section 2(e) below.] If the county does have such a program, ask whether you have to appear before a judge at arraignment to ask for traffic school, or whether you can arrange it with the court clerk.

Municipal Court
Palo Alto-Mountain View   **COURTESY NOTICE**
270 Grant Ave Rm 204
Palo Alto CA 94306

Traffic citation MV50864 issued on 01/13/9_ has been filed with the court. You may post and forfeit bail in the sum of $56 by mailing check or money order payable to the Municipal Court, in the enclosed envelope within 20 days from the date of the citation. Bail forfeiture closes the case. If you wish to appear in court you must appear in this office within 20 days from the date of the citation to arrange an appearance date.

Office Hours: 8:30 a.m. to 4:00 p.m.

Failure to comply with the instructions within the specified time will result in a bail increase and you will not be permitted to renew your driver's license.

Please disregard this notice if this citation has been paid or you have appeared in court.

Failure to comply with these instructions may result in a warrant for your arrest with an increase in bail.

B0025640 D 03/26/9_

DO NOT SEND CASH

---

2. Deciding How to Plead

Before you go to the clerk's office, decide how you want to plead. There can be as many as five options to choose from: not guilty, guilty, nolo contendere, forfeiting bail without a plea, and accepting traffic school instead of a plea. By deciding ahead of time which way you want to plead, you'll know what kind of hearing to ask for when you get to the clerk's window. For example, if you want to plead "not guilty" you may want to bypass the arraignment and request a trial with the officer present. (See Section B, below.) If you want to opt for traffic school, you may be able to tell the clerk immediately and be done with it.

Each of the possible plea options is discussed below.

a. Not Guilty

Under our legal system, it is always your legal right to plead not guilty whether or not you think you really are. You can do this by mail [see Section B(4) below], at the court clerk's office [see Section B(3) below], or at arraignment (see Section C, below).

By pleading not guilty, all you're saying is that, since you're presumed innocent, you're going to insist on your right to have the prosecution prove *every* element of its case. For example, if you plead not guilty to a charge that you violated the Basic Speed Law by doing 38 mph on Market Street, where the speed limit is 25 mph, it's legally equivalent to saying:

- I wasn't driving a motor vehicle down Market Street; and

- the speed limit wasn't 25 mph; and

- I wasn't going over 25 mph.

Even if only one of these denials is true (or even if none of them are), you're not doing anything wrong by pleading not guilty. You're merely demanding that they prove every element against you.

b. Guilty Pleas

Formal guilty pleas to infractions are rare, but are more common in misdemeanor cases. Most people charged with infractions simply fork over the forfeited bail to the clerk without entering any plea at all. (See Section B, below.)

One exception to this is the so-called "guilty with an explanation" plea, where a person pleads guilty but tells his or her story to the judge at an informal hearing at arraignment, hoping to get a reduced or suspended fine.[1] Unfortunately, this is generally not a good idea. Even if a sympathetic judge reduces or "suspends" the fine, the offense still goes on your driving record if it's one of those types of violations that gets reported to the DMV, and your insurance rates may rise, depending on the offense. Thus, the "guilty with an explanation" plea is usually used by ill-prepared people who do not want to take another trip down to the courthouse for trial.

Just as a plea of not guilty constitutes a denial of the truth of every element of a charge, a guilty plea constitutes an admission of each element.

You should never plead guilty to a charge arising out of an accident in which you were involved. Should you be sued, your guilty plea can be used against you. Instead, you should either forfeit bail (see below) or plead nolo contendere if you don't want to fight the ticket.

However, for minor parking, equipment or registration violations that don't normally go on your driving record, you don't have that much to lose by pleading "guilty with an explanation," except perhaps a small fine.

c. Nolo Contendere

Remember how former Vice President Spiro Agnew pleaded nolo contendere (pronounced "no'lo contend'-er-ray") to not paying income tax on the money he was accused of having received as bribes? Even though his nolo contendere plea had the same effect as a guilty plea for criminal purposes, it prevented the IRS from using a guilty plea against him in a later civil suit over back taxes. Similarly, if you're ever cited for a non-felony Vehicle Code violation arising out of an accident and you don't want to fight the ticket, you can plead nolo contendere, sometimes referred to as "no contest," at arraignment.

Bear in mind, that a plea of nolo contendere does have exactly the same consequences as a guilty plea with regards to the amount of the fine, extra penalties on future offenses, your driving record at the DMV, and the effect on your insurance rates.

Some judges do not like to see people plead nolo contendere and will try to prevent them from doing so. If the judge won't let you, tell her that there was an auto accident (if true). If that doesn't convince the judge, then plead not guilty; you can change it later if you get a more intelligent judge at trial. Of course, if you have to go that far, you may decide to fight it all the way.

d. "Forfeiting Bail" (Just Paying the Fine)

Showing up at the clerk's window to pay your ticket (or mailing in the fine, for parking tickets) has the same effect as pleading guilty, except that it cannot be used against you in a lawsuit arising out of an accident.[2] If the violation is one of those that's normally reported to the DMV [see Chapter 3, Section

---

[1] This is not really a special kind of plea. All you're doing when you tell the judge you're pleading "guilty with an explanation" is 1) pleading guilty, 2) giving up your right to a delay of at least six hours before sentencing (see Chapter 14), and 3) offering evidence in mitigation at what is now a sentencing hearing.

---

[2] This is because you are only forfeiting bail by arranging not to contest the ticket. You are not pleading guilty.

A(2)], it will appear on your driving record, and will count as a prior conviction for all purposes. Your insurance rates are also likely to rise.

e. Traffic School with Dismissal

In some counties, rather than fighting or paying off a ticket, you can sign up for traffic school and have the violation erased from your driving record. (All that goes on your record is a notation you've been to traffic school and when—information disclosed only to courts, to prevent people from using this option more than twice over a certain period.) Not all counties allow this, and the procedure varies from county to county.

Generally, you have to opt for traffic school at some early stage of the case. Some counties require you to sign up for traffic school with the clerk, while others require you to go to an arraignment and request traffic school instead of entering any kind of plea. After you've successfully completed traffic school and a notice of completion is sent to the court, the traffic charge will be dismissed and will not show up on your record. You can't opt for traffic school twice in a 12-month period (VC § 1808.7); some counties require a longer period.

Note: If you don't opt for traffic school at the beginning of your case, you miss your chance. That is, you can't fight, and then—after you lose—decide you'd rather go to traffic school. Don't confuse this type of arrangement with the case where you plead or are found guilty and are sentenced to attend traffic school. If you plead guilty, the charge does appear on your record and your attendance is merely part of your sentence (perhaps instead of a fine). (See VC § 42005.)

Note: No court may legally withhold from the DMV any record of a violation to which you've pleaded or been found guilty, in exchange for your attendance at traffic school.[3] So, if you're ever required to sign up for traffic school at an arraignment where the judge insists that you plead guilty first, and promises to "sentence" you to traffic school, don't fall for it. Plead "not guilty" instead.

Traffic school is conducted not by the court, but by local high schools, private organizations, and in some cases local police departments. The court can charge you up to $24 just to "refer" you to traffic school, and you also have to pay the school itself. That charge is between $20 and $50.

Also, there is usually a limit on how often you can take traffic school. Many counties require you to take the advanced (and more expensive) course if it's your second or third attendance at traffic school within a specified number of years.

During the course (which might be several evening classes spaced over one or two weeks, or all day on a Saturday), you get to hear lectures, see "ketchup movies" (referring to the substance most used to simulate blood and gore), and take quizzes to prove that you now understand how to drive properly.[4] It's all somewhat simple-minded, but there are people who have found much of the information to be valuable. Traffic safety, intelligently presented, has a lot going for it.

Warning: If you do opt for traffic school, "willful failure" to sign up for and complete it is a misdemeanor (VC § 42005).

---

[3]VC §§ 1803, 1803.5, 42005. A dismissal of your case in exchange for your attendance at traffic school is the only legally-recognized way to prevent an offense from counting against your driving record. Even then, a court has to report to the DMV when dismissals are obtained this way, but these reports aren't available to the public (or insurance companies) and can't be used as "points" upon which to base a license suspension.

[4]A number of traffic schools in the San Francisco Bay area rely on professional comedians and pointed humor rather than "ketchup" to get their point across.

3. Deciding What Kind of Hearing You Want

If you decide to contest your ticket, there are several kinds of hearings available. You can have a formal "in-person" trial with the officer present. You can have an "informal hearing" at arraignment, although this is not recommended. Finally, in some courts, mostly in non-urban areas, you can contest your ticket through the mail.

a. Formal Trial with Officer Present

As we've stated before, in most cases, you should insist on a trial with the officer present. By doing so, you get the advantage of being able to challenge the officer's assertions in court, and most importantly, you gain the very real possibility that the officer will not show up to testify against you, and your case will be dismissed.

A trial for an infraction is held in a Municipal Court or Justice Court with a judge or "commissioner" presiding. You are notified where and when to appear. Be on time. When your case is called, you (and your witnesses, if any) and the officer walk up behind the table, raise your right hands and are "sworn in." There is usually no prosecutor. The officer tells his story first. His job is to testify to facts that establish all the required elements of the case. After he's finished, you have an opportunity to cross-examine him. You can ask him questions on matters he has testified to, and on new matters that might help you establish a defense (e.g., to establish the excellent weather and visibility in a Basic Speed Law case).

After you finish cross-examining, you get your turn to explain what happened. You will probably want to contradict the officer's testimony by establishing other facts that tend to disprove one or more elements of the offense. You may also want to establish facts that constitute a defense even if everything the officer said was true. Some judges will then give the officer a chance to cross-examine you.

After all the testimony has been given (including that of witnesses) the judge usually gives the decision. Some judges will instead try to "take the case under advisement," with your permission. If the judge finds you guilty, she will usually, at the same time, tell you what the fine will be. (You can, however, insist on the right to be sentenced between six hours and five days later. See Chapter 14, Section A)

In some places minor traffic cases are still prosecuted by bored assistant district or city attorneys, but in most courts, the police officer prosecutes the case himself merely by testifying.

If you decide you want a formal trial be sure to read Chapters 11 and 12.

b. Informal Hearing

The second kind of hearing you can get is an informal hearing, which usually is held at the same time as arraignment. If you're ever asked by a court clerk, or by a judge at arraignment, whether you prefer a formal trial or an informal hearing, be careful. You may think that the distinction involves things like whether you testify from a witness stand or just tell your story from behind a table, or whether the case against you is presented by the police officer or by a deputy district or city attorney. An informal hearing will very likely sound good to you. Unfortunately, the nice-sounding word "informal" may mean little more than that you give up your right to insist on the officer's coming to testify against you. Indeed, you have very little to gain by giving up your right to a formal hearing. Since moving violations go on your record, you should usually insist on the formal trial with the officer present. A surprising number of tickets are beaten by people who insist that the officer show, and have their cases dismissed when he doesn't.

However, if you do go to arraignment and have signed up for an informal hearing, watch other people's cases and notice whether they are often found not guilty by a particular judge. If they are, you too may want to go ahead with the "informal" hearing before that judge.

But if it appears to you that the judge is prone to find people guilty, consider changing your mind when your name is called and asking for a formal trial with the officer present. Traffic court judges who want people to accept informal hearings won't get many takers if they convict everyone and assess heavy fines. But be careful. If the judge's "leniency" only takes the form of reduced fines or "suspended" sentences (you're found guilty and pay no fine—but it still goes on your record), forget it. You may save money on the fine now, but you'll pay more in increased insurance rates later. Also, insist on a formal trial if you see the judge consistently taking cases "under advisement." This usually means he found the defendant guilty but doesn't have the guts to tell the person directly.

In sum, an informal hearing is better than no hearing at all, but not much better. If you're serious about fighting your ticket, you'd generally be better off by proceeding directly to formal trial with the officer present, unless you're fighting low-fine parking tickets that aren't worth a lot of trouble (since they don't go on your driving record). If the choice is between paying the fine and putting up a little fight, you might want an informal hearing and hope to get a lenient judge at arraignment.

c. "Trial-by-Declaration" (VC § 40902)

In some cases, the law allows traffic-court "trials" without actually requiring anyone to show up in court. A person accused of a nonalcohol-related infraction (i.e., all moving violations other than open-container violations, etc.) may contest a ticket by telling his or her story in a letter to the court. Unfortunately the law only provides that courts *may* set up this type of procedure—it doesn't *require* them to do so, except for violations where the person lives more than 100 miles from the court or the place where the citation was issued. Even so, some courts have adopted this procedure without requiring that a person who uses it live 100 miles away.

One advantage of telling your story in writing is that you can take time to draft a convincing, well-thought-out defense, which may sound better to the judge than the oral testimony of an inexperienced, nervous defendant. A second, and even bigger, advantage is that you get two chances to be found not guilty. If you start off with written testimony and are found guilty, you can demand and get a regular trial (called a "trial de novo") with the officer present. Thus you have nothing to lose.

The procedure for requesting a "trial by written declaration," as it's sometimes called, may vary. The first step is to ask the court clerk whether it exists regardless of whether you live 100 miles away or not. (If you do live 100+ miles away, the first step may be convincing the clerk that VC § 40902 requires the court to use this procedure when you first arrange to fight your ticket.) If you have no specific problems of the type that should be dealt with at an arraignment, you should insist that the clerk allow you to plead not guilty under § 40519. Then, instead of arranging for a trial date, you should arrange to bring in or mail your statement to the clerk. If you're lucky, you should be able to handle the entire matter by mail (and telephone, if necessary) in just two transactions.

In order to stand any chance of beating the ticket by "written declaration," you'll have to do more than just deny the charge. For example, in a typical radar speeding case, your written statement is going to have to show a little sophistication and might look something like the sample on the next page.

Several weeks (or months) later, you'll receive a notice in the mail telling you of the judge's decision. If the notice says that you've been found guilty, you have the right to go to the courthouse in person and arrange for a regular trial with the officer present. It is important to do this as soon as possible. If you wait too long (like a month or more), you'll find that your right to a new, formal trial has vanished. The new trial is handled in exactly the same way as any traffic trial. However, two things should be kept in mind. First, if the judge is the same, file a "Peremptory

Challenge" disqualifying him (see Chapter 11, Section C) as soon as you can, or ask the judge at trial to disqualify herself on the grounds that she has already decided issues in the same case. Second, never agree to an "informal" trial without the officer present; that's essentially what you had before, and you lost.

Warning: Handling tickets by mail. Whenever you handle a ticket by mail, rather than going down to the clerk's window in person, be sure to send all of your correspondence, fines or court papers by certified mail, return receipt requested.

Do this even if you're simply paying a fine. If you only use regular first class mail, you have no way of knowing whether your papers ever reached their destination. If they didn't, you may face additional fines and possibly additional charges against you for failing to respond to your ticket in time –and the court won't listen to your claims that your correspondence got lost in the mail. Paying the small fee for certified mail is cheap insurance against hundreds of dollars in fines in the future.

WRITTEN DECLARATION FOR "TRIAL BY DECLARATION"

October 2, 199_
123 Plumbumped Drive
Santa Barbara, California

Traffic Docket
Municipal Court of Alameda County
Fremont-Newark Judicial District
Fremont, California

Re: People v. Lenny D. Leadfoot, Municipal Court No. A036912-B
    Traffic Citation-Fremont Police Dept. No. 44-12345

Declaration of Defendant Lenny D. Leadfoot Pursuant to
Vehicle Code § 40902 (Trial by Written Declaration)

To the Judge or Commissioner of the Traffic Docket:

[If applicable:] Pursuant to Vehicle Code Section 40902, I wish to exercise my right to trial by declaration with regard to a Vehicle Code infraction citation. I reside over 100 miles from your court (or from where the alleged offense occurred).

On September 20, 199_, at approximately 10:30 a.m., I was driving my 1966 Volkswagen, License No. 123ABC, west on Breezy Boulevard, a four-lane divided highway, between Drag Boulevard and Zoom Street. I was in the right-hand lane. The weather was clear and dry. There was no traffic in my direction other than a large panel truck (visible in my side view mirror) in the left lane, several car lengths behind me. The truck overtook and passed my vehicle shortly before I crossed the Zoom Street intersection.

Approximately two blocks past Zoom Street, I was stopped by Officer Stickler of the Fremont Police Department. He informed me that he had determined my speed on his hand-held radar unit to be 45 mph, the posted prima facie speed limit being 35 mph. He said that he had read my speed at the Breezy Boulevard-Drag Boulevard intersection from the intersection at Zoom Street, which a street map will show is 500 feet away. Officer Stickler responded to several of my questions by stating that the radar beam width was "about six degrees," and that his unit had been "calibrated recently with this little knob," pointing to the "calibrate" position on the controls of the unit. He said he hadn't used a tuning fork, and that he didn't have one in his possession. He also indicated that his unit was capable of reading speeds of both oncoming and receding traffic.

I believe that there exists a reasonable doubt as to the accuracy of Officer Stickler's radar reading. As can be seen from the diagram below, a six-degree beam width at 500 feet will indiscriminately read speeds of vehicles across a width of 55 feet—all four lanes of traffic.

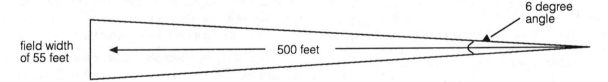

The radar unit may therefore have been reading both speeds of traffic in my direction (including a truck target much larger and more likely to reflect radar beams than my small Volkswagen) and the heavy traffic in the other direction. This being so, it is doubtful that the speed he recorded was mine. Furthermore, even if I were traveling at 45 mph, the weather was clear and dry, and there was very little traffic in my direction on a divided four-lane road. The intersections of Breezy Boulevard with Drag Boulevard and Zoom Street are both controlled by stoplights. Under these conditions, 45 mph was a safe speed at which to drive (although I doubt that I was going that fast). The truck which overtook and passed my vehicle did so safely even at its higher speed.

Finally, my research efforts at City Hall have failed to yield any record of a traffic survey justifying the 35 mph speed limit within the past five years.

Also enclosed is the declaration of Wilhelmina D. Witness.

I declare under penalty of perjury under the laws of the State of California that the foregoing is true and correct and that this written statement was signed by me on October 2, 199_.

Lenny D. Leadfoot

**WRITTEN DECLARATION OF
WITNESS FOR TRIAL BY DECLARATION**

October 2, 199_

Traffic Docket
Municipal Court of Alameda County
Fremont-Newark Judicial District
Fremont, California

Re: People v. Lenny D. Leadfoot,
    Municipal Court No. A0369 12-B
    Traffic Citation-Fremont Police Dept.
    No. 44-12345

Declaration of Wilhelmina D. Witness
Pursuant to Vehicle Code § 40902
(Trial by Written Declaration)

To the Judge or Commissioner of the Traffic
Docket:

   On September 20, 199_, at approximately
10:30 a.m., I was riding as a passenger in
an automobile driven by Lenny D. Leadfoot.
Mr. Leadfoot was relaxed and not driving
very fast for conditions. There were no
other cars on the road in our direction of
travel that I could see, other than a large
truck which passed us on the left shortly
before we crossed the Zoom Street
intersection. We were talking as we drove
westbound on Breezy Boulevard in Fremont.
As we drove past Zoom Street, Mr. Leadfoot
said that a police officer was pulling us
over. I was surprised because I didn't know
why we being pulled over. We drove to the
side of the road and waited for the
officer. I asked Mr. Leadfoot why we were
being pulled over, and he did not know.

   The officer approached the car. He told
Mr. Leadfoot he was driving 45 mph in a 35
mph zone. I was surprised because I didn't
think that we were going that fast. I still
don't think so.

   I declare under penalty of perjury under
the laws of the State of California that
the foregoing is true and correct.

DATED: October 2, 199_

                    Wilhelmina D. Witness

B.   Seeing the Court Clerk

NOW THAT YOU'VE found out the county's procedure from your phone call or visit to the clerk's office, and now that you've decided how you want to plead and what kind of hearing you want, you're ready to see the clerk to take care of your ticket. At the clerk's window you can either pay your fine and go home, sign up for traffic school (if you qualify), arrange a date for your arraignment, if you want one, or set up a date for a formal trial.

   You should probably wait at least a week after you receive the ticket before you visit the clerk's office. It sometimes takes this long for the officer's copy of the ticket to reach the court, and the court personnel will refuse to deal with the matter until they have received it. In some counties, you may even have to wait longer because the county waits to obtain your record from the DMV in Sacramento before it forwards the officer's copy of the ticket to the clerk.

   Note: Don't avoid seeing the clerk out of fear she'll have you arrested on the spot for a traffic warrant on this or another case. First, most traffic-infraction failures to appear are nowadays just reported to the DMV (which will suspend your license until you get the matter resolved) without any warrants being issued. Second, you can usually call the county sheriff in advance to see if they have any warrants against you. Third, even if there are minor warrants against you, most courts will give you time to post bail.

1. Should You Bypass the Arraignment?

The major decision you'll have to make at the clerks window is whether you want to set a date for an arraignment. An arraignment (a-rain'-ment) is a brief proceeding where you are informed of your rights and of the charge against you (usually the Vehicle Code section number and a very brief explanation of where and when you allegedly violated it). You are also asked if you wish to sign up for traffic school or whether you want to enter a plea—that is, guilty, not guilty or nolo contendere. If you plead not guilty, a date is set for your trial.

If you don't want to contest your ticket, there's no need to set up a date for arraignment. Merely go to the clerk's window and pay your fine or request traffic school if your county offers that option. [In some counties you can't request traffic school at the clerk's window. Instead, you have to set up an arraignment first, and request traffic school at the arraignment. See Section A(2), above.]

If you do want to fight your ticket you can either set up an arraignment or bypass that step and proceed directly to a formal trial with the officer present. Most court clerks won't tell you that you have this choice. If you want to plead not guilty, you can enter your not guilty plea at the clerk's window and set up a date for trial at that time, bypassing the arraignment. (See Section 3, below.) In fact, you do not even need to go to the clerk's window—you can enter your not guilty plea by mail, and have the court notify you of your trial date. (See Section 4, below.) However, when going the mail route, you give up your right to a speedy trial. [See Section C(1)(d), below.]

However, before you decide to bypass the arraignment, be aware that it is an important step for assuring certain rights. You should attend it if you want any of the following:

- to have your rights read to you;

- to request that the place of trial be changed to another court (usually the one at the county seat) —see Section D(2)(c) of this chapter and Chapter 17, Section C. This request must be made at the arraignment;[5]

- to demand that the charges be dismissed on the grounds that there has already been too much delay on the part of the court personnel—see Section D(2)(a) of this chapter. This motion does not have to be made at the arraignment, but the arraignment is the only time for you to ask the judge to set up a separate hearing, prior to trial, for a "speedy trial motion";

- to insist that a "verified complaint" be filed, in certain accident-citation or parking cases where it's required but hasn't been done—see Section D(2)(d) of this chapter.

Other reasons for going to an arraignment include:

- not having the bail money to post under VC § 40519 (you may need to post bail to avoid the arraignment, as we discuss below);

- wanting to request traffic school in exchange for a dismissal of the charge if the county doesn't allow it at the clerk's window;

- pleading nolo contendere to a violation arising out of an accident. [See Chapter 9, Section A(4), and Section A(2) of this chapter on pleading "nolo contendere".]

Finally, some people elect to go to arraignment to have an "informal hearing," without the officer present, on the same day as the arraignment. As explained above, this is generally not recommended.

If you're still unsure whether you want an arraignment, read Section C, below.

---

[5]PC § 1462.2.

2. Setting Up an Arraignment Date

If you decide you do want an arraignment, ask the clerk to schedule one. Make sure that the time and date the clerk gives you is on the arraignment calendar, not the trial calendar. Some courts schedule arraignments at night, but clerks usually won't put on you the night arraignment calendar unless you specifically ask for it.

3. Bypassing the Arraignment (A Shortcut)

If you do not want an arraignment—that is, you wish to contest your ticket and don't plan to make any of the motions mentioned above—simply tell the clerk that you wish to plead "not guilty" right now as provided by VC § 40519(a), thereby "waiving" the arraignment. You have this right, as long as you assert it *before* the last day for appearance stated on your Notice to Appear. Emphasize that you want your next appearance to be a trial with the officer present and that you're willing to post bail. You will probably have to pay the amount of the fine as bail, though some courts may let you by without paying it. Unlike forfeited bail in traffic cases, this bail really is bail (that is, a deposit to guarantee your appearance) and will be returned to you if you're eventually found not guilty. If you're found not guilty, your bail should be refunded in six to eight weeks. If you simply don't show up, you'll lose your bail and be charged with an additional misdemeanor for failing to appear. [See Chapter 7, Section B(3).]

Note: In avoiding a separate court date for arraignment, you give up your right to insist on a trial within 45 days afterward. If you opt for this procedure, the court clerk may schedule your trial date months away.

The clerk is required to set a trial date—not merely an arraignment date[6]—if you ask for it. If the clerk hassles you about this, be persistent and tell him to read VC § 40519(a). Or, ask to speak to a supervisor. Keep going up the ladder until you get results.

4. Bypassing Arraignment, by Mail

You can also bypass your arraignment by mail [VC § 40519(b)]. The procedure is similar to that just described, except its all done in writing. You send a personal check for the proper amount of the bail. If you received a courtesy notice, the bail amount will be listed. Otherwise, you'll have to call the clerk and ask. The amount should be the same as the bail to be "forfeited" if you were to choose to just pay the fine.

Along with your check, you send a note giving the case number of your ticket or courtesy notice, and clearly indicate that you are pleading not guilty. This should be mailed by certified mail (return receipt requested) at least five days before the deadline for you to appear (as stated on your ticket). The clerk's office is then supposed to notify you by mail (postmarked at least 10 days before) of your trial

---

[6]Court clerks will often sign you up for the arraignment without telling you. In some courts, they do so to pressure you into accepting an "informal" hearing procedure. [See Section A(3)(b) of this chapter.]

date. (By bypassing the arraignment you give up your right to a speedy trial.)

Your note to the clerk should look something like this:

June 10, 199_

Traffic Clerk
Municipal Court
Los Angeles Judicial District
Traffic Division, Downtown Branch
Los Angeles, California

RE: Los Angeles Police Dept.
    Citation No.LA-12345
    dated June 1, 199_;
    Your Docket No.L-123456789-A.

Dear Sir or Madam:

This is in regard to the above citation I received in Los Angeles on June 1, 199_. I hereby waive the arraignment, and in accordance with § 40519(b) of the Vehicle Code plead not guilty to the charge of violating § 22350 of the Vehicle Code. I request a trial date for a trial with the officer present.

Pursuant to my telephone conversation yesterday with Ms. Donna Nuthin of your office, I am enclosing a check for bail in the amount of $52.

Sincerely,

Sara Speedaway
123 Market Street
Santa Ana, CA 90123

Be sure to keep a carbon or photocopy of the letter for your records, and to save all certified mail receipts.

If your court district allows a "trial by declaration," you might be able to handle your whole case by mail. [See Section A(3), above.] Call the court clerk and ask whether this option is available. [See Section A(1), above.]

C. Arraignment

THE REST OF THIS CHAPTER discusses the arraignment and the procedural requests (called "motions") you can make at arraignment. If you've already decided to bypass arraignment. [See Section B(1-4) above], you can go directly to the next chapter. If you are still undecided, keep on reading to get a better idea of what an arraignment involves.

1. Telling You Your Rights

One of the most important parts of the arraignment is to inform you of your basic legal rights. These include the right to be represented by an attorney, to cross-examine the officer, to subpoena witnesses, to have your case tried within 45 days, and to have a jury trial in a misdemeanor case.

Usually the judge will read these rights to the group of defendants in the courtroom when court begins, or a clerk will pass out a printed sheet containing this information. Rarely will the judge recite these rights to a defendant individually.

(Note: By reading this book, you're already getting a pretty good idea of what those rights are, so there's no need to schedule an arraignment just to hear someone read them to you.)

When your case is called, the judge will ask you whether you understand these rights. Answer yes only if you really do. If you say you understand something, but really don't, you won't be allowed to complain about it later. Similarly, don't sign forms until you know what you are signing. Below is a sample "Advice of Rights" form.

Occasionally, a judge may ask you to "waive" (give up) your rights. She may, for example, announce that unless you object, it will be assumed that you want an informal hearing in which the citing officer will not be present for you to cross-examine. [See Section (3), below.)] Or, due to a very crowded court calendar, your trial will be scheduled more than 45 days ahead, unless you object. [See Section (4), below, for advice on when you should and shouldn't give up this right.] So listen carefully, and don't mistakenly give up these important rights.[7]

2. Entering a "Not Guilty" Plea

Once the charge is read to you and you have claimed or waived certain rights, the judge or clerk will ask you how you plead. Your answer should almost always be "not guilty." [If you intended to plead guilty, you should have just paid your fine to the clerk without taking time off work to go to an arraignment. [See Section (A)(2) above.] However, in some courts, where having the charge dismissed and

going to traffic school is an alternative to entering a plea, you may want to tell the judge you prefer traffic school "in lieu of a plea." If the judge insists that you plead guilty first, don't do it—the offense will go on your record. Plead not guilty instead.

Occasionally, you might be asked about prior offenses, or "priors" (earlier violations on your record).[8] This is called "charging a prior," and lays a basis for raising your fine above that for a first-time offense in the event you're found guilty of the current charge. You should always deny the prior offenses. This is perfectly proper, even though you may really have forfeited bail or been convicted of the prior offense. You're not committing perjury (lying under oath) any more than when you plead not guilty. When they ask if you have any prior convictions, simply say, "I deny the validity of any prior convictions." All you're doing is requiring the prosecution to prove the existence of priors by locating the original court records, which is often difficult to do. (See Chapter 14.)

---

[7]Although the law technically requires that procedural rights in criminal cases must be waived "expressly," not merely by silence, traffic court judges do take a few "shortcuts" now and then. Since court reporters usually don't attend traffic court arraignments, it's often difficult for you to prove that your waiver wasn't "express." One recent court case held that a person pleading guilty to a traffic ticket is entitled to the same procedures employed for guilty pleas in regular misdemeanor cases. *People v. Mathews* (1983) 139 Cal.App.3d 537. See also PC § 19.7.

---

[8]The Court of Appeal has held that a court violates a defendant's rights against self-incrimination when it asks him or her about prior offenses. *Municipal Court v. Superior Court* (1988) 199 Cal.App.3d 19, 244 Cal.Rptr.591.

ADVICE OF RIGHTS—TRAFFIC VIOLATIONS

The following represents a summary of the rights you have as a defendant in this Court. If you do not understand these rights, be sure to request a further explanation from the court.

Each defendant has the following rights:

(1) To have the complaint or citation read in open court.

(2) To be represented by legal counsel at all stages of the proceedings and to be allowed a reasonable time to obtain an attorney. If you are charged with a misdemeanor and are indigent, the Court will appoint an attorney to represent you.

(3) To plead guilty or not guilty or nolo contendere. A plea of nolo contendere has the same effect as a plea of guilty except that it cannot be used against you in a civil action.

(4) To confront and cross-examine witnesses who would testify against you.

(5) To the use of subpoena power of the Court to compel the attendance of witnesses on your behalf.

(6) A constitutional privilege against self-incrimination; you cannot be compelled to be a witness about the matter.

(7) To have your case tried within 45 days of your plea.

(8) If you are charged with a misdemeanor, you are entitled to a jury trial.

(9) If you plead guilty or nolo contendere (no contest) you have the right to delay sentencing for six hours and sentence must be imposed within five days. Since it may be inconvenient to return to court for sentencing, the Court will assume that you prefer to be sentenced immediately unless you request a later date.

(10) If you desire to admit guilt and to give an explanation to the Court, you may do so after entering your plea of guilty. Your plea of guilty, however, is an admission of each element of the offense, and your explanation will be considered only in determining the appropriate penalty.

MAXIMUM PENALTIES

If you are convicted of any infraction, you may be fined $260. For a second conviction within one year, you may be fined $520. A third conviction within one year carries a maximum penalty of $650. A fourth conviction may be treated as a misdemeanor. Your license may also be suspended as a consequence of a conviction for certain violations.

Misdemeanor convictions of § 23103 (reckless driving) and 23109 (speed exhibition or contest) carry possible sentences of 90 days in jail and a fine of $2,600, plus a possible license suspension. Other misdemeanors, including violations of §§ 12500 (driving while not licensed) and 40508 (a) (failure to appear) are punishable by six months in jail and a fine of $2,600.

I HAVE READ THE ABOVE ADVICE OF RIGHTS AND UNDERSTAND THE SAME. I FURTHER UNDERSTAND THAT IF I SHOULD PLEAD GUILTY OR NOLO CONTENDERE, I WILL BE GIVING UP THE RIGHTS SET FORTH IN §§ (2) THROUGH (8) ABOVE.

SIGNED _____

ADDRESS _____

CITY _____ ZIP CODE _____

TELEPHONE _____

3. The Informal Hearing Option (Infractions Only)

Some courts encourage you to agree to an informal hearing, without the officer present, on the same day as the arraignment. As we've said before, this is rarely in your best interest. You generally have a better chance of beating a ticket in a formal trial where the officer may well fail to appear. The only times you should agree to an informal hearing are when you're fighting low-fine parking tickets that aren't worth a lot of trouble (since they don't go on your driving record), or when the judge conducting the informal hearings finds people not guilty at least half the time on moving violation charges, in cases called before yours.

hair pin tern

Note: If the judge appears to be encouraging informal trials, make sure he doesn't assume that you want one. All you have to say is "I plead not guilty, Your Honor, and request a trial with the officer present."

If you do decide to have an informal hearing, the procedure is simple; you merely tell your story to the judge. Your best shot at beating a ticket is to testify to facts that legally excuse you of the charge, as opposed to denying that you committed an "element" of the offense. The reason for this is that by agreeing to substitute the officer's copy of the

ticket for his testimony, you have basically admitted to the truth of what's stated on the face of the ticket. For example, if the ticket says you were doing 45 in a 35 mph zone, you stand a better chance of being found not guilty if you establish that 45 mph was a safe speed under the circumstances (road width, traffic, weather, visibility, etc.), rather than by arguing that you were only doing 33 mph. If you disagreed with what was stated on the ticket, you should have insisted on a trial with the officer present so you could have exposed his untruths by cross-examination. On the other hand, when you say that it was safe to go 45 mph, you're dealing with an issue not specifically addressed by the brief information on the face of the ticket, and the judge or commissioner isn't faced with a conflict between your story and the ticket. And since the officer isn't present to contradict you, you may have a decent chance of winning.

People sometimes confuse an informal hearing with "pleading guilty with an explanation." But these are very different procedures. In the informal hearing, you believe you are not guilty, and your explanation (i.e., your defense) shows why. You could be found not guilty, in which case nothing is reported to the DMV, and nothing goes on your driving record. In pleading guilty with explanation, you're basically saying, "Yes, I'm guilty" (and that goes on your DMV record), "but please give me a break on the fine." In actuality, you should have gone to an informal hearing (if not a formal one) and seen whether you couldn't beat the charge altogether. Pleading "guilty with an explanation" is never recommended.

4. "Waiving Time" for Trial-Setting

The law requires that a trial date be set within 45 days from the date of the arraignment.[9] Traffic court judges who are faced with too many trials within this time will try to get you to waive your right to a

---

[9]PC § 1382(c); see also *Arreola v. Municipal Court* (1983) 139 Cal.App.3d 108.

speedy trial. They may ask something like, "Do you waive time for trial?" If you say no, the judge is required to set it within the 45-day period. One reason for not waiving time is that if, on the trial date (usually pretty close to the end of the 45-day limit), you show up and the officer doesn't, it's impossible for the judge to arrange for re-subpoenaing the officer and still have a trial within the 45-day limit. As a result, the judge must dismiss the charge against you. If you do agree to waive time, however, for one of the reasons set out below, the judge can reset the trial for a later date and force you to come in again.[10]

If the trial date is inconvenient for you, tell the judge. She will very likely set a later date. If that later date is more than 45 days off, the judge will require you to waive time as a condition for the delay.

Seasoned trial lawyers often try to get trials delayed and then delayed again. The theory is that if the delay is long enough, memories fade, witnesses die or move away, and police records get routinely destroyed, with the result that the prosecution has a tough time trying to prove its case.[11]

You may also want to postpone the trial if you know when the officer will take a vacation. Many standard-form tickets have a space for the citing officer to fill in his vacation dates. Many officers simply neglect to fill this in, but when they do, it's meant as a signal to the court personnel not to schedule the trial during that period. If at arraignment the court personnel aren't too wide awake, however, and the officer's vacation period is not too far off (two or three months at the most), you might want to ask for a trial date that happens to fall within the officer's vacation period. If the judge doesn't see what you're up to (even if he does, there is nothing he can do, other than refuse your requested date), the judge may agree to the proposed trial date on the condition that you waive time for trial. When the trial comes and the vacationing officer doesn't show, you are in a good position to protest vigorously about how you had to lose a day's pay and drive 25 miles ("which is punishment enough, Your Honor") and request a dismissal "for lack of prosecution."

---

[10]On the other hand, even if you have waived time, some—but not all—judges will dismiss the case "in the interest of justice," since forcing you to appear three times, once for arraignment, and twice for trial, is too much to ask. But this practice is entirely up to the judge.

[11]Don't ever try to beat a traffic ticket by ignoring it for two years, then showing up, posting bail, pleading not guilty and asking for a trial. While it's true that by this time, the officer who ticketed you will have forgotten everything and the record of the ticket, having been routinely destroyed, will be unavailable to refresh his memory, you'll end up losing in the end because:

a. you'll face the misdemeanor charge of failure-to-appear [which is quite serious—see Chapter 7, Section (B)(3)].

b. you might be physically arrested before then on a warrant; and

c. your driver's license might be suspended.

So this is definitely *not* recommended.

D. Requests You Can Make at Arraignment

IN CERTAIN SITUATIONS, there are issues you should raise at arraignment, in order to protect your rights.

1. Requests You Can Make Before Pleading Not Guilty

In cases in which you've received a ticket as the result of an accident, and in photo-radar cases, you may wish to seek dismissal of the case even before pleading guilty, if the prosecution has not filed the proper documents.

a. Demanding That a "Verified Complaint" Be Filed

Now let's look at a variety of situations in which a "verified complaint" must be filed.

i. Citations Issued as the Result of an Accident

- *Where a "Notice of Violation" is Issued*

In every criminal case, including traffic infraction cases, a document called a "complaint" (or its legal equivalent, which contains the charges against you) must be filed with the court by the district attorney.[12] In most traffic cases, this requirement is deemed fulfilled by the filing of the Notice to Appear signed under penalty of perjury by the officer who cited you [VC § 40513(b)]. There is one major exception to this rule, however. This is where you've been issued a citation following an accident in which you're involved, but the officer didn't observe the violation. In this situation, it's to your advantage to slow things down (perhaps permanently), by insisting that the district attorney take the time and trouble to file a formal complaint in these cases.

---

[12]PC § 949. See also VC § 40513, indicating when a Notice to Appear is the legal equivalent of a complaint.

If an officer wishes to charge you with an offense, he can legally do so only by giving you a type of ticket called a "Notice of Violation." (Many officers mistakenly use a "Notice to Appear" form; we address this further below.) When a Notice of Violation is issued after an accident by an officer who didn't witness the accident [see Chapter 2, Section D(2)], a formal written complaint must be prepared, signed and filed by the district attorney's office if you do anything other than plead guilty. This is specifically required by VC § 40603. In practice, this is almost never done, so that no case has been legally filed. If you are in this category (i.e., you were cited with a Notice of Violation after an accident that the officer didn't see first hand, and no complaint has been filed), simply say the following to the judge you enter your not-guilty plea:

"Your Honor, the Notice of Violation indicates that it was issued as the result of an accident not observed by the officer, and § 40603 of the Vehicle Code requires that a verified complaint be issued before the court can proceed further—unlike the case with a Notice to Appear on a violation observed by the officer. The court, therefore, has no jurisdiction to proceed."

The judge should then order that no further proceedings occur. If not, simply plead not guilty. Later, at trial, you can still argue (if the officer or necessary witnesses appear) that the court has no jurisdiction in the absence of the complaint required by VC § 40603.

- *Where a "Notice to Appear" is Issued*

Unfortunately, in many accident cases unwitnessed by the police, the police improperly mail the wrong form—a Notice to Appear (the form used for regular violations the officer observes, with a place for your signature)—several days or weeks after the accident. You can tell it's the wrong form if it has a place on it for your signature, and it's obviously unsigned by you. Often the officer will write the word "mailed" or "accident" or "complaint to be filed" in the space where your signature should be. This practice, though used by many police departments, is illegal (funny how obedience to the law seems to apply only to you), according to a published 1976 opinion of the California Attorney General.[13] Since it isn't the proper legal form, it isn't the legal equivalent of a complaint, under VC § 40513(b), and a complaint still must be filed.

Should this happen in your case, you will have to prepare a written objection called a "demurrer," in order to preserve your rights. (We show you how to do this later in this section.) When your case is called, you should state:

"Your Honor, rather than entering a plea, I would like to file a demurrer with the court at this time on the basis that a Notice to Appear is not a legal substitute for a complaint in an accident case such as mine. According to Penal Code Section 1003, a demurrer can be filed at arraignment, and so I would like to do that now."

You then hand your papers to the clerk. The judge may ask you if you've served a copy on the district attorney. Your reply should be:

"No, Your Honor. Section 1003 seems to require the demurrer be presented, and served on the prosecutor, at arraignment only."

If there's no prosecutor there (usually there isn't in traffic court), say:

"Since there is no prosecutor here, I believe the district attorney's office has impliedly given up the right to service."

If a prosecutor is present, hand her a copy of your papers. Then, you should say:

"Your Honor, Penal Code Section 1006 requires that the demurrer be heard immediately."

Even though this is true, the judge will probably set a hearing on it for another time, and may also

require you to provide the district attorney's office with a copy.

When you do get a court hearing on your demurrer, you should say:

"Your Honor, the basis of this demurrer is that it's apparent from any lack of signature on the Notice to Appear (or the word "mailed" or "a accident" in the place for your signature) that it was issued in a situation where a completely different form is required, a Notice of Violation, under Vehicle Code Section 40600, and that a verified complaint is required for the matter to proceed. According to an attorney general opinion this is illegal and such a Notice to Appear is not a legal substitute for a complaint."

If the judge rules against you, plead not guilty. If the judge agrees, though, the district attorney might file a verified complaint. However, district attorneys' offices often will neglect to do so even then.

Another rational and perhaps even more effective way to deal with an unsigned citation issued as the result of accident—whether called a Notice to Appear or a Notice of Violation—is to ignore it. Since you didn't sign it, you never promised to appear in court. Of course, a warrant may be issued for your arrest (or your driver's license suspended), perhaps after being spit out by a computer unaware your citation was never signed. If this happens and you're arrested, you can sue the county. On the other hand, some courts do properly computer-code these citations as "unsigned" and this may not happen. If no actual complaint is issued for a year, the statute of limitations will have expired.

A sample demurrer follows:

---

[13]56 Ops. Cal.Atty.Gen. 355 (1976).

David W. Brown
1201 Ninth Street
Monterey, CA 93940
Tel: (408) 555-1234
Defendant in Pro Per

MUNICIPAL COURT OF CALIFORNIA, COUNTY OF MONTEREY
MONTEREY DIVISION

THE PEOPLE OF THE STATE
OF CALIFORNIA,

          Plaintiff,

  -vs-

DAVID W. BROWN,

          Defendant.

Case No. A1234567

DEMURRER TO
"NOTICE TO APPEAR";
POINTS AND AUTHORITIES

[Penal Code § 1004(2)]

Defendant hereby demurs, pursuant to PC § 1004(2), to the Notice to Appear herein, on the ground that it does not conform to the provisions of PC §§ 950 and 952, or VC § 40513. As the Notice to Appear indicates on its face that it was not issued at the scene, pursuant to VC §§ 40500 et seq, it is not a statutory substitute for a complaint under § 40513(b).

WHEREFORE, defendant prays that this demurrer be sustained.

DATED: March 15, 199__

        DAVID W. BROWN
        Defendant in Pro Per

POINTS AND AUTHORITIES

Statement of Facts

According to the face of the Notice to Appear herein, prosecution of the instant case was initiated following an automobile accident that was not observed by the citing police officer. The officer who later came to the accident scene commenced prosecution herein by the filing of a Notice to Appear unsigned by defendant. The place normally reserved on the Notice to Appear for the defendant's signature does not contain a signature, but rather the officer's notation in the place for signature, indicating the notice was mailed (following an accident) and not presented at the scene. As this Court's records should indicate, a copy of the Notice to Appear was filed with the Court and was mailed to defendant with a demand that he respond to it. No complaint has been filed.

Argument

I.   DEFENDANT'S DEMURRER IS PROPERLY BEFORE THE COURT

Defendant is charged with an infraction. A defendant may demur to a misdemeanor complaint or other accusatory pleading. PC § 1002. This is true as to infractions as well. See PC § 19.7.

Accordingly, unless there exists a statutory provision to the contrary, a criminal complaint or its equivalent is required in a prosecution for an infraction to the same extent it is required in a prosecution for a misdemeanor; thus, a defendant may similarly demur to such a complaint, as permitted by PC §§ 1002 et seq.

Here, the demurrer is authorized under § 1004(2), the ground being failure of the Notice to Appear to comply with PC § 950 or 952.

The demurrer can only be presented at arraignment, the defendant's first appearance, and the statute thus contemplates

III. A NOTICE TO APPEAR, ISSUED IN A DEFENDANT'S ABSENCE, UNSIGNED BY AND MAILED TO HIM, IS NOT A LAWFUL SUBSTITUTE FOR THE COMPLAINT REQUIRED TO INITIATE A MISDEMEANOR OR INFRACTION PROSECUTION.

These proceedings were initiated by the filing in court of what purports to be a Notice to Appear, unsigned by defendant, filled out in his absence subsequent to an automobile accident, and mailed to him. Other than this notice, no complaint or other accusatory pleading was filed.

The procedure erroneously followed by most law enforcement agencies, whereby a Notice to Appear is issued in the defendant's absence and mailed to him following an accident investigation, has no basis in law and is contrary to the scheme set forth in §§ 40500 et seq and 40600 et seq of the California Vehicle Code.

Where the Notice to Appear is properly used in accordance with §§ 40500 et seq, i.e., where the officer has observed the alleged violation and effected a traffic-stop "arrest," it is a proper substitute for a complaint. VC § 40513(b). According to VC § 40513(b), however, that is true only where a properly-used Notice to Appear has been prepared on "a form approved by the Judicial Council." Again, this occurs only where the officer has observed the violation and obtained a written promise to appear from the accused. It is not authorized by the Judicial Council for a use the law does not intend.

Where the officer has not observed the violation, but has reason to believe, after observing the aftermath of a vehicle collision, that a driver has committed a violation, he or she may only issue a Notice of Violation, which when filed must still be followed by the filing of a complaint (unless the defendant pleads guilty).VC §§ 40600-40603.

---

service on the prosecutor only if one is present at arraignment. PC § 1003. (Where the prosecution chooses not to appear, then such service is waived by the prosecution.) The demurrer then "must be heard immediately," with a continuance granted only for "exceptional cause" as entered in the minutes. PC § 1006.

II. INTRODUCTION

Only when a police officer observes a violation of a misdemeanor (or an infraction), is he or she empowered to make an arrest.* Pursuant to VC §§ 40500 et seq, the officer then issues a Notice to Appear, which the defendant signs and promises to appear in court; the officer then releases the defendant. Where this form is properly used for the purpose intended, VC § 40513(b) allows it to be the legal substitute for a complaint.

Where an officer believes, based on his or her investigation of a traffic accident, that a violation he or she did not observe occurred, the officer may not use a Notice to Appear. Instead, a "Notice of Violation" can be issued by the officer. VC §§ 40600 et seq. A Notice of Violation does not substitute for a complaint, because under § 40603, the prosecution must file a verified complaint for jurisdiction to attach, unless a guilty or nolo contendere plea is entered.

Here a Notice to Appear was misused, since the officer did not observe the accident or alleged violation. A Notice to Appear is a statutory substitute for a complaint only where it is used as intended. VC § 40513(b). Therefore, defendant has not been legally charged with an offense.

---

*For the purpose of apprehending traffic violators, such an "arrest" occurs when the officer merely pulls over the suspect on the highway. People v. Superior Court (1972) 7 Cal.3d 186, 200.

The distinction between a § 40500 Notice to Appear and a § 40600 Notice of Violation is substantial. Though no published appellate decision analyzes this distinction, an excellent treatise on the distinction can be found in 59 Ops. Cal.Atty.Gen. 355 (1976). Following a detailed analysis of the three ways (Notice to Appear, Notice of Violation, and verified complaint) by which misdemeanor or infraction prosecutions can be initiated, the writer concluded that "[t]he terms Notice of Violation and Notice to Appear, as contained in Vehicle Code section 40600, are not synonymous" and that the mailing of a Notice to Appear to a driver "after an accident investigation does not fully comply with legal requirements." Id. at 356. The opinion notes at 359 that "the dissimilarities between the two citation procedures are basic and prevent the substitution of one notice for the other," listing the dissimilarities as follows:

(1) There can be no arrest in order for a Notice of Violation to issue; an arrest is required before a Notice to Appear can issue.

(2) Before a Notice of Violation can issue, the issuing peace officer must have completed a 40-hour POST-approved accident investigation course; there is no such training requirement before a Notice to Appear can issue.

(3) Notices of violation are used only in connection with traffic accident investigations; notices to appear are not so limited.

(4) Notices of violation are used only when the offense was not committed in a peace officer's presence; notices to appear are not similarly restricted.

(5) Notices of violation are not required to be signed by the suspect and no crime is committed if the suspect fails to appear as directed in the notice; notices to appear must be signed by the suspect and failure to appear as directed is a misdemeanor.

(6) Failure to appear after being issued a notice of violation will not result in arrest until the suspect is given a second opportunity to voluntarily appear; failure to appear after signing a Notice to Appear can result in the suspect's arrest without further notice.

Finally, the opinion, at 362, deals with the question as to whether a mailed Notice to Appear following an accident investigation may be used in lieu of the notice-of-violation procedure, to accident violations not observed by the officer. The opinion states in this regard:

Your specific question is whether the following procedure would be authorized under present law. The investigating officer prepares his report after making an investigation of a traffic accident to which Section 40600 applies. The report may conclude that there is a probable cause to believe a suspect has committed one of the applicable misdemeanors or violated one of the applicable ordinances. The report is submitted for administrative review.

If the reviewer concludes there is probable cause, your question is whether a Notice to Appear must be used as the accusatory complaint. Could the suspect be mailed the Notice to Appear using a copy thereof as an accusatory complaint?

In light of our analysis we conclude that this procedure is not authorized. In order to use the Vehicle Code Notice to Appear as a complaint, Section 40513 subdivision (a) requires that it must first have been prepared, delivered and filed with the court. Section 40500 subdivision (a) outlines the circumstances under which a Notice to Appear is prepared, i.e., whenever a person is arrested for a non-felony Vehicle Code or local ordinance violation and he is not immediately taken before a magistrate. Section 40504 subdivision (a) outlines the circumstances under which a Notice to Appear is delivered, i.e., it is delivered to the arrested person and, when the arrested person signs the notice, he is released from custody. Section 40506 refers to the notice being filed with the court and with the policy agency involved by the arresting officer. Thus, the statutory scheme creating the Notice to Appear contemplates its use even as a complaint only when there has been a prior arrest.

IV. EVEN IF THE MAILED NOTICE TO APPEAR IS TREATED AS A PROPERLY-ISSUED NOTICE OF VIOLATION UNDER VEHICLE CODE SECTION 40600, IT IS STILL NOT A LAWFUL SUBSTITUTE FOR A COMPLAINT.

Granting that a Notice of Violation pursuant to §§ 40600 et seq should have been used instead of a Notice to Appear, and ignoring the officer's failure to deliver the notice at the accident scene, as required by § 40603, let us hypothetically treat the mailed Notice to Appear as a properly-issued Notice of Violation. Is this Notice of Violation a lawful substitute for a complaint? Unless the defendant pleads guilty or nolo contendere to it, the answer is no, because § 40603 still requires the filing of a verified complaint in such situations, for jurisdiction to attach, when the defendant does something other than plead guilty or nolo contendere.

According to the above-quoted statute, a Notice of Violation is a lawful substitute for a verified complaint only if the defendant pleads guilty or nolo contendere, or waves the filing of a verified complaint in writing. As defendant has done neither of these, the so-called Notice to Appear in the instant case, even if deemed a Notice of Violation, is not a lawful substitute for a complaint. Since a complaint (or legal substitute) is essential for jurisdiction (see PC § 949; VC §§ 40513, 40603; Anger v. Municipal Court (1965) 237 Cal.App.2d 69; Gavin v. Municipal Court (1960) 184 Cal.App.712), the court is without jurisdiction.

CONCLUSION

For the foregoing reasons, the Notice to Appear filed herein is not a lawful substitute for a complaint under VC § 40513(b), because it is not the form the Judicial Council prescribed in the situation where an officer does not observe a violation, but simply investigates an accident. As no actual complaint has been filed, as required by Section 40603 in such "accident" cases, the Court is without jurisdiction to hear the matter.

Dated: March 15, 199_

DAVID W. BROWN
Defendant in Pro Per

ii. Photo-Radar Cases

Another situation in which Notices to Appear are improperly used by police departments, and in which you may be able to use a demurrer to get the case dismissed before even entering a plea, is in a case where "photo-radar" has been used. As we saw in Chapter 4, Section B(2), a radar unit placed in a police vehicle is connected to a camera which photographs the license plate of the offending vehicle, as well as the driver. No police officer pulls you over; instead, a computer-generated Notice to Appear is mailed to the registered owner of the vehicle.

Aside from fighting that sort of ticket on the merits, as discussed in Chapter 4, you may wish to try to nip the ticket in the bud before even pleading not guilty. Although no case law specifically provides for this, some attorneys have successfully beaten such tickets on the ground that, in this situation, a copy of the mailed Notice to Appear is not a legal substitute for a complaint.

Again, the way to attack this lack of a complaint is by filing a demurrer. When your case is called, you should state:

"Your Honor, rather than entering a plea, I would like to file a demurrer with the court at this time on the basis that a Notice to Appear is not a legal substitute for a complaint in a photo-radar case such as mine. According to Penal Code Section 1003, a demurrer can be filed at arraignment, and so I would like to do that now."

You then hand your papers to the clerk. The judge may ask you if you've served a copy on the district attorney. If so, say:

"No, Your Honor. Section 1003 seems to require the demurrer be presented, and served on the prosecutor, at arraignment only."

If there's no prosecutor there (usually there isn't in traffic court), say:

"Since there is no prosecutor here, I believe the district attorney's office has impliedly given up the right to service."

If a prosecutor is present, hand her a copy of your papers. Then, you should say:

"Your Honor, Penal Code Section 1006 requires that the demurrer be heard immediately."

Even though this is true, the judge will probably set a hearing on it for another time, and may also require you to provide the district attorney's office with a copy.

When you do get a court hearing on your demurrer, you should say:

"Your Honor, the basis of this demurrer is that it's apparent from the court's file in this case that the supposed Notice to Appear was issued in a situation where only a verified complaint may be used. This is a photo-radar case in which there was no traffic stop, so that the Notice-to-Appear procedure in VC §§ 40500 through 40502 is inapplicable, and no complaint has been filed.

If the judge rules against you, plead not guilty. If the judge agrees, though, the district attorney might file a verified complaint. However, district attorneys' offices often will neglect to do so.

As with unsigned accident citations, you might want to consider ignoring the mailed Notice to Appear. Since you didn't sign it, you never promised to appear in court. Of course, the city may then file a complaint and ask that a warrant be issued for your arrest (or your driver's license suspended), perhaps after being spit out by a computer unaware your citation was never signed. If no actual complaint is issued for a year, the statute of limitations will have expired.

A sample demurrer follows:

Phoebe Photon
123 Main Street
Pasadena, CA 91100
Tel: (818) 555-1234
Defendant in Pro Per

MUNICIPAL COURT OF CALIFORNIA, COUNTY OF LOS ANGELES
PASADENA JUDICIAL DISTRICT

THE PEOPLE OF THE STATE
OF CALIFORNIA,

      Plaintiff,

-vs-

PHOEBE PHOTON,

      Defendant.

Case No. 123456

DEMURRER TO
"NOTICE TO APPEAR"
POINTS AND AUTHORITIES

(Penal Code § 1004(2))

Defendant hereby demurs, pursuant to PC § 1004(2), to the Notice to Appear herein, on the ground that it does not conform to the provisions of PC §§ 950 and 952, or VC § 40513. As the Notice to Appear indicates on its face that it was not issued pursuant to an arrest per VC §§ 40500 et seq, it is not a statutory substitute for a complaint under § 40513(b).

WHEREFORE, defendant prays that this demurrer be sustained.

DATED: March 15, 199_

PHOEBE PHOTON
Defendant in Pro Per

POINTS AND AUTHORITIES

Statement of Facts

This is a "photo-radar" speeding case. The defendant was mailed a copy of a purported "Notice to Appear." This form is not approved by the Judicial Council for this purpose. It is to be used only in conjunction with an "arrest" in which the citing officer apprehends the alleged violator. An officer's name is typed or machine-printed on the form, and defendant's signature does not appear in the promise-to-appear position of the form. No complaint has been filed.

ARGUMENT

I.   DEFENDANT'S DEMURRER IS PROPERLY BEFORE THE COURT

[This part is identical to Part I of the previous demurrer to be used in accident cases.]

II. INTRODUCTION

Only when a police officer observes a violation of a misdemeanor (or an infraction) is he or she empowered to make an arrest.* Pursuant to VC §§ 40500 et seq, the officer then issues a Notice to Appear, which the defendant signs and promises to appear in court; the officer then releases the defendant. Only where this form is used as intended by the Judicial Council does VC § 40513(b) provide that it is a legal substitute for a complaint. VC § 40513(b) allows it to be the legal substitute for a complaint.

The prosecution here was not initiated by a lawfully-issued Notice to Appear presented to or signed by defendant. Instead, the matter was commenced by the mailing of a printed notice to

---

*For the purpose of apprehending traffic violators, such an "arrest" occurs when the officer merely pulls over the suspect on the highway. People v. Superior Court (1972) 7 Cal.3d 186, 200.

The Notice to Appear is authorized by § 40500 of the Vehicle Code. It is supposed to be used only where a person is "arrested" for any violation of [the Vehicle] Code not declared to be a felony." The Notice to Appear cannot be used unless there is an arrest in this sense. As an officer generally may arrest a person suspected of having committed a misdemeanor or infraction only when he has observed the offense and the perpetrator, and as a Notice to Appear can be issued only by an officer who has "arrested" the suspected offender, it follows that a Notice to Appear can be issued only when the citing officer has observed the violation and the perpetrator and apprehended the latter.

It is only when the Notice to Appear is properly used in accordance with § 40500 et seq, on a form intended for that purpose by the Judicial Council, that it is a lawful substitute for a complaint. VC § 40513(b).

The Judicial-Council Notice to Appear form was never intended for use as a citation to be issued in a defendant's absence and mailed to him or her. That form is intended to be filled out by the arresting officer at the scene of a traffic-stop, noncustodial arrest, to be signed by the officer under penalty of perjury, and then to be signed by the defendant as a promise to appear. Only VC §§ 40600 et seq provide for the issuance of such notices after the fact, and then only in accident cases.

In other words, a formal complaint is necessary unless a proper Notice to Appear has been prepared on "a form approved by the Judicial Council." However, the Judicial Council has not promulgated a form to be mailed to the defendant in non-accident cases, for the simple reason that no statute authorizes the

defendant. This procedure is not authorized, and the document is not a lawful substitute for a complaint. Prosecution in the instant case could only have properly initiated either by 1) the filing of a formal complaint, or 2) the issuance to defendant (at the scene, following apprehension by an officer who observed the alleged violator's identity) of a Notice to Appear signed by the officer and on which the defendant promised to appear. Since neither has occurred, the Court is without jurisdiction to hear the case.

III. A NOTICE TO APPEAR, ISSUED IN A DEFENDANT'S ABSENCE, UNSIGNED BY AND MAILED TO HIM, IS NOT A LAWFUL SUBSTITUTE FOR THE COMPLAINT REQUIRED TO INITIATE A MISDEMEANOR OR INFRACTION PROSECUTION.

There are two ways for a police officer to initiate a prosecution against a person the officer believes committed a misdemeanor or infraction Vehicle Code violation. The first, and usual, way is to issue a "Notice to Appear" to the motorist who the officer has allegedly observed commit the offense. The officer observes the alleged violation, and the alleged perpetrator, and apprehends that person. The officer then prepares a Notice to Appear, which the alleged violator must sign to obtain his or her release following this type of "arrest" (stated as such in §§ 40500 et seq). The original of the true Notice to Appear, filed with the court, constitutes a lawful substitute for a verified complaint, even in the face of a not-guilty plea. VC § 40513(b).

This method is only intended for the situation where the officer immediately stops and apprehends the alleged violator. The second way, more common for offenses that are not traffic infractions, is to file a complaint on which a warrant is issued by a magistrate for the defendant's arrest.

mailing of any type of violation notice, or Notice to Appear, to the registered owner in photo-radar cases.

The procedure erroneously used here is analogous to the procedure used where an officer mails a citation to a driver following an accident investigation, pursuant to VC §§ 40600 et seq. The analogy is important because the Attorney General has determined that in such cases a mailed "Notice to Appear" is not a lawful substitute for a complaint. An excellent discussion in this regard can be found in 59 Ops. Cal.Atty. Gen. 355 (1976).

Following a detailed analysis of the three ways (Notice to Appear, Notice of Violation, and verified complaint) by which misdemeanor or infraction prosecutions can be initiated, the writer concluded that "[t]he terms 'notice of violation' and 'notice to appear' as contained in VC § 40600 re not synonymous" and that the mailing of a "Notice to Appear" to a driver "does not fully comply with legal requirements." Id. at 356. The opinion concludes that a mailed Notice to Appear, used in a situation for which it was not intended by the Judicial Council (namely other than after an officer apprehends an alleged violator for a violation allegedly observed) is not a lawful substitute for a complaint.

Since a complaint (or legal substitute) is essential for jurisdiction (see PC § 949; VC §§ 40513, 40513, 40603; Anger v. Municipal Court (1965) 237 Cal.App.2d 69; Gavin v. Municipal Court (1960) 184 Cal.App.712)), the court is without jurisdiction.

CONCLUSION

For the foregoing reasons, the notice filed herein is not a lawful substitute for a complaint under VC § 40513(b), because it is not the form the Judicial Council prescribed in the situation where an officer does something other than apprehend the violator and then and there determines his or her identity. As no actual complaint has been filed, the Court is without jurisdiction to hear the matter.

Dated: March 15, 199_

PHOEBE PHOTON
Defendant in Pro Per

2. Requests You Can Make After Pleading Not Guilty

At arraignment, after pleading not guilty, there are certain requests you should make in certain situations:

- Where the offense can be charged as a misdemeanor or infraction (such as failure to appear [VC § 40508(a)] or driving without a valid license [VC § 12500(a)], or where it's your fourth infraction within a year, you can insist it be charged as a misdemeanor where you have a right to a jury trial. **Note:** See cautionary note below (Section a).

- Where you insisted the officer cite you to appear in the court at the county seat (see Chapter 17) and he refused, you should ask that the case be transferred there. If the judge refuses, ask her to set a date for your motion for change of venue.
- Where there have been months of delay before arraignment, you can ask the judge to set a date for your motion to dismiss for violation of your right to a speedy trial.

In any of these situations, you should *briefly* summarize the legal basis for your request. Judges who hear traffic cases are often pretty impatient with defendants who make long statements. A bored, impatient judge might stop you before realizing the valid legal point you're making.

Note: Formal motions and legal arguments are rarely heard at arraignment. [Demurrers of the type mentioned in Section 1(a)(ii) above are supposed to be the only exception.[14]] The only thing you should do at arraignment is plead not guilty, briefly state your request (transfer to county seat, or dismissal), and ask the judge to set a hearing on the matter.

a. Demanding a Jury Trial in Certain Cases

A very few offenses, most notably failure to appear [VC § 40508(a)], driving with an invalid license [VC § 12500(a)], or driving with a license suspended for failure to appear (VC § 14601.1), can be charged as misdemeanors (punishable by up to six months in jail and a $2,600 total fine) or as infractions. Many courts have begun charging these offenses as infractions. The advantage to you is a lower maximum possible penalty; the disadvantage is you have no right to a jury trial.

You do have the right, under PC §§ 17(d)(1) and (2) to "elect to have the case proceed as a misdemeanor" (after having been "informed of [your] rights," which rarely occurs), and to have the matter tried as an infraction, only "with the consent of the defendant." This means that when you are charged with any of these offenses, you can have a jury trial. The advantage is that prosecutors will then be forced to deal with you in order to avoid what is, for them, a low-priority item.

> **Example:** You're charged with violating the Basic Speed Law (VC § 22350), an infraction. Since you waited too long to respond to the citation, you're also charged with failure to appear [VC § 40508(a)]. Because the system wants to keep the case in high-volume, low-cost traffic court, the failure-to-appear is charged as an infraction. You can insist it be charged as a misdemeanor and demand a jury trial (and even a public defender, if your income is low enough). The case will then be assigned to a real judge (not a "commissioner" or "referee") and a prosecutor, and set for a "pretrial conference." Once you tell them you'll insist on your right to a jury trial, the judge and prosecutor may offer to drop one charge if you'll plead guilty to the other for a promised low fine.

---

[14]PC §§ 1003, 1006.

Warning: When you raise the stakes this way, you also risk being sentenced to jail, if found guilty, by a vindictive judge angry at you for bogging down the system this way. On the other hand, few judges are really this bad, and county jails are usually so filled to capacity so as to discourage judges for jailing people for first-offense minor misdemeanors such as these. The choice is up to you.

As we also saw in Chapter 7, Section B(5), VC § 40000.28 and the case of *People v. Shults* (1978) 87 Cal.App.3d 101 allow you to insist that a fourth infraction committed in a year be charged as a misdemeanor. When you plead guilty, and claim you've had at least three other infraction convictions based on three prior offenses that occurred within a year of your receiving this fourth ticket, the judge is required to hold a hearing to determine if you've really had the three prior convictions. At such a hearing, a certified copy of your DMV print-out should suffice for this purpose.

Again, though, this can be dangerous. A judge who has just spent two days on a jury trial for your fourth speeding offense in a year may convince himself that a few days or months in jail would slow you down.

b. Demanding Transfer to the County Seat

As we discuss in Chapter 17, a person being cited for a Vehicle Code offense often has the right to demand of the officer writing the ticket that they go to court at the "county seat" rather than at some other court nearer to where the offense supposedly occurred. And almost all police officers—with the exception of Highway Patrol officers—either are ignorant of that law or simply refuse to follow it.

When this happens, the person cited will probably have to make a formal motion—discussed in Section E (2) of this chapter—to transfer the case to the county seat court.

Note: You have a right to have this motion granted *only* if you demanded the county seat from the officer when you were stopped. To preserve your right to make such a motion, you must demand

transfer at arraignment.[15] This would be done by saying something like this:

"Your Honor, I plead not guilty, and, pursuant to Penal Code Section 1462.2 and Vehicle Code Section 40502(b), I request that this case be transferred to the county seat. I live/work closer to the county seat than to this court, and I made a timely demand of the officer for the county seat, which he refused. If Your Honor won't transfer it now, I request the matter be set for my motion for change of venue."

The judge should then either order the case transferred or set a date for such a motion. If the judge sets a motion hearing for the same day as the trial, but a few minutes before, he's setting you up to deny the motion and find you guilty. Ask him to set it several weeks beforehand. If he won't, then you probably should disqualify that judge from hearing your motion, by filing a peremptory challenge. [See Chapter 11, Section C(3).]

road hog.

c. Requesting a Hearing on a Motion to Dismiss for Lack of a Speedy Trial

Occasionally, in courts in larger cities, court clerks faced with crowded dockets will refuse for months to allow a person charged with a traffic offense to attend arraignment. This is often because the law requires that you be given a trial date no later than

---

[15]PC § 1462.2.

45 days after the arraignment and not-guilty plea, unless you "waive time" for trial.[16] In places where the system is so bogged down, clerks would rather delay the date your statutory right to a speedy trial begins.

However, if this forced waiting goes on for too long, the clerk is still denying you a speedy trial. Under the state and federal constitutions, you have a right to a speedy trial even though no clear-cut law applies to require trial within a certain number of days. This means that if any sort of lengthy "pre-arraignment" delay occurs, and your ability to defend your case suffers as a result, you have a right, after arraignment, to make a motion to dismiss the case on the basis that your constitutional right to a speedy trial was violated before arraignment.

This motion is proper in some cases, even where you've failed to appear in response to a ticket, if the system has taken no action against you for over a year.[17]

We cover this subject in more detail in Section E of this chapter. So, if at arraignment you think you should make a motion to dismiss on the basis that your right to a speedy trial was denied because of pre-arraignment delay, you should ask the judge to set a date for hearing on your motion.

d. Other Motions

The above is certainly not a complete list of the types of technical issues you can raise at and/or after arraignment. Pretrial motions in criminal cases are often brought on numerous other grounds, such as motions to suppress evidence based on an unlawful search by a police officer.[18] However, other than those listed above, there are few motions applicable to traffic cases.

E. Motions After Arraignment

IF YOUR REQUEST at arraignment resulted in the judge setting a hearing date on a motion, you will have to prepare for the hearing on that motion. Also, if the judge refused to set a hearing date, or otherwise brushed you aside without setting a hearing, you will have to schedule such a hearing through the court clerk.

Most courts hear such motions one or two days during the week on what's called a "law-and-motion calendar." Almost all such motions deal with criminal matters more serious than traffic infractions. Some courts schedule motion hearings in traffic cases during the same period they conduct arraignments. To find out which days motions are heard in traffic cases, call the court clerk. If the person has no idea what you're talking about (which is very likely), ask to speak to a supervisor! Keep going up the ladder until you get results. If this fails, contact the "criminal" court clerk for this information.

Once you get a date and courtroom number for your motion to be heard, you'll have to write them in on the Notice of Motion form you file. Try to prepare the motion papers at least two weeks before the hearing date so that the district (or city) attorney's office won't be able to complain about insufficient time to prepare and respond to the motion.

1. General Rules on Preparing Motions

The best way to tell the judge about the facts and legal reasons why your motions should be granted is

---

[16]PC § 1382(c).

[17]*Serna v. Superior Court* (1985) 40 Cal.3d 239.

[18]See PC § 1538.5.

to put it all in writing in a standard legal format, properly "serve" it on the prosecutor and file it with the court clerk. The standard legal format for this requires all of the following:

- a "Notice of Motion" to tell the prosecutor's office that you're going to have your motion heard at the date, time, and place of arraignment;

- a "Declaration" listing certain facts entitling you to the granting of the motion (e.g., you asked the citing officer to send the ticket to the "county seat," but he refused);

- "Points and Authorities," a fancy name applied to a short legal essay, citing laws or court cases as to why, in light of the facts presented in the Declaration, the judge should grant the motion; and

- a "Proof of Service," on which a person other than you states she mailed a copy of all the above to the prosecutor's office.

All this looks nice if typed double-spaced on line-numbered legal paper, as are the samples that follow. You can usually get line-numbered legal paper at any good quality office supply store. But, it's okay to type neatly on ordinary typing paper. After you sign the papers, make two sets of photocopies, one set for yourself, and one for the prosecutor's office. Then have someone else put the copies in a stamped envelope addressed to the Office of the District Attorney nearest to the court where your motion will be heard, (or in some cases the office of the City Attorney[19] of the city in which you were ticketed—call the court clerk to find out which), and mail the envelope. This process is called "serving" the papers. You are not allowed to do this for yourself.

The person "serving" your papers must be over 18 and either work or reside in the county in which she mails the letter. When the papers have been mailed, this person must also fill out a Proof of Service, stating under penalty of perjury that she mailed the copies, is over 18 and lives or works in the county where they were mailed.

Once all this is done, you should file the original motion papers and Proof of Service with the traffic court clerk. Do this at least two weeks before the arraignment date. You may get a few strange looks from clerks who aren't used to people filing motion papers in traffic cases. If so, be firm and insist the paper be accepted.

Common Sense Note: Most judges are very comfortable dealing with attorneys and very uncomfortable when facing a non-lawyer who makes legal arguments. In the following pages we offer guidelines, suggestions and sample legal documentation, for the purpose of allowing you to advance your legal rights without the need for a lawyer. The judge may react to your presentation in any number of ways, from hostile questioning about fine points of law, to bored indifference, to complete interest. Obviously we can't predict how your judge will react. The point is, don't worry if things go awry when you appear before the court on your own behalf. The fault is not necessarily in you or in this book. Just keep plugging ahead the best you can.

Now, let's see how to prepare the papers that are necessary for each kind of motion.

---

[19]In some cities, most notably Los Angeles, the offense is prosecuted by the City Attorney for the city in which you were ticketed. This is almost always true for city ordinance (e.g., parking) violations.

✓ CHECKLIST FOR FILING A MOTION
(Follow *all* steps.)

1. ____ Type up a Notice of Motion from the sample we provide, substituting your name, the court's name (municipal or justice court), county, judicial district and courtroom number, your case number and motion date assigned by the arraignment judge or obtained from the clerk.

2. ____ Tailor the Declaration and the Points and Authorities to fit the facts of your case, making sure everything you say in them is true.

3. ____ Don't forget to sign and date them.

4. ____ Type a Proof of Service with the prosecuting agency's address listed, but don't fill it out or sign it.

5. ____ Make *two* sets of photocopies of the above documents.

6. ____ Have an adult friend mail one set of photocopies to the office of the prosecuting agency (district attorney or city attorney), mailing it in the county where she lives or works. Then she should fill out and sign the original of the Proof of Service.

7. ____ Go to the court clerk and file the original of your set of papers (the set with the Proof of Service filled out by your friend). Ask the clerk to "file-stamp" your remaining set of photocopies, so you'll have proof that you filed the originals.

8. ____ When you go to arraignment, remind the judge of your motion and ask for a dismissal (or transfer, depending on the motion), or—if the judge doesn't want to hear the case then and there—for a postponement of the motion hearing to another date.

9. ____ Be prepared to answer any questions the judge may have about what you said in your papers.

---

2. Various Types of Motions

The following motions are the most common types made after pleading not guilty at arraignment. Each one may or may not apply to your particular situation.

a. Motion for a Transfer to the County Seat

As discussed in Chapter 17, Section C, one of the best strategies in fighting a traffic ticket involves getting your case transferred to a different court—the one at the county seat.

Vehicle Code Section 40502(b) requires a citing police officer to list on the ticket as the "place to appear" the court at the county seat, requested by the person getting the ticket. Unfortunately, many local police officers are unaware of this requirement and will refuse to specify the county seat court on the ticket. This means you'll have to go to arraignment at the court the officer specified, and request a "change of venue" to the county seat.

You must request the transfer at arraignment, otherwise you'll lose the right.[20] Also, if you failed to make such a request at the time the officer gave you your ticket, you can't request it for the first time at arraignment.

Preparing the Papers

The papers for your motion to change venue to the county seat should look something like this:

---

[20]PC § 1462.2.

DECLARATION

I, MICHAEL MOVER, declare:

1. I am the Defendant in the above-entitled action.

2. On December 6, 199_, I was driving my vehicle in a westerly direction on California Street in Mountain View when I was stopped by Officer J. Friday of the Mountain View Police Department. Officer Friday got out of his vehicle and indicated his intention to cite me for a speed law violation. I immediately told Officer Friday that I desired to have the court at which I would be directed to appear be the one at the county seat, namely the court at San Jose, pursuant to Section 40502(b) of the Vehicle Code. I informed him that the court at the county seat in San Jose was closer to my principal place of business at 123 Silicon Street, Santa Clara, California, which was and is my principal business address where I am employed as an electronics technician. Officer Friday told me he would not do so because the address of the Palo Alto court was already printed on his citations. He told me to "take it up with the court clerk."

3. I then told Officer Friday that he was required to specify the court as the one in San Jose, and I offered him a photocopy of Vehicle Code Section 40502(b), but he refused to read it, replying, "I already know all I need to know in the Vehicle Code." He then indicated again that he would specify the Palo Alto court as the one at which I should appear.

4. Officer Friday then prepared a traffic citation or Notice to Appear in which the court at which I was directed to appear was, contrary to my repeated requests, the Palo Alto court. I was then handed the citation book so that I could sign the citation and promise to appear.

Michael Mover
950 California Street
Mountain View, CA 94010
Tel: (415) 555-5678

MUNICIPAL COURT OF CALIFORNIA
SANTA CLARA COUNTY JUDICIAL DISTRICT,
PALO ALTO FACILITY

THE PEOPLE OF THE STATE
OF CALIFORNIA,

Plaintiff,

-vs-

MICHAEL MOVER,

Defendant

Case No. A1234567B

NOTICE OF MOTION FOR
CHANGE OF VENUE TO COUNTY
SEAT; DECLARATION; POINTS
AND AUTHORITIES

TO: PLAINTIFF, THE PEOPLE OF THE STATE OF CALIFORNIA, AND TO THE DISTRICT ATTORNEY FOR THE WITHIN-NAMED COUNTY:

PLEASE TAKE NOTICE that on the date set for arraignment herein, January 16, 199_ at 9:00 a.m. in Department 33 of the above-entitled Court at 270 Grant Avenue, Palo Alto, California, Defendant will move the Court for an order transferring the place of trial in this action to the Municipal Court at San Jose, California.

This motion is made on the ground that Defendant, upon having been arrested for the offense charged, requested that the court at which he be directed to appear be specified as the court at the county seat, and that pursuant to § 40502(b) of the Vehicle Code, the said court is therefore the proper court for trial of this action.

This motion is based on the pleadings, records and files in this action, the accompanying Declaration and Points and Authorities, and on oral and documentary evidence to be presented at the hearing on the motion.

DATED: January 2, 199_

MICHAEL MOVER
Defendant in Pro Per

POINTS AND AUTHORITIES

ARGUMENT

I.   WHEN A NOTICE TO APPEAR IS ISSUED BY A PEACE OFFICER FOR
       VIOLATION OF THE VEHICLE CODE, THE OFFICER MUST SPECIFY THE
       PLACE OR APPEARANCE AS THE COURT AT THE COUNTY SEAT, IF SO
       DEMANDED BY THE PERSON CITED.

When a peace officer cites a person for violation of a
Vehicle Code, issuing a Notice to Appear, the place for appearance
is governed by Section 40502 of that Code, which states in
pertinent part:

       § 40502. [Place to Appear] The place specified in the Notice
       to Appear shall be...:

       (b) Upon demand of the person arrested,* before a municipal
       court judge or other magistrate having jurisdiction of the offense
       at the county seat of the county in which the offense is alleged
       to have been committed... [Emphasis added]

Subdivisions (a) and (c) of Section 40502 respectively name
the "nearest or most accessible" magistrate or a "person
authorized to receive a deposit of bail" as other places that may
be specified as the place to appear. With respect to these two
choices, the decision apparently lies within the arresting
officer's discretion. Subdivision (b), however, requires the place
to appear to be the county seat whenever 1) the arrested person's
residence or business address is closer to the county seat than to
the nearest municipal or justice court, and 2) the arrested person
demands that the place to appear be the county seat. In Smith v
Municipal Court (1959) 167 Cal.App.2d 534, 538, the similar
wording of former Section 739(c) of the Vehicle Code was construed

*A person is "arrested" within the meaning of §§ 40500 through 40504 "when
the officer determines that there is probable cause to believe that an offense
has been committed and begins the process of citing the violator to appear in
court. People v. Superior Court (1972) 7 Cal.3d 186, 200, 101 Cal.Rptr. 837.

---

5. I then signed my name on the citation, promising to appear
as directed, and wrote the words: "COUNTY SEAT REQUESTED AND
REFUSED."

I declare under penalty of perjury under the laws of the
State of California that the foregoing is true and correct.

DATED: January 2, 199__

_____
MICHAEL MOVER

The court at the "county seat" is a court located within the city limit of the city in which the seat of government of the county is located. Government Code Section 23600. See also People v. Beltran (1981) 124 Cal.App. 3d 335. In this county, that city is San Jose.

DATED: January 2, 199_

Respectfully submitted,

MICHAEL MOVER
Defendant in Pro Per

---

to require that "[i]f a demand therefore is made by the arrestee, the officer must specify as the place of appearance a municipal court within the judicial district at the county seat or at the demand of the arrestee, before a magistrate in the judicial district..." [Emphasis added]

Whichever court is so demanded is the proper court for trial. Here, defendant requested that the court at the county seat be that place, but the citing officer refused to comply.

II. WHEN THE ARRESTING OFFICER HAS REFUSED TO COMPLY WITH A DEMAND FOR APPEARANCE AT THE COUNTY SEAT COURT, THE ACTION MUST BE TRANSFERRED THERE FROM THE NON-COUNTY-SEAT COURT WHEN SUCH TRANSFER IS REQUESTED AT ARRAIGNMENT.

Section 1462.2 of the Penal Code states that "Except as provided by the Vehicle Code," the proper court for the trial of a misdemeanor is in the judicial district in which the offense is alleged to have occurred. The fact that this section specifically refers to the Vehicle Code shows that the Legislature contemplated provision of Vehicle Code Section 40502 as determining trial venue for Vehicle Code offenses where a Notice to Appear is issued. Section 1462.2 states that when the action is commenced in a court other than the proper court for trial, it may nevertheless be tried there, "unless the defendant, at the time he pleads, request an order transferring the action or proceeding to the proper court." It continues, "If after such request it appears that the action or proceeding was not commenced in the proper court, the court shall order the action or proceeding transferred to the proper court." The proper time for making the motion is therefore immediately following a not-guilty plea at arraignment. In Smith, the court stated that the respondent court "was without discretion to deny the motion to transfer..." [167 Cal.App.2d at 541].

The papers are prepared, served and filed in accordance with the instructions above, in Section 1. Don't forget to prepare a Proof of Service to be signed by the person who mails the papers to the prosecutor's office. See the Motion Checklist in Section E (1) above.

What to Say in Court

At the hearing on your motion, say to the judge:

"I request a change of venue to the municipal (or justice) court at the county seat. I already made this request at arraignment, as required by Penal Code Section 1462.2. The legal basis for my request is stated in my Declaration and Points and Authorities Your Honor has on file."

At this point, the judge should grant your request to transfer the case. If someone from the District Attorney's office is there, she may argue the legal merits of your request. Nevertheless, the law is pretty clear. If the judge refuses to transfer, and insists on a trial in his court, you will have grounds for an appeal if you're eventually found guilty. [See Chapter 16, Section A(4).]

Be sure to follow all the steps outlined in the Motion Checklist appearing in Section E(1).

b. Disqualifying the Trial Judge

One of the least known surprises in California law is that everybody gets one free shot at disqualifying a judge. You don't have to prove that the judge is unfair or biased, you just have to believe it. You might have heard that a particular judge is unfair or rude, sides with police officers over defendants, metes out heavy fines, or worse. If you anticipate that the judge at arraignment will assign your case to such a judge, Section 170.6 of the Code of Civil Procedure allows you to file a "Peremptory Challenge." This is simply a typed statement in which you say you think that the particular judge is "prejudiced," either against you personally or against your "interest."

Although the law refers to this type of written request as a "motion," it does not require a hearing. You just file it with the court clerk prior to trial. [You can also wait and file it just before trial, if the case hasn't been specifically assigned to a particular judge or commissioner before that. See Chapter 12(C)(2)(b).]

```
DEBORAH DEFENDANT
123 Fell St.
San Francisco, CA 94137
(415) 555-1234

Defendant in Pro Per


        MUNICIPAL COURT OF CALIFORNIA, COUNTY OF SAN FRANCISCO
                SAN FRANCISCO JUDICIAL DISTRICT


                                    )
THE PEOPLE OF THE STATE             )    No. A-123456-F
OF CALIFORNIA,                      )
                                    )    PEREMPTORY CHALLENGE
                      Plaintiff,    )    [CCP § 170.6]
vs.                                 )
                                    )
DEBORAH DEFENDANT,                  )
                                    )
                      Defendant.    )
        _____)


I.   DEBORAH DEFENDANT, DECLARE:

     1. I am the defendant in the above-entitled action.

     2. I believe the Hon. Homer D. Hangemhigh, the judge or

commissioner before whom the above-entitled matter is assigned to

or pending before, is prejudiced against my interest, so that I

cannot have a fair trial before such judge or commissioner.

     WHEREFORE Defendant requests, ex parte, per CCP Section

170.6, that the said judge or commissioner be disqualified from

hearing the above-entitled matter.

     I declare under penalty of perjury under the laws of the

State of California that the foregoing is true and correct.

DATED: October 10, 199_


                                    _____
                                    DEBORAH DEFENDANT
```

You should only use this Peremptory Challenge when you're really certain that you do not want to appear before that particular judge or commissioner and you're not worried about getting someone even worse (since you're only allowed one challenge).[21] Also, many judges take a dim view of defendants disqualifying one of their colleagues, and the second

---

[21]Actually, you're only limited to one challenge where you believe the judge is prejudiced but can't prove it. You're entitled to another challenge "for cause" if you can prove a particular judge is prejudiced (for example, he implied that he'd "get you" the next time you come before him). You have to ask for a hearing before another judge for the purpose of determining if the judge is truly prejudiced against you. This type of challenge "for cause" is fairly complicated and beyond the scope of this book. (See CCP § 170.3.)

judge might, perhaps unconsciously, hold this against you.

When you must file the Peremptory Challenge depends on how your case is assigned to a particular judge. If your case is assigned for trial or other hearing to a particular courtroom presided over by a judge you don't want, it's best to file your Declaration as soon as possible afterward.[22]

Simply file the Challenge (filled out with the name of the judge you don't want) with the clerk. You don't have to have a copy mailed to the prosecutor beforehand, and you don't have to prepare a Notice of Motion or Proof of Service.

At this point, your case should be assigned to a different judge.

c. Motion to Dismiss—Long Delay Before Arraignment

If an unusually long amount of time (at least four months)[23] is allowed to pass between the time you were ticketed and your arraignment, and you diligently tried to get a court date earlier, you can make a motion at the arraignment for a dismissal of the charge on the ground that you were unconstitutionally deprived of your right to a "speedy trial." Court clerks in some counties absolutely refuse to begin processing a case, and won't assign you an arraignment date, until you receive a courtesy notice in the mail and bring it to them. If there's a delay of several months in getting this out, an unconstitutional "pre-arraignment delay" will have occurred, and you will be entitled to a dismissal. Also, if you can show in your Declaration that this delay

"prejudiced" (hurt) your case, your chances of getting your case dismissed will be higher, but such a showing is not necessary.

Example: Your Aunt Agatha was riding with you when you were cited, in January, for doing 45 mph in a 35 mph zone. If you'd been able to go to trial in February or March, Aunt Agatha would have been able to testify to your approximate speed, that you were just keeping up with traffic, and that the weather and road conditions made your speed safe. However, various court clerk delays that were not your fault caused your trial to be scheduled for May. Unfortunately, Aunt Agatha moved to her sister's home in Missouri in April and will not be available to testify. Your inability to get the early trial date has therefore hurt your case.

Preparing the Papers

Below is a sample of what the papers for a "Motion to Dismiss" should look like in this situation.

The Declaration should list the pertinent facts relating to the delay, and should be written to truthfully reflect what happened in your case. (We suggest that you use your own words and not copy the example word for word.) Finally, you will have to make at least two sets of copies of the motion papers. A friend of yours will have to fill out and sign the original of a Proof of Service and mail one set of the copies to the district or city attorney's office. Then you'll have to go down to the courthouse and file the set of originals.

---

[22]If your case is assigned to a specific judge at least 10 days before trial, you must file your Challenge five days before trial. (Another time limit that may apply is that the challenge must be filed within 30 days after the case was so assigned.) This is true only if the case is assigned to a particular named judge (not just a numbered courtroom), and that judge's courtroom is not used by other judges. [See *Bouchard v. Insona* (1980) 105 Cal.App.3d 768, 164 Cal.Rptr. 505; *Retes v. Superior Court* (1981) 122 Cal.App.3d 799, 176 Cal.Rptr. 160]. Also, in one-judge courts (such as justice courts), it must be filed within 30 days of your first appearance at arraignment. Otherwise, the Peremptory Challenge can be filed immediately before trial.

[23]See *Rost v. Municipal Court* (1960) 184 Cal.App.2d 507.

DECLARATION

I, PATIENCE FAULTLESS, declare:

1. I am the defendant in the above-entitled action.

2. On January 15, 199_, I was stopped while driving my motor vehicle, and was cited by a police officer for a violation of § 22350 of the Vehicle Code. I was presented a copy of the Notice to Appear in this action by that officer.

3. While so driving, I was accompanied by Mrs. Agatha Aardvark, who would have been able to testify on my behalf to the speed of my vehicle and to the traffic, weather and road conditions at the time.

4. On January 16, 199_, I appeared at the office of the Clerk of the Municipal Court at 2120 Grove St., Berkeley, California, as directed, and requested a court date for arraignment. The deputy clerk to whom I spoke refused to assign me a court date, made a notation on the Notice to Appear that the matter was "Continued to 28 Feb. 199_." I again appeared at the office of the above-mentioned Clerk of the Municipal Court, as directed, and requested a court date for arraignment. A deputy clerk again refused to assign me a court date, made a second notation on the Notice to Appear that the matter was "Continued to April 11, 199_" and told me to come back on that date. She informed me that I would be unable to obtain a court date until I had received a "courtesy notice" in the mail.

5. On April 2, 199_, Mrs. Agatha Aardvark moved permanently to Joplin, Missouri, and will therefore be unable to testify at any trial of the within matter.

PATIENCE FAULTLESS
950 Parker St.
Berkeley, CA 94710
(415) 555-1234

Defendant in Pro Per

MUNICIPAL COURT OF CALIFORNIA, COUNTY OF ALAMEDA
BERKELEY-ALBANY JUDICIAL DISTRICT

THE PEOPLE OF THE STATE) No. B 0025640 D
OF CALIFORNIA,)
          Plaintiff,) NOTICE OF MOTION TO
) DISMISS; DECLARATION;
vs.   ) POINTS AND AUTHORITIES
)
PATIENCE FAULTLESS,)
          Defendant.)

TO: PLAINTIFF, THE PEOPLE OF THE STATE OF CALIFORNIA, AND TO THE DISTRICT ATTORNEY FOR THE WITHIN-NAMED COUNTY:

PLEASE TAKE NOTICE that on the date set for arraignment herein, May 9, 199_, at 9:00 a.m. in Department 2 of the above-entitled Court at 2120 Grove Street, Berkeley, California, Defendant will move the Court for dismissal of the above-entitled action.

This motion is made on the ground that Defendant has been denied a right to a speedy trial under Article I, § 15 of the California Constitution and the Sixth Amendment of the United States Constitution.

This motion is based on the pleadings, records, and files in this action, the accompanying Declaration and Points and Authorities, and on oral and documentary evidence to be presented at the hearing on the motion.

DATED: April 10, 199_

Respectfully submitted,

_____
PATIENCE FAULTLESS
Defendant in Pro Per

POINTS AND AUTHORITIES

ARGUMENT

I. THE CONSTITUTIONAL RIGHT TO A SPEEDY TRIAL IS SELF-EXECUTING AND IS NOT LIMITED OR RESTRICTED BY STATUTE.

Although the various provisions of Penal Code Section 1382 constitute the Legislature's implementation of the constitutional right to speedy trial after arraignment, that implementation does not necessarily encompass all the constitutional protections. The courts have held that the constitutional provision for speedy trial is "self-executing." In Barker v. Municipal Court (1966) 64 Cal.2d 806, the California Supreme Court stated: "It is unnecessary that petitioners, in asserting their constitutional rights to a speedy trial, rely on specific statutory provisions."

Citing Barker, the court in Zimmerman v. Superior Court (1967) 248 Cal.App.2d 56, stated that certain Penal Code Sections (§§ 686, 802, 1050) "are merely 'supplementary to and a construction of' the Constitution [citation omitted]. So, too, are Sections 1381, 1381.5, 1382 and 1389 establishing maximum periods within which defendants must be brought to trial."

In People v. Flores (1968) 262 Cal.App.2d 313, the Court held that "(e)xcessive, unexcused delay is a ground for dismissal of a criminal charge, even though the particular delay is not specifically covered by a statute requiring mandatory dismissal. The defendant...repeatedly insisted upon the prompt disposition of this cause." (In the instant case, defendant did precisely this, but was thwarted by court personnel at every turn.)

---

6. On April 9, 199_, I received a "courtesy notice" in the mail. This was fifty-three (53) days subsequent to my first appearance before a deputy clerk of the Municipal Court.

I declare under penalty of perjury under the laws of the State of California that the foregoing is true and correct.

DATED: April 10, 199_

PATIENCE FAULTLESS

[Note: Even though some earlier California appeals courts say you need to show your ability to defend was hurt by the delay, this is no longer the only factor (see Points and Authorities on next pages). Courts are supposed to consider four factors, including the length of and reasons for the delay, your record of insistence on a speedy trial, and finally, prejudice to your case. In the face of a long delay for no good reason, you might not have to show prejudice. So you should use this motion—making appropriate changes in wording your Declaration and Points and Authorities—even if you can't show that a witness moved away or some other type of "prejudice" to your case.]

II. THE CONSTITUTIONAL RIGHT TO A SPEEDY TRIAL ATTACHES AT THE TIME AN ACCUSED IS STOPPED ON THE HIGHWAY AND CITED FOR A TRAFFIC VIOLATION.

The People will perhaps argue that, even for constitutional purposes, the right to a speedy trial runs only from the date of filing of a criminal complaint. This oft-cited rule, however, is only an example of the general principle that the time begins to run when a person becomes an accused (see Serna v. Superior Court (1985) 40 Cal.3d 239). When an arrest is made pursuant to a warrant, this will always be the case. But virtually all arrests* arising out of traffic violations occur before any complaint is filed.

In the case of In re Mugica (1968) 69 Cal.2d 516, the California Supreme Court stated, "The basic policy underlying the constitutional guarantee to a speedy trial is to protect the accused from having criminal charges pending against him an undue length of time." The interest in not prolonging the pendency of criminal charges requires that such time should begin to run when the defendant is unequivocally informed that a criminal charge will be brought. This is what a Notice to Appear does. It is issued in conjunction with an arrest, and constitutes a statutory substitute for a complaint (Vehicle Code § 40513(b)). This being so, an arraignment within a reasonable time of arrest is still required, even when the accused is not in custody. Therefore, an unreasonable delay between the time of issuance of a Notice to Appear on a traffic violation and the time the accused is allowed

---

* In traffic infraction cases, an arrest occurs when the officer determines there is probable cause to believe that an offense has been committed and begins the process of citing the violator to appear in court. People v. Superior Court (1972) 7 Cal.3d 186, 200.

to appear at arraignment will require dismissal upon the making of a timely motion.

III. A SHOWING OF PREJUDICE CAUSED BY THE DELAY IS NOT REQUIRED.

A three-month delay from the time defendant was cited to the time she was permitted to request arraignment for a traffic citation is not reasonable, and has prejudiced her ability to present her case; a potential witness has moved away. However, such prejudice need not always be shown. Rather, it is only one of four factors that a court must consider.

[Note: Use the above first paragraph, or something similar, only if your case has been hurt by clerk-caused delay.]

The United States Supreme Court in Moore v. Arizona (1973) 414 U.S. 25, 26-27, rejected the requirement of a showing of prejudice to one's defense as a necessary element in reversing a conviction for an unconstitutional abridgment of the Sixth Amendment right to a speedy trial, stating:

> The state court was in fundamental error in its reading of Barker v. Wingo and the standard applied in judging petitioner's speedy trial claim. Barker v. Wingo expressly rejected the notion that an affirmative demonstration of prejudice was necessary to prove a denial of the constitutional right to a speedy trial...
>
> * * * * * *
>
> Moreover, prejudice to a defendant caused by delay in bringing him to trial is not confined to the possible prejudice to his defense in those proceedings. Inordinate delay, may...create anxiety in him, his family, and his friends...(quoting Barker v. Wingo (1972) 407 U.S. 514).

In Barker v. Wingo, supra, the court listed four factors to be considered in evaluating a speedy-trial motion: 1) the length of the delay, 2) the prosecution's justification for it, 3) the defendant's insistence on a speedy trial, and 4) prejudice to

---

defendant's case, a factor not determinative if the other three militate in favor of dismissal.

In Serna v. Superior Court (1985) 40 Cal.3d 239, the California Supreme Court, citing Moore, stated, "The defendant need not establish actual prejudice as a prerequisite to a hearing at which the evidence relevant to this balancing process is heard."

Finally, it makes little difference whether the delay is the fault of court personnel or the prosecution itself. People v. Kerwin (1972) 23 Cal.App.3d 466, 469. Accordingly, the within action should be dismissed.

DATED: April 10, 199_

Respectfully submitted,

PATIENCE FAULTLESS
Defendant in Pro Per

PROOF OF SERVICE

I, JOHN SMITH, declare:

1. I am over the age of eighteen and not a party to the within action.

2. My residence address is 1234 El Monte Ave., Berkeley, California, in the county within which the mailing herein mentioned occurred.

3. On April 25, 199_, I served the within Notice of Motion to Dismiss, Declaration, and Points and Authorities on the plaintiff by placing true copies thereof in a separate sealed envelope, with the postage thereon fully prepaid, in the United States Postal Service mailbox at Berkeley, County of Alameda, California, the said envelope being addressed to:

Office of the District Attorney
County of Alameda
2120 Grove Street
Berkeley, CA

I declare under penalty of perjury under the laws of the State of California that the foregoing is true and correct.

DATED: April 26, 199_

JOHN SMITH

What to Say in Court

When you get to the courtroom, sit down and wait until your case is called. Then step forward. The judge will ask you to enter a plea. Respond with:

"I am making a motion to dismiss for lack of a speedy trial. The legal basis for my request is stated in the Declaration and Points and Authorities that Your Honor has on file, and copies of which have been served on the district (or city) attorney. They indicate that over three months have passed since I was able to get this arraignment date."

After that, you should mention how your case was hurt by the delay, or emphasize that the U.S. Supreme Court in *Moore v. Arizona* and the California Supreme Court in *Serna v. Superior Court* said that a showing of "prejudice" isn't necessary to prevail under a constitutional speedy trial theory. At this point, if someone from the district attorney's office is present, she will probably object. That person may say something like "the time for speedy trial should be counted from the time of arraignment, not from when you were cited." You should respond that the cases you cited in your Points and Authorities deal with a constitutional right to speedy trial beginning from the time of arrest, which for traffic ticket purposes, is when you were ticketed.

If you are fortunate enough to have been assigned a conscientious, intelligent judge, you might just have to answer a few questions relating to your legal theories. If the judge hasn't read the papers, he may quickly go over them, or you may be asked to briefly summarize the legal basis of your motion. Never read directly from your Points and Authorities. It's simply too boring. To prepare yourself, spend an hour or two the night before going over your main points. Be sure you are prepared to state them to the judge succinctly. If you are afraid of forgetting a point and feel more secure with notes, write your principal points on an index card for quick reference. Relax. You are not being judged on your speaking abilities—only on the law.

If the judge grants your motion, your case will be dismissed and you win. If not, he may postpone the hearing on the motion to another date. (If the judge simply denies the motion, he will set a trial date.

d. Motion to Dismiss—Long Delay Before Arrest for Misdemeanor

You can also claim your right to a speedy trial was violated because the police took too long to arrest you after you ignored a ticket. If you ignore a ticket or refuse to pay a fine, you can be charged with a misdemeanor and a warrant can be issued for your arrest. [See Chapter 7, Section B(3).] Fortunately, neither the police nor the prosecutor's office take the trouble to go to your home and arrest you. (It's much easier—and cheaper—to send you threatening notices and have the DMV put a "hold" on your driver's license renewal.) The charge might remain pending for several years, whether your driver's license is suspended or not.

If you haven't been arrested within a year after being charged with failure to appear, you should move for a dismissal on the ground that your right to a speedy trial has been violated. In this case, you do not have to convince the judge that your ability to defend against the charge has been compromised ("prejudiced") because of the delay. If it's been less than a year but more than four months since you were charged with failure to appear, you still might be able to have your case dismissed if you can convincingly show that your ability to defend yourself has been seriously prejudiced by the delay.

Note: When you're finally arrested on an old charge, or voluntarily go to court because the DMV either suspends or won't renew your license until you do (see Chapter 15, Section D), you should make your Motion to Dismiss at your arraignment.

Preparing the Papers

The papers you will have to prepare for this kind of speedy trial motion are very similar to the ones you just saw in the previous example. The Notice of Motion and Proof of Service forms are prepared the same way. The Declaration and Points and Authorities for this kind of motion should look something like this:

POINTS AND AUTHORITIES

I. THE CONSTITUTIONAL RIGHT TO A SPEEDY TRIAL IS SELF-EXECUTING AND IS NOT LIMITED OR RESTRICTED BY A STATUTE

[This section should be the same as part I of the previous points and authorities, excluding the last paragraph.]

II. THE CONSTITUTIONAL RIGHT TO A SPEEDY TRIAL ATTACHES AT THE TIME A PERSON BECOMES AN ACCUSED, AND THE POLICE HAVE AN AFFIRMATIVE DUTY TO SERVE ARREST WARRANTS IN A TIMELY FASHION, WHERE THEY CAN DO SO THROUGH ROUTINE, UNCOMPLICATED INVESTIGATION.

For constitutional purposes, the right to a speedy trial runs from the date of arrest or filing of a criminal complaint. A Notice to Appear, signed by a police officer charging a Vehicle Code violation is the equivalent of a complaint under Vehicle Code Section 40513(b). If the prosecution thereafter makes no serious attempt to physically arrest the defendant on a warrant within a year, after the Notice is filed with the court, that delay is "presumptively prejudicial" to the defendant's right to a speedy trial, and the charges must be dismissed on motion. _Serna v. Superior Court_ (1985) 40 Cal.3d 239. In _Serna_, the court summarized its holding by stating, "delay between the filing of a misdemeanor complaint and the arrest and prosecution of a defendant which exceeds the statutory period of limitation is unreasonable and presumptively prejudicial…" The same standard applies to delay between the filing of a Notice to Appear and trial.

In this case, over a year has elapsed since the Notice to Appear was filed with this court, and since a bench warrant was issued as a result of the failure to appear, the defendant has made no attempt to evade arrest. The defendant has lived at the same address, and has held steady employment at the same business address. The authorities could have easily served the defendant

DECLARATION

I, LANE TURNER, declare:

1. I am the defendant in the above-entitled action.

2. On February 1, 199_ I became aware that a misdemeanor complaint charging me with a violation of Vehicle Code Section 40508(a) had been filed in the above-entitled court on January 2, 199_.

3. Since June 12, 199_ and until the present date, I have regularly resided at 950 Parker Lane, El Cajon, California, the address on file with this court.

4. Since April 3, 199_ and until the present date, I have been employed at 123 Industrial Drive, El Cajon, California, and was there regularly during working hours.

5. I made no attempt to avoid any arrest.

I declare under penalty of perjury under the laws of the State of California that the foregoing is true and correct.

DATED: February 14, 19_

_____ LANE TURNER

[Note: Again, you should make this motion even if you can't show "prejudice" to your case, such as a witness moving away, but your chances of winning will be lower. Adjust this Declaration and your Points and Authorities to reflect your own situation.]

with the arrest warrant at either location but failed to do so. In such circumstances, where the State has failed to fulfill it's affirmative duty to serve its warrants, the court should dismiss the charges. See _People v. Mitchell_ (1972) 8 Cal.3d 114, 104 Cal.Rptr. 348; _Jones v. Superior Court_ (1970) 3 Cal.3d 734, 737, 91 Cal.Rptr. 578, 580.

In _Jones v. Superior Court, supra_, the court found a delay in service of an arrest warrant to be unreasonable The court noted that "there was no evidence that [Jones] attempted to avoid arrest." _Jones, supra_, 3 Cal.3d at p. 738. "He was under no obligation to go to the police station, and his failure to appear cannot justify an otherwise unreasonable delay in apprehending him... Petitioner was not in hiding and his whereabouts could have been discovered by routine, uncomplicated investigation." _Jones, supra_, 3 Cal.3d at p. 741.

Finally, it makes little difference whether the delay is the fault of court personnel or the prosecution itself. _People v. Kerwin_ (1972) 23 Cal.App.3d 466, 469. Accordingly, the within action should be dismissed.

DATED: February 14, 199_

Respectfully submitted,

_____
LANE TURNER
Defendant in Pro Per

Finally, the Proof of Service goes on the last page. It should look like the one at the end of the previous set of speedy-trial motion papers. All these papers are prepared with copies mailed to the prosecutor and the original filed with the court clerk.

What To Say In Court

When your case is called at arraignment, you simply say:

"Your Honor, I plead not guilty and request dismissal for lack of a speedy trial under the rule of Serna v. Superior Court. My Declaration, and Points and Authorities indicate that over a year has elapsed since the complaint was filed, and no attempt has been made to arrest me."

Again, either mention how the delay has hurt your case, or that the _Serna_ case says you don't have to show that it did. It will then be up to the prosecution to explain why they didn't arrest you. Unless they respond with something to the effect that you changed your address and were concealing yourself, the judge should dismiss the case.

Note: If you were arrested, taken to jail, and not released on bail, you would go directly to court for arraignment, without having had time to prepare a written motion. If that happens, you can (and should) make the motion orally at arraignment, remembering to tell the judge about the 1985 California Supreme Court case of _Serna v. Superior Court_. Also, you should ask the judge to let you testify under oath as to how the delay hurt your ability to defend against the charge. If all else fails, ask the judge to reschedule the hearing on your motion for another day.

Summary

The procedures for setting up the motion for hearing at arraignment, and for preparing, filing and serving the papers on the prosecutor are the same as those in the Motion Checklist provided in Section E (1).

e. *Motion to Dismiss—Long Delay After Arraignment*

Another type of "speedy trial" motion for dismissal has to do with delay occurring after arraignment. It should be made if you haven't gone to trial within 45 days after your arraignment and you didn't waive your right to have a trial within that time.

In this case, of course, your arraignment will already have occurred without your having obtained a hearing date from the judge and you will have to obtain such a date from the clerk.

Your motions papers should look something like the ones that follow.

What To Say To the Judge

When your motion is called, and it seems that the judge has read your papers, you probably will only need to respond to any questions asked. There's no use repeating what you've already said. If, however, the judge hasn't read your papers, simply say:

"Your Honor, I'm moving for a dismissal under Penal Code § 1382. More than 45 days have passed since I was arraigned, I never waived time for trial, and I still haven't had a trial."

Unless the prosecutor can show a very good reason for the delay, your case will probably be dismissed.

DANIEL DEFENDANT
950 Parker St.
San Jose, CA 95129
(408) 555-6789

Defendant in Pro Per

MUNICIPAL COURT OF CALIFORNIA, COUNTY OF SANTA CLARA
SANTA CLARA COUNTY JUDICIAL DISTRICT, SAN JOSE BRANCH

THE PEOPLE OF THE STATE		No. A5675675B
OF CALIFORNIA,		
	Plaintiff,	NOTICE OF MOTION TO
		DISMISS FOR LACK OF
vs.		PROSECUTION; DECLARATION;
		POINTS AND AUTHORITIES
DANIEL DEFENDANT,		
	Defendant.	[Penal Code § 1382]

TO: PLAINTIFF, THE PEOPLE OF THE STATE OF CALIFORNIA, AND TO THE DISTRICT ATTORNEY FOR THE WITHIN-NAMED COUNTY:

PLEASE TAKE NOTICE that on August 1, 199_ at 9:00 a.m., in Department 12 of the above-entitled Court at 955 Ruff Drive, San Jose, California, Defendant will move the Court for dismissal of the above-entitled action.

This motion is made on the ground that more than 45 days have elapsed since the arraignment, and that Section 1382 of the Penal Code therefore requires that the action be dismissed.

This motion is based on the pleadings, records, and files in this action, the accompanying Declaration and Points and Authorities, and on oral and documentary evidence to be presented at the hearing on the motion.

DATED: July 17, 199_

_____
DANIEL DEFENDANT
Defendant in Pro Per

POINTS AND AUTHORITIES

Defendant is charged with a violation of the Vehicle Code constituting an infraction. PC § 17 requires that "all provisions of law relating to misdemeanors shall apply to infractions," the only exceptions being that infractions are not triable by a jury, nor is a defendant entitled to the assistance of a court-appointed attorney.

Section 1382(c) of the Penal Code requires that a criminal action must be dismissed "when a defendant in a misdemeanor (and hence also an infraction) case in an inferior court is not brought to trial...within 45 days after his arraignment...unless the defendant requests or consents to a later date." See Arreola v. Municipal Court (1983) 139 Cal.App.3d 108; Beasley v. Municipal Court (1973) 32 Cal.App.3d 108; Castaneda v. Municipal Court (1972) 25 Cal. App.3d 588; Hankla v. Municipal Court (1972) 26 Cal.App.3d 342.

Accordingly, more than 45 days having passed without trial since defendant was arraigned, and defendant not having waived time for trial or caused the delay, the complaint herein must be dismissed.

DATED: July 17, 199_

Respectfully submitted,

_____
DANIEL DEFENDANT
Defendant in Pro Per

DECLARATION

I, DANIEL DEFENDANT, declare:

1. I am the defendant in this action.

2. I was arraigned in Department 8 of the Municipal Court for the Santa Clara County Judicial District (San Jose Branch) on June 2, 1992 and pleaded not guilty to the charges pending against me. The presiding judge, Hon. Timothy Handimafine, set the trial for July 15, 1992 at 2:00 p.m. in Department 9.

3. On July 15, 199_ at 2:00 p.m., I appeared for trial in this action in Department 33 of the said court, Commissioner Raymond Cunningone presiding. The said commissioner informed me that Officer Greg Gettem, who was scheduled to appear as a witness against me was on vacation and that trial would have to be postponed. He continued the trial to August 5, 199_ over my objection.

4. More than 45 days have elapsed since I was arraigned on July 15, 199_ and I have still not had a trial in this action.

5. I have not been responsible for any of the delay herein mentioned, and have not waived time for trial under Section 1382 of the Penal Code.

I declare under penalty of perjury under the laws of the State of California that the foregoing is true and correct.

DATED: July 17, 199_

_____
DANIEL DEFENDANT
Defendant

F.   After Your Motion Is Granted or Denied

AFTER YOUR HEARING on a motion, the judge might give the decision right away, or may want to read the papers and think it over. The decision will either be to "grant" or "deny" the motion.

1.   Denied Motions

If your motion is denied by the judge, you can bring the judge's error to the attention of a higher court in one of two ways. The easier choice is simply to go to trial. If you're found guilty, you can appeal to the superior court appellate division and raise the errors, in the hope of getting your case reversed. One problem with this (especially if you're complaining about having been denied the right to a speedy trial) is that, in addition to showing that the judge was legally wrong in denying your motion, you may also have to show that you were put at a serious disadvantage because of the ruling (for example, that your key witness moved away during the excessive delay). Appeals are also fairly complicated, and the chances of success aren't high.

The alternative is to bring a separate lawsuit, requesting the superior court to order the municipal or justice court to grant your motion.[24] This is called a "mandate" or "prohibition" proceeding, and is fairly complicated. It is only worth the trouble in very serious cases. Entire books have been written about these types of proceedings.[25]

2.   Granted Motions

Obviously, if you win a Motion to Dismiss, it's the end of the case—you win without having to go to trial. If you win a Motion for Transfer to the county seat, prepare to wait. Then prepare to wait some more. If you're lucky, the judge's order to the clerk to transfer the case will baffle and befuddle the clerks, and may cause your case to be delayed for several months. This kind of delay works to your advantage because it increases your chances of eventually winning at trial (memories fade, police officers quit the force or transfer), and maybe even of getting your case dismissed for delay.[26] Still, unless your successful motion was one for dismissal, you'll need to prepare for trial. And that's what the next few chapters are about.

---

[24]You may have noticed that many of the cases cited in the book involve the municipal court, like *Smith v. Municipal Court*, brought against a municipal court after an incorrect ruling on a motion.

[25]See *Witkin, California Procedure* (3d Ed.) p. 628 et seq. A particularly helpful set of books is produced by "CEB" (Continuing Education of the Bar). Ask the law librarian how to find the latest CEB books on bringing writs of mandate or writs of prohibition.

---

[26]The *Fajardo* case cited in footnote 14 of Chapter 17 was won on a speedy-trial motion following a 1-1/2-year delay by the Santa Clara County District Attorney in getting the case transferred out of Palo Alto to the county seat at San Jose.

11

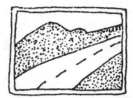

PREPARING FOR TRIAL

IN THIS CHAPTER we tell you how to prepare for a formal trial with the officer present. This is the type of proceeding you think of when you hear the word trial, where evidence is presented by both sides and a judge or jury decides who should prevail. Other types of proceedings such as "informal hearings" and "trials by declaration," which don't involve the give and take of an adversarial proceeding in a courtroom, are covered in Chapters 9 and 10.

A.   Overview of Formal Infraction Trial With Officer Present

AS WE'VE STATED BEFORE, in most cases where you choose to contest your infraction ticket, you should insist on a formal trial with the officer present. By doing so, you get the advantages of being able to challenge the officer's assertions in court, and most importantly, you gain the very real possibility that the officer will not show up to testify against you, and your case will be dismissed. Before we tell you to how to prepare for this kind of trial, it will be helpful to get an overview of the entire process.

A trial for an infraction is held in a municipal court or justice court with a judge, "commissioner" or "traffic referee" presiding. You are notified where and when to appear. Be on time. When your case is called, you (and your witnesses, if any) and the officer walk up behind the table, raise your right hand and are "sworn in." There is usually no prose-cutor. The officer tells his story first. His job is to testify to facts that establish all the required ele-ments of the case. After he's finished, you have an opportunity to cross-examine him. You can ask him questions on matters he has testified to, and on new matters that might help you establish a defense (e.g.,

to establish the excellent weather and visibility in a Basic Speed Law case). Don't argue with him.

After you finish cross-examining, you get your turn to explain what happened. You will probably want to contradict the officer's testimony by estab-lishing other facts which tend to disprove one or more elements of the offense. You may also want to establish facts which constitute a defense even if everything the officer said was true. Some judges will then give the officer a chance to cross-examine you.

After all the testimony has been given (including that of witnesses) the judge usually gives the deci-sion. Some judges will instead try to "take the case under advisement," with your permission. If the judge finds you guilty, she will usually, at the same time, tell you what the fine will be. (You can, how-ever, insist on the right to be sentenced between six hours and five days later. See Chapter 14, Section A.)

There are several variations to this scenario. For example, a few courts expect the officer, you, and any witnesses, to testify from the witness stand next to the judge's bench. This may seem like a small matter, but you'd be surprised how many people who are capable of doing a good job in the some-what relaxed atmosphere behind a table, stumble, stutter, and mumble incoherently when they must speak from a witness stand. Often people who will use notes when standing behind a table will aban-don them when testifying from a witness stand, thinking somehow it's impermissible. This is a mis-take. Nobody cares whether you use notes. In fact, you're probably a lot better off using them, thus making sure you don't omit important details. The judge may even be impressed that you are so well organized.

In some places minor traffic cases are still prose-cuted by bored assistant district or city attorneys, but in most courts, the police officer prosecutes the case himself merely by testifying. Finally, trials for misdemeanor violations are almost always very "formal." They will include a court reporter, a prosecuting attorney, a witness stand, and a jury, unless you specifically "waive" (give up) those rights. [See Chapter 13, Section (A).]

B. Putting Your Case Together

MOST PEOPLE WHO DEFEND themselves in traffic court think that all they need to do is tell a good story to the judge and they will be found not guilty. They couldn't be more wrong. Although it is true in theory that the "burden of proof" in a traffic case is on the police officer (or assistant district attorney), in practice almost everything a police officer says is believed, and you have the heavy burden of proving him wrong.[1] Your job is made even more difficult by the fact that police officers are very skilled at giving courtroom testimony and at stretching the truth when they have to.

To overcome these difficulties it's important that you be well prepared ahead of trial. This chapter will show you how to prepare for the two most important things you must do at trial. These are:

1. Put on a very convincing display using your own testimony and other evidence to raise a "reasonable doubt" about whether you are guilty. Depending on the situation, you may have to prepare notes, research laws, take pictures on the scene, bring witnesses and practice giving your own testimony beforehand; and

2. Show, by cross-examining the officer, that his story raises some doubts. To do this, you will have to learn how to cross-examine.

1. Gathering Your Notes and Research

The first step in preparing for your trial is to write down everything you can remember about the traffic violation. It's best to do this while it's still fresh in your memory, preferably as soon as you or the officer leaves the scene or as soon thereafter as possible.[2] (See Chapter 17, Section E.) You may also want to take pictures of the scene from different angles and locations, if it's relevant to your case. In Chapters 4 through 8, we showed you how to figure out the elements of your violation and determine your best defense. Try especially hard to remember the details of those facts which relate to your defense.

2. Diagrams, Maps and Pictures

Diagrams or maps of the place where you allegedly committed the violation are always useful, particularly in speeding cases. Many officers use diagrams, and some ticket formbooks are even printed with a little intersection for the officer to fill in. If you use a diagram, you'll be better equipped to illustrate inaccuracies in the officer's testimony. In radar cases,

---

[1]The only time the so-called "presumption of innocence" really works is when the officer doesn't show and can't prove you guilty. The charges are then usually dismissed.

[2]Of course, we realize that many readers will only be reading this book long after the fact of the ticket being given. If you want to be better prepared in the event you receive a ticket in the future, read Chapter 17.

you can show how the radar beam might have intercepted targets other than your vehicle. Where radar wasn't used, you can indicate how the officer's vehicle overtook yours at a higher speed. In defending against traffic signal and stop sign violations you can point to the place where the green light turned yellow or where you stopped at the sign. For turning violations you can show how far away the oncoming or cross traffic was when you made your turn.

Your diagram should include the intersection, stop signs or signals, dividers, crosswalks, limit lines and the location of parked vehicles, and should indicate the approximate widths of the streets and lanes. The locations of moving vehicles (yours, the officer's, and maybe of oncoming or cross traffic) are indicated either with movable markers (cut out of colored paper or cardboard) or by drawing an arrow with a felt-tipped pen as you testify.[3] Here's a sample diagram of an intersection:

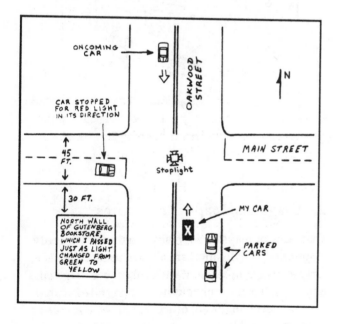

In speed violations where you were paced by the officer over a long stretch, a diagram of the road should show intersections, familiar buildings or

other landmarks, and should indicate the distance traveled between the places where you first saw him and he stopped you.

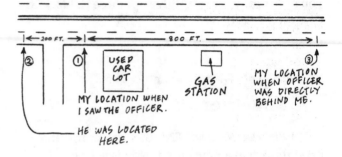

During your testimony, you'll be pointing out the various things you observed about the location and the movements you made. When you come to the place in your testimony where you have a picture of the actual scene, stop and show the picture to the judge.

If nothing else, your manner of presentation of maps and pictures will suggest that you're prepared and sure of yourself.

3. Preparing Your Witnesses

You have the right to bring as a witness anyone who was present and observed the situation in which you allegedly committed a violation. This will usually be someone who was in the car with you.

Before you go to trial, ask your potential witness to tell you her version of what happened. Then go over your version of the facts to make sure you won't be contradicting each other. This does not mean your witness should lie to adjust her story to fit yours. However, if your stories are too far apart, you probably shouldn't ask this person to testify. There is nothing wrong with going over testimony with your potential witness. Attorneys would never go to court without first preparing their witnesses.

Instruct your witness on how the testimony should be organized and emphasized. Acquaint

---

[3]Some courtrooms have chalk boards or large pads of drawing paper you can use, but don't count on it.

your witness with the various elements of the case and your defense. Her testimony should not duplicate yours word for word, but should support the parts of it to which both of you can truthfully testify. Inform your witness that there's a slight possibility (especially if a prosecutor is handling the case) that she will be asked to step outside the courtroom when you testify, in order to prevent her from adjusting her testimony to be consistent with yours. (You also have the right to insist on this procedure when there are two or more prosecution witnesses to testify against you.)

Warn your witness to answer truthfully if she's asked at trial whether she discussed the testimony with you in advance. Experienced prosecutors use this question to trick an inexperienced witness into telling an obvious lie so as to suggest the witness was lying all along.

Finally, instruct your witness to tell the truth even if it appears that her testimony will hurt your case. Then, if the prosecutor asks her what you told her to say, she can truthfully say that you said "tell the truth, even if it hurts."

4. Subpoenaing Witnesses

A "subpoena" is a document which requires a witness to appear in court at the time and place of your trial. Failure to appear can result in arrest and jail or fine for contempt of court.

There are two situations where you may want to "subpoena" a witness: 1) if a witness wants to testify on your behalf but needs to be excused from work or school, or 2) if the potential testimony of a person who doesn't want to testify is absolutely essential to winning your case.

If an unwilling witness's testimony isn't absolutely essential, you probably shouldn't subpoena her unless her testimony is crucial and you're sure she won't lie even if annoyed with you for dragging her into court. Why? You don't want to be stuck with a "hostile witness" who will delight in getting revenge by damaging your case.

To have the court issue a subpoena, go to the clerk as far ahead of time as possible, preferably two to three weeks before your trial date, and ask that a subpoena be issued. Give the clerk your case name (*People v. Your Name*), case number, your scheduled trial date and courtroom number, and the name and address of the person(s) you're having subpoenaed. The clerk may prepare the subpoena, or may simply hand you a blank form on which to fill in the appropriate information. After the information is placed on the subpoena, the clerk should "issue" it by putting the court's seal on it and giving it to you. A sample subpoena is shown on the next page.

There is another kind of subpoena besides a regular subpoena—a "subpoena duces tecum." The subpoena duces tecum orders the witness not only to appear in court, but also to bring certain papers, books, items, or other type of evidence along. The same subpoena form is used for this as for a regular subpoena, with a box next to the words "DUCES TECUM" checked. For a subpoena duces tecum, you will also need to indicate on a separate declaration what items you want the subpoenaed person to bring, and why it's necessary to subpoena the items. A sample declaration follows.

Note on "Serving" Your Subpoena: The subpoena or subpoena duces tecum must be "served" on the person subpoenaed. This is done by any person over 18, other than you. (A defendant cannot serve a subpoena in her own case.) You can even insist that a police agency—which has jurisdiction over the area in which the subpoena is to be served—serve the subpoena. For unincorporated areas of a county, that's the sheriff, and for cities, it's that city's police department. This must be done without charge (PC § 1328). To do this, you must mail the original and a copy of the subpoena to the police department, with instructions to serve the copy at the address you give, and to fill out the Proof of Service on the back of the original, which is returned to you for filing with the court. But be warned. Most law enforcement agencies are backlogged, and your subpoena may still be sitting in an officer's in-basket long after your trial has been held.

FOR COURT USE ONLY

ATTORNEY OR PARTY WITHOUT ATTORNEY (Name and Address):

STANLEY SAFESPEED   TELEPHONE NO.
950 Parker Street   (415) 555-1234
Berkeley, CA 94710

ATTORNEY FOR (Name):   Defendant in Pro Per

Insert name of court, judicial district or branch court, if any, and post office and street address:

MUNICIPAL COURT OF CALIFORNIA, COUNTY OF ALAMEDA
BERKELEY-ALBANY JUDICIAL DISTRICT
2120 Grove Street, Berkeley, California 94704

Title of case:

THE PEOPLE OF THE STATE OF CALIFORNIA v.
STANLEY SAFESPEED

CASE NUMBER: A-123456-B

SUBPENA (CRIMINAL OR JUVENILE)

[X] DUCES TECUM

THE PEOPLE OF THE STATE OF CALIFORNIA, TO (NAME): Terrence Ticketer

1. YOU ARE ORDERED TO APPEAR AS A WITNESS in this action at the date, time, and place shown in the box below UNLESS you make a special agreement with the person named in item 3:

a. Date: May 1, 1991   Time: 3:00 PM   Dept.: 2   Div.:   Room:
b. Address: 2120 Grove Street, Berkeley, California 94704

2. AND YOU ARE
a. [ ] ordered to appear in person.
b. [ ] not required to appear in person if you produce the records described in the accompanying affidavit and a completed declaration of custodian of records in compliance with Evidence Code sections 1560, 1561, 1562, and 1271. (1) Place a copy of the records in an envelope (or other wrapper). Enclose your original declaration with the records. Seal them. (2) Attach a copy of this subpena to the envelope or write on the envelope the case name and number, your name and date, time, and place from item 1 (the box above). (3) Place this first envelope in an outer envelope, seal it, and mail it to the clerk of the court at the address in item 1. (4) Mail a copy of your declaration to the attorney or party shown at the top of this form.
c. [X] ordered to appear in person and to produce the records described in the accompanying affidavit. The personal attendance of the custodian or other qualified witness and the production of the original records is required by this subpena. The procedure authorized by subdivision (b) of section 1560, and sections 1561 and 1562, of the Evidence Code will not be deemed sufficient compliance with this subpena.
d. [ ] ordered to make the original business records described in the accompanying affidavit available for inspection at your business address by the attorney's representative and to permit copying at your business address under reasonable conditions during normal business hours.

3. IF YOU HAVE ANY QUESTIONS ABOUT THE TIME OR DATE FOR YOU TO APPEAR, OR IF YOU WANT TO BE CERTAIN THAT YOUR PRESENCE IS REQUIRED, CONTACT THE FOLLOWING PERSON BEFORE THE DATE ON WHICH YOU ARE TO APPEAR:
a. Name: Stanley Safespeed   b. Telephone number: (415) 555-1234

4. WITNESS FEES: You may be entitled to witness fees, mileage, or both, in the discretion of the court. Contact the person named in item 3 AFTER your appearance.

DISOBEDIENCE OF THIS SUBPENA MAY BE PUNISHED BY A FINE, IMPRISONMENT, OR BOTH. A WARRANT MAY ISSUE FOR YOUR ARREST IF YOU FAIL TO APPEAR.

FOR COURT USE ONLY

CLERK STAMPS HERE

     CLERK SIGNS HERE
     (SIGNATURE OF PERSON ISSUING SUBPENA)

Date: CLERK DATES   CLERK STAMPS HERE

    (TYPE OR PRINT NAME)
    (TITLE)

(See reverse for proof of service)

SUBPENA
(CRIMINAL OR JUVENILE)

Form Adopted by Rule 982
Judicial Council of California
982(a)(16) (Rev. January 1, 1991)

Penal Code § 1326 et seq.
Welfare and Institutions Code, 11 341, 664, 1727

Space Below for Use of Court Clerk Only

Name, Address and Telephone No. of Attorney(s)

Attorney(s) for ....

MUNICIPAL COURT OF CALIFORNIA, COUNTY OF ALAMEDA
BERKELEY-ALBANY JUDICIAL DISTRICT
2120 Grove Street, Berkeley, California 94704

CASE NUMBER

The People of the State of California vs.

SUBPENA (CRIMINAL)

Defendant(s)

Name(s):   Address(es):

You are hereby commanded to appear in the above-named court located at 2120 Grove Street, Berkeley, California

on _____ at _____ m.,

to testify as a witness in the above-entitled criminal action.

Dated _____

(SEAL)

By order of court.

CHARLES E. McCAIN, Clerk

By _____, Deputy

Disobedience to this subpena may be punished as a contempt of court.

ORDER
OUT-OF-COUNTY WITNESS

(Required for out-of-county witnesses served 150 miles or more from court, or otherwise as provided in Penal Code Section 1330.)

Upon reading the affidavit or declaration of _____

On file, and proper cause appearing, it is ordered that each witness above named attend a session of this court as a witness in this criminal action.

Dated _____

_____
Judge

(See reverse side for Proof of Service)

SUBPENA (CRIMINAL)

Rev. 1/1/71   Pen. C. Secs. 1326-1332

3. It is essential to my defense that the above items be produced at trial in order that I may demonstrate with them that radar speed measuring units produce false and spurious readings and do not accurately measure speeds of moving objects, including the vehicle I was driving when cited for the alleged violation.

I declare under penalty of perjury under the laws of the State of California that the foregoing is true and correct.

DATED: April 1, 199__

_____
STANLEY SAFESPEED

STANLEY SAFESPEED
950 Parker St.
Berkeley, CA 94710
(415) 555-1234

Defendant in Pro Per

MUNICIPAL COURT OF CALIFORNIA, COUNTY OF ALAMEDA
BERKELEY-ALBANY JUDICIAL DISTRICT

THE PEOPLE OF THE STATE OF CALIFORNIA,

        Plaintiff,

vs.

STANLEY SAFESPEED,

        Defendant.

NO. A-123456-B

DECLARATION IN SUPPORT OF ISSUANCE OF SUBPOENA DUCES TECUM

I, STANLEY SAFESPEED, declare:

1. I am the defendant in the action of People v. Safespeed, No. A-123456-B, pending before the Municipal Court for the Berkeley-Albany Judicial District.

2. I seek to have the clerk of the court issue a subpoena duces tecum requiring Officer Terrence Ticketer of the Berkeley Police Department to appear at the time and place for the trial in this action, set forth on the said subpoena duces tecum, and bring with him the following items:

a. The hand-held radar unit with which he alleges he determined my speed.

b. The instruction manual stating how the said radar unit is to be operated.

c. The tuning forks or other devices with which he calibrated the said radar unit on the day of the alleged violation.

If you want to subpoena the radar unit or manual of the officer who cited you, two copies of the subpoena must be delivered to that officer's supervisor. If you want to subpoena police records of any kind, the two copies must be delivered to the supervisor of whomever has control of the records. You can also insist that the police department serve the subpoena on their own appropriate employees. To do this, you give the police agency the original and two copies and a letter of instruction. In this case, your original and copies must reach the police agency at least five days before the court hearing (PC § 1328). Here are some sample letters to accomplish this:

Dan Driver
123 Main St
Salinas, CA 93900

April 1, 199_

Monterey Police Department
Pacific & Madison Streets
Monterey, CA 93940

RE: People v. Driver
    Monterey Municipal Court No. 1234567

Dear People:

    Enclosed are an original and a copy of a subpoena for service on Wilma Witness, of 1200 Ninth street, Monterey. The best time to serve Ms. Witness is between 6:00 p.m. and 8:00 p.m. on weekdays.

    Please fill out the Proof of Service on the back of the original and return to me.

Sincerely,

Dan Driver

Rhonda Roadie
456 7th Street
San Jose, CA 95110

May 1, 199_

Monterey County Sheriff
240 Church Street
Salinas, CA 93940

Re: People v. Roadie
    Monterey Municipal Court No. 23456789

Dear People:

    Enclosed are an original and two copies of a subpoena duces tecum for service on your custodian of records. Please give two copies of the subpoena duces tecum to his/her immediate supervisor and return the original to me with the Proof of Service filled out.

    Thank you for your cooperation.

Sincerely,

Rhonda Roadie

Where a police department fails to comply with a subpoena (such as by refusing to produce the radar manual), you should ask at trial—if the officer who cited you shows up to testify against you—that the case be continued and that the officer be directed to produce the items sought. [See Section C(2), below.] (Obviously, if no officer shows up to testify against you, you should instead ask the judge to dismiss the case against you.)

C. Motions You May Want to Make Before Trial

DEPENDING ON THE CIRCUMSTANCES, you may wish to make certain requests of the judge before trial.

1. Requesting a "Continuance" (Postponement)

A "continuance" is a postponement of a scheduled court appearance (usually a trial). You might want your trial date postponed because you won't be prepared on the scheduled trial date, you'll be out of town, or are ill, or, better still, you've just discovered the days the officer will be on vacation and you want the trial held then.

Unless you've informed the prosecutor or officer in advance, most requests for a continuance which are made on the day of trial will be denied. However, it is usually not difficult to arrange for a continuance if you plan ahead. You should make your written request at least several weeks before trial whenever possible. Send a copy to the officer's police agency, or to the district or city attorney's office if it prosecutes traffic cases or your case involves a misdemeanor violation. Such a letter might look like this:

```
123 Parker St.
Berkeley, CA 94710
May 5, 199_

Clerk, Municipal Court
Berkeley-Albany Judicial District
2120 Grove Street
Berkeley, California

Re: People v. Safespeed, #A-123456
    Trial Date: June 1, 199_

Dear Sir or Madam:

    I am scheduled to appear for trial in
the above matter on June 1, 199_.
Unfortunately, I will be out of town on
that date due to my employer's insistence
that I attend a two-week seminar in New
York between May 28th and June 11th. I
therefore request that trial be continued
to June 15th, or as soon as possible
thereafter as it can be scheduled. Please
inform me as to whether the continuance
will be granted and any new trial date and
time.

Sincerely,

Shirley Safespeed

cc: Officer G. Growlski
    Berkeley Police Department
```

If you don't receive a reply at least a week before the scheduled trial date, call the court clerk. If the continuance hasn't been granted (or if dealing with the clerks proves fruitless), you'll have to appear in court on the trial date. It is best to be prepared to go to trial, although you can ask for a continuance again. The continuance will probably be granted if you show your copy of the letter as proof that you notified the police and/or the district/city attorney of your request well in advance. Of course, there is always a chance that if the officer doesn't show, and the judge doesn't notice your letter in the file, he might dismiss the case (since it will look like you showed up ready for trial but the officer didn't). So, you may want to wait to see whether the officer shows before raising your request.

You may also want to ask for a continuance where 1) the officer who cited you shows up, *and* 2) he or another officer you've subpoenaed have failed to produce material you've demanded in your subpoena, or a witness you've subpoenaed simply failed to show. For example, the officer failed to bring the manual for the radar unit, which you subpoenaed earlier. (Of course, if the officer who cited you doesn't show, you should ask that the case be dismissed.) The best time to request a continuance on this basis is when your case is called before the trial starts, after having asked the officer or other person if they brought all material listed in the subpoena duces tecum.

2. Responding to a Prosecution Request for a Continuance

Occasionally, because of an officer's scheduled vacation or other anticipated reason for his absence, the district attorney or police agency will ask for a postponement of the trial date and will notify you by mail. If you receive such a notice, figure out whether the letter indicates that the court has already granted the continuance, or whether the agency is merely stating that the officer won't be showing up and you needn't go. If the court date has been changed, you should receive a notice from the court, not merely the prosecuting or police agency. If the letter only indicates that the prosecution wants a continuance, you may want to show up in court on the trial date —"ready" for trial—to object. Be prepared to point out that you had to make arrangements well in advance to take time off from your job (at a loss of pay) on the day originally scheduled for trial and that you don't relish the thought of doing it again. If you're lucky, the judge may then dismiss the case.

3. Preparing a Motion to Disqualify the Judge

As we noted in Chapter 10, you can disqualify a particularly unfair or hard-line judge merely by preparing and using a Peremptory Challenge. This is your right.[4] The time to use the Challenge depends upon whether your case is specifically assigned 10 days or more in advance to a particular judge (as opposed to a particular courtroom or department). If it's not, and as long as the court district has more than one judge, you can move to disqualify the judge just before your trial begins. Otherwise you have to make the motion at least five days in advance.

---

[4]See *Bouchard v. Insona* (1980) 105 Cal.App.3d 768, 164 Cal.Rptr. 505 and *Retes v. Superior Court* (1981) 122 Cal.App.3d 799, 176 Cal.Rptr. 160.

```
DARLENE DISQUALIFIER
950 Parker Road
Los Angeles, CA 90000
(213) 555-6789

Defendant in Pro Per


        MUNICIPAL COURT OF CALIFORNIA, COUNTY OF LOS ANGELES
                  LOS ANGELES JUDICIAL DISTRICT


THE PEOPLE OF THE STATE          )
OF CALIFORNIA                    )       No. M123221-B
                                 )
                                 )
                   Plaintiff,    )       PEREMPTORY CHALLENGE
vs.                              )       [CCP § 170.6]
                                 )
DARLENE DISQUALIFIER,            )
                                 )
                   Defendant     )
_____ )


    I, DARLENE DISQUALIFIER, declare:

    1. I am the defendant in the above-entitled action.

    2. On September 12, 199_, the date of trial herein, it became

known to me that the Hon._____ was scheduled to

try the above-entitled matter as judge or commissioner.

    3. I believe that the aforesaid judge or commissioner, before

whom the trial in the above-entitled matter is pending, is preju-

diced against my interest so that I believe that I cannot have a

fair and impartial trial before such judge, court commissioner or

referee.

    WHEREFORE, Defendant requests ex parte, per CCP Section

170.6, that the said judge or commissioner be disqualified from

hearing the above-entitled matter.

    I declare under penalty of perjury under the laws of the

State of California that the foregoing is true and correct.

DATED: September 12, 199_

                                  _____
                                  DARLENE DISQUALIFIER
                                  Defendant in Pro Per
```

However, in courts with only one judge (justice courts), the Peremptory Challenge must be filed at least 30 days before trial. [See Chapter 10, Section D(2)(d).]

If you are able to make your Peremptory Challenge the day of the trial (because your case wasn't assigned to a definite judge sufficiently in advance of trial), fill out your challenge in advance except for the name of the judge and the date of the trial (the date next to item "2." and on the last line before the signature). Then, when you show up at the courthouse for your trial and discover the name of your judge, fill it in at that time. Once presented with the challenge, the judge will have to transfer the case to another courtroom. If no other judge is available, the case will have to be postponed to another day when one is available. Once you find out this information the trial date information can be filled in.

Hedge Note: Assuming your case is not the first to be heard, you can observe the judge who will be hearing your case and decide whether she seems to be dealing fairly with other cases. If so, leave your challenge in your briefcase and have your trial. If you decide, before your case is called, that the judge is more likely than not to find you guilty, produce the Challenge when your case is called.

Another Hedge Note: If traffic court trials are regularly held by one judge or commissioner, so that you know in advance where your trial will be held and which judge or commissioner will hear it, it might be helpful for you to go to the courthouse and watch traffic trials held by the same judge several days before your case is to be heard. If the judge seems unfair or finds people guilty even when they have a good defense, you may want to prepare and file your Peremptory Challenge.

Note: It should be obvious that if the officer doesn't show up—even if you dislike the judge—you should not use the Challenge, but rather should just ask the judge to dismiss the case.

D. Preparing to Deal With the Officer's Testimony

IN TRAFFIC OFFENSE TRIALS, the testimony of the police officer who cited you is the most important part of the prosecution's case. The officer's story will usually follow this pattern: he will testify that he was parked or driving, minding his own business ("writing a report" or "observing traffic") when he just happened to observe you committing all the elements of the particular violation. He will probably also embellish this with testimony relating to traffic and road conditions, to establish why the violation was hazardous to other vehicles, pedestrians, etc.

Your job is to cast doubts on the officer's testimony through careful cross-examination or, in some cases, have the testimony excluded entirely, on the basis of a legal "objection."

1. When Should You Raise an "Objection"?

Despite what you've seen on television, there is very little reason to interrupt the prosecutor's questions or the officer's testimony with all sorts of legal objections. "Objections" are based on formal "rules of evidence" which dictate what kind of evidence can and cannot be considered by the court. These rules are complicated and not entirely logical. In most cases, even if you were to raise a valid objection to the officer's testimony, it would probably just irritate the judge (or jury) and do you more harm than good. However, in speed violation cases where the officer(s) used radar to nab you, there are two types of objections you might want to raise.

a. Radar Evidence and the Engineering and Traffic Survey Requirement

For Basic Speed Law violations [except in 15 mph, 55-65 mph, and 15 and 20 mph school zones, 25 mph "senior" zones, and on "local streets and roads," the officer cannot testify about the use of radar until he has introduced into evidence a certified copy of an engineering and traffic survey justifying the speed limit where you were nabbed.[5] If he tries to testify, without doing this, object by saying something like:

---

[5]See Chapter 4, Section B, for the legal basis of this requirement.

"Your Honor, I object to the introduction of radar testimony on the ground that Officer Gettem has failed to lay the foundation by proving an engineering and traffic survey as required by § 40803 (b) of the Vehicle Code."

It is not enough for the officer to just testify that such a survey was conducted, unless he helped conduct it.[6] His testimony about the study should be objected to on the basis that it's "hearsay" and not the best evidence. (The "best evidence" rule requires production of the survey itself.)

Some courts, particularly those in Santa Clara County, will allow radar speed convictions without introduction of a survey, unless you insist that one be introduced. If you object about the absence of a survey, the judge will probably quickly mumble something about "judicial notice" of a copy of the survey filed with the court. If this happens, you should at that time politely object to the judge taking judicial notice of the document without it being produced in court, and you should insist on seeing the survey itself. It must then be produced.[7] Don't settle for anything less than a certified copy. (A true certified copy bears an original signature of some city or county employee stating the copy is a true copy of the original.) Some courts take shortcuts by keeping only a list of streets which have been certified. This is not enough, and such a list should be objected to as "hearsay." The actual survey itself might not be located anywhere near the courtroom. If the judge seems inclined to postpone the case to allow the prosecutor or officer to produce the survey, you should argue that the prosecutor or officer should have come to court prepared, and complain of the hardship of having to stay longer or come back another day.

If the officer does produce the survey, check the date to see if it was done within five years prior to your ticket. Also check to see if it contains the fol-

lowing items (listed under VC § 627), required in a valid survey of that portion of roadway:

(1) Prevailing speeds as determined by traffic engineering measurements.

(2) Accident records.

(3) Highway, traffic and roadside conditions not readily apparent to the driver.

If the survey requirements are not met, or the survey is not introduced into evidence, remind the judge that under VC § 40805, he has "no jurisdiction" to find you guilty, even if the radar evidence is admitted.

b. *Hearsay Evidence in Aircraft Speed Detection*

In situations where an officer in an aircraft radios your car's speed and description to an officer in a patrol car, the officer in the car cites you for going at a speed he may not have personally observed. When tickets given in this type of situation are contested, both officers have to show up in court—the one who issued the ticket, and the ones who determined the speed, without whose testimony the first officer's evidence would be insufficient. Be prepared to object to such evidence as hearsay if the officer who cited you starts testifying about the speed some other officer—who isn't also in court—told him you were going.

The hearsay testimony may take any one of the following forms: 1) the ground-based officer testifying as to what the aircraft-based officer told him your speed was, or 2) the aircraft-based officer testifying as to his knowledge of the distance between highway markings on the ground (by which he calibrated his aircraft speedometer or timed your car's passage across a known distance), or 3) either of the two officers testifying in writing by written affidavit. Be ready to object to any evidence of this kind as "hearsay."

---

[6]See *People v. Sterritt* (1976) 65 Cal.App.3d Supp.1, 135 Cal.Rptr. 522.

[7]*People v. Peterson* (1986) 181 Cal.App.3d Supp.7, 226 Cal.Rptr. 544.

2. Cross-examining the Officer— Basic Strategy

You have the right to ask an arresting officer questions in order to get him to clarify his testimony or to bring out other facts. But be careful. Cross-examination can often backfire because the person you're examining has a lot of experience in courtroom testifying. The last thing you want is the officer to elaborate and embellish his story. The best way to prevent this from happening is to ask the officer specific questions—not questions like "what happened then?" or "why did you stop me, anyway?" Your purpose is to get him to say things which will indicate that his powers of observation were not perfect, or which will show either the probable absence of an element of the offense, or a possible defense to it.

The key to effective cross-examination is preparation. Before you go to trial, make a list of questions you intend to use at trial, using the sample questions provided below as a guide. Develop your cross-examination step-by-step, beginning with the least important questions and ending with the most important ones. You need to use errors, lapses of memory and outright lies discovered in cross-examination to try to sway the judge to see your point of view. If you don't have a specific purpose in mind when you ask a particular question, don't ask it. And be careful—your questions should never include an admission ("where were you when I ran the stop sign?"). They should be non-committal

instead ("where were you when you claim I ran the stop sign?").

The questions below are representative of the types of questions to ask in trials involving common traffic violations. If the situation in which you were cited is not covered in this chapter, try to develop a set of questions to show how the officer could have been mistaken in his observations.

Make a list of questions you intend to use and bring it with you to trial. But don't use the list as a rigid guide.[8] Depending on how things go, be prepared to drop any that, in light of the officer's responses, will not work in your favor. If the officer is evasive, be prepared to bear down with more specific questions until you either get the answer you want to or force the officer to lie. Also, keep in mind that many officers are skilled at using your cross-examination of them to give you harmful answers and to tell more of their own story.

One of the basic rules of cross-examination is that you should almost never ask a question to which you yourself don't know the answer. Unexpected answers can often do more harm than good. Of course, you are likely to get a few unexpected answers now and then. When you do, you'll have to decide whether to just switch to the next line of questioning or ask more detailed questions, trying to force the officer to give specific answers.

You can ask almost anything you want, so long as the answer you're seeking is in some way relevant to a particular element or defense. Never argue with the officer or assume an antagonistic stance. If the officer answers a question untruthfully, or gives a ridiculous answer, ask more direct questions.

Example

Your Question: *Officer, how far from my vehicle were you when you initially took your radar reading?*

_____

[8]Many judges and officers have said that too many people who use this book blindly run through the cross-examination questions listed here, without much thought on how the questions relate to their own situation. Don't fall into this trap. It bores and sometimes angers judges.

Officer's Answer: *500 feet.*

Wrong Response: *Officer, you know very well that the radar beam width at that distance can't differentiate between vehicles in adjacent lanes.* [This is argument, and isn't allowed during the cross-examination phase.)

Right Response: *Question: Officer, you previously testified to a beam angle width of six degrees. Isn't it true that at 500 feet from your radar unit the beam will be over 50 feet across?*

Next Question: *Aren't individual lanes much narrower than 50 feet?*

3. Cross-Examination Questions to Test the Officer's Power of Observation

The basis for all traffic violations lies in the perceptions of the officer. Thus, the more you can establish that there are some things he doesn't remember as to where, why and how he stopped you, the more doubt you raise as to the truth of those parts of his story that seem to establish the elements of the violation. The following is a list of some of the types of general questions you might want to ask in order to test the officer's knowledge of the location and conditions where he observed you. Review these sample questions before trial, and leave out those which would be irrelevant in your case. Don't ask them in a boring, monotonous way, either, lest you drive the judge batty. Also, be prepared to leave out any questions which the officer answered in his initial testimony.

Sample Questions

1. Where were you located when you first saw my vehicle?

2. Where was my vehicle when you first saw it?

3. Was your car (or motorcycle) parked or moving at the time?

4   *[If parked]* Was your engine idling, or was it off?

5. *[If off]* What did you do to start your vehicle?

The more extraneous things you can get him to admit he did, the more doubt you may be able to cast on how hard he was concentrating on you.

6. Did you turn on your lights?

7. Did you use your two-way radio?

8. Did you start your engine just before you saw the alleged violation, or during? *[If just before, you can argue later that he made up his mind to stop you before he saw any violation. If during, he might have been too busy starting it to observe things very well. If idling, you can later argue that he was already intent on stopping someone regardless of whether he saw a violation.]*

9. *[If moving]* In which lane were you traveling?

10. In which direction were you going?

11. How fast were you driving? *[Leave this one out for speeding violations.]*

12. Did you have a clear view of the traffic on the road when you claim you observed the violation?

13. Was there any other traffic on the road other than your vehicle and mine?

14. *[If other traffic]* Could you describe the traffic in front of your vehicle? On either side of you?

Try to ask questions regarding the number and types of other vehicles on the road and their movements. The more specific you can get him to be, the more likely he may not have observed your car accurately, since he was watching everything else.

15. How fast was the flow of his traffic?

16. *[If slower than your vehicle]* Did you see my vehicle passing any others?

If he says other traffic was slower than you, but that you weren't passing other vehicles, he's contradicting himself. If he says you did pass other vehicles, ask him for specifics (type of vehicle, color, make). He won't remember.

If he says he was traveling at the same speed as, or faster than your vehicle, your over-the-limit (but under-55) speed might have been safe, and therefore legal under the Basic Speed Law.

If he says there was no other traffic, again, your over-the-limit speed might be considered to have been safe under the circumstances.

17. Do you consider yourself to have fairly well-developed powers of observation and memory for details concerning weather, and road conditions?

18. What were the weather conditions when you saw my vehicle?

Don't ask this one if you're charged with a Basic Speed Law violation and there was fog, rain or snow, since a safe speed under those conditions may be even less than the posted speed limit. But for other violations, bad weather—especially rain on his windshield—could have impaired the officer's ability to observe.

19. Then, ask the officer about every possible detail and hazard on the road, but leave out hazards that were really there. This way his answers will make it seem like the roadway was pretty safe, or that he can't remember all the details. Possible road conditions include:

- highway width
- divider strips or islands
- sharp curves
- dips or hills
- railroad crossings
- road repairs in progress
- obstructions in the road
- soft shoulders
- spilled liquids
- pedestrians, bicyclists or animals in the road.

4. Cross-Examination Questions for Specific Offenses

The remainder of your cross-examination of the officer should be directed to undermining his testimony on the specific elements of the offense, and with getting him to admit any circumstances justifying your supposed violation. For example, in radar speeding cases, you might want to bring out the officer's lack of familiarity with his radar unit. The types of cross-examination questions depend on the violation charged. Sample questions for the most frequent violations are listed below.

a. Speed Violations in General

The following questions relate to how the officer measured your speed: was it visual observation, clocking you with his speedometer, radar, or a combination of these? The officer will undoubtedly testify as to which method he used. The questions apply to violations of the maximum speed law [VC § 22349(a)—over 55, or 65 on certain Interstate freeways] as well as the Basic Speed Law (VC § 22350).

Visual Speed Estimation: If the officer estimated your speed only through visual observation (believe it or not, this is accepted by some judges), you might want to ask the following questions:

1. Over what distance did you see my vehicle travel?

It might have been so short as to render an accurate speed estimate unlikely.

2. Did my speed change at all as you observed me?

If he says you slowed down after you apparently saw him, the original high estimate was good only over a short distance. If he says your speed suddenly went up or down at various places, ask him to elaborate in detail and describe those places; few officers have that good a memory.

3. Was my vehicle traveling toward you, away from you, or across your line of vision?

It's more difficult for the officer to estimate the speed of vehicles moving in a more or less direct line toward or away from him than of vehicles traveling across his field of vision.

4. Have you ever participated in controlled tests where you were asked to estimate vehicle speeds?

Most officers have not participated in such tests. If he says he has, ask whether he always guessed the exact speed correctly. If he says "yes," he's obviously lying—no one could be that perfect; if he says "no," you can later argue that he admits to mistakes in past estimations.

Speed estimated by following you (without radar): If the officer's estimate of your speed was based on his own speedometer reading while following you, the following questions may be helpful:

1. Over what distance did you follow my vehicle at a steady rate of speed?

The shorter the distance, the less likely he got an accurate reading.

2. Was the distance between your car and mine always constant?

If he says "yes," he's obviously mistaken, since he had to close in on you as he began to follow you. Try to get him to admit that he closed in to pull you over. But if he says no, it suggests that he may have been reading the speed as his car was bearing down on yours at a higher speed.

3. Did you observe your speedometer during this time?

4. Was the speed you observed constant?

5. How long before you cited me was the speedometer in your patrol car (or motorcycle) last calibrated? *[The longer the better.]*

6. Has it been calibrated since the day you cited me?

If the officer tries to get away with simply saying "it was accurate," he's bluffing. No speedometer in the world is accurate within one mile per hour at all speeds; there's always some variation between true speed and the reading over at least part of the speedometer's range. It might be accurate at one speed, but perhaps two, three or four or more mph off at other speeds. Ask the officer to answer the question.

7. Did you bring a record of the speedometer calibration with you today? *[He almost never will.]*

8. Are you aware that speedometer accuracy is affected by tire circumference?

9. Are you also aware that tire circumference is affected by tire pressure and wear? *[It is unlikely the officer will say no.]*

10. Then isn't it fair to say that speedometer accuracy is affected by tire pressure and wear?

11. Were your tires' pressures checked when your speedometer was calibrated? *[Probably not.]*

12. Were they checked on the day you cited me? *[Probably not.]*

13. Are you aware that a tire's air pressure depends on its temperature at the time?

14. Have the tires on your patrol car been rotated, or have any of them been changed since the last speedometer calibration?

Note: If the officer's rear tire (on a rear-wheel drive car) was slightly smaller on the day he cited you (due to wear, lower pressure or lower temperature) than when the speedometer was checked, it will have given an erroneously high reading on the day you were cited.

Speed Estimated by Radar: If the officer used radar, you can use these questions in attempting to show that he doesn't really know how it works, that he was not careful about maintaining his unit's accuracy, and that the speed measured may not have been yours. If you plan to make extensive use of any of these questions, go back and reread Chapter 4, Sections B and F, on radar speed detection.

1. Does your radar unit have a control which allows you to "lock in" a speed onto the readout?

2. *[If yes]* Did you show your unit's speed to me when you stopped me? *[Only ask if he did not—then ask why he didn't, if he could have locked in the reading.]*

3. Could you please describe briefly how speed-determining radar works?

4. Could you explain the meaning of the "Doppler effect"?

5. Isn't it true that delicate and sensitive electronic measurement instruments such as radar units must be calibrated often to make sure they're accurate?

6. Did you calibrate your unit immediately before and after you measured my alleged speed?

If he didn't, it suggests sloppiness and inaccuracy. If he says he did, he most likely only used the internal calibrate control, not a tuning fork.

7. How exactly did you calibrate the unit?

8. *[If he says he turned a switch to the "calibrate" position on his instrument or states that he calibrated it "internally."]* You mean, you didn't use a tuning fork?

9. Isn't that merely an internal calibration without reference to an external source?

10. Doesn't the radar unit's manufacturer recommend calibration with a tuning fork?

11. Isn't a tuning fork certified as accurate by a testing laboratory a better check than the unit's internal electronics?

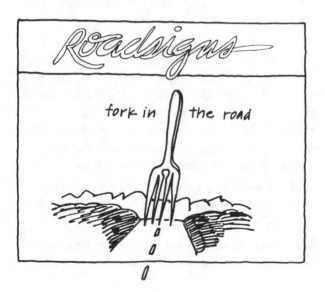

Roadsigns

fork in the road

12. *[If he says he used a tuning fork]* Did you calibrate your unit with a tuning fork immediately before and after you cited me? *[Usually he will have done it with a tuning fork only at the beginning and end of his shift.]*

13. Isn't it true that there are certified tuning forks available in increments of 5 mph from 25 mph to 100 mph?

14. What was the certified speed for the tuning fork you used?

If it's much different from the speed he says he clocked you at, you can later argue that tuning-fork-checked accuracy at one speed is not a guarantee of accuracy at a different speed.

15. When was the tuning fork itself last calibrated by an independent testing laboratory?

16. Do you have a certificate of accuracy for this particular tuning fork?

17. Has your radar unit ever malfunctioned in any way?

18. *[If he says no]* Then it's never been taken to the shop for repairs?

19. *[If he says it hasn't]* Not even for routine maintenance? *[If he says it has, try to pin him down as to the type of malfunction, getting him to go into detail.]*

20. Have you ever in your professional experience been able to obtain an apparent speed reading on the unit by aiming it at anything other than a moving vehicle?

21. Isn't it true that nonmetallic surfaces can sometimes reflect radar beams?

22. And if those surfaces are in motion, they can cause a spurious reading on a radar unit, can't they?

23. Isn't it true that windblown tree limbs or even leaves can sometimes reflect radar signals to generate a spurious reading? *[Don't use this unless it was very windy the day you were cited.]*

24. Even blowing dust or rain can sometimes do this, can't it?

25. Do you know what a harmonic frequency is?

26. Are you aware that harmonic frequencies of nearby radio transmissions, for example from CB sets, can cause spurious radar readings?

27. Did you know that electrical interference from nearby power lines or transformers or even high-voltage neon lights can generate such spurious readings?

28. Wouldn't it be possible for you to determine the speed of a train or low-flying airplane with your unit if you aimed the beam at it?

29. What's the maximum range, in thousands of feet, of your radar unit?

30. What is the beam width of your radar unit in degrees?

Don't settle for an answer in "lanes"—the beam width in lanes varies with the beam distance. You can calculate the approximate width of the beam at the end of its range by using the formula:

beam width = 17.4 x maximum range x beam width[9]
(feet)   *(thousands of feet)*   *(degrees)*

If he doesn't know the beam width in degrees, ask him how much wider the beam gets for each thousand feet distance from the radar unit. You can try to quickly calculate the beam width at the maximum range; then ask:

31. So then, at the maximum range, where you can still determine a target's speed, the width of the beam is about ____ feet, isn't it?

32. Isn't that wider than one lane of traffic?

33. Isn't this wide enough to reflect beams from low-flying aircraft or nearby trains? *[Only use this if you were cited near railroad tracks or an airport.]*

34. When you aim your radar unit at a nearby object, your unit's antenna will pick up signals reflected from other more distant sources, won't it?

35. Isn't your unit supposed to track the strongest reflected signal?

36. Did you know that a more distant, but larger, vehicle may reflect a stronger signal than a smaller nearby vehicle?

37. When you estimated my vehicle's speed, were you first observing my vehicle or your radar unit?

38. *[If your vehicle]* So, then, you had already assumed I was exceeding the speed limit before you took a radar reading?

39. *[If the radar unit]* So, you had already formed an opinion of my speed before looking up at my vehicle?

40. Did you see my vehicle directly, or just in your rearview mirror? *[Only ask this if he aimed his radar antenna behind him while parked.]*

41. *[If in the rearview mirror]* How many inches wide is your rearview mirror? How many feet were your eyes from the mirror?

The angle of view of the rearview mirror, in degrees, will be:

$$\text{Angle (degrees)} = \frac{5 \text{ x mirror width } (inches)}{\text{eye-mirror distance } (feet)}$$

42. So then, the angle of view of your mirror is about ___ degrees, isn't that so? *[Try to pin him down to some figure near 30 degrees.]*

43. Isn't this much larger a field of view than your radar beam width?

44. How do you know your unit was aimed exactly at my vehicle and not at something else you saw in your rearview mirror?

45. You certainly couldn't see whether the beam was hitting my vehicle, could you?

---

[9] This is derived as follows: At low angles, sine or tangent of an angle approximately equals the angle, in "radians" (6.28 or 2x pi "radians" = 360 degrees of arc.) Therefore, the angle (in radians) about equals the beam width divided by the distance. Or, the beam width about equals the angle (in radians), multiplied by the distance. If we use degrees (360 in a circle) instead of radians (only 6.28 in a circle), we must multiply by 6.28/360 (about 0.0174). If we use thousands of feet for distance, the overall conversion factor becomes 17.4.

46. Have you ever heard the term "cosine angle factor" as applied to speed-measuring radar?

47. Isn't it true that the cosine angle factor refers to an error in speed measured when the beam is aimed at an angle—other than directly—to the path of the moving object?

Actually, this error always works in your favor by causing an inaccurately low radar reading. This can be shown using trigonometric manipulations, but it is very difficult to explain why it's so. If the officer says something like, "but the error is always in the motorist's favor," but otherwise doesn't seem too knowledgeable, try to get him to illustrate why this is so. It's fairly difficult to explain properly. It may be he "knows" this because his chief told him so.

48. Could a completely untrained person use your radar unit accurately? *[The answer will almost always be no.]*

49. Could you please describe the training you've had in the use of radar? *[All officers will try to build up the two-hour pep talk they received into an intense "seminar."]*

50. How long ago did you have this training?

51. How long did the training last?

52. Did you have supervised "hands-on" instruction out on the road?

53. Were there examinations?

54. Have you participated in any tests where you used radar to measure a vehicle's speed, then were told the correct speed? *[Almost never; if he says yes, try to get him to give precise details.]*

Speed detected from aircraft: Where your car's speed was detected from an aircraft, your cross-examination should shed doubt on the speed the officer determined for the aircraft (and therefore your car as he followed), the officer's knowledge of distance between highway markings (based on hearsay?), his identification of your vehicle, and the patrol car officer's having picked out the right vehicle from among other traffic. Here are a few sample questions:

1. Officer Aircop, didn't you testify that you calculated the aircraft speed by timing its passage across highway markings?

2. And you did this before you finally determined my vehicle's speed?

3. If a headwind had suddenly slowed the aircraft after the timing, wouldn't you have had to redetermine your slower speed?

4. How much time passed between the time you calibrated the speed of the aircraft and the time you paced my vehicle? Are you certain the wind speed did not change during this time?

5. You didn't actually measure the distance between the highway markings on the ground, did you? *[If not, ask]* So your knowledge of the distance between the markings is based on other than your own observations, isn't it? **Note:** If the officer simply timed the passage of your car between two highway markings (as opposed to following you after using the markings to get aircraft speed), an illegal speed trap was used, as prohibited by VC § 40802(a). You should then ask the judge to dismiss the case. See Chapter 4, Section B(2).

6. When you identified what you say was my vehicle, you didn't actually read a license plate number, did you? *[Only ask if he failed to testify to this earlier on "direct."]*

7. *[If no license number read from air]* Was there other traffic? *[If yes, ask]* Could you describe each of the other vehicles by make and color? *[If he can't, then he can't say for sure there weren't other cars like yours.]*

8. Officer Groundcop, isn't it true that you were first alerted to my vehicle only because of the radio report from the officer in the aircraft? *[Don't ask if he testified otherwise earlier.]*

9. *[If answer to question 7 is yes and officer in patrol car did not testify that he paced you after hearing the radio report]* So then, your knowledge of my speed was based solely on the radio report, correct?

b. "Basic Speed Law" Questions

If you were cited for going over the posted speed limit but under 55, it's still possible to be acquitted if you can show that it was safe under the conditions at the time to drive at a higher-than-posted speed. This doesn't mean you have to admit you were going over the limit—just that it would have been safe to do so.

Before you lunge ahead and prepare to ask the officer all sorts of questions related to road, traffic and weather conditions, think about the conditions where you were cited, and leave out any questions if the answers could damage your case. For example, if it was raining or foggy, don't ask anything about the weather. Also, don't ask anything about the traffic if it was fairly heavy, unless it can help shed doubt as to which vehicle the officer was pointing at with a radar unit. Similarly, leave out questions relating to road conditions for two-lane winding, hilly roads. Sample questions are as follows:

[If the traffic was light]

1. Was there a lot of traffic in my direction?

2. How many vehicles were there in my lane?

3. How many behind me? In front of me?

4. What was the average distance between vehicles?

5. *[If at a time far removed from morning, noon or evening rush hour]* Was there any rush hour traffic on the road?

[If there was some traffic]

6. Wasn't most of the traffic going at about the same speed you say I was going?

7. Did you see my vehicle pass any others? *[Don't ask if you did pass other vehicles. If he says "yes," ask him to describe them in detail.]*

8. *[Only if he says you weren't passing other cars]* So then, I was going slower, or at least at the same speed as the other traffic, correct?

9. *[If there was no rain]* Was the road pavement dry?

10. *[If there was no rain or fog, etc.]* Was the visibility satisfactory?

11. *[If you were ticketed in the daytime and if it wasn't even overcast]* Was the sun shining? Were clouds obscuring it?

12. *[If you were cited at night but the road was well lit]* Are there street lights along this stretch of road? Were they lit?

13. *[If the road had at least two lanes in your direction]* How many lanes did the road have? How many in my direction?

14. *[If the road was divided by a median or barrier]* Did the road have a divider or barrier down the middle?

15. *[If there were no intersections near where you were cited]* Were there any intersections nearby?

16. *[If there were intersections but all were controlled by stoplights]* There were no uncontrolled intersections nearby, were there?

17. Were there any sharp turns in the roadway? *[Ask only if there weren't.]*

18. Were there any hills obscuring the view from the roadway? *[Again, ask only if there weren't.]*

19. How many pedestrians were in the area? *[Ask only if there were a few, and none were crossing or trying to cross the road.]*

20. Were any pedestrians crossing the road? Trying to cross? *[Ask only if none were.]*

If the road, traffic and weather conditions really were good, the foregoing line of questions should help your case. Of course, the best time to make your case in this area is when you testify, and this will be covered in the next part of the chapter.

c. Running a Stoplight (VC § 21453)

This is a fairly straightforward offense—either the officer observed a traffic light which was red when you entered the intersection (i.e., when the front of your car drove across the "limit line" or cross street) or he didn't. The following questions are directed at showing something inconsistent in the officer's observations of your speed and distance from the intersection:

1. Did you see my vehicle when the green light turned yellow? *[If he says he didn't, then he could have seen you only two or three seconds before he says you ran the red light, shedding doubt on his ability to see something happen so fast.]*

2. For how many seconds does the yellow light stay on?

You should find out the answer ahead of time by going back and timing the light. If the officer guesses too brief a duration for the yellow light, it will help you. If he says he doesn't know, ask him to estimate. If he still won't volunteer an answer, his powers of observation aren't that good.

3. How fast, in your opinion, was I traveling?

4. How many feet from the intersection was my vehicle when the green light turned yellow.

Note: At trial, you can then make a little calculation, preferably with a pocket calculator. First, you multiply the speed the officer says you were going by the number 1.47 to get that speed in feet per second.[10] Then divide this number into the number

of feet he says you were from the intersection when the green light turned yellow, to get:

$$\text{Time } \textit{(seconds)} = \frac{\text{distance when turned yellow } \textit{(feet)}}{1.47 \times \text{speed } \textit{(mph)}}$$

If this number, in seconds, is less than what he says the duration of the yellow light is (or what you can later truthfully testify it is if you timed it), then you would have made it into the intersection while the light was still yellow.

If the officer was on a cross street at right angles to your direction of travel, he probably didn't see the traffic signal facing you, but assumed that when his red light changed to green, your yellow light changed to red. If this seems to be the case, ask:

5. Could you see the signal lenses facing my direction of traffic from your location? *[If he says yes, stop here. But if he says no, ask:]*

6. Then why do you say I entered the intersection on a red light if you couldn't see my light? *[He will undoubtedly say his light went green.]*

7. So you assumed my light turned from yellow to red at that time? *[Yes.]*

8. Did you examine the signal to determine whether the light in my direction was properly coordinated so as to turn red when the one in your direction turned green? Did you do this immediately before or after you cited me?

Very few officers check the lights for coordination. If the officer did not, it sheds doubt as to whether the light was really red when you entered the intersection.

d. Running a Stop Sign (VC § 22450)

For this violation, there are usually only two issues:

1. Whether you came to a complete stop behind the "limit line" (or "prolongation" of the intersecting street curb lines), and

2. Whether there was a regulation stop sign controlling traffic in your direction.

---

[10] This is because there are 5,280 feet in a mile and 3,600 seconds in an hour. 5,280/3,600 = 1.4666 . . . (about 1.47).

The questions you ask the officer should focus on his powers of observation. He will probably claim that you failed to stop. You will claim you did stop and that he wasn't properly observing you. The discussion in Section D(2)(d) below should cover this adequately.

e. Illegal Turns (VC §§ 22100-22106)

These sections deal mainly with "unsafe" turns (usually left turns) at intersections which "constitute a hazard" to other drivers and allegedly aren't made "with reasonable safety." Whether a particular driver really commits such a violation is a matter of subjective interpretation. Therefore, you should ask the same sorts of questions you would ask in Basic Speed Law violations and bring out conditions that show your turn was done safely. The following questions should be helpful.

1. Was the intersection controlled by a speed limit? What color was the signal when I entered the intersection? [Ask these only if you had the right of way.]

2. Did I come to a complete stop in the intersection before turning? [Ask only if you did—it tends to show you were being careful.]

3. How many feet was the oncoming vehicle from me when I made the left turn?

4. How fast was the oncoming traffic moving?

Based on the answers to 3 and 4, the time you had, in seconds, to make the turn before being hit by the oncoming traffic is equal to:

$$\frac{\text{distance of oncoming vehicle from yours (feet)}}{1.47 \times \text{speed of oncoming traffic (mph)}}$$

If this works out to five seconds or more, you can later argue that there was plenty of time for you to turn safely.

5. Was my turn signal flashing? [Ask only if it was.] For how long?

6. Did any vehicle blow its horn in response to my turn? [Ask only if none did.]

7. Did the oncoming vehicle slow down, in your opinion, because of my turn? [He will almost always answer yes.]

8. Did that vehicle screech its tires? [Ask only if it didn't.]

9. Isn't it true that many safe drivers slow down at intersections out of general caution, whether or not someone up ahead is turning?

E. Testimony Presented on Your Behalf

UNLIKE THE PROSECUTION, which has to prove all the elements of the offense, your testimony need only disprove one. For example, in speeding violations, your best approach might be to establish that the officer's estimate of your speed was incorrect. In Basic Speed Law violations, you might want to establish that the speed the officer says you were going was safe. Or that the speed limit signs weren't properly posted.

You're not required to testify, but it's a good idea. Though they won't admit it, judges assume that a defendant who refuses to testify must be guilty. And given that the odds are stacked against traffic court defendants, your testimony can only help.

It's a mistake to write down your testimony and recite it verbatim in court. Reciting it word for word from memory is also not a good idea—it will sound like a canned speech. Instead, draw up an outline of your testimony and fill in the gaps in a normal, relaxed manner. (There is absolutely nothing wrong with using notes while you testify.[11]) Practice your clear, smooth presentation in front of a relative, friend, or a mirror.

1. Maximum Speed Violations (Over 55 VC § 22349)

This type of violation is most often committed on the freeway where CHP officers try to pace your speed, checking it against their own speedometers. Your only defense is that you weren't really going over 55 (65 on portions of certain interstate freeways). Whether or not it may have been safe to do so is not legally relevant. If you do nothing more than testify that you were looking at your speedometer (which you might even have road-calibrated using the mile signs and a stopwatch—see Chapter 4, Section C) and that it indicated less than 55 mph, the judge will almost always believe the officer's word over yours.

However, many overzealous CHP officers will drive over the speed limit while bearing down on you and read their own faster speed. That way, even though both your speedometer and the officer's may have been correct, his might read a steady speed

higher than yours during the time he was gaining on you. [How this works is explained in detail in Chapter 4, Section C(1).] Thus, both you and the officer may be testifying truthfully as to your respective speedometer readings, so the judge doesn't have to disbelieve the officer to find you not guilty.

2. "Basic Speed Law" Violations (VC § 22350)

When you're charged with going over the speed limit, but less than 55 mph, you can attack both the officer's estimate of your speed, and also attempt to show that a speed over the limit would have been safe. And you don't have to admit that you were going over the limit—that's for the prosecution to prove. After you testify as to what you thought your speed actually was, you might then point out that "Even if I was going slightly faster than that, it was safe to do so because.... " As we say in Chapter 4, Section C(2), this claim would be backed up with testimony as to favorable road, weather and traffic conditions. As part of your testimony, you should list any of the following conditions—if they applied when you were cited—which might render a higher speed safe:

1. The alleged violations occurred at a time when very little vehicle or pedestrian traffic was on the road. Very early morning hours are best, but in general, times other than rush hours (7-9 a.m., 11:30-1:00 p.m., 4-6 p.m.) are also good. The time you were cited will be listed on the ticket.

2. There was little or no other traffic in your lane, in your direction, or on the whole road, for at least a half mile.

3. There was no cross traffic at uncontrolled (stop sign only) intersections.

4. You were in the "fast lane" (lane no. 2 of 2 lanes).

5. The weather was clear (no rain, fog, hail, etc.).

6. The road was dry.

---

[11]Note, however, that the police officer or prosecutor can ask the judge for permission to review your notes.

7. If at night, the road was well-lighted by regularly spaced street lamps.

8. There were no sharp curves, hills, dips or other such "natural" road defects requiring a slower speed.

3. Running a Stoplight (VC § 21453)

When you're accused of running a red light, the only issue is usually whether your vehicle entered the intersection when the light changed from yellow to red. This means the front bumper of your vehicle must have passed into the cross street just after the light changed. The best type of testimony is outlined as follows:

1. You were driving at the speed limit.

2. You were only several car lengths from the intersection when the green light turned yellow.

3. You didn't think you could safely stop the car, either because you feared being rear-ended by the tailgater behind you, or because you were afraid you'd come to a stop inside the intersection.

4. You proceeded through the yellow light cautiously.

5. You looked up at it and noted that it hadn't yet changed to red as your car entered the intersection. (A diagram might be very useful.)

Note: Needless to say, you should only testify as to the above if you can do so truthfully. Your argument might be that had you braked as soon as the light turned yellow, you would have come to a stop right in the middle of, or beyond, the intersection. Also, if you can testify to the distance you were from the light when it changed from green to yellow, the duration of the yellow light, and your car's speed, you may be able to show that you could only have entered the intersection while the light was still yellow. [See Chapter 5, Section A(2).]

4. Running a Stop Sign (VC § 22450)

As we saw in Chapter 5, Section A(1), the issue is simply whether you came to a complete stop behind the limit lines or entrance to the intersection. The more you go into detail about what happened while you were stopped, the more believable your testimony. Things like this, if true, might help:

1. You saw the stop sign, slowed down, and came to a complete stop.

2. You stopped behind the white limit lines painted on the road, or, if none, behind the entrance to the intersection.

3. You noticed a slight amount of cross traffic, and inched forward a few feet for a better look at it, where you stopped again.

4. You looked left and right, waited until it appeared safe, and drove forward.

A defense that occasionally works is that the stop sign was obscured and you couldn't see it until it was too late. Perhaps untrimmed tree leaves or branches obscured the stop sign. If you were unable to see it, you can argue that you lacked the necessary "criminal negligence" to be guilty of the offense.

5. Illegal Turns (VC §§ 22100-22106)

When you're accused of having made an "unsafe" or "hazardous" turn at an intersection, you might want to testify—to the extent you truthfully can—as follows:

1. If the road had two or more lanes in your direction and you had to change lanes to turn, you signaled and looked in your rear or side view mirror before doing so.

2. You used your turn signal at least 100 feet (6-8 car lengths) before turning.

3. You had the right of way, either because the light was green for a left or right turn, or that you stopped on a red light before turning right.

4. You proceeded into the intersection cautiously, watching oncoming traffic if you were turning left, or for cross traffic from the left if you were turning right.

5. You came to a complete or near stop in the intersection (or at least proceeded cautiously) for a left turn, or at the entrance to the intersection for a right turn on a red light.

6. There was no oncoming traffic (for a left turn) within several car lengths of the other side's entrance to the intersection, or no cross traffic from the left (for a right turn).

7. Your turning movement was smooth, neither too sharp, nor too wide.

8. You finished your turn in the proper lane of the street you turned onto—the far right lane for a right turn, and the left or middle lane for a left turn.

6. Other Offenses

To list detailed summaries of proper testimony for all the offenses listed in Chapter 5 would take more space than would be justified. Generally, in order to outline your "direct" testimony for other offenses, the first step should be to carefully analyze the Vehicle Code violation you're charged with, breaking the offense down into its "elements." Then, try to plan your testimony—to the extent you can truthfully testify—around those elements. You should especially concentrate on any elements (e.g., "posing a hazard," driving "unsafely") which call for a measure of subjective interpretation. Finally, outline your testimony.

F. Cross-Examination by the Prosecution

IN REGULAR CRIMINAL TRIALS, where procedure is more formal than in traffic court, the prosecuting attorney gets a chance to cross-examine any person who testifies. This seldom occurs in most traffic court trials because infraction cases are usually prosecuted by police officers instead of prosecuting attorneys. A few judges give the police officer the opportunity to cross-examine, an opportunity most officers decline, if only because they're so sure they'll win without it. If the officer does try to cross-examine you or a witness, you might want to object on the grounds that he's not an attorney. It should be remembered that the officer doesn't really represent the state as a prosecutor. He's only a witness there to tell his side of the story. A person can prosecute a case by cross-examining a witness only if she is a plaintiff (one who files charges) or a defendant, or the proper attorney. (You can cross-examine the officer because you're the defendant.) If you wish to object, say something like the following:

"Your Honor, I object to Officer Shultz cross-examining me on the ground that he is neither the true plaintiff nor its attorney—he's just a witness." [If the judge suggests you're out of line, you might ask whether she will permit your non-attorney witness to cross-examine police officers.]

Assuming you or your witnesses have to respond to cross-examination questions, keep the following things in mind:

1. Don't respond in an evasive, hostile or argumentative manner—keep your cool.

2. Keep your answers as short as possible, and don't volunteer unnecessary information. You don't always have to be tricked into answering yes or no— you have the right to answer the question fully. But any new information you add opens the door for more questions.

3. Tell the truth. Obvious as this may sound, people still think they can get away with "stretching the truth." The last thing you'll want is for the prosecutor to expose a lie. This is likely to happen when

you are less than truthful in response to a question to which the prosecutor already knows—and can prove—the answer.

G. Final Argument

AFTER YOU (AND YOUR witnesses, if any) have completed testifying, or after any cross-examination by the prosecution, both you and the prosecutor should have a chance to summarize your case. This is where you explain to the judge (or jury in a misdemeanor case) why there's a reasonable doubt as to whether you had committed at least one of the elements of the offense, and possibly also how you

have proven a defense. Basically, you are reviewing and summarizing the main points you had been trying to make all along at trial. You can also argue points of law, citing cases or statutes which support your position.

Before trial, outline your final argument on a sheet of paper. But don't feel bound by it. Be sure your outline is flexible enough to include unexpected statements made by the officer during his testimony.

Unfortunately, many judges are quite narrow-minded about allowing traffic court defendants to "argue" their case in a closing statement. Such judges have developed the view that only lawyers are capable of understanding and making legal arguments, and will jealously try to keep everyone else out.

If the judge refuses to let you make your final arguments or cuts you off before completion, you should politely but firmly assert your right to make a legal argument. There is a case which says that even defendants in informal traffic court have this right.[12] You might not want to cite the case, however, for if you merely ask to be allowed to make a closing argument and the judge says no, you have a good chance of getting your conviction reversed on appeal. [See Chapter 16, Section B(11).]

---

[12]In *People v. Douglas* (1973) 31 Cal.App.3d Supp. 26, 106 Cal.Rptr. 611, an appellate court reversed a conviction for running a stoplight because the traffic court refused to allow the defendant to argue his case. Also, see the U.S. Supreme Court case of *Herring v. New York* (1975) 422 U.S. 853, 95 S.Ct. 2550.

12

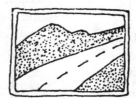

TRIALS BEFORE A JUDGE (WITHOUT A JURY)

A. Introduction

SINCE JURY TRIALS ARE available only for misdemeanors and not for infractions, most traffic violations are heard before a judge alone. As a general
rule, these judge trials are conducted relatively
informally. However, if a prosecutor is present
(usually in a misdemeanor case where you didn't
ask for a jury or in the few counties which insist on
prosecutors), the trial will be more formal. First we
provide you an overview of each type of trial. Then
we get into specifics.

1. Traffic Trials Without a Prosecutor (Infractions Only)

In traffic trials without a prosecutor, the clerk first
calls the case and you and the police officer go
forward. Before testimony begins, you may wish to
make any of the last-minute motions (e.g., for
continuance, dismissal, judge disqualification) that
we discuss in Chapter 11, Section C, if you feel it's
necessary. You can also "move to exclude" multiple
prosecution witnesses from the courtroom while the
remaining witness testifies.[1]

The judge allows the officer to tell his side of the
story in narrative form, perhaps asking a few
questions afterward. You then should be given an
opportunity to cross-examine the officer with relevant questions. Some judges may not remind you of
this, but they must let you do so if you insist. At this
time, you tell your side of the dispute, and any
witnesses you have tell their version, after which the
judge might ask a few questions.

Finally, the judge announces his verdict of guilty
or not guilty. If he finds you guilty, he will usually
pronounce sentence (a fine) right away, unless you
ask for a postponement.

2. Nonjury Trials Prosecuted by a District (or City) Attorney (Misdemeanors and Infractions)

All misdemeanor cases are prosecuted by district or
city attorneys. While trials in infraction cases usually
are prosecuted just by the officer, occasionally a
prosecutor will appear. In such infraction cases, and
in misdemeanor cases where the defendant has
given up the right to jury trial, here's how the trial
proceeds.

The clerk calls the case, and you and the prosecutor go forward. Again, this is the time to make any
last minute motions to request a continuance, a
dismissal, a change of venue, the disqualification of
the judge, and to ask for the exclusion of multiple
prosecution witnesses from the courtroom.

The prosecutor, then you, are permitted to make
opening statements summarizing what you each
intend to prove. (These are often dispensed with in
trials without a jury.)

The prosecution puts on its case by asking
questions of its witnesses. After each prosecution
witness testifies, you are given the chance to cross-
examine her.

After the prosecution's witnesses have testified,
you can give an opening statement if you hadn't
given one earlier. Also, if you feel the prosecution
didn't prove its case, you can ask for an acquittal
right then. If your request is denied, you then
present your case by testifying in narrative form as
to your version of events. The prosecutor may cross-
examine you, just as you cross-examined the
prosecution's witnesses. Any witnesses you may
have give their testimony, after which the prosecutor
cross-examines them.

The prosecutor, then you, make the final closing
arguments, summarizing the testimony and relating
it to the applicable law. After your argument, the
prosecutor can make another "rebuttal" argument.
The judge then announces his verdict. Unless you
want to be sentenced right away, the judge will set a
later time for sentencing.

---

[1]These kinds of motions are commonly called "motions in limine"
(pronounced *in-lim'-in-nee*).

Although the above formats are found respectively in police-officer-prosecuted infraction trials and D.A.-prosecuted misdemeanor trials, some courts are run more formally (or informally) than others. Each of these formats is discussed in greater detail in Section C, below.

B. Understanding the Courtroom

TRAFFIC COURT TRIALS are generally conducted in standard courthouses in courtrooms which look much like those on television. In addition to the judge (or commissioner), a clerk and a bailiff will normally be present. They sit at tables immediately in front of the judge's elevated bench, or slightly off to the side. The clerk's job is to keep the judge supplied with necessary files and papers, and to make sure that proceedings flow smoothly. In more formal trials, there also may be a court reporter present, who keeps a word-by-word record of proceedings. Such records are seldom kept in traffic court.

Courtrooms are divided about two-thirds of the way toward the front by a sort of fence known as "the bar." The judge, court personnel and lawyers use the area on one side of the bar, and the public, including people waiting for their cases to be heard, the other side. You are invited to cross the bar only when your case is called by the clerk. Then you come forward and sit at the long table, known as the counsel table, facing the judge. What happens next depends on whether yours is a formal or informal trial. In informal trials, your witnesses accompany you to the counsel table. At more formal trials, they remain behind the bar (as does the officer) and testify at the witness stand only when their names are called. In some informal traffic court hearings, you will be asked to raise your right hand and swear to tell the truth before the judge arrives. In others, and in all formal trials, you or your witnesses will only be sworn in just before testifying.

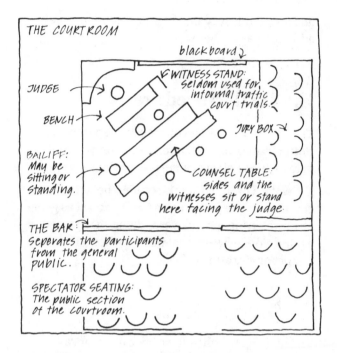

THE COURTROOM

blackboard

JUDGE

WITNESS STAND: seldom used for informal traffic court trials.

BENCH

JURY BOX

BAILIFF: May be sitting or standing.

COUNSEL TABLE: sides and the witnesses sit or stand here facing the judge.

THE BAR: Seperates the participants from the general public.

SPECTATOR SEATING: The public section of the courtroom.

In nearly all traffic court trials, you, your witnesses and the prosecution will present the case from the long table; you do not sit in the witness box next to the judge. Many people feel that it is polite to stand while addressing the judge, but this is not a requirement and you should do what feels most comfortable to you.

Common Sense Note: Many people react to the negative experience they have had with our traffic court system by appearing hostile and angry in court. This sort of attitude, while understandable, is almost sure to be counterproductive. Judges are used to "lawyerly attitudes"—that is, to people who separate themselves emotionally from the cause they are arguing—and will often punish (decide against) people who make "a scene." A little conviction that you are right can be refreshing against this background of work-a-day cynicism, and can be very effective, but don't overdo it. As a general rule, judges have a low tolerance for emotion.

Also, when you address the judge, you should say, "Your Honor," or, if you can't bring yourself to do that, "Sir" or "Ma'am." Silly as it sounds, many judges have fragile egos, and are so used to being addressed this way that it grates on them to be addressed any other way.

C. Trial Procedure

THIS SECTION TAKES you step by step through a traffic court trial, with information on your options at the various stages of the proceedings.

Note: Throughout this section, the terms "prosecutor" and "the prosecution" will be used as general terms referring to whoever is doing the prosecuting against you, whether that be the police officer or a district or city attorney.

1. Clerk Calls the Case

The trial begins when the clerk calls your case, usually by saying "People v. [your name]." The clerk (or sometimes the judge) will then recite the bare facts of the case, perhaps something like "you are charged with a violation of Sec. 22350 of the Vehicle Code—the Basic Speed Law—on October 24, 1987, by driving 45 mph in a 35-mph zone on the 400 block of Main Street in the City of Ventura."

2. Last Minute Motions

Before the prosecution begins its case, you might want to make one or more of the motions discussed in Chapter 11, Section C. These include requesting a continuance, disqualifying a judge, asking for dismissal because of delay, and moving the trial to the county seat.

a. Lack of Prosecution (If the Officer Fails to Show Up)

Since you're presumed to be innocent until proven guilty, your case should be dismissed if no one is able to testify to your guilt—namely the officer. If the officer fails to show, you should ask the judge to dismiss the case "for lack of prosecution," perhaps complaining about how you've been severely

inconvenienced by having to take time off work. Such requests are often granted. They are denied, and the case postponed to another date, only where the officer has a very good excuse, both for not showing and not notifying the court beforehand—such as when the officer's wife had to be rushed to the hospital to give birth.

b. Disqualifying the Judge

If when your case is called you have decided you probably cannot get a fair shake from the judge, commissioner or traffic referee, and the officer is present, this is your last opportunity to disqualify the judge by presenting a Peremptory Challenge if you haven't done so already. Simply say, "Your Honor, I wish to file this Peremptory Challenge," and hand it to the clerk.

If the judge is a actually a volunteer lawyer serving as "pro tem" judge, you do not need to do this. Simply tell him you don't consent to his hearing the case—if the officer shows.

c. Excluding Multiple Witnesses

Once in a while the prosecution will have more witnesses than just the police officer. In addition to freeway aircraft patrol situations, this is likely to happen if you encountered two police officers on patrol when you were cited. Also, if you were involved in an accident, other drivers or bystanders—in addition to the officer—may be asked to testify against you. Needless to say, it will work against you if each of the prosecution witnesses recites a similar version of the facts but a version different from yours. On the other hand, if the testimony of a witness is inconsistent with another's, it will help your case.

If the witnesses are allowed to stay inside the courtroom and watch each other testify, their stories may indeed become very similar. For this reason, you should make a "motion to exclude multiple witnesses" from the courtroom. Such a request will always be granted, and will mean that while any prosecution witness testifies, all others must wait outside.

Note: A "Motion to Exclude" works both ways. Any witnesses you have must also then wait outside while you or another testifies. (You can minimize this disadvantage by waiting until after they testify to give your own testimony; you can't be excluded from the courtroom because you're the defendant.)

d. Asking That a Reporter or Recorder Be Used

According to the case of *In re Armstrong* (1981) 126 Cal.App.3d 565, a misdemeanor defendant has the right to insist that a court stenographer (reporter) be present to take verbatim notes of the proceedings, or that a tape recorder record them. Penal Code Section 19.7 says that unless there is a law that specifically provides otherwise for infractions (such as PC § 19.6 removing the right to a jury trial in infraction cases), misdemeanor rules apply to infractions.

Since there is no law specifically allowing infraction proceedings to proceed without a reporter or recorder present, the *Armstrong* rule applies to infractions the same way it applies to misdemeanors. The purpose of this particular rule is to allow for preparation of a "transcript" of the trial proceedings if you need to appeal. If the judge refuses to allow a court reporter to be present, ask to be allowed to use your own pocket tape recorder, if you have one. Unless the judge has a good reason to deny this, she must allow it [California Rules of Court, Rule 980(c)].

e. Requesting a Continuance If Your Subpoena Is Not Obeyed

If you've subpoenaed a witness for trial and that person does not appear, you should request a continuance—but only if the officer who cited you

shows up. Also, if a person on whom you served a subpoena duces tecum ordering him/her to produce certain documents fails to do so, you can ask the judge to postpone the case and order that person to bring the requested material.

3. Opening Statements

Before testimony is presented, both the prosecution and the defense have an opportunity to make an opening statement, stating how they intend to prove each element of the case.

a. The Prosecution's Statement (Only in Trials Prosecuted by a Lawyer)

In trials prosecuted by the deputy district or city attorney, the prosecution may give an "opening statement," stating how he intends to prove each element of the case. But since most trials are prosecuted by a police officer, opening statements are rare. Police officers cannot make them, and prosecutors usually "waive" them. A simple opening statement for the prosecution might go something like this:

"Your Honor, the People will show, through the testimony of Officer Ted Ticketem of the Los Angeles Police Department, that the defendant, Stanley Safespeed, while driving a red 1987 Corvette, drove approximately half a mile down Wilshire Blvd., where posted speed limit signs indicate the prima facie safe speed to be 35 miles per hour, at a speed in excess of 50 mph, in violation of the Basic Speed Law. Officer Ticketem will testify that while parked and observing traffic, he saw Mr. Safespeed weaving in and out of traffic at a high rate of speed, endangering pedestrians and other drivers. The officer gave chase for at least a half mile, during which time he clocked Mr. Safespeed's vehicle as traveling 53 miles per hour."

An opening statement indicates what the prosecutor intends to bring out when he questions the officer on "direct examination." The prosecutor doesn't testify that Mr. Safespeed did those things, but simply lays the groundwork for the officer (or maybe other witnesses as well) to testify to that effect.

b. Your Opening Statement

If the prosecutor does make an opening statement, you have the right to either give one immediately following, or "reserve" it for when you begin to put on your testimony. As a practical matter, you probably should reserve your opening statement. By doing so, you have the opportunity to work it around the officer's testimony. Moreover, by giving your statement right after the prosecution's, you'll be revealing your strategy in advance. (A sample reserved opening statement is given in Section 5, below.)

Even when a prosecuting attorney does not make an opening statement or isn't even present (the usual situation), you still have the right to present an opening statement before you testify. Some people feel an opening statement helps them organize their presentation.

4. The Prosecution's Testimony

After any opening statements, the officer who cited you will testify. In most traffic trials, he will be testifying from the counsel table. In more formal trials, he will testify from a witness stand.

You can interrupt if you have a legitimate legal objection to the propriety of particular types of testimony (see below). However, you should never

interrupt with "He's lying!" or "That's not true!" You'll get the chance to testify later.

a. Your Objections to Certain Types of Testimony

You have little to gain from making technical objections, even if you know how to make them. Most objections to testimony are made on one of four grounds:

1. The testimony is irrelevant to anything which needs to be proven;

2. It relates to something or someone other than what the person testifying observed, and is therefore "hearsay";

3. The question asked of a witness assumes facts not in evidence. (For example, when an officer testifies that your car exceeded the 35 mph speed limit but hasn't testified that the speed limit was 35, as evidenced by posted signs, he's assuming a fact—that the speed limit was 35—which hasn't been testified to yet.); or

4. The foundation necessary to testify to a particular fact hasn't been introduced. (For example, a photograph of the scene of the alleged offense, by itself, proves nothing. However, your testimony that you took the picture at a certain day and time representative of traffic conditions at the time you were stopped establishes a "foundation" of fact that gives meaning to the photograph.)

Watch the officer carefully to see if he's using notes. Many officers use notes scribbled on the back of their copy of the ticket to refresh their memories. If the officer does this, you have a right to object on the basis the officer hasn't "laid the foundation" necessary to use the notes. First he must testify he needs the notes to refresh his memory, at which point you have a right to see them.

The two most important objections likely to be made in traffic court fall under the last of these grounds.

In the last chapter, we told you how to prepare to make an objection to radar evidence in speeding cases. It is important that you object whenever a police officer starts testifying about his radar unit's speed reading, unless the original or certified copy of a traffic and engineering survey justifying the speed limit has already been introduced into evidence. [See Chapter 11, Section D(1)(a).] Making this type of objection in formal trials is fairly easy—you just wait for the prosecutor to ask any question relating to radar and immediately object before the officer can answer, on the ground that the prosecution hasn't "laid the foundation under VC § 40803(b)" for the introduction of radar evidence.

Unfortunately, in most trials involving speed violations the officer just tells his side of the story instead of responding to questions. This makes it very difficult to stop him before he testifies to the speed reading on his radar unit. You should therefore be ready to jump in with your objections at the slightest hint from the officer that he is going to try to get in his radar evidence without providing a traffic study. Your objection might be phrased like this:

"Excuse me, Your Honor, I would like to object to Officer Growlski's proposed testimony on his use of radar, on the ground that he hasn't laid the foundation by introducing a traffic and engineering survey justifying the speed limit. Under Sec. 40803(b) of the Vehicle Code, he is required to do this."

5. Your Cross-Examination

After the officer is finished, you get to cross-examine him along the lines suggested in the previous chapter. If you haven't read Section D of the previous chapter, you should do so now. Remember to be polite and non-argumentative. If he gives an unexpected answer, don't argue with him. Either ask more detailed questions if you think he's lying, or just go on to the next line of questioning. Ask him simple questions that require short and direct answers—don't ask vague questions that give him a chance to tell more of his story. If he tries to do that, politely interrupt with "Thank you" or "I think you've answered my question." If he persists in trying to tell more of his story—rather than responding to the question—remind him that he already had a chance to do that when he gave his direct testimony.

If the case is handled by a prosecuting attorney, he will have the chance to ask more questions of the officer after you finish. This is called "redirect examination," and the questions are supposed to relate only to the matters you brought up during your cross-examination. If the prosecutor takes advantage of his right to redirect examination, you, too, get another turn—called "recross-examination"—to ask more questions of the officer. Again, the scope of your questions is limited to matters brought out by the prosecutor on redirect examination. Theoretically, this could go on forever, but since the scope of the questions is limited to what the other side asked just before, it eventually ends. In fact, in traffic cases, it rarely goes beyond one recross and one redirect examination.

6. Motion for Acquittal

Once in a while, particularly where the violation is complex, the officer may forget to testify about one of the elements. Keep a little checklist of the elements of the charged offenses in front of you. Check off each element as he testifies to it after you've finished cross-examining the officer and ask yourself whether he has failed to testify to one or more of the elements. If so, turn to the judge and say something like:

"Your Honor, I move for an acquittal on the ground that Officer Gettem has failed to establish all the elements of the offense."

Then explain which elements of the offense are unsupported by any testimony. If you're correct, there's a slight chance the judge will find you not guilty. On the other hand, the judge may simply allow the officer to supply the missing testimony. But you have nothing to lose by trying.

Note: In radar speed violation cases, the requirement of the introduction of an engineering and traffic survey into evidence is considered an "element" of the case. [See VC § 40803(b) and Chapter 4, Section B.] If a survey was not produced as required, this should be pointed out at this time as well, in support of a motion for acquittal.

7. "Reserved" Opening Statements

If, at the beginning of the trial, you reserved your opening statement, now is the time to make it, before you give your testimony. If you decide to give an opening statement, summarize what you (and your witnesses, if any) intend to prove. Stan Safespeed's opening statement might sound something like this:

"Your Honor, I will show, primarily through my own testimony, that I ascertained my speed to be approximately 35 miles per hour on Wilshire Boulevard, by occasionally glancing at my speedometer as I was driving, and that my speedometer, as shown by a subsequent calibration, was accurate at that speed reading. I will also testify to the fact that Officer Ticketem suddenly raced up behind me, nearly rear-ending my vehicle, and that is the sole cause of his own high speedometer reading.

Finally, I will show that the road was well-constructed and lit, that the traffic was moderate, that the weather was clear and dry, and that therefore, even if I was going over 35 miles per hour, I was still traveling at a safe speed."

Notice that this statement is only a preview of the testimony that will follow. It is important not to confuse the opening statement (a summary of what you intend to prove) with the proof itself.

8. Your Testimony

In most informal trials, you will simply stand up at the counsel table, look at the judge, and present your testimony. Don't hesitate to look down at your notes, but if possible, don't read directly from them. In formal trials, you'll be testifying from a witness stand.

When you're finished giving your testimony, pause for an instant (or step down from the witness stand). Then, if you have any other witnesses, introduce them. Your witnesses can either testify in the same narrative fashion in which you testified, or, if you prefer, you can ask them to respond to your questions.

In more formal trials, the prosecutor may insist that your witnesses' testimony only be in response to your questions. Unless you were going to question them anyway, you should object to this request. Simply say that you're unfamiliar with "direct examination" techniques, and that (if there's no jury) the judge will be able to disregard objectionable testimony anyway. If you choose—or are required—to have your witnesses respond to questions, and particularly if a prosecuting attorney is conducting the case, here are some hints that will make things go easier:

a. Think about the key facts to which your witnesses will testify, and arrange them in topical or chronological order. Try to save the more important questions for last.

b. Build a foundation for later questions using the expected answers from earlier questions.

c. Avoid irrelevant details.

d. Don't ask questions which assume facts "not in evidence." (This means, don't ask "How hard was it raining?" unless there has already been testimony that it *was* raining.)

e. Don't ask leading questions. In other words, don't put words in your own witnesses' mouths or ask questions which seem to instruct them on how to answer. (Instead of asking "The road surface was dry, wasn't it?" or "Was the road dry?" ask "What was the condition of the road surface?")

Don't ask questions which call for "hearsay." Don't ask your witness to recite what she was told by someone else, unless that someone else was the police officer *and* it helps your case.

9. Cross-Examination by the Prosecution

After you and any witnesses have testified, the D.A. (if present), or sometimes the judge, may question any or all of you. If the police officer tries to do this, you should object on the ground that he is only a witness, not licensed to practice law, and that courtroom cross-examination certainly constitutes the practice of law. (See Chapter 11, Section F.) If your objection is overruled, you must answer the officer's questions.

Any response by you or your witnesses on cross-examination should be given courteously, truthfully, and as briefly as possible. Contrary to old Perry Mason episodes, you don't have to give a "yes" or "no" answer. After all, what if the prosecutor asked you whether you knew you were speeding? Both "yes" and "no" are bad answers. You have a right, for example, to say you knew you weren't speeding because you were continually glancing at your speedometer, or to briefly explain your answer.

Caution! Don't be hostile toward the person cross-examining; it may hurt your case. You do have the right, however, to politely object to any question which is abusive, assumes facts not in evidence, or asks irrelevant information or hearsay. Keep your objections to a minimum, objecting only when your or your witness' response to the question would be damaging to your case—not just for the sake of proving you would have made a dynamite lawyer if you hadn't decided to be a professional bowler, or whatever. Finally, remember that any matters brought up during cross-examination can be clarified by your giving further testimony.

10. Closing Statements

After all the evidence is presented, both the prosecution and defense will have opportunity to make a closing statement.

a. The Prosecution's Statement

In trials conducted by a prosecuting attorney, she will probably give a closing argument as to why you're guilty. She will explain how the officer's testimony (and maybe even some cross-examination testimony given by you or your witnesses) "proves beyond a reasonable doubt" each element of the offense and disproves any defenses you've raised.

If a police officer tries to give a closing statement, you can object on the ground that this involves the practice of law. If the officer is nevertheless permitted to make a statement, listen closely. The officer is definitely not permitted to introduce new testimony. If he does, object.

b. Your Closing Statement

Whether or not a prosecutor or police officer gives a closing argument, you have an absolute right to make one. Unfortunately, and unfairly, this fact is often ignored by traffic court judges. If the judge tries to deny you this right, politely but firmly insist on it, unless it is absolutely clear that you have won your case. If the judge interrupts to tell you a closing argument isn't allowed, you have two choices. You can cite *People v. Douglas*[2] as authority that a closing statement must be allowed in traffic cases, or you can simply submit to the judge's unlawful refusal to hear a final argument. Then you'll have a good chance of getting your conviction reversed on appeal. [See Chapter 16, Section A(11).] However, all you'll win on appeal is a right to a new trial.

Your closing statement should basically summarize how at least one of the elements of the offense hasn't been proven beyond a reasonable doubt or how you have proven a defense. It might help to explain first how the law you're accused of having violated can be broken down into its various elements. Then explain how:

1. The officers' testimony failed to show that one or more of the elements was present; or

2. Your own testimony (and that of any other witness) has shown that one or more elements did not exist despite the officer's testimony; and/or

3. Testimony has established one or more defenses to the charge.

To begin your closing argument, say to the judge: "My closing argument is as follows: …" (You always give your closing argument standing up at the counsel table, even if you testified from the witness stand.)

c. Prosecution's Rebuttal

In formal trials, the prosecution gets to make a *second* closing statement after you've given yours. They get two shots at convincing the judge, but you only get one. This is usually justified on the ground that the prosecution has the burden of proving you guilty and thus should have the last word.

11. The Verdict

After all the evidence and closing statements have been presented, the judge must announce her verdict. When the judge doesn't have the guts to tell you to your face that you've just been found guilty (or sincerely wishes to think the matter over), she may try to take the case "under advisement." But she cannot do this without your permission. If the judge makes the mistake of "taking the matter under advisement" without asking you if it's okay, don't remind her of this mistake. You can appeal if you're found guilty. The conviction will almost certainly be reversed,[3] and the case will probably be dismissed. [See Chapter 16, Section A(12).]

If the judge takes the case under advisement, call or visit the court about once a week to find out the verdict. You must appeal within 30 days from when the judge files the verdict with the court clerk. Court clerks have a nasty habit of waiting two or three weeks before notifying you by mail. With the mail as slow as it sometimes is, this can leave you with very little, or no, time in which to appeal.

If the judge finds you not guilty, you don't have to pay any fine and are entitled to a refund of any bail you may have posted. Such refund should reach you (speedily) in two to six months.

---

[2]In *People v. Douglas* (1973) 31 Cal.App.3d Supp. 26, 106 Cal.Rptr. 611, an appeals court reversed a conviction for running a red light because the trial judge "ignored, talked-over and otherwise refused to acknowledge the defendant when he attempted to make a closing summation."

[3]*People v. Kriss* (1979) 96 Cal.App.3d 913, 158 Cal.Rptr. 420.

12. The Sentence

Most traffic court judges will try to assess a fine immediately after announcing a guilty verdict. However, you have the right to wait at least six hours before sentencing, unless you agree otherwise.[4] If the judge doesn't ask your permission, you have grounds to have the sentence vacated and be resentenced. (See Chapter 14, Section A.) Obviously, then, you wouldn't want to exercise this option unless the sentence is too harsh.

13. Reporting Obnoxious Judges

Unfortunately, quite a few judges take offense at non-lawyers who represent themselves competently and thoroughly in traffic court. Since most judges are old men, born and schooled in another era, they will, at times, cut off cross-examination and final argument, interrupt repeatedly, stare off into space while you present your case, ridicule you, and perhaps comment on how honest and believable the police officer is, compared to you, the liar.

Even in the face of this sadly too-frequent behavior, you can have the last word. Everyone in the court, whether accused of a traffic violation or not, has the right to complain about the behavior of the official presiding over the trial, by simply writing a letter. If your complaint is about a "commissioner," "traffic referee" or "pro-tem judge" (lawyer filling in as a judge, with your consent), your complaint should be to the "presiding judge" of the Municipal Court. Look in the phone book under the Municipal Court for the county, preferably under the sub-heading for "court administration," or something similar. Call that number, ask who the presiding judge of the court is, and ask for his or her mailing address.

If your complaint is about an actual judge, it should be made to the Commission on Judicial Performance. This agency has the power to censure or even remove judges for misconduct. Although it handles judicial discipline cases about as laxly, weakly and meekly as the State Bar used to handle lawyer-discipline cases, and although it usually acts only in the face of repeated complaints, the Commission on Judicial Performance has disciplined a tiny handful of judges for extreme misconduct—including one for going on record as stating he always believes police officers over traffic-court defendants.[5] The Commission's address is 1390 Market St., Suite 304, San Francisco, CA 94102.

One word of caution. Anyone in authority who receives a complaint about a judge or commissioner is wary of disgruntled people whose primary complaint is that the person complained of didn't believe their story at trial. This doesn't mean that if you lose in traffic court you shouldn't complain about a judge's or commissioner's improper behavior. However, you should be ready to point to specific things he or she did, in your own case or perhaps even in other cases you saw in court the day you were there, which showed a biased, prejudiced, or tantrum-oriented judge or commissioner. This would include:

- assisting the prosecution to extremes, in the prosecution of the case;

- yelling, shouting or snapping at you when you made appropriate objections;

- repeatedly cutting off your right to thoroughly cross-examine the officer with relevant questions;

- genuine inattentiveness as you presented your side of the case (staring off into space, pushing your exhibits off to the side without looking at them, etc.);

- refusal to allow you to give a closing statement, or repeated hostile interruptions during it;

- finding people guilty in contested trials more than 90% of the time (you might want to sit through all the cases and keep track);

- frequent comments that suggest the judge or commissioner believes all traffic-court defendants

---

[4]PC § 1449.

[5]See *Furey v. Commission on Judicial Performance* (1987) 43 Cal.3d 1297, 240 Cal.Rptr. 859.

guilty and/or always believes police officers over other individuals.

If you were found guilty by such a judge or commissioner, don't hesitate to say so, but be sure to give a factual basis for believing your complaint may be valid nevertheless. Be sure to give specific facts such as dates, times, case names and/or number, and perhaps a few direct quotes from the judge or commissioner, if you can recall them.

If you do complain, feel free to send a copy of your letter to the judge or commissioner, though you don't have to. In fact, sending a copy to the judge, while noting at the bottom of your letter that you are doing so (for example, with "cc: Judge O.B. Noxious") will give your complaint letter a little more credibility. You cannot be held in contempt of court for doing so, and if nothing else, you may have an effect on that judge's behavior in the future.

13

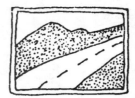

HANDLING A MISDEMEANOR CHARGE: ARRAIGNMENT TO JURY TRIAL

A. Introduction

WHEN YOU'RE CHARGED with a misdemeanor, you have the right to a trial by jury. As a general rule, a person accused of committing a misdemeanor stands a better chance of being acquitted by a jury than by a judge. That's why defendants accused of driving under the influence almost always demand a jury trial.[1]

The format of a jury trial is similar to a formal non-jury trial (described in Chapter 12). The chief differences are that jury trials require the selection of jurors prior to trial and the jury must be "instructed" (after testimony and closing statements) on how to determine whether you're guilty.

However, before you start thinking about doing your own jury trial, keep the following in mind: First, jury trials in misdemeanor cases are much more difficult than ordinary non-jury trials for infractions. This is especially true since the state will be represented by an experienced prosecutor—who knows all sorts of subtle and underhanded ways to sway juries. Second, the stakes are higher. A misdemeanor conviction for such offenses as drunk or reckless driving or speed contest or exhibitions, will give you a criminal record and will cause your insurance to be cancelled or the rates drastically increased.[2] Doing your own jury trial should be a last resort, and only because you can't find an attorney you can trust or afford. (See Chapter 9, Section B.)

B. Arraignment

THE FIRST COURTROOM appearance in a misdemeanor case is arraignment. Unlike infraction arraignments, misdemeanor arraignments cannot be waived. The most important things that occur at arraignment include pleading not guilty and requesting a jury trial.

1. Entering Your Plea

An arraignment in a misdemeanor case is similar to that for an infraction, *except* you can't bypass it and you aren't allowed to have an "informal hearing"

---

[1]If you're accused of a misdemeanor, particularly driving under the influence of alcohol or drugs, where the potential consequences are severe, you may decide to hire a lawyer. If your income is low, the court will appoint a lawyer to defend you at no cost. (See Chapter 9, Part B.)

[2]This will not be true for the misdemeanor of failure-to-appear [VC § 40508(a)], when charged as a misdemeanor. (See Chapter 7, Section B.) Still, if you're found guilty of that offense after a jury trial, a judge may sentence you to pay a high fine or even to serve several days in jail.

(described in Chapter 10). With misdemeanors, the time you're arraigned depends on whether you were issued a Notice to Appear (see Chapter 2, Section D) or were released on bail. If you were issued a Notice to Appear, the matter is handled in much the same way as an infraction, in that you must show up in court on or before the date and time indicated, to arrange with the clerk for an arraignment.[3] If you were released on bail from jail after having been arrested, your release papers should indicate your arraignment date. If you're jailed and not released (perhaps because you can't make bail), your arraignment must occur within two days after your arrest, excluding weekends.[4] It is a brief proceeding where you are informed of your rights and of the charge against you (usually the Vehicle Code section number and a very brief explanation of where and when you allegedly violated it). You are also asked to enter a plea—that is, guilty, not guilty, or nolo contendere.

Guilty pleas are more common in misdemeanor cases than in infractions, since a court appearance is required. You can't just forfeit bail to the clerk like you can with an infraction. If you don't want to fight the charge, you still have to go before a judge and plead guilty.[5]

But you should never plead guilty to a misdemeanor at arraignment. It's far better to plead not guilty and then try to work out a deal later to plead guilty to a "lesser offense" in exchange for a prosecutor's promise not to charge you with a more serious offense. (If you plead not guilty, you can always change your plea after arraignment.) If you're charged with drunk driving, for example, you might be well-advised to offer to plead guilty to the

less serious misdemeanor of reckless driving instead. Or, if the initial charge was reckless driving, you might offer to plead guilty to the infraction of violating the Basic Speed Law. (See Section C, below, on "making deals.")

You should never plead guilty to a charge arising out of an accident in which you were involved. Should you be sued, your guilty plea can be used against you. Instead, you should plead nolo contendere if you don't want to fight the ticket.

If you need time to consult an attorney for advice, tell this to the judge, who will postpone the arraignment for several days.[6] Simply say, "Your Honor, I haven't had time to consult with a lawyer. Could I please have this arraignment continued for several days?"

2. Demanding a Jury Trial

Once you plead not guilty, you should request a jury trial. In theory, when you're charged with a misdemeanor, the case should be set for a jury trial, without your having to specifically demand one. In theory, you'll wind up with a non-jury trial in a misdemeanor case only if you expressly waive (give up) that right. However, mistakes do happen. Some judges automatically set some less serious misdemeanors (such as failure to appear[7] or reckless driving) for non-jury trial because they assume that people representing themselves prefer it. Don't go along with this. If you're charged with a misdemeanor, it doesn't hurt to add "and I request a

---

[3]The appearance date and time on your ticket is more likely to mean an actual arraignment date and time—not merely a deadline to see the clerk—when a misdemeanor is charged. The practice varies between courts, and it's always best to phone or see the clerk at least a few days before the date, to ask about this.

[4]PC § 825. Unfortunately, this means that a person arrested on a Friday need not be arraigned until Tuesday—four days later.

[5]You may also avoid a trial in a misdemeanor case by pleading nolo contendere (no contest). This results in a conviction but doesn't constitute an admission that you were guilty. The purpose of this type of plea is discussed below.

[6]See PC § 990.

[7]Failure to appear can be charged as an infraction, but only with your consent. [See Chapter 7, Section B(3), and PC §§ 17(d) and 19.8.] Unfortunately, many judges don't ask you whether you consent to having it tried as an infraction, and in doing so, you give up your right to a jury trial. In this situation, you should insist that the offense be charged as a misdemeanor and insist on a jury trial, if you really wish to contest the charge. On the one hand, this exposes you to the higher penalties for misdemeanors, including a possible jail sentence if you're convicted. On the other hand, a prosecutor forced to deal with this type of minor charge as a misdemeanor may be willing to plea bargain with you rather than go to the trouble of having a jury trial.

jury trial" after the initial, "Your Honor, I plead not guilty."

In most counties, the judge won't give you a trial date right away, but will set a date for a court appearance called a "pretrial conference." [See Section C(1), below.] (In fact, pretrial conferences are so common in jury cases that if the judge simply sets the case for trial, she may have mistakenly assumed you waived a jury trial; if that happens, you should remind the judge you requested a jury trial since the offense is a misdemeanor, and ask whether a pretrial conference should be scheduled.)

As with infractions, the case must be tried within 45 days of your arraignment, unless you specifically "waive time." [See Chapter 10, Section C(1).] If you don't waive time, the judge will schedule any pretrial conference soon enough so that if negotiations fail, the case will go to trial within 45 days of the arraignment. The date for trial will be set at that time.

3. Other Requests You Can Make at Arraignment

The arraignment is also the place at which you can request any of the following:

- the place of trial changed to another court (usually the one at the county seat)—see Chapter 10, Section D(1), and Chapter 17, Section C;

- a court-appointed lawyer (only in misdemeanor cases if you haven't enough money to pay for a lawyer [see Chapter 9, Section B(2)];

- your case moved from a particular judge you feel will be prejudiced against you. [See Chapter 10, Section E(2).]

Read the passages referenced above to decide whether you might want to make any of these requests. Also, read the sections on legal research in Chapter 9, Section B(4).

C. Making Deals

SINCE JURY TRIALS can be time consuming for all concerned, the prosecutor (and maybe the judge, too) has an incentive to work out a deal with you. For example, the prosecutor might offer to drop some charges if you plead guilty to one or two others. Thus, she may agree to reduce a serious misdemeanor charge (such as driving under the influence) to a less serious one (like reckless driving—if your blood alcohol wasn't too high) or reduce a misdemeanor (reckless driving, or speed contest, or exhibition of speed) to an infraction (ordinary speeding).

1. Negotiating

Most such negotiations occur either at a "pretrial conference" in the judge's chambers, or are sometimes held impromptu just before trial, in a corner of the hallway outside the courtroom or in a nearby office.

But even though most "plea bargaining" occurs just before trial, there's nothing to prevent you from approaching the prosecutor before then to see if she is willing to reduce or dismiss one or more charges (and "recommend" a small fine to the judge) in exchange for a guilty plea. About a week after you've pleaded not guilty and demanded a jury trial, you should try to find out the name of the prosecutor who will be handling your case. This information should be available from the district (or city) attorney's office, a branch of which might be located in or near the courthouse building. Once you have the prosecutor's name, you will find it easier to get past the receptionist whenever you phone that office regarding your case.

If you plan to negotiate with the prosecutor, whatever you do, remember: it's important to let her know that you're well-prepared to go through with a jury trial, but you're willing to listen to alternatives other than pleading guilty to everything you're charged with. For example, if you're charged with a speeding infraction and a failure-to-appear misdemeanor for which you've demanded a jury trial, you might offer to plead guilty to just one charge, provided a low fine is recommended to the judge and the other charge is dismissed. Or, if you're charged with a misdemeanor such as speed contest, or exhibition of speed or reckless driving, you might offer to plead guilty to a reduced charge of simple speeding.

Other points to remember while negotiating are:

a. Do not plead guilty to everything you're charged with, on the promise of a lesser fine and/or no jail sentence. If you're charged with two or more offenses, at least one of which is a jury-triable misdemeanor, you have a lot of bargaining power; you can insist on going to a jury trial if the prosecutor won't dismiss one charge in exchange for pleading guilty (or nolo contendere) to the other.

b. Do not lay everything "on the table" by telling the prosecutor every detail of your defense strategy.

c. Never agree to plead guilty to anything when the police officer hasn't shown up to testify. (This will be rare, however, in misdemeanor cases.)

d. Never make any admission of guilt before a deal is formalized (see below).

Example: You talk to a deputy district attorney who says "Come on now—just between us—you were drunk as a skunk, weren't you?" Don't say, "Sure." If you do and a deal is not made, the prosecutor can testify to your admission in court. Even if a deal is made, there's still no reason to

admit any facts about your case to any one. So don't. All you should do to keep your part of the bargain is plead "guilty" when the judge asks you how you plead.

2. How a Deal Is Formalized

Without plea bargaining, the courts would become so clogged with cases where jury trials were demanded, that many cases would have to be dismissed for not being tried within the 45-day time limit.[8] Still, no one wants to talk much about this "necessary evil," and formal records of plea bargains are not kept. What happens once a deal is made is simply that a prosecutor requests permission to dismiss or reduce one or more charges "in the interests of justice," and indicates your intention to plead guilty to a reduced charge. Sometimes the prosecutor may also recommend a particular punishment.

Although the judge does not have to agree to the dismissal or reduction of charges, nor to the recommended punishment, he almost always will.[9] Then the judge asks you a few questions to find out if you understand that you're giving up your right to trial by pleading guilty (to the reduced charge), and that the prosecutor's "recommendation" in regard to your sentence is just that and does not bind the judge. Although this statement seems to give the judge free reign to sentence you more harshly than you bargained for, that almost never will happen. If it does, you will be given the opportunity to withdraw your guilty plea, plead not guilty instead, and go to trial before a different judge without any reference being made to your withdrawn plea.

---

[8]This has already happened in Ventura County because of the D.A.'s policy against plea bargaining.

[9]If the judge does not, he will say so and give you a chance to withdraw your offer to plead guilty.

D. Selecting the Jury

IN THIS SECTION, we'll look at the jury-selecting process—basic procedures, questions you ask potential jurors, presenting challenges to disqualify a prospective juror who you believe is strongly prejudiced against you, and making peremptory challenges to exclude certain groups of people without having to prove prejudice.

1. The Basic Procedure

Many lawyers believe that selecting the members of the jury is the single most important phase of the trial. It begins as soon as your case is called, after any preliminary motions are taken care of.

Before trial, the potential jurors will normally be seated in a "jury assembly room" waiting to be called. However, in some courts, they may be milling around in the corridors or be seated inside the courtroom with you before court begins. If you find that the people sitting around you are potential jurors, don't try to influence them. But be your pleasant and charming best. Brief idle conversation won't hurt, as long as you don't talk about your case. Don't tell anyone you're a defendant unless asked.

When your case is finally called and it's clear that no compromise can be reached, the first 12 people from the group of potential jurors will take their seats. If the court provides you with a list of all the names (and occupations) of the potential jurors, write down the name of each juror on a chart as they are seated. (Usually they are seated in two rows of six chairs each.) Later in the selection process, if a juror is disqualified and a new one takes the seat, you can cross out the name of the person who left and enter the new name. (Many lawyers prefer to write the jurors' names on small adhesive "post-it notes" attached to the appropriate place on a jury seating chart. This allows easy removal of the post-it note and replacement with a blank one when a juror is excused, a method superior to crossing out and re-writing juror information in the small space provided.)

Unfortunately, thanks to the passage of Proposition 115 by the voters in the June 1990 election, judges no longer have to allow the prosecution or defense to question prospective jurors.[10] Instead, the judge may elect to ask all the questions himself or herself. However, many judges ask prospective jurors only perfunctory questions relating to occupation, spouse's occupation, previous experience with the criminal justice system and acquaintance with police officers and attorneys. This procedure is called "voir dire" ("vwar deer," French for "to speak the truth"). The questions will be to the entire panel and to individual jurors. If the answers to any of these questions indicate blatant prejudice, you and the prosecutor can ask the judge to excuse that person "for cause." If the prejudice is more subtle, or you or the prosecutor just doesn't like the potential juror's attitude, a "peremptory challenge" can be used to excuse the juror. Both you and the prosecutor are allowed to exercise six "peremptory"

---

[10]CCP § 223, as amended by Proposition 115 in June 1990. Although part of this initiative was voided by the California Supreme Court in December 1990, this aspect (and others) remain in effect.

MUNICIPAL COURT JURY PANEL CHART			Peremptory Challenges			Only for Offenses Punishable by Over 90 Days in Jail			

No. | 1 | 2 | 3 | 4 | 5 | 6 | 7 | 8 | 9 | 10

Date	Case No.	People of State of Calif. vs.	Plntf. Dfndnt.						

1	2	3	4	5	6
7	8	9	10	11	12

challenges if the maximum term of imprisonment you're facing is 90 days or less in jail (e.g., speed contests or exhibitions). Ten such challenges are allowed if the maximum jail time is more than 90 days (e.g., driving under the influence, failure-to-appear).

Some judges, particularly ones in smaller counties, will allow you and the prosecutor to ask questions of the prospective jurors themselves. Others will not, and may insist that you specify more areas you want the judge to cover. Still others may allow you to ask a few specific questions. If so, start by asking the entire panel particular questions related to their possible prejudices or biases that the judge or prosecutor have not asked. (A sample list is indicated below.) If there are any potential jurors with serious prejudices against defendants (or in favor of police officers), the answers to your questions will hopefully reveal this and the judge will excuse that particular juror "for cause." (This way, you don't have to use one of your peremptory challenges.) The answers given by the potential jurors (including the tone of voice, hesitancy to

answer particular questions, scowls, bad or good vibes in general) may guide you in deciding whether to exercise a peremptory challenge to get rid of someone you don't want to hear your case. Questioning jurors also gives you the opportunity of educating them about general principles of law. (See Section 2, below.)

After you've used "for cause" and/or peremptory challenges to affect the make-up of the jury, it becomes the prosecutor's turn again.[11] The prosecutor will be particularly concerned about the new jurors who have replaced those you excused. If he or she excuses any of the jurors, you have another turn. This goes on until both sides are satisfied with the make-up of the jury, or run out of challenges.

---

[11]This means that if after you've excused several jurors, you're satisfied with the jury make-up and "pass" the selection to the prosecutor, then, if the prosecutor excuses no more jurors, the selection is over. It might be over before you think, so you'd better be sure that you're satisfied with the jury make-up each time you "pass" to the prosecutor.

2. Questions to Ask on "Voir Dire"

If you are permitted to question the potential jurors, start by asking their name, occupation and place of employment, whether they're married, and if so, their spouse's occupation (unless you've already been given this information by the court, or the judge or prosecutor has established it). After you've noted all this on a jury seating chart, you should ask the panel general questions, similar to the following:

a. Do any of you have any objections to sitting here as jurors in a misdemeanor traffic violation case? Please raise your hand if you do.

b. Do any of you object to the fact that I will be representing myself without an attorney?

c. Are any of you aware of the fact that in order to find me guilty of the offense I'm charged with, the prosecution must prove beyond a reasonable doubt *every single element* of its case?

Note: This sort of question is designed more to "educate" prospective jurors, than to lead to an answer that will give you useful information. One important aspect of voir dire is to inform jurors— some of whom may assume you're guilty, or you wouldn't have been arrested in the first place—that you're "presumed innocent," that the prosecution must prove you're guilty, that the prosecution must prove everything it is required to prove, and that it must do so "beyond a reasonable doubt." Many prospective jurors do not realize this, and may need such gentle reminders. Of course, if a juror's answer

suggests disagreement with, or total ignorance of, all these rules, the answer may help you decide to exercise a peremptory or for-cause challenge against the juror. (See Sections 3 and 4, below.)

d. Are there any of you who have trouble believing that a person is innocent until proven guilty beyond a reasonable doubt on the basis of the evidence?

e. Will you each commit yourself to honor the constitutional guarantee that a person is not guilty, unless the prosecution proves each element of the offense beyond a reasonable doubt?

Note: As with question (c) above, the purpose of questions (d) and (e) is mostly to educate the jurors by reminding them of their obligations in this regard. Each should at least nod his or her head. If any juror gives you bad vibes in this regard, you may want to use a peremptory challenge.

f. Do you all understand that my being accused of a violation is no evidence at all of guilt?

g. Have any of you ever been employed as a law-enforcement officer or security guard?

h. Do any of you have friends or relatives who have been employed as a law-enforcement officer or security guard?

i. Do any of you have friends or relatives who have been employed in a district attorney's office?

j. Are there any among you who would believe the word of a police officer solely because he is a police officer, over my own testimony?

k. Do any of you believe that police officers are incapable of mistaken observations?

l. Do any of you believe police officers always tell the entire truth?

m. Have any of you ever sat on a jury previously where the defendant was charged with the offense I'm charged with?

n. Have any of you ever been involved in an automobile accident which you believe was caused by someone breaking the law?

o. Are there any of you who don't drive at least 10 thousand miles each year?

p. Are there any among you who have never been cited for a moving traffic violation? **Note:** You might want to reject a juror who's never been subject to the indignity, or, you may want to reject a person who too-quickly paid the fine because he "knew he was guilty."

The above questions are only examples. Depending on the facts of your particular case and the offense with which you're charged, you could come up with others. For example, in drunk driving cases, you might ask general questions as to whether any of the potential jurors occasionally take a drink. (You would want to exclude a teetotaler.)

If any of the jurors indicate, whether by nodding, raising a hand, or even by a facial expression, an affirmative answer to a question, be prepared to follow up. Address the particular juror by name, if possible. You might say:

"Ms. Jones, I noticed you seemed to nod yes when I asked you if you had any friends or relatives who were police officers. Could you elaborate on that?"

Depending on the answer, you might want to ask further questions to expose a possible anti-defendant or pro-police prejudice. If you decide to excuse that particular person, use one of your peremptory challenges. If the juror's prejudice is blatant, ask the judge to excuse the juror for cause.

3. Challenges for Cause

If a prospective juror *strongly* indicates that he is prejudiced against defendants, would believe the word of a police officer over yours no matter what, or thinks you have to prove yourself innocent, you should ask the judge to disqualify that person for cause. Be polite when you do so, or you'll only succeed in alienating the remaining jurors. However, you're likely to find that it's a rare person who will outright admit his prejudices so clearly that you can successfully challenge that person for cause. Also, the

law of disqualification for cause is complicated and beyond the scope of this book. If you believe a juror is so prejudiced that he should be disqualified for cause and the judge doesn't disqualify that person, you will have to trust your instincts and use one of your peremptory challenges. Don't cause a scene with the judge.

4. Peremptory Challenges

You have the right to excuse prospective jurors for any reason or for no reason. You should exercise peremptory challenges with care, however, because you only have a limited number of them—six or ten. [See Section C(1) above.] Though you should rely on your instincts, you probably would be wise to consider exercising peremptory challenges to exclude the following types of people:

a. Present and former police officers and security guards;

b. Anyone who has ever worked in a prosecutor's office, including lawyers;

c. Relatives or close friends of the above;

d. Teetotalers in drunk driving cases;

e. Anyone who has ever been involved (or has a close friend or relative who has been involved) in an accident caused by someone else charged with the offense you're charged with (especially if it's drunk driving);

f. People whose dress and/or lifestyles are much more conservative than yours;

g. People who don't drive or who have never received a traffic ticket;

h. People who obviously resent being called for jury duty;

i. People you feel uneasy about but don't know why.

When you excuse a prospective juror, be polite. Simply say something to the judge like, "The Defense would like to thank and excuse the fifth juror, Ms. Smith."

E. Trial Procedure

AFTER THE JURY IS selected, the 12 jurors are "sworn in." Then, the trial proceeds in much the same way as a trial before a judge. (See Chapter 12.)

1. Opening Statements

The opening statements are presented in the same way noted in the previous chapter, but you address the jury instead of the judge. Since jurors obviously know less about the law than most judges, an opening statement is advisable. You can give it right after the prosecutor gives (or waives) hers, or you can reserve it until just before you put on your testimony. If you want to make an opening statement, don't read it while shuffling or stooping—look at the jury members directly. Refer to your notes only from time to time. Be sure you have already practiced it at home with friends. The important

thing to remember is that your bearing will probably have a much greater effect on a jury than it would have on a judge.

2. The Prosecution's Testimony

In jury trials, the officer will always testify in response to the prosecutor's questions, never by narrative. You should avoid all but the most crucial objections. Studies have shown that jurors are more likely to rule against the side that makes the most objections, everything else being equal. Jurors resent anyone trying to keep them from hearing evidence and even if you do successfully object and keep certain evidence out, they are likely to be able to guess the answer to the question objected to, and will probably attach a lot more importance to the answer than they would if you'd just let it pass.

There are several areas where the general rule of not objecting may not be appropriate. These include:

a. When the prosecutor tries to introduce radar evidence of your speed without having first introduced into evidence a traffic and engineering survey justifying the speed limit. [See Chapter 12, Section C(4)(a).] (**Note:** Only when a speeding offense is charged as a misdemeanor because of three prior violations in a year will a jury be involved.)

b. Where questions are extremely vague, confusing or unintelligible.

c. Where a prosecution witness is asked questions which are so "leading" that the prosecutor is really supplying all the testimony in the question. As we pointed out in Chapter 12, Section C(8), a leading question is one which implicitly "instructs" the witness how to answer. To cite the Chapter 12 example, questions stated as "The road surface was dry, wasn't it?" or "Was the road dry?" are leading; "What was the condition of the road surface?" is not.

Note: Do not use this objection unless the overall pattern of the prosecution's questions are leading. If you object to each leading question, you will not only make the judge and jury impatient, but also, when it's your turn to ask questions, the prosecutor may probably fight fire with fire, harassing you with objection after objection about the form of your questions. Prosecutors can play this game a lot better than you can, so think twice before you object.

cross walk →

cross walk

3. Your Cross-Examination

When you cross-examine the prosecution's witnesses, be courteous but firm. If the officer tries to tell more of his story, you might gently interrupt with "Please answer the question—you've already had a chance to tell your story; I'd appreciate it if you wouldn't try to influence the jury any further." (Juries hate to be influenced.) Otherwise, the cross-examination should be pretty much the same as in trials before a judge, as discussed in Section C(5) of the previous chapter.

4. Motion for Acquittal

As we saw in Chapter 12, Section C(6), a motion for acquittal is used when the prosecution has failed to establish the elements of the violation. Since jury trials are always handled by trained prosecuting attorneys (who use checklists to make sure they don't forget anything important), this will almost never occur.

5. "Reserved" Opening Statement

If you "reserved" your opening statement at the beginning of the trial, this is the time to make it— before you present your testimony. [See Chapter 12, Section C(7).]

6. Your Testimony

Your testimony in a jury trial should also be pretty much the same as it would be before a judge, with two important exceptions:

a. Be sure to look directly at the jury from time to time while you do your best to look sincere without being phony. Throughout your trial, your demeanor should reflect that you are an honest, law-abiding citizen who has been wrongly accused.

b. You may be able to exert subtle influences on the jury by sprinkling your testimony with slightly relevant personal details with which one or more members of the jury might identify. For example, if you were on your way to a church function when you were pulled over, and there are a few churchgoers in the jury, casually mention the fact, but don't overplay it. Jurors also tend to like firefighters, medical personnel and teachers. However, if you're an undertaker, bill collector or insurance salesman, you may be wise to keep your occupation to yourself.

Finally, while judges often train themselves to remain totally expressionless even while hearing the most blatant lie (lest they be accused of being prejudiced) at least some of the jurors will probably be a little more transparent. Be alert for signs on jurors' faces that might suggest confusion or disbelief, and adjust your conduct accordingly. For example, if a part of your testimony evokes snickers, don't refer to that part in your final argument.

When your testimony is completed, and after the prosecutor has cross-examined you (see Section 7, below), introduce any other witnesses who will testify on your behalf. As we saw in Section C(8) of the previous chapter, the prosecutor might insist that your witnesses testify only in response to questions you ask, as opposed to the narrative fashion in which you testified. You should object to this request and tell the judge you're unfamiliar with the way such questions should be asked. You should be prepared to ask non-objectionable questions just in case the judge sides with the prosecutor in this point. [See Chapter 12, Section C(8).]

7. Cross-Examination by the Prosecution

When it's your time to be cross-examined by the prosecutor, listen carefully to the question. Do not guess at an answer you don't know. Ask the prosecutor to repeat questions you don't understand. On the other hand, do not purposely avoid answering reasonably clear questions; otherwise the jury will think you are being evasive. Do not show discourtesy or anger toward the prosecutor, even if she tries to irritate you. If she is obnoxious and you remain polite, it may well arouse the juror's sympathies on your behalf. Otherwise, your response to cross-examination should be the same as in non-jury trials.

F.   Jury Instructions

AFTER YOU PRESENT your evidence, but before the beginning of closing arguments, you can (and should) submit proposed "jury instructions" to the judge to be read to the jury. If you don't, the judge will most likely read a standard-format "multi-purpose misdemeanor jury instruction," plus one or more relating specifically to the offense(s) you're charged with. These jury instructions are listed in a book referred to as "CALJIC."[12] This book contains jury instructions appropriate to all sorts of criminal trials, and which are referred to by number. The general purpose misdemeanor jury instruction is called CALJIC 16.000,[13] and includes general instructions dealing with respective duties of the judge and jury, types of evidence, weighing evidence and determining credibility of witnesses, and the presumption of innocence. Somewhere in the middle of all this, the judge inserts instructions relating to the particular offense charged. The judge must also add other instructions suggested by you or the prosecutor if they accurately reflect the law and are relevant to the charge.

You should request that the following CALJIC instructions be given to the jury in the following situations:

- **2.72:** You should always request this one. It tells the jury that the prosecution must prove each element of the case. In your argument, you should also emphasize that each element must be proven beyond a reasonable doubt.

- **2.61:** If you've chosen not to testify, this instruction tells the jury that you simply thought it was unnecessary to testify because of the poor state of the prosecution's evidence. The jury should therefore not make any assumptions of guilt based on your not testifying.

- **2.91:** If you're trying to establish that the police officer saw someone else commit the violation but mistakenly nabbed you (such as in certain reckless driving or speed exhibition or contest

---

[12]*California Jury Instructions, Criminal* (abbreviated CALJIC) available at any law library.

[13]The following CALJIC jury instructions relate to the following offenses: 16.630—driving without being licensed; 16.640—driving while license is suspended or revoked; 16.830—driving under the influence of alcohol; 16.840-16.841—reckless driving; 16.850—driving under the influence of drugs; 16.860—speed contest; 16.870—exhibition of speed; 16.880—failure to appear. The appropriate instruction will be read by the judge.

cases), this tells the jurors the prosecution must prove that you're the person who committed the offense.

- **1.20:** When you're charged with *willful* failure to appear or pay a fine (VC § 40508), this instruction explains to the jury what "willful" means.

- **2.50:** If the prosecution has pointed to prior offenses you've committed, this instruction tells the jury that the prosecutor has done so only to elevate the penalty if you're convicted of the present offense. The jury must not assume you are more likely of having committed the present offense because of these other violations. [Read Chapter 10, Section C(2), and Chapter 14, Section B(1), before you do this.]

You should request these jury instructions by number. It is also proper for you to ask the judge to use a jury instruction not in the CALJIC book, as long as it is relevant to the case. You must do this in writing. We suggest that you try to get the judge to use the following instructions:

1. You must not consider the testimony of a law enforcement officer to be more believable than that of the defendant solely because that person is a law enforcement officer.

2. In order to find the defendant guilty as charged, you must find beyond a reasonable doubt, first, that she committed all the acts required to commit the offense, and second, that she either had a specific intent to commit those acts or was criminally negligent in committing them.

Note: You should use this in all cases except where the statute specifically requires "willful" behavior. You may have a hard time getting the judge to accept this instruction if he believes that willfulness or criminal negligence doesn't have to be shown for traffic violations. If the judge refuses, you may have grounds for appeal.

3. In order to find that the defendant drove in excess of a safe speed you must find beyond a reasonable doubt, first, that she was driving a motor vehicle, and second, that she drove at a speed higher than that which it is presumed to be safe. A speed is presumed to be safe if it is posted on properly-displayed speed-limit signs or stated by the Vehicle Code to be safe for a given type of area (such as a school zone or a residential area). However, you must find the defendant not guilty if you believe she has shed a reasonable doubt as to whether the weather, road or traffic conditions rendered the speed at which she was driving unsafe.

Note: Only use this when you're charged with violating the Basic Speed Law (not going over 55 mph). Since this violation is an infraction, you will only have a jury trial if you had three prior violations within a year and this is charged as a misdemeanor, or if the judge allows the jury to try this violation along with some other misdemeanor you were charged with at the same time.

1. How to Request Jury Instructions

To request one or more jury instructions, submit a written form to the judge before the closing statements to the jury begin. Your request for jury instructions should be prepared in advance before the day of your trial, and might look something like this:

```
RALPH LEADFOOT
950 Parker St.
Berkeley, CA 94710
(415) 555-1234


          MUNICIPAL COURT OF CALIFORNIA, COUNTY OF ALAMEDA

             BERKELEY-ALBANY JUDICIAL DISTRICT


THE PEOPLE OF THE STATE      )   NO. A-123456
OF CALIFORNIA,               )
                             )
                 Plaintiff,  )   REQUEST FOR JURY
                             )   INSTRUCTIONS
vs.                          )
                             )
RALPH LEADFOOT,              )
                             )
                 Defendant.  )
_____)


     Defendant, RALPH LEADFOOT, hereby requests that the jury be instructed

with the following CALJIC instructions:

     2.50
     2.61
     2.72
     2.91
     16.000.

     Defendant further requests that the following additional instructions be

given:

     1. You must not consider the testimony of a law enforcement officer to

be more believable than that of the defendant, or any of his witnesses,

solely because that person is a law enforcement officer.

     2. In order to find the defendant guilty as charged, you must find

beyond a reasonable doubt, first, that he committed all the acts required to

commit the offense, and second, that he either had an intent to commit those

acts or was criminally negligent in committing them.

DATED: March 31, 199_

                                     _____
                                     RALPH LEADFOOT
                                     Defendant in Pro Per
```

G. Closing Arguments

AFTER ALL THE EVIDENCE is presented, both you and the prosecutor will have the opportunity to present closing arguments. Here we give you a sample closing argument that you can adapt to suit your own particular case.

1. The Prosecution's Argument

During the prosecutor's closing argument, remain calm—poker-faced if you can. Don't express outrage, indignation, derision, or any other emotion, no matter how horribly the prosecutor distorts the truth. Just listen carefully to the prosecution's arguments so that you can respond to them in your own closing argument, which comes next.

2. Your Argument

Your closing argument to the jury serves two purposes. First, you should explain how the evidence isn't sufficient to prove your guilt (or actually disproves it) and second, you should rebut statements made by the prosecutor in her arguments. Reread the closing statement information in Chapter 12, Section C(10).

Be sure to emphasize to the jurors that each element of the offense must be proven "beyond a reasonable doubt," which is something in-between a "great" doubt and a "mere" or insignificant doubt. But with a little glib talk, you can infer that a "reasonable" juror (everyone considers him/herself to be reasonable) who has any doubt at all about any element of the offense must find you not guilty. Remember, it only takes one stubborn juror to produce a "hung" jury. Part of your argument might go something like this:

Ladies and Gentlemen, since I know that I'm innocent of the offense(s) charged, I'm contesting it/them here. Attorneys are very expensive, and so I'm defending myself. Not being familiar, as is the prosecutor, with all the legal technicalities and rules of trial procedure, I researched the nature of criminal trials, since I wanted to present the case as best I could. The most important thing I learned about American criminal trials—and we are all taught this—is that the prosecution must prove a defendant guilty—as to each and every element of the offense—beyond a reasonable doubt. [Now, describe the elements of the offense and how, in light of the evidence presented, why doubt remains. This is the most important part of your argument!]

The doctrine of "reasonable doubt" means that if you have any doubt as to whether any of those elements is true, and you feel that such doubt is reasonable, you must find me not guilty. You are not necessarily saying "I'm absolutely sure he's innocent," but rather, "The prosecution has failed to prove everything it has to prove beyond a reasonable doubt."

I submit that the evidence indicated sheds a reasonable doubt on my guilt. The prosecutor, in her statement to you, merely repeated the police officer's testimony. But this is only part of the evidence. I [and my witnesses] also testified, and I know I was telling the truth. You must not believe a police officer's powers of observation to be infallible just because he's a police officer, or that he's incapable of exaggerating a little. When the prosecutor repeated what the officer said, she didn't disprove any of the evidence I (and my witnesses) presented. She wants you to give the officer's word complete credibility, and my word none. If the law required this, we wouldn't need trials at all! We could all just have automatic guilty verdicts.

I'm asking you to consider all the testimony—mine and that of my witnesses included.

Now, when the prosecutor argues the case again —she gets another chance while I only get this one—she may tell you that I have a lot to gain, and that therefore the officer's story is more believable than mine. I ask you to take this with a grain of salt. Even though official "quota systems" were supposedly outlawed quite a few years ago, it's no secret that police officers are promoted at least partly on the basis of the average number of violations they charge people with every month. [Some prosecutors may object to this. If this happens, simply drop the point and go on.]

I have no hard feelings toward the officer, and I know that part of the reason he's on the roads is to protect us from hazardous drivers, but he's not infallible, and in this particular case, he was mistaken. [Now, briefly reiterate the key areas in which he was mistaken, and also rebut any of the points the prosecutor made in the initial argument to the extent you feel it will help you.]

Since I'm not an attorney, I could not present this case as smoothly and professionally as the prosecutor; nor did I know when to object to any evidence she might have improperly introduced [use this only if you made no objections and the prosecutor made some]. *Still, I hope you will examine all the evidence and apply it to each element the prosecution has to prove.*

You may recall that in the beginning of this case, you each indicated you would honor the constitutional guarantee that a person is not guilty until and unless the prosecution proves each element beyond a reasonable doubt. Indeed, in this case, the prosecution has come up far short in doing this. In retiring to the jury room, I ask you to do your duty in this regard and to enter a verdict of not guilty. Thank you."

This may seem a bit long-winded but it goes pretty fast when you're talking. Feel free to change it to suit your particular case. It's wise to practice this sort of statement a number of times before you go to court.

3. The Prosecution's Rebuttal Argument

Since the prosecution has the burden of proof, it gets two shots to argue its case to the jury. The second one is intended to allow a rebuttal to the things you covered in your argument. Sometimes the prosecutor won't exercise this opportunity.

H. The Judge Instructs the Jury

FINALLY, THE JUDGE will instruct the jury from the standard instructions, plus any that were accepted from suggestions by you or the prosecutor. Then the bailiff will take the jury into the jury room to deliberate. The longer they take, the better for you. When they come back, they will announce a verdict. The judge will thank and excuse them. If you are found guilty, the judge will set a time for you to appear for sentencing. It's improper for her to sentence you right then and there unless you agree to it, and in many cases you shouldn't. (See Chapter 14, Section A.)

14

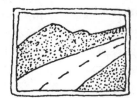

SENTENCING

A. Time for Sentencing

THE LAW PROVIDES for a cooling off period between the time you're found (or plead) guilty and the time the judge (or traffic commissioner) sentences you. Unless you agree otherwise, the judge must wait at least six hours before sentencing you.[1]

Often, however, traffic court judges will ignore this rule and sentence people immediately. Since most people are unaware of the requirement,[2] very few object. But the law is clear. If you are sentenced too soon, you can ask the judge to "vacate" the sentence on the ground that she hasn't waited the six hours (unless you have waived this right). If the

---

[1]PC § 1449.

[2]A judge must inform you of this right if you represent yourself, but not if you have an attorney. *People v. Wilson* (1963) 60 Cal.2d 139, 32 Cal.Rptr. 44.

judge refuses, the sentence is nevertheless invalid and can be vacated on appeal. Unfortunately, however, the fact that the sentence will be vacated doesn't mean that the underlying conviction is wiped out. It is not, and you will just be resentenced.

There are several advantages to insisting the judge wait at least six hours before sentencing. First, it gives you a chance to figure out whether you have legal cause to ask for a new trial. When you come back for sentencing, you have the right to orally make a "motion for a new trial" and explain your legal reasons why. Secondly, if you face a license suspension, the postponement will give you time to contact a friend who can drive you home from court. Finally, there's even a chance that a bureaucratic snafu will develop that you can use to your advantage. Unless you're found guilty early in the morning, six hours later will probably be after the court closes for the day and the judge will have to set up a sentencing appointment for another day. If the judge sets sentencing time more than five days away, you may be entitled to a whole new trial, perhaps before a different judge.[3] If your sentencing is delayed more than five days, quickly state "Your Honor, in view of the sentencing not having occurred within five days of conviction, I move for a new trial under PC § 1202." You must do this quickly, before the judge has a chance to sentence you. If she doesn't grant a new trial, you can have the conviction reversed on appeal and get a new trial.

Now that we've told you of the advantages of insisting on a six-hour delay, here is one large disadvantage. By requesting the court to set up another court appearance, you are creating trouble for the court bureaucracy. Recognizing this, the judge may decide to exercise her discretion and impose a larger fine than would have otherwise been the case (even though she's not supposed to punish you for exercising your rights). Our advice is to insist on your six-hour delay only when it will

truly serve a purpose, and not just to throw a monkey-wrench into the court machinery.

Remember: If you agree to have the judge "think your case over," and decide on your guilt or innocence in your absence, none of the above applies. You just receive a notification by mail indicating whether you are guilty, and if so, what the sentence will be.

B. Possible Sentences

IN CHAPTERS 3 THROUGH 8 we set out the possible penalties for the main traffic offenses. Go back to your section and review the maximum and probable penalties for your violation. Absent a plea bargain, the sentences listed in those chapters are what you should expect at your sentencing hearing.

1. Repeat Offenses[4]

As we pointed out in Chapter 3, the fines are higher for a second or third Vehicle Code infraction within 12 months.

Fortunately, though, a judge may not increase an infraction fine beyond the first-time limit on the basis of prior offenses unless either the prosecution initially alleged that you had prior convictions—almost never done in traffic court—[and provides court records showing convictions—see Chapter 10, Section C(2)] or you admit the prior violations shown on your driving record.[5] If the prosecution does not attempt to prove the constitutional validity of your prior offenses (they rarely do), the judge can only raise your fine above that for a first-time offense if:

1. He looks at your DMV record;

---

[3]PC § 1202.

[4]VC § 42002.

[5]VC § 42004. See also *In re Tahl* (1969) 1 Cal.3d 122, 81 Cal.Rptr. 557. A prior offense based on a guilty plea is not valid for the purpose of increasing your sentence unless you expressly waived your right to trial, the right of confrontation, and the right against self-incrimination. *People v. Matthews* (1983) 139 Cal.App.3d 537.

2. Then asks whether you've had any prior violations within the last 12 months; and

3. You answer yes.

You do not have to answer "yes," but if you say "no," it will look like you're lying. If you're afraid the judge will try to raise your fine on the basis of prior convictions, simply say, "Your Honor, I deny the validity of any and all prior convictions." Then, should your fine be higher than the first-time infraction maximum, you should move to vacate the sentence on the ground that you did not admit to any priors. (See Section 3 below.) If that fails, you can and should appeal the sentence. [See Chapter 16, Section B(15).]

2. Inability to Pay

If you're sentenced to pay a fine you cannot afford, tell the judge. The judge can authorize that the fine be paid in installments or at a later date. You can't be sent to jail for inability to pay a fine,[6] but you can be jailed for either refusing to pay or for failing to come to court with a sufficient explanation of your inability to pay.[7] "Inability to pay" does not mean you have to be totally destitute, but rather that you

or your family would have to do without the basic necessities of life—food, clothing, and shelter—if you were forced to pay the fine. Be prepared to tell the judge about your earnings, expenses and property, and why payment of a fine or installment would be a real hardship on you or your family.

If you can pay a fine but refuse to, the judge can order you to spend one day in jail for each $30 of the fine you don't pay [VC § 42003(b)].

If you can't afford to pay the fine, the judge can restrict your driving for up to 30 days until it is paid [VC § 40508(c)]. This can only be done for one period of up to 30 days, even if you still can't pay the fine after that. If this penalty prevents you from earning a living, either because it is impossible for you to get to and from work or because you have to drive as part of your job, ask the judge immediately to modify the order to allow you to drive at least for that purpose. Driving while your license is impounded is punishable by fine (or even five days in jail) as contempt of court.

Note: The DMV will also refuse to renew your driver's license if notified by the court that you "willfully failed to pay" your fine. The court will notify the DMV of this on all reportable Vehicle Code violations (see Chapter 6 for violations *not* reported to the DMV), unless the judge determines that you were unable to pay the fine [VC §§ 12807(c), 40509(b)].

3. Traffic School

In Chapter 9, we indicated that in some counties you can go to "driver improvement" or "traffic school," as an alternative to being tried, and the violations you are charged with will then not appear on your DMV record. Remember that this is not the same as being sentenced to attend traffic school. When you plead or are found guilty of a violation, the judge may offer to sentence you to attend traffic school instead of paying a fine. If you get to traffic school by this route, your conviction will still go on your record. In making your choice, you should consider that traffic school will take some time to complete,

---

[6]*In re Antazo* (1970) 3 Cal.3d 100, 89 Cal.Rptr. 255.
[7]VC § 40508(b). See Chapter 7, Section B(3).

and there will probably be a charge, which may make it as expensive as paying your ticket. Furthermore, if for some reason you're unable to complete traffic school, you can be charged with willfully failing to attend traffic school, a misdemeanor with a maximum penalty $1,000 fine plus six months in jail (VC § 42005).

4. Judge-Imposed License Suspensions and Restrictions

As we mentioned in Chapters 4-8, some infractions and all misdemeanors can result in court-ordered license suspensions from up to 30 days (for first-time infractions) to up to three years for some drug and alcohol related offenses.

Note: In practice, license suspensions are extremely rare for first or even second-offense speeding infractions, except where your speed is very high—like 100 mph on the freeway or 50 mph in a school zone.

A judge cannot suspend your license for a period longer than he would for a first-offense violation unless you admit the prior offense (or it is proved by the prosecution). So, for example, reckless driving (without bodily injury) or a speed violation, the judge can only suspend your license for longer than the 30-day maximum for a first offense if you admit to the prior offense or the prosecution proves its constitutional validity.

Note: Driving while your license is suspended is a misdemeanor punishable on a first offense by a fine of up to $1,000 and up to six months in jail. [See Chapter 7, Section B(4).]

In drunk driving cases, the judge also has the power to restrict your driving privileges, for up to 90 days on a first offense and up to a year-and-a-half on a second offense, to allow you to drive only to and from your work (and *in* your work if you drive in the course of your occupation) as a condition of probation. (See Chapter 8, Section B.) Violating that restriction is a ground for revoking your probation, which could result in suspension of your license.

5. Jail and Probation

As we saw in Chapters 3 through 8, you cannot be sentenced to jail for committing an infraction, but you can be for committing a misdemeanor. Six months is the maximum sentence authorized for most Vehicle Code misdemeanors, but sentences that long are rarely given.[8]

Some misdemeanors, like reckless driving, provide for a mandatory jail sentence of "not less than" a certain number of days. However, the judge usually has the discretion to grant you probation and suspend all, or part, of the jail sentence. But, there are a few exceptions. One is that a judge must, as a "condition of probation," require a repeat under-the-influence offender to serve two days in jail (VC § 23165). (See Chapter 8.) Also, a person convicted of driving while her license was suspended for an under-the-influence violation must go to jail for at least 10 days (VC § 14601.2). [See Chapter 7, Section B(4).]

---

[8]One such situation is where a person originally charged with a felony-manslaughter, or drunk driving causing injury or death—agrees to plead guilty to the misdemeanor. There the judge may impose a fairly long jail term.

In many cases, judges will allow persons sentenced to jail to serve the time on weekends. You or your attorney should request this if you would otherwise lose time from work.

If you are sentenced to jail for a Vehicle Code misdemeanor, you are entitled to have your sentence "stayed" for at least 24 hours, on request (VC § 42004.5). The judge can only refuse this request if she believes that you would not return to serve the jail sentence.

For most offenses, a judge can grant probation, usually by imposing a sentence and "suspending" all or part of it. However, you should clearly understand that if the terms of probation are violated, you have to serve the original sentence. The judge can also grant probation without imposing a sentence, and if the terms of the probation are violated, you go back before the judge to be sentenced.

Probation terms may also include going to jail or paying a fine. For example, a person convicted of driving under the influence must be sentenced to a suspended sentence of six months in jail, with probation, the conditions being the payment of a $375 fine, spending 48 hours in jail, and staying out of trouble for the next three years. Probation can last for three years, but if the judge doesn't specify, it only runs for one year.

C. Motions to Vacate Sentence

IF THE JUDGE SENTENCES you harshly, you can move to "vacate" the sentence if: 1) you were sentenced over your objection within six hours after being found guilty, or 2) you were assessed a penalty higher than the maximum for the first offense and you didn't admit to any prior offenses and the prosecution didn't prove them. You should make this motion right after the judge improperly sentences you. However, if for some reason you had failed to object then, you should file a written

motion to vacate the sentence as soon as possible thereafter.

The procedure for preparing and filing such a motion is the same as that given in Chapter 11 for other motions. First, a court date is obtained from the clerk. Then, you type a Notice of Motion, Points and Authorities, and Proof of Service, preferably on numbered legal paper. Make two sets of copies, and have a friend mail one set to the district (or city) attorney. The original set (including a Proof of Service signed by your friend) is then filed with the clerk.

The following sample motion papers list two separate grounds for moving to vacate the sentence. The first is that the judge refused a request to postpone sentencing for at least six hours. The second ground is that the fine is greater than that for a first-time infraction, even though no prior offenses were proved or admitted. If your situation involves only one of these grounds, you should prepare your Notice of Motion and Points and Authorities accordingly.

What to Say in Court

If your motion is to vacate the sentence because the judge sentenced you too soon, you should say:

Your Honor, I'm moving to vacate the sentence on the ground that I was not sentenced between six hours and five days as required by Penal Code § 1449. I call attention to the Points and Authorities I've submitted.

If you're moving to vacate a sentence greater than that for a first-time offense because no prior offenses were proved by the prosecution or admitted by you, say something like this:

Your Honor, I'm moving to vacate the sentence of a $200 fine on the ground that the fine is higher than the $100 maximum for a first-time infraction, yet no priors were proven, nor did I admit to any. I call attention to the Points and Authorities, I've submitted.

If your motion is denied, you can appeal your sentence. But even if you win this appeal, the appeals court will still allow the conviction to stand and will merely order the trial court to sentence you properly.

PATRICIA PRIOR
950 Parker St.
Berkeley, CA 94710
(415) 555-1212

MUNICIPAL COURT OF CALIFORNIA, COUNTY OF ALAMEDA

BERKELEY-ALBANY JUDICIAL DISTRICT

THE PEOPLE OF THE STATE
OF CALIFORNIA,
        Plaintiff,

vs.

PATRICIA PRIOR,
        Defendant.

NO. A-123456 - B

NOTICE OF MOTION
TO VACATE SENTENCE;
POINTS AND AUTHORITIES

TO: PLAINTIFF, THE PEOPLE OF THE STATE OF CALIFORNIA,
AND TO THE DISTRICT ATTORNEY FOR THE WITHIN-NAMED COUNTY:

PLEASE TAKE NOTICE that on March 6, 199_ at 9:00 a.m. in Department 2 of the above-entitled Court, at 2120 Martin Luther King, Jr. Way, Berkeley, California, defendant PATRICIA PRIOR will move to vacate the sentence imposed in the above-entitled action, on the grounds that:

1. Sentence was imposed immediately after pronouncement of verdict without defendant's consent, in violation of Section 1449 of the Penal Code; and

2. The sentence imposed is in excess of that permitted by law in the absence of allegation and proof, or admission by defendant, of prior Vehicle Code infractions.

This motion is based on this Notice of Motion and attached Points and Authorities, and on the pleadings, records and files in this action.

DATED: March 1, 199_

                    PATRICIA PRIOR
                    Defendant in Pro Per

POINTS AND AUTHORITIES

Statement of Facts

On February 22, 199_, defendant was convicted of violating Section 22350 of the Vehicle Code, an infraction. No prior offenses were alleged in the complaint. The verdict of guilty was pronounced in open court by the Honorable Hugo Humorless, who sentenced defendant to a $200 fine immediately thereafter. Judge Humorless neither requested defendant to waive time for sentencing, nor did defendant waive such time. She did, however, deny any prior Vehicle Code offenses when asked by Judge Humorless, who replied, "Well, I see one here on the form from the Department of Motor Vehicles. This being your second offense in a year, I'm fining you $200 plus a $280 penalty assessment."

Argument

I.   A SENTENCE IMPOSED ON A PRO PER DEFENDANT WITHIN SIX HOURS OF A GUILTY VERDICT MAY BE SET ASIDE ON MOTION, ABSENT A WAIVER OF TIME FOR SENTENCING BY DEFENDANT.

When a defendant has been convicted of a misdemeanor, the court must set a time for sentencing that is between six hours and five days from the time of pronouncement of the verdict. Penal Code § 1449. The same post-conviction procedures apply to infractions. See Penal Code § 19.7.

While time for sentencing can be waived, there can be no waiver by a pro per defendant unless the right is explained to her and she consents to be sentenced immediately. People v. Wilson (1963) 60 Cal.2d 139, 32 Cal.Rptr. 44.

If the defendant is sentenced earlier than the statute allows, the sentence may be vacated on motion. See In re Elsholz (1964) 228 Cal.App. 2d 192, 39 Cal.Rptr. 356.

Accordingly, since the record shows defendant appeared in pro per and did not indicate a knowing waiver of the time for sentencing,

PROOF OF SERVICE

I, JOHN SMITH, declare:

1. I am over the age of eighteen and not a party to the within action.

2. My residence address is 1200 Shattuck Ave., Berkeley, California, in the county within which the herein-mentioned mailing occurred.

3. On March 1, 199_ I served the within Notice of Motion to Vacate Sentence and Points and Authorities on plaintiff by placing true copies thereof in a separate sealed envelope, with the postage thereon fully prepared, in the United States Postal Service mailbox at Berkeley, County of Alameda, California, the said envelope being addressed to:

Office of the District Attorney

County of Alameda

2120 Martin Luther King, Jr. Way

Berkeley, California 94704

I declare under penalty of perjury under the laws of the State of California that the foregoing is true and correct.

DATED: March 1, 199_

JOHN SMITH

---

the sentence herein must be vacated.

II. THE MAXIMUM FINE FOR A VEHICLE CODE INFRACTION IS $100 PLUS PENALTY ASSESSMENT, ABSENT ALLEGATION AND PROOF OR ADMISSION BY DEFENDANT OF A PRIOR CONVICTION OF SUCH AN INFRACTION.

The maximum fine for conviction of a Vehicle Code infraction is $100 for the first offense, $200 for the second, and $250 for the third, plus any penalty assessments. [VC § 42001(a).] In general, a defendant cannot be given the higher maximum penalty for a second or later offense unless the prior offense is 1) alleged in the complaint, and 2) either proved at trial or admitted by the defendant. See People v. Ford (1964) 60 Cal.2d 772, 794, 36 Cal.Rptr. 620; People v. Ratner (1944) 67 Cal.App.2d Supp. 902, 153 P.2d 790; 39 Ops. Atty. Gen. 13 (1962). The complaint herein, a police officer's citation or "Notice to Appear," obviously does not allege any prior infractions.

It is true that for Vehicle Code offenses, Section 42004 of that code authorizes the court to use a written report from the Department of Motor Vehicles showing prior convictions. However, the section states that "the communication is prima facie evidence of such convictions, if the defendant admits them...." [Emphasis added.]

By implication, the DMV report does not establish the prior convictions (or bail forfeitures) unless the defendant admits them. If the defendant denies such priors (or is not even asked about them), the DMV report is insufficient to establish such priors. In the instant case, defendant did not admit any priors. Accordingly, she may be fined only $100 (plus penalty assessments), and the $200 fine (plus penalty assessments) must be set aside.

Respectfully submitted,

PATRICIA PRIOR
Defendant in Pro Per

DATED: March 1, 199_

D. If You Appeal

APPEALING THE DECISION does not automatically postpone the sentence. Judges will seldom, if ever, "stay" (postpone) a fine while your appeal is pending. They simply require you to pay and refund your money in the event the conviction is reversed. Jail sentences, license suspensions, and forced attendance at traffic school, however, cannot be so easily undone if your conviction is reversed. Ask the judge to stay these if you plan to appeal.

15

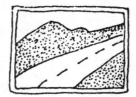

LICENSE SUSPENSIONS BY THE DMV

UNDER CERTAIN CIRCUMSTANCES, the Department of Motor Vehicles may suspend or revoke your license. This chapter deals with when and how this can happen, and what you can do about it.

A. Too Many Violations or Accidents

THE MOST COMMON TYPE of license suspension occurs when a person gets too many "points" on his or her driving record, by having too many moving-violation convictions and/or reported accidents within too short a time.

1. The "Point Count" System

The DMV can suspend or revoke your license if, at a hearing, it is determined that you're a negligent driver. In order to determine whether a driver is negligent, the DMV uses a point count system. Moving violations and accidents reported by a police officer to be your fault count as one point. Violations which count as two points include reckless driving, hit-and-run, driving under the influence, driving the wrong way on a freeway or other divided highway, driving over 100 mph, or participating in a speed exhibition or contest (VC § 12810). You are considered negligent if you have four or more points in any 12-month period, six or more in any 24-month period, or eight or more points in any 36-month period.[1] This includes accidents or violations in any state or U.S. Territory and Canada, if they're reported to the DMV.[2] (See Chapter 3, Section C.)

---

[1]VC § 12810.5. Certain categories of truck or bus drivers (those with "Class 1" or "Class 2" licenses) are allowed up to 6, 8 or 10 points in 12-month, 24-month, or 36-month periods, respectively, to the extent the violations occurred during the driving of a truck or bus for which a Class 1 or 2 license is required. However, violations involving truck or bus driving count for 1-1/2 or 3 points each, rather than the ordinary 1 or 2 points, respectively.

[2]VC § 13363. See Chapter 3 on out-of-state tickets and Chapter 6 on federal tickets.

If your license is suspended for this reason, you may be required to periodically post proof of insurance with the DMV for three years following the lifting of the suspension, in order to get your license back and keep it.

2. Other Criteria for Suspension

Even if your point count isn't high enough to classify you as "negligent," the DMV can still consider suspending or revoking your license for any of the following reasons (VC § 13800):

a. You were involved in an accident that involved death, injury, or "serious damage to property"; or

b. You were involved in three or more accidents in any 12-month period; or

c. You were convicted of any of the following offenses (VC §13361):

• a second offense of ordinary reckless driving (VC § 23103);

• hit-and-run (VC § 20002); or

• vehicular manslaughter [PC § 192(c)].

d. You violated restrictions imposed on your license (like refusing to wear glasses as required while driving)[3] or allowed someone else to use your license.

3. Your Right to a Hearing Before Suspension

Whenever the DMV decides to suspend your license for having too many points on your records, you have the right to a hearing where you can present evidence and argue against the proposed suspension.[4]

---

[3]VC § 13360.

[4]VC §§ 13950, 14100, 14101.

a. Requesting a Hearing

In most cases, the DMV will notify you that your license will be suspended or revoked unless you immediately write them a letter and request either a formal or informal hearing.[5] If you don't demand a hearing within 10 days from the date the notice was mailed, you give up your right to have one (VC § 14103). Such a letter might look something like this:

Jason D. Wason
123 Parker St.
Sacramento, California

June 25, 199_

Department of Motor Vehicles
2415 First Avenue
Sacramento, California 95817

Re: Proposed Driver's License Suspension,
    Driver's License # S053435.

Dear Sir or Madam:

   This is in response to your letter of March 3, 199_ in which your office proposed to suspend my driver's license on the ground that I am a negligent driver. Pursuant to § 14100 of the Vehicle Code, I request that an informal hearing be held so that I may present evidence on my behalf in opposition to the proposed suspension.

Sincerely,

Jason D. Wason

You can demand either an informal or a formal hearing in your letter. The only significant advantages of a formal hearing are that the issues are set forth in writing and the proceedings are recorded or transcribed. This makes it easier to appeal a decision to suspend your license. Since, however, an appeal from the DMV's decision to suspend is unlikely to be successful (because it is so discretionary under the law), an informal hearing is sufficient for most purposes.

b. The Hearing

In most cases, the hearing will take place in a little room at an office of the Department of Motor Vehicles in your county. When you get there, you will probably see the hearing referee seated at a desk or the end of a long table. You and any witnesses you bring will be seated in front of the desk or at the table. At formal hearings, a stenographer or a recording device will be there to make a record of the hearing.

   The referee will introduce herself. If you have witnesses, tell the referee. If any of your witnesses do not show, you can ask for the hearing to be held over to another day. The referee will consider how crucial your witness is and make a determination.

   Note: Witnesses can be very important. If, for example, you have too many violation points in too short a time, a couple of reputable people who will testify that you are an excellent driver will be a great help. But choose your witnesses well. Lenny Lowrider and Walter Wino aren't going to help you much, while Fred Firefighter probably will. If attending the hearing would be inconvenient, your witnesses can file written statements. You can also request the DMV to issue subpoenas to compel their attendance (VC §§ 13952, 14100). The referee will then summarize the case as it appears in the file. After you are sworn in (it is perjury to lie at the hearing), you will be asked to present your case.

   An informal hearing is more informal and easygoing than a traffic court trial. Except for hearings based on your refusal to take a blood, breath or urine test following an arrest for drunk driving (see Section B of this chapter), no one will be there to testify against you. Even in a formal hearing, the referee might allow you to testify to any information that may be important, though in a court of law it might not be admissible. This means you can present your case entirely in writing if you want (VC § 14104). But don't do this unless you

---

[5]VC §§ 13950, 14100, 14101.

know you'll be too nervous to present a coherent case in person. It's better to present your evidence to the referee face-to-face. You will need to convince the referee that there are sound reasons why your license shouldn't be suspended or revoked.

Here are some examples of the types of evidence you may want to present:

- Any circumstances in the violations counted against you that tend to cast you in a favorable light;

- Why an accident the DMV is counting against you wasn't your fault;

- Evidence that you drive a great many miles—personal and business— each year;

- How your livelihood depends on your ability to drive;

- Statements by employers or other "responsible" people as to how carefully, cautiously and conservatively you drive;

- Evidence of a recently-completed defensive driving, driver training, or other driving-related courses; or

- Physicians' reports of your physical condition and ability to drive.

Discuss your points clearly. The referee may ask you questions to help you explain your case. If you have any evidence to present, such as a doctor's statement, a driver training certificate, a written statement from someone who couldn't appear, or anything else, present it.

Then, any witnesses you have will be given a chance to testify. At an informal hearing, a witness just makes his statement to the referee. (This is one of the advantages of the informal hearing procedure.) At a formal hearing, however, you must have each witness testify in response to your questions and you will not be allowed to use "leading questions" that suggest what the answer should be.

After each witness presents his testimony, the referee might ask questions.

During the hearing, stick to the points you are trying to make. Don't get carried away in unnecessary detail. Don't feel you have to rush through. You'll have plenty of time to explain your position.

The referee can suspend or revoke your license or grant "probation." The terms of the probation can include a suspension, the issuance of a probationary license which is subject to certain restrictions, or the requirement that you take a driver education course.[6] At the end of an informal hearing, the referee may give a decision. More likely, and always after formal hearings, it will take up to two weeks before you receive a notice in the mail.

c. *Further Review of the Decision*

You may appeal the referee's decision after an informal hearing by writing a letter to the hearing board within 15 days of the effective date of the decision. Instructions on how to go about this will be included on the notice you receive of the referee's decision (VC § 14105.5). Your license suspension will be stayed while this appeal is pending. The appeal is merely a process where an appeals board or other DMV employees look at the referee's hearing report and any written evidence you presented. You do not have an opportunity to present further evidence or argument on your behalf, and it is likely that the referee's decision will be affirmed. But you have nothing to lose by appealing.

If you have a formal rather than an informal hearing, the referee's decision is automatically sent to an assistant to the director of the DMV for approval. This happens without your having to do anything, and the decision is mailed to you from there. Thus, after you receive the notice, your only further avenue of appeal is through the court system.

Although you can have the superior court review the DMV's final decision (from a formal hearing, or from the appeal following an informal hearing), the courts seldom reverse the DMV. The superior court procedure is extremely formal and

---

[6]VC §§ 14250, 14250.5.

complicated, and is beyond the scope of this book. It should be handled by an attorney. Strictly speaking, this type of proceeding does not involve an appeal, but rather an original lawsuit against the DMV in which you seek a "writ of mandate" to prevent it from suspending your license. The lawsuit must be brought within 90 days of the DMV's decision.[7]

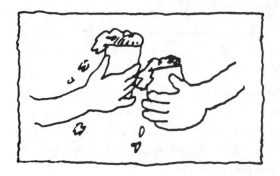

B. Driving Under the Influence

AS WE SAW IN CHAPTER 8, your license can be suspended by the DMV for four months or a year (if you had a previous conviction or suspension within the past seven years) for driving with a blood alcohol of 0.08% or above. The officer who arrests you serves you the suspension notice—effective in 45 days. To contest it, you must apply to the DMV for a hearing within 10 days. At the hearing the issues are:

1. The officer had "reasonable cause" to believe you were driving under the influence or with a blood alcohol over 0.08%;

2. You were placed under arrest (almost never in dispute); and

3. You were in fact driving a motor vehicle while under the influence or with a blood alcohol level over 0.08%.

The procedure for these hearings is similar to that for other license-suspension hearings (see Section A), except that the issues are limited to those discussed above.

If you are also charged criminally with driving under the influence, you should request a hearing in order to avoid a suspension. An acquittal in court will entitle you to a lifting of the suspension.

At the DMV hearing, you should object if the hearing officer attempts to introduce the officer's police report as evidence, in the police officer's absence. (Police officers often are not subpoenaed or don't show up for such hearings.) You may do this when the attempt is made, or at the close of the hearing officer's case. The hearing officer may then try to continue the case at another date, at which time he'll hope to have the officer there. You should object to this also. If you were acquitted in a criminal case, or the matter was dismissed, you should have copies of those court records with you. If you do testify at such a hearing, your testimony can be used against you in any DUI criminal case that may be pending. For that and other reasons, you should be represented by a lawyer at this stage.

C. Refusal to Take a Blood, Breath or Urine Test

AS WE DISCUSSED in detail in Chapter 8, California has an "implied consent" law. Driving a vehicle on the road implies that you consent to a blood, breath or urine test for blood alcohol. Also, if you took a breath test and passed it, and the officer had "reasonable cause" to believe you were under the influence of drugs, you "implicitly" consent to another test of your blood or urine. If you refuse to take at least one of the three tests, the DMV suspends your license for a year, in addition to any

---

[7]VC § 14401(a). See also CCP § 1094.5. How to handle "writ" cases is thoroughly discussed in Witkin, *Criminal Procedure*, and *California Civil Writs*, by CEB (Continuing Education of the Bar), available in virtually all California public law libraries.

suspension for driving under the influence. If you suffered a previous suspension or were convicted of driving under the influence (or plea-bargained reckless driving) within the previous seven years, the suspension is for an additional two years. If you suffered two such convictions or suspensions within the previous five years, your license is revoked for an additional three years. This is true even if you're found not guilty of the current charge (VC § 13353). The officer who arrests you serves you the notice of suspension; to contest it, you must apply to the DMV within 10 days for a hearing.

At the hearing, the issues are whether all of the following occurred:

1. The officer had "reasonable cause" to believe you were driving under the influence or with a blood-alcohol over 0.08%;

2. You were placed under arrest (almost never in dispute);

3. You refused to submit to and complete any of the three tests; and

4. You were told that failure to complete at least one test would result in a license suspension.

The procedure for implied consent hearings is similar to that for other hearings, except that the issues in an implied consent hearing are limited to those discussed above (VC § 13353). A hearing must be initiated by you after you receive the suspension notice from the officer (or the DMV if the officer didn't give it to you).[8] Unlike other DMV hearings, which can be held anywhere you want in California, "implied consent" hearings must be held in the county where you were arrested.

In almost all implied consent hearings, the main issue is whether your refusal to take the test was reasonable. Did the police fail to give you a choice of properly-administered tests, or fail to warn you of the consequences of refusing to submit to one of them?

Reasonable excuses for not taking the tests include:

• The police didn't really give you a choice of tests; perhaps they coerced you to take a certain one (usually a blood test);

• They refused to afford you privacy in giving a urine sample (see Chapter 8, Section D);

• They failed to tell you your license would be suspended if you refused to take one of the tests;

• They didn't have the proper equipment or personnel (such as a urine specimen bottle or a person licensed to withdraw blood samples) available for the test you insisted on.

Note: If you were taken to a hospital because you needed medical treatment, you can't use this excuse if the test you insisted on (e.g., a breath test) wasn't "feasible" there.[9]

Excuses which definitely *won't* work include:

• Not being able to pass urine, give blood or blow hard enough into the breathalyzer. If you cannot complete a particular test, you have to submit to one you can complete. (Also, if you pass a breath test and the officer reasonably believes you were on drugs, you have to submit to another test of blood or urine (VC § 23157.5).

---

[8]See sample letter in Section A(3)(a) of this chapter.

[9]VC § 23157(a)(3). This provision helps the police to coerce people into taking the more accurate blood test if they are taken to hospitals.

- Refusal to take the test until your attorney or physician shows up. You have the right to have an attorney present eventually, and to have a private physician give you an additional test later, but you cannot condition the test on either one showing up.

- Insistence on taking two or three tests or none at all.

- Being too drunk to understand the police explanations.

"Implied consent" hearings are notoriously difficult to win, especially in cases where the officer, who says he read you your rights and saw you refuse all tests, shows up to testify against you. The DMV hearing referee will almost always believe the officer, instead of you, on any point where your testimony differs from the officer's. Also, case law over the years has severely limited the types of technicalities you can raise at these hearings.

In any event, since a license suspension of at least six months (two or three years, respectively, if you have one or two prior convictions for drunk driving and/or plea-bargained reckless driving) is very severe, and since you may want to have a formal hearing in order to better preserve your right to have a court review the DMV's decision, you may want to hire an attorney to represent you at the hearing. (See Chapter 9, Section B.) But be aware that your chance of winning this type of hearing is exceedingly slim, and you may be better off saving your money to cope with any fines or other economic hardships you are likely to face.

D. Automatic Suspension or Revocation

SOMETIMES THE LAW requires that the DMV suspend or revoke a driver's license regardless of the particular circumstances. (The only significant difference between a "suspension" and a "revocation" is that a "suspension" is for two years or less and a "revocation" is for three years or more.) In the following situations, since the suspension or revocation is automatic, there is no opportunity for a hearing.

1. Conviction of a Felony Where a Vehicle Was Used

The DMV is required to revoke or suspend your license for at least one year when you're convicted of any felony (other than felony driving under the influence, covered below) in which a motor vehicle was used, including manslaughter and hit-and-run where death or injury resulted. After the one year is up, you have to prove to the DMV that you're covered by insurance, in order to get your license back [VC § 13350(c)].

2. Conviction of Driving Under the Influence—Injury or Death

As we saw in Chapter 8, a drunk driver who kills or injures someone in an accident can be convicted of either a felony or a misdemeanor. Either way, the DMV must impose the following license suspensions or revocations [VC §§ 13352(a), (4), (6)]:

DRIVING UNDER THE INFLUENCE— RESULTING IN INJURY OR DEATH

FIRST OFFENSE	Suspension for one year.
SECOND OFFENSE (including earlier non-injury DUI offenses as a prior conviction):	Revocation for three years—or when participating in an alcohol treatment program, one-year suspension followed by a two-year license restriction, where you can only drive to, from and in your work.
THIRD OFFENSE (also including non-injury DUI's as priors):	Revocation for five years.

After the period of suspension or revocation, you'll have to prove to the satisfaction of the DMV, that you're covered by auto insurance in order to get your license reinstated. And, in the case of second or third offenses, you'll need to show that you've satisfactorily completed a one-year alcoholism treatment program.

3. Conviction of Misdemeanor Driving Under the Influence—No Death or Injury

For misdemeanor driving under the influence (or with over 0.08% blood alcohol), not involving death or injury, the DMV must suspend or revoke your driver's license as follows:[10]

KEEP
RIGHT

DRIVING UNDER THE INFLUENCE—NOT RESULTING IN INJURY OR DEATH

FIRST OFFENSE:	Six-month suspension only if ordered by the court.
SECOND OFFENSE (within 7 years) (including reckless driving plea-bargained from DUI as a prior conviction):	Suspension for 18 months unless application is made to the DMV for a "restricted" license allowing driving only to, from, and in your work, and to and from an alcoholism treatment in which participation is required [VC §13352.5(a)].
THIRD OR FOURTH OFFENSE (within 7 years) (including plea-bargained reckless driving as a PRIOR):	Revocation for three years (third offense) or four years (fourth offense).

After the suspension or revocation period for second or third offenses, you have to prove to the DMV that you're insured before you're allowed to drive again.

4. Conviction of Other Offenses

If you're convicted of reckless driving or hit-and-run involving bodily injury, vehicular manslaughter, or any felony in which a motor vehicle is used, the DMV must revoke your license. Also, revocation is required if you're convicted of three reckless driving and/or hit-and-run offenses within any 12-month period. Finally, a six-month or one-year suspension (or restriction, to allow driving only to, from and in your work) is required for respective second or third offenses, within three years, of driving over 100 mph.[11]

---

[10]VC §§ 13352(a)(1), (5) and (7).

[11]VC §§ 13350(a), 13351, 13355.

5. Not Having Insurance

In addition to the laws allowing you to be fined if you drive without insurance, a separate law allows the DMV to suspend your license for a year if you're involved in an accident—regardless of who was at fault.

a. Accidents

Whenever you're involved as a driver in an automobile accident where over $500 in property damages (to any one person) results, or if anyone (including yourself) is injured or killed, you are required to report the accident to the DMV within 10 days (VC § 16000). (Forms for this purpose are available from any DMV office or from your insurance company.) If you don't file the report, and the DMV finds out about the accident (if it's reported by the other driver or the police), your license will be suspended until you either file the report or provide proof that you're covered by auto insurance. The DMV will also suspend your license, until you show proof you were insured at the time of the accident, if the police report or other driver's report claims you weren't insured.[12]

Even if you were driving someone else's vehicle, you must still report the accident yourself, because you were the driver. That means you must also report the owner's insurance information if you weren't insured for the vehicle yourself. If the owner won't provide that information, you should remind him or her that to fail to provide you with it under those circumstances is a criminal offense (VC § 16050.5).

Even if you do file an accident report within the required 10 days, you will still have your license suspended for one year if you weren't covered by insurance at the time of the accident—whether or not you were at fault. Even after the year is up, you still don't get your license back until you show the DMV proof that you've obtained auto insurance.

Any lapse in your insurance for the next three years will be reported by your insurance company to the DMV, which will suspend your license again.[13] (See Subsection c, below.)

However, you can get the one-year suspension reduced to a restriction under which you can drive only to, from and in your work, or to and from a hospital or doctor for recurring medical treatments if a physician certifies that you have a "serious health problem." To do this, you must pay a $250 penalty to the DMV and get insurance right away. (You can also drive your minor children to and from school if the principal certifies that public transportation to and/or from school is not readily available.) This sort of restriction still lasts a year, and after that you must keep your insurance in force or your license will be suspended.[14]

b. License Suspension Proceedings Resulting from Accidents[15]

The DMV will mail you a notice of its intent to suspend your license for not reporting an over-$500 or injury accident, or for not being covered by insurance. The suspension takes effect within 15 days unless you either:

1. Send the DMV a form (available from your insurance company) that you've since obtained insurance; or

2. Make a written demand for a hearing. (See Section A.)

If you weren't insured, you have nothing to lose by demanding a hearing, and the DMV can't suspend your license on the basis of the other driver's written statement of the accident.[16] The only

---

[12]VC §§ 16004, 16070. One exception to this is that if you were driving a vehicle owned by your employer, your employer must report the accident (VC § 16002).

[13]VC §§ 16070, 16072.

[14]VC §§ 16072, 16076-16078.

[15]Although the Legislature has allowed other insurance laws to expire (probably temporarily), this law remains in effect. You are still required to have auto insurance, even though one enforcement mechanism has lapsed. This one has not.

[16]*Daniels v DMV* (1983) 33 Cal.3d 532. If no one shows up personally to testify about the accident, you can object to the DMV referee's attempt to "introduce" the other driver's written statement into the record. You can also refuse to testify yourself.

issues on which you will be allowed to present evidence at such a hearing are:

1. Whether you were a driver in an accident resulting in over $500 worth in damages to any one person, or in injury or death; and

2. Whether you were insured at the time.[17]

Unfortunately, the DMV considers it irrelevant whose fault the accident was, and will not let you present any evidence in that regard.[18] This means that if you can't afford auto insurance and have an accident that's entirely someone else's fault, you can still lose your license for a year—and for up to three years after that, if you can't find affordable insurance.

c. Convictions of Insurance Law Violations

As we have already stated, conviction of a violation of the new insurance law (not having insurance when stopped for a moving violation, VC § 16028) will result not only in a fine, but also in the imposition of a three-year insurance-posting requirement.[19] For three years following the conviction, you will have to notify the DMV, as a condition of keeping your license, of the name of your insurer and policy number.

Falsely reporting insurance information (VC § 16029) is a misdemeanor punishable not only by a fine of up to $500 and a jail sentence of up to 30 days, but also by a court-imposed one-year license suspension or restriction allowing you to drive only to, from, and in your work. This one-year period will be followed by a similar three-year period within

which you must keep the DMV notified of your insurance as a condition of keeping your license. (See Chapter 5, Section F, for more discussion of insurance requirements.)

E. Holding a License in Abeyance

THE DMV WILL HOLD your driver's license in limbo, either by refusing to renew it, or by suspending it, if you:

- fail to answer to a moving violation ticket you've signed;
- fail to pay a fine a judge sentenced you to pay; or
- fail to pay a civil court judgment arising out of an auto accident.

Your license will be returned or renewed once you remedy these problems.

1. "Failure-to-Appear" on a Ticket You Signed

When you violate a written promise to appear by ignoring a ticket you signed, the court to which the ticket is sent will also charge you with the misdemeanor of failure to appear. It will then notify the DMV of this charge.[20] The DMV will then suspend your license until you have all the original and failure-to-appear charges "adjudicated"—cleared with the court by either forfeiting bail, or by contesting the charge and then winning—or losing and paying the fine (VC § 13365).

Even if, for some reason, the court has neglected to notify the DMV of your failure to appear, or the DMV simply hasn't gotten around to suspending your license, you may still have a problem when it comes time to renew your driver's license. The DMV will refuse to issue you a renewal license until you have both the original and the failure-to-appear

---

[17]VC § 16075. A corporation or person who has either posted a $30,000 bond or deposit with the DMV, or who is "self-insured" and owns 25 or more vehicles, is exempt from this insurance requirement. (See VC §§ 16052-16056.)

[18]In 1972, the California Supreme Court ruled in the case of *Rios v. Cozens* 7 Cal.3d 792, 103 Cal.Rptr. 299, that the DMV's refusal to consider fault was unconstitutional. Since then, however, the license-suspension laws were overhauled in a way that make the refusal to consider fault constitutional. See *Anacker v. Sillas* (1977) 65 Cal.App.3d 416, 135 Cal.Rptr. 537.

[19]As of this writing, the Legislature has failed to pass a law that would extend this mandatory proof-of-insurance law (VC § 16028). It is expected, however, that the Legislature will reinstate the requirement as we describe it here in mid 1991.

---

[20]VC §§ 12807(c), 40509(a), 16030(a).

charges adjudicated [VC § 12808(b)]. If you've waited until the last day to renew your license, and you decide to contest the matter, you may find yourself out of luck. It may take one or two months before you have your trial on both the original violation and the failure-to-appear charge. If you want the court clerk to send the "clearance" certificate (which tells the DMV not to suspend or hold your license on account of the particular violation) to the DMV right away, you'll have to appear in court and plead guilty to both charges—including the misdemeanor of failure to appear—or pay the fine.[21]

2. Unpaid Parking Tickets

Similarly, the DMV will refuse to renew your auto registration (not your driver's license) if you ignore a parking ticket.[22] In order to get your registration renewed, you'll have to either fight the parking ticket in court and win, or pay the fine plus a hefty "administrative fee." (You can also pay this directly to the DMV, which will then forward the money to the proper court.) If someone else's tickets are holding up registration of a vehicle you recently purchased, you won't have to pay the tickets that person got if you sign a statement to that effect, under penalty of perjury.[23]

3. Failure to Pay a Judge-Imposed Fine

If you were found or pleaded guilty on a ticket, and were fined by a judge or traffic commissioner, the court will report a failure to pay the fine to the DMV [VC § 40509(b)].This applies only to offenses that are normally entered on your driving record—including all moving violations. (See Chapter 3.) When you apply for a renewal license, the DMV will refuse to renew it until you pay the fine [VC § 12807(d)].

4. Not Paying Off an Accident-Related Court Judgment

Your license can be suspended (without a hearing) for failing to pay off all or a certain portion of a civil court judgment arising out of a lawsuit filed against you as the result of an auto accident. You can't get your license back until you pay off the required amount and provide the DMV with proof that you're insured [VC §§ 16250-16381, CCP § 117.24 (Small Claims Court)].

---

[21]Santa Clara county has adopted a local court rule under which the clerk will issue the "clearance" to the DMV right away—even if you choose to contest the ticket—provided you post the bail, which you don't have to forfeit.

[22]VC § 4760. However, no failure-to-appear charge is involved unless you personally were cited while in or near the vehicle and signed an actual Notice to Appear.

[23]VC §§ 40208-40210, 41102(d), 5602. In San Francisco, where parking space is so rare that virtually everyone parks illegally and accrues many unpaid tickets, a custom has developed where two people with lots of tickets sell their cars to each other. Both can then truthfully sign the statement, and no tickets hold up the respective registrations.

16

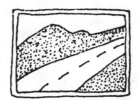

APPEALING A CONVICTION

AFTER YOU'VE BEEN FOUND guilty of a misdemeanor or infraction in municipal or justice court, you have the right to appeal the decision to the superior court. Doing your own appeal is very time-consuming and complicated, even more so than preparing and arguing a written pretrial motion. You will have to prepare quite a bit of paperwork and attend at least two hearings.

Your chances of getting your conviction reversed on appeal are low. Appellate court judges do not review the evidence of the case again. Even if the trial judge made a mistake in believing the police officer over your truthful testimony, the higher court will not reverse the decision. Appeals courts overturn a conviction only if the trial court improperly ruled on a point of law.[1] For example, if the judge insisted on hearing the case after you properly filed a Declaration of Prejudice, she committed a legal error and the appeals court will reverse. Errors of law commonly made by traffic court judges are listed in Section B, below.

Moreover, it's not enough to merely note in your appeal that the judge made a legal error. Usually you also have to show that your ability to present

your case was "prejudiced" (i.e., "compromised," or hurt) as a result of the judge's error. For example, if the judge erred in denying your motion to dismiss the case for excessive delay of the trial, you usually have to show that the delay actually hurt your case. (This might happen if a witness died, moved away, or simply forgot important details.)

Finally, you will have to become familiar with legal research and writing techniques and spend some time in a law library. To learn more about this, it is highly recommended that you read *Legal Research: How to Find and Understand the Law* by Stephen Elias, available from Nolo Press. This book shows you how to look up cases and statutes, how to see if they are up-to-date, and how to use all sorts of secondary sources, such as law reviews, legal encyclopedias and law texts. Chapter 9, Section B(4), also explains how to find cases (court decisions) or statutes. It is important that you read the cases cited in this chapter before relying on them, to be sure that they apply to your specific fact situation.

Before you begin, remember that a successful appeal may only get you a new trial. However successful appeals on some grounds, such as insufficiency of the evidence or violation of your right to a speedy trial, will terminate the case. A few cases suggest that a reversal of a traffic-infraction conviction should *always* terminate the case—on the

---

[1] Appeals courts are often skeptical of "pro per" appeals which tend to argue the facts rather than the law.

basis that an appeal is punishment enough, given the minor nature of the offense.[2] However, many appeals courts have not followed this suggestion.

Below, we tell you which grounds on appeal will result in termination of the case, and which ones may result in a retrial. If your appeal is one that may only get you a new trial, you may not want to go to the trouble. On the other hand, if you request termination of your case in your brief, the appeals court might agree to do it in the interests of justice.

A. Possible Grounds for Appeal

HERE IS A LIST OF the most likely bases for appealing traffic court decisions, with a few comments about each. It is not intended to be complete. Included with each appeal ground is the appropriate authority—statute or case(s). Use these legal references as a starting point in your legal research; they are not the exclusive authority on the subject. And remember, don't try to use one of these bases of appeal unless it applies to your particular fact situation.

1. Pre-Arraignment Delay

You can appeal on this ground when there was a delay of several months before your arraignment, you weren't responsible for the delay, you made a timely motion to dismiss that was denied, and your presentation of the case suffered as a result of the delay. [See Chapter 10, Section E(2)(c).] See the following cases: *In re Mugica* (1968) 69 Cal.2d 516, 72 Cal.Rptr. 645; *Barker v. Municipal Court* (1966) 64 Cal.2d 806, 51 Cal.Rptr; *People v. Valenzuela* (1978) 86 Cal.App.3d 427, 150 Cal.Rptr. 314; *People v. Guaracha* (1969) 272 Cal.App.2d 839, 77 Cal.Rptr. 695; *People v. Flores* (1968) 262 Cal. App.2d 313, 68 Cal.Rptr. 669;

Zimmerman v. Superior Court (1967) 248 Cal.App.2d 56, 56 Cal.Rptr. 226. A reversal on this ground will terminate the case. It will not be sent back for retrial.

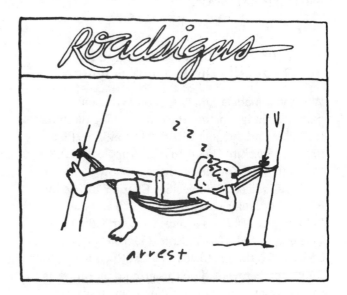

2. Pre-Arrest Delay

If a misdemeanor complaint was filed against you in court (usually for failure-to-appear), but the police didn't arrest you until at least a year had passed, you should have made a motion to dismiss at your arraignment. (See Chapter 10.) If such a motion was denied, and your presentation of the case suffered as a result of the delay, you should appeal. See *Rost v. Municipal Court* (1960) 184 Cal.App.2d 507, 7 Cal.Rptr. 869, and *Rice v. Superior Court* (1975) 49 Cal.App.3d 200, 122 Cal.Rptr. 389 [Felony case, but same rule applicable]. In *Ibarra v. Municipal Court* (1984) 162 Cal.App.3d 853, 208 Cal.Rptr. 783, the appeals court held that a court must hold a full evidentiary hearing on whether the defendant's case was hurt as a result of pre-arrest/pre-arraignment delay. [See also *People v. Rogers* (1981) 120 Cal.App.3d Supp. 7, 174 Cal.Rptr. 313.] In *Serna v. Superior Court* (1985) 40 Cal.3d 239, the court said that a one-year delay preceding arrest is presumed to hurt the defendant's case. Also the U.S. Supreme Court case of *Moore v. Arizona* (1973) 414 U.S. 25, 94 S.Ct. 188, 38 L.Ed. 2d 183 says that your ability to present your case doesn't have to have suffered in

---

[2]See *People v. Kriss* (1979) 96 Cal.App.3d 913, 921 and *People v. Binghinatti* (1975) 55 Cal.App.3d Supp. 5, 7.

order for your conviction to be reversed on account of unconstitutional delay. [See Chapter 10, Section D(2)(b).] Again, a successful appeal on this ground will terminate the case.

3. Your Peremptory Challenge to Disqualify the Judge Was Ignored

When you made a timely motion to disqualify a particular judge, before she did anything on the case, the judge had "no jurisdiction" to continue. [See *Brown v. Swickard* (1985) 163 Cal.App.3d 820, 209 Cal.Rptr. 844.] You do not have to show your case was "prejudiced" by this. [See Chapter 10, Section E(2)(b).] We refer you to CCP § 170.6 and the following cases: *Retes v. Superior Court* (1981) 122 Cal.App.3d 799, 176 Cal.Rptr. 160; *Bouchard v. Insona* (1980) 105 Cal.App.3d 768, 164 Cal.Rptr. 505. If your conviction is reversed on this ground, the appeals court can send the case back for a new trial.

4. Your Motion for Transfer to the County Seat Was Ignored

A non-county seat judge who ignores a proper request for transfer of a case to the county seat has "no jurisdiction" to conduct the trial. You don't have to prove that your case was compromised by this [VC §§ 40502 and 40601 (accident citations)]. [See Chapter 10, Section E(2)(a).] We refer you also to *Smith v. Municipal Court* (1959) 167 Cal.App.2d 534, 344 P.2d 931. In *People v. Beltran* (1981) 124 Cal.App.3d 335, 177 Cal. Rptr. 262 and Government Code § 23600, "county seat" is defined. Again, if your conviction is reversed on this ground, the appeals court can order a retrial.

5. Delay after Arraignment

If you didn't go to trial until more than 45 days after your arraignment had passed, you didn't waive your right to a speedy trial, and you weren't responsible for causing the delay, you may get your

conviction reversed. However, you had to have objected to the delay before trial, and your presentation of the case had to have suffered because of the delay. See PC § 1382 and the many cases in the annotations, including *Rhinehart v. Municipal Court* (1984) 35 Cal.3d 772, 200 Cal. Rptr. 916; *Arreola v. Municipal Court* (1983) 139 Cal.App.3d 108, 188 Cal.Rptr. 529; *Castaneda v. Municipal Court* (1972) 25 Cal.App.3d 588, 102 Cal.Rptr. 230; *Hankla v. Municipal Court* (1972) 26 Cal.App.3d 342, 102 Cal.Rptr. 896; and *Beasley v. Municipal Court* (1973) 32 Cal.App.3d 1020, 108 Cal.Rptr. 637. [See also Chapter 10, Section E(2)(e).]

6. Improper Use of Speed Trap Evidence

If the officer testified that he used radar to determine your speed, but failed to either: a) properly introduce into evidence a traffic and engineering survey justifying the speed limit on the section of the street where he nabbed you, or b) establish that the street was a statute-defined "local street (or) road," you should have objected to his testimony at trial. [See Chapter 11, Section D(1).] If you objected, but the judge convicted you after allowing this testimony, you should appeal on this ground. [See VC §§ 40801-40805, particularly § 40803(b).] Also, read the cases of *People v. Halopoff* (1976) 60 Cal.App.3d Supp.1, 131 Cal. Rptr. 531; *People v. Sterritt* (1976) 65 Cal.App.3d Supp.1, 135 Cal.Rptr. 552; *People v. Flaxman* (1977) 74 Cal.App.3d Supp.16, 151 Cal.Rptr. 799; *People v. Abelson* (1980) 104 Cal.App.3d Supp. 16, 164 Cal.Rptr. 369; and *People v. Peterson* (1986) 181 Cal.App.3d Supp.7, 226 Cal.Rptr. 544. [Also see Chapter 4, Section B(1).] The failure of the officer to do one of the above is actually a failure to present evidence on all the essential elements required to be proved [under Section 40803(b)] when radar is used. This will support an appeal for an insufficiency of evidence. (See Section 7, below.) In such cases, a new trial is barred under the "double jeopardy" clause of the Constitution. *Burks v. U.S.* (1977) 437 U.S. 1. Thus, if you win an appeal, your fight is over.

7. Verdict Not Supported by Evidence

For some fairly complex Vehicle Code violations with lots of elements, it's possible that the officer failed to establish every element of the violation. If you can analyze the section you were charged with (see Chapter 2 , Section B) and find at least one element to which the officer didn't testify at all, then the evidence wasn't sufficient to convict you (unless you inadvertently supplied the missing element in your own testimony). [See Chapter 12, Section C(6).] If this is the case, no retrial is allowed and you win, period. (See Ground 6, above.)

Note: Don't confuse this with trying to get the appeals court to "reweigh" the evidence. As long as there is *any* evidence in the record to support the conviction, the conviction will be upheld. For example, if you were charged with failing to yield the right of way at an intersection controlled by a stop sign (VC § 21802), and the officer testified that a stop sign was there, the appeals court won't reverse a guilty verdict, even if you and three other witnesses testified that there was no stop sign. However, if the officer never testified that a stop sign was there, one essential element would be completely unproved, and the verdict of guilty would not be supported by the evidence.

8. Judge Acted as Prosecutor

In *People v. Carlucci* (1979) 23 Cal.3d 249, 152 Cal. Rptr. 439, the California Supreme Court suggested that trials conducted without a prosecutor were proper, but only "if the conduct of the court, including its questioning of the witnesses, is fair and properly limited in scope." See also *People v. Municipal Court* (1990) __Cal.App.3d__, __Cal.Rptr.__, and *People v. Daggett* (1988) 206 Cal.App.3d Supp.1, 253 Cal.Rptr. 195. (Read the excellent dissent, in any event.) This means that if the judge was very prosecution-oriented in cross-examining you, or in reminding the officer to supply testimony important to the prosecution, the judge went too far and the conviction might be reversed. See also *People v. Handcock* (1983) 145 Cal.App.3d

Supp. 25, 30, 193 Cal.Rptr. 397 and *People v. Ferguson* (1981) 126 Cal. App.3d Supp. 22, 30-31, 179 Cal.Rptr. 437. If you win on this basis, the case may be ordered retried.

9. Judicial Bias

If the judge indicated from the beginning of the trial that she thought you were guilty, you were denied a fair trial and are entitled to a reversal. It is very hard to prove judicial bias, however. See CCP § 170.1 and cases interpreting it, including *Pacific and Southwest Conference of United Methodist Church v. Superior Court* (1978) 82 Cal.App.3d 72, 147 Cal.Rptr. 44 and *Taliaferro v. Taliaferro* (1962) 203 Cal.App.2d 642, 21 Cal.Rptr. 864. Winning on this ground may result in a retrial.

10. Refusal to Allow Relevant Testimony

You may have found that judges often refuse to allow testimony by "expert witnesses." Expert witnesses are people who because of their education, training, or experience can testify as to the reliability of certain types of evidence. In traffic cases, defendants will sometimes bring in engineers or scientists to testify as to the fallibility of radar speed-measuring devices. A judge who does not give the expert witness a chance to establish her qualifications to testify may be in error. See Evidence Code § 720, *People v. McDonald* (1984) 37 Cal.3d 351, 208 Cal.Rptr. 236. However, a judge's determination that the person is not qualified to testify as an expert will probably be affirmed by an appeals court. See *People v. Kelly* (1976) 17 Cal.3d 24, 130 Cal.Rptr. 144 and *Cooper v. Board of Medical Examiners* (1975) 49 Cal.App.3d 931, 123 Cal.Rptr. 563. Even if you win on this ground, the case may be retried.

11. Refusal to Allow Final Argument

In *People v. Douglas* (1973) 31 Cal.App.3d Supp. 26, 106 Cal.Rptr. 611, the Appellate Department of the

Los Angeles County Superior Court reversed a traffic court conviction because the judge refused to allow the defendant to make a closing argument. In *Herring v. New York* (1975) 422 U.S. 853, 95 S.Ct. 2550, 45 L.Ed. 2d 593, the U.S. Supreme Court reversed a felony conviction (after a non-jury trial) because the trial judge refused to allow a concluding statement by the defendant's lawyer. Closing statements are always allowed in misdemeanor trials, and the same provisions of law apply to infraction trials. See PC § 19.7 and *People v. Matthews* (1983) 139 Cal.App.3d 537, 188 Cal.Rptr. 796. [Also see Chapter 11, Section G, and Chapter 12, Section C(10).]

12. Refusal to State Guilty Verdict in Open Court

In *People v. Kriss* (1979) 96 Cal.App.3d 913, 158 Cal. Rptr. 420, the Court of Appeal ruled that a judge must state the decision (i.e., guilty or not) in open court while you're there—unless you give the judge permission to take the case under advisement. If you didn't give the judge this permission, the appeals court will reverse your conviction. (See Chapter 12.) The appeals court may order the case retried. However, in the *Kriss* case, the court ordered the case terminated in light of the minor nature of the traffic infractions involved.

rush hour

13. Sentenced Too Early

If you were sentenced right after the judge found you guilty (as usually occurs in traffic court), but the judge didn't ask you about giving up your right to be sentenced at least six hours later, you can make a motion to vacate the sentence. (See Chapter 14.) If your motion is denied, you can appeal the sentence —but the conviction will remain. See PC § 1449 and *In re Elsholz* (1964) 228 Cal.App.2d 192, 39 Cal.Rptr. 356. However, the appeals court will probably only vacate the sentence and send the case back for resentencing. You therefore gain very little from an appeal on this ground, unless the sentence imposed was unusually harsh.

14. Sentenced Too Late

If you were sentenced more than five days after being found guilty and you moved for a new trial on that specific point, just before being sentenced, the appeals court should reverse the conviction and order a retrial. See PC § 1449 and *People v. Cheffen* (1969) 2 Cal.App.3d 638, 82 Cal.Rptr. 658 and *People v. Von Moltke* (1931) 118 Cal.App. 568, 5 P.2d 917. (Also see Chapter 14, Section A.) However, this is extremely rare in traffic cases.

15. Sentence Greater than Maximum for First-Time Infraction

If the judge sentenced you to pay more than the basic first-offense infraction fine of $100 plus penalty assessment, but the prior offenses on which he based this heavier fine were neither 1) alleged and proved at trial, nor 2) admitted by you, you should have moved to vacate the sentence. If you did, but the judge refused to change it, the appeals court should order the trial court to do so. See *People v. Ford* (1964) 60 Cal.2d 772, 794, 36 Cal. Rptr. 620, and VC § 42004. See also *In re Tahl* (1969) 1 Cal.3d 127, 81 Cal Rptr. 557, and *People v. Matthews* (1983) 139 Cal.App.3d 537, 188 Cal.Rptr. 796. [See also Chapter 14, Section B(1).] Your case will be sent back for resentencing.

16. Excessive Delay in Appeal

If the trial court judge, the clerk, or the prosecutor, delays for several months any step of the appeal [such as "settling" the statement of trial proceedings,[3] or transmitting it and other papers (the "record") to the appeals court], you might be able to file a motion in the appeals court to have the conviction reversed and ordered dismissed. See *People v. Jenkins* (1976) 55 Cal.App.3d Supp. 55, 61, 127 Cal.Rptr. 870, *People v. Ruhl* (1976) 63 Cal.App.3d Supp. 6, 134 Cal.Rptr. 62, and *People v. Binghinatti* (1975) 55 Cal.App.3d Supp. 5, 127 Cal.Rptr. 310. The cases of *Ruhl* and *Binghinatti*, as well as *People v. Kriss* (1979) 96 Cal.App.3d Supp. 26, 106 Cal.Rptr. 611, have also held that the case should not be sent back to the trial court for a new trial, but rather should be dismissed. The appellant, in having to appeal such a minor violation, has suffered enough.

B.   The Steps in an Appeal

PROSECUTING AN APPEAL involves the filing of at least three written documents: a Notice of Appeal; a Proposed Statement on Appeal in the Municipal Court; and an opening brief in the appeals court once the case is transferred there.

1.   The Notice of Appeal

The appeal is started by filing a Notice of Appeal[4] with the clerk of the municipal or justice court in which you were found guilty. The Notice of Appeal is a one-page form simply stating that you are appealing the "judgment of conviction," the sentence, or both. It includes the date of conviction and the offense of which you were found guilty. Unlike other papers you file, you don't have to mail a copy to the prosecution. However, you must file it within 30 days of the date you were found guilty. This requirement can cause problems if you allow the judge to take your case under advisement and have the decision mailed to you. If you're not informed of the result in court, call the clerk every few days to find out whether you were found guilty.

If possible, you should file the appeal with the clerk of the municipal or justice court in which you were found guilty, within a few days of the date of the conviction. The Vehicle Code requires court clerks to notify the DMV of convictions within 10days, whether they're appealed or not.[5] In a few courts, however, the practice is to put off notifying the DMV of your conviction until and unless it comes back affirmed by the appeals court. This means that where this is the practice, you won't have the conviction on your record while the appeal is pending, which may help you if you already have a few other violations on file. However, to take advantage of this, you must file your Notice of Appeal with the clerk of the municipal or justice court in which you were found guilty, within 10 days, and hope the court has not yet notified the DMV before the 10-day limit. A sample Notice of Appeal follows.

---

[3]See Section C(2) below.

[4]California Rules of Court, Rule 182.

[5]VC § 1803. If the conviction is reversed on appeal, the traffic court clerks send a corrected notice to the DMV (VC § 1803.3).

```
DAVID W. BROWN
950 Parker St.
Berkeley, CA 94710
(415) 555-1212

Defendant and Appellant in Pro Per

        MUNICIPAL COURT OF CALIFORNIA, COUNTY OF ALAMEDA

              BERKELEY-ALBANY JUDICIAL DISTRICT

THE PEOPLE OF THE STATE   )    No. B 000836-C
OF CALIFORNIA             )    NOTICE OF APPEAL
                          )
              Plaintiff,  )
                          )    [Penal Code § 1466,
                          )    Rule 182]
vs.                       )
                          )
DAVID W. BROWN,           )
                          )
              Defendant.  )
_____)


TO THE CLERK OF THE ABOVE-ENTITLED COURT:

    PLEASE TAKE NOTICE that defendant DAVID W. BROWN hereby appeals to

the Superior Court of California, County of Alameda, from the final

judgment of conviction for violation of § 22350 of the Vehicle Code,

rendered in this action on October 10, 199_.

DATED: October 15, 199_


                              _____
                              DAVID W. BROWN
                              Defendant and Appellant in Pro Per
```

```
* This Penal Code citation is just a procedural statute that allows you to appeal.
  It doesn't vary with the offense and should appear on your Notice of Appeal.
```

2. Statement of Proceedings

Every appeal from a trial court is required to have some kind of written record of what happened at the trial. In serious criminal cases, the record is a written transcription of the testimony. In traffic cases, however, there is usually no court reporter present. The law thus allows the use of a "Settled Statement." A Settled Statement is a legal document that briefly lists your grounds for appeal and summarizes the proceedings, including testimony and other evidence relevant to those grounds. It is the result of a three-step process whereby:

a. The appealing defendant (appellant) prepares a "Proposed Statement" of what happened at trial, or if relevant, at arraignment or motion hearing;

b. The prosecution prepares its own version of what happened; and

c. The judge who presided at the trial "settles" the differences between the two versions, ruling as to what will be accepted as a final "Settled Statement" to be transferred to the appeals court.

Your "Proposed Statement" must be filed with the municipal or justice court at which you were found guilty within 15 days after you file the Notice of Appeal. It must contain a brief statement of each legal ground for your appeal, and a summary of that part of the proceedings in which you claim the legal error occurred—whether at arraignment, a motion hearing or trial.[6]

For example, if the basis of your appeal is that the judge had no jurisdiction to hear the case, all you need is a statement as to when and how you made the request to disqualify the judge and what the judge said in denying it. Or, if your appeal is based only on the judge's refusal to let you make a closing argument, your statement need only indicate that you requested the opportunity to make a closing argument and that the judge refused to let you do so.

On the other hand, if one of the grounds for your appeal is insufficiency of the evidence, improper admission of radar evidence, refusal to allow relevant testimony, judicial bias, or any other ground relating to much or all of what happened throughout the trial, you will have to prepare a more extensive statement of the proceedings. For example, in appealing on the basis of a denial of a speedy trial, you will want to show how the judge's error compromised or "prejudiced" your ability to defend by including in your statement that one of your witnesses said she couldn't remember important details (that might have helped you had the trial been held earlier).

The proposed statement should not retell all your testimony in detail, nor should it include evidence you forgot to present at trial. You should only mention in detail the testimony relevant to your appeal. (If leaving out testimony that isn't relevant would seem to leave an awkward gap, you can briefly refer to it, however.) In summarizing the testimony, you will often have to rely on your memory, since most traffic courts do not use court reporters or even tape recorders. In those courts that do electronically record the proceedings, you should be able to purchase a copy of the tape from the court clerk for $10 to $15. You can then listen to the tape and write down a brief summary of the proceedings, or even a verbatim record. The procedures for this are listed in Rule 187.5, California Rules of Court.

If the judge allowed you to record the trial proceedings yourself, with a hand-held recorder [as permitted by Rule 980, California Rules of Court—see Chapter 12, Section C(2)(d)], you can use that recording in the same way, as an aid to drafting your Proposed Statement.

Finally, you must have a friend serve a copy of the Proposed Statement on the prosecution [either by mail or delivery to the district (or city) attorney's office] and fill out a Proof of Service attached to the back of the original. You can then file the whole set of papers with the court.

A sample Proposed Statement on Appeal follows:

---

[6]California Rules of Court, Rule 184.

DAVID W. BROWN
950 Parker St.
Berkeley, CA 94710
(415) 555-1234

Defendant and Appellant in Pro Per

MUNICIPAL COURT OF CALIFORNIA, COUNTY OF ALAMEDA

BERKELEY-ALBANY JUDICIAL DISTRICT

THE PEOPLE OF THE STATE OF CALIFORNIA,	No. B008836C
Plaintiff,	PROPOSED STATEMENT ON APPEAL
vs.	
DAVID W. BROWN,	
Defendant	

GROUNDS ON APPEAL

Defendant, DAVID W. BROWN, the appellant herein, submits the following Proposed Statement on Appeal pursuant to Rule 184 California Rules of Court:

The grounds on which appellant intends to rely are:

1. The Court was without jurisdiction to try defendant, following his request at arraignment, that the action be transferred to the Municipal Court at the county seat; and

2. The Court was without jurisdiction to find defendant guilty after having admitted, over his objection, testimony based on the use of speed-detection radar, when no foundation engineering and traffic survey had been properly introduced into evidence.

STATEMENT OF EVIDENCE AND PROCEEDINGS

Appellant, in support of his grounds of appeal, sets forth the following statement of the proceedings held and the evidence taken in this action.

ARRAIGNMENT

Arraignment of defendant in this action commenced in the within-entitled Court on September 5, 199_ at 9:00 a.m., in Department 3, the Hon. T.M. Handimafine presiding. Defendant entered a plea of not guilty to the charge of violating Vehicle Code § 22350, an infraction. Defendant then requested that the action be transferred to the Municipal Court at the County Seat, at 600 Washington Street, Oakland; defendant stated that he based this request on the ground that such court was the proper court for trial because of his demand to the citing officer that the Notice to Appear specify that court as the place to appear, pursuant to Vehicle Code § 40502(b). Defendant referred the court to his previously-filed Notice of Motion for Change of Venue to County Seat and supporting Declaration and Points and Authorities, included in the record herein. Defendant's request for transfer to the county seat was denied, and trial was set for October 10, 199_ at 2:00 p.m. in Department 3 of the within-entitled court.

TRIAL

Trial of this action commenced on October 10, 199_ at 2:00 p.m., in Department 3 of the within-entitled court before the Hon. T.M. Handimafine, without a jury. No counsel was present on plaintiff's behalf, defendant was present in propria persona, and neither party made an opening statement.

PROSECUTION'S CASE

As the prosecution's only witness, Officer John Smith of the Berkeley Police Department testified that he was parked facing north on Milvia Street, where a posted sign indicated a speed limit of 35 mph. He further stated that he observed a vehicle driven by defendant traveling at what he thought was a speed in excess of 35 mph, and raised his hand-held radar unit to measure the vehicle's speed.

At this time, defendant objected to the introduction of Officer

Smith's radar-based testimony on the ground that the foundation had not been laid for introduction of such evidence by proper introduction of a engineering and traffic survey justifying the speed limit, as required by Vehicle Code § 40803(b) and the case of People v. Halopoff (1976) 60 Cal.App.3d Supp.1. The Court overruled the objection, stating that it was up to defendant to show the nonexistence of an engineering and traffic survey, and that in any event, one had been made. The Court then allowed Officer Smith to continue with his testimony.

Officer Smith continued that his radar unit indicated defendant's vehicle's speed to be 46 mph, that he gave chase and stopped defendant in order to issue him a citation.

On cross-examination, Officer Smith, in addition to answering questions not relevant to this appeal, admitted that defendant had requested that he list the court at which defendant be directed to appear as the county seat. Officer Smith also admitted that he refused this request because the address of the Berkeley court was already printed on his citation forms.

DEFENDANT'S CASE

Though not relevant for the purpose of this appeal, defendant took the stand to testify that he had been driving at a speed of 35 mph, as indicated by his speedometer, and that the specific road, weather and traffic conditions in any event rendered even a substantially higher speed to be safe. No cross-examination of defendant was conducted.

VERDICT AND SENTENCE

The Court then found defendant guilty as charged and sentenced him to pay a fine of $85 including penalty assessments.

DATED: October 15, 199_   Respectfully submitted,

_____
DAVID W. BROWN
Defendant and Appellant in Pro Per

PROOF OF SERVICE

I, RICHARD MILLER, declare:

1. I am over the age of eighteen and not a party to the within action.

2. My business address is 123 Galvez Street, Oakland, California, in the county within which the herein-mentioned mailing occurred.

3. On October 15, 199_ I served the within Proposed Statement on Appeal by placing a true copy thereof in a separate sealed envelope, with the postage thereon fully prepaid, in the United States Postal Service mailbox at Oakland, County of Alameda, California, the said envelope being addressed to:

Office of the District Attorney

County of Alameda

1225 Fallon St.

Oakland, California 94612

I declare under penalty of perjury under the laws of the State of California that the foregoing is true and correct.

DATED: October 15, 199_

_____

RICHARD MILLER

3. Prosecution's Proposed Statement

If the district or city attorney's office disagrees with your Proposed Statement, it must prepare, file, and serve on you, within 10 days,[7] its own Proposed Statement.[8] This is very difficult for the prosecution to do in traffic cases where no prosecutor —just the officer—was present at trial. To find out what happened, the prosecution must interview the officer, who may have forgotten all sorts of details or may even be on vacation. The officer cannot prepare the Proposed Statement since he's not a lawyer.

4. Hearing to Settle the Statement

After your Proposed Statement and that of the prosecution (if any) have been filed with the court, a hearing is set to reconcile the two versions. This hearing takes place before the same judge who found you guilty. A few judges have been known to try to sabotage defendants' appeals by arbitrarily accepting the prosecution's version.[9] If this happens, stick to your guns. Explain in detail the circumstances surrounding the disputed part of the trial, so as to refresh the judge's memory.[10] After all, you're in a better position to remember than either the judge (who hears lots of cases and is likely to confuse or forget what happened) or the prosecutor (who also handles numerous cases and was probably not even there).

The facts of the case, as the appeals court will see them, are fixed at this hearing. You can't turn around later and base your appeal on anything not contained in the final record.

5. The "Settled Statement"

After the final Settled Statement has been worked out, it will be up to you to prepare it and submit it to the judge.[11] The Settled Statement on Appeal (also called an "Engrossed Statement") must be filed with the clerk of the municipal or justice court in which you were found guilty within five days. It should be in the same format as the Proposed Statement, but at the end, a separate sentence should be added, saying: "The within Settled Statement on Appeal is hereby certified as correct." This should be followed by a place for the judge to date and sign the statement. "Judge of the Municipal [or Justice] Court," should be printed directly beneath the line.

---

[7]Fifteen days if your proposed statement was served by mail (CCP § 1013).

[8]California Rules of Court, Rule 185.

[9]Some judges even go so far as to "strike" from the statement any ground of appeal they disagree with. This, however, is prohibited by Rule 187 of California Rules of Court, and you should point this out to the judge.

[10]In *People v. Jenkins* (1976) 55 Cal.App.3d Supp. 55, 61, 127 Cal.Rptr. 870, the appeals court stated that "if there was no court reporter at the trial and a Settled Statement cannot be drafted which will afford an adequate basis for appellate review, the defendant is entitled to a new trial as a matter of due process." The court also said ,"Where there are conflicts as to what transpired at the trial, the court must resolve the dispute as to the facts and see to it that a single unified statement is prepared which sets forth the evidence and testimony received at the trial. To assist him in carrying out his responsibility to prepare an accurate statement of the evidence, the trial court may rely on the appellant's proposed statement, the respondent's proposed amendments, and his own notes or memory of the defendant. If a reporter was present, the trial judge may order the testimony read to him to refresh his memory. As a last resort, the trial judge may recall witnesses to give testimony anew." See also Rule 187.5 (g)(3), California Rules of Court on the judge using any sound recordings to refresh her memory. As we saw in Section C of Chapter 12, the case of *In re Armstrong* (1981) 126 Cal.App.3d 565, requires that a court reporter be present at your trial if you insist. This may irritate the judge, but the availability of a verbatim record will keep the judge from trying to wreck your appeal by refusing to certify an accurate Settled Statement.

[11]California Rules of Court, Rule 187.

Also, as with your Proposed Statement, a copy should be served on the prosecutor and a Proof of Service filled out.

6.   Transfer to the Appeals Court

After the Settled Statement has been signed by the trial judge, and the record of documents put together by the trial court clerk, the case file is transferred to the Appellate Department of the Superior Court for the county in which the trial court is located.[12] The clerk will send you a notice of the transfer. The notice will also list your new appeals case number (entirely different from your traffic court case number, which should be used on everything you file in the appeals court, including your "Opening Brief." You have 20 days from the time the notice says the record was transferred (not from the time the clerk sent out or you received the notice) to file your brief.

7.   Your "Opening Brief"

Your opening brief will present your arguments as to why the trial judge committed one or more legal errors, which resulted in "prejudice" to your case.

The brief must have a cover, be typed (triple-spaced) on numbered 8-1/2 by 11" legal paper, and cannot be more than 15 pages long.[13] It must be accompanied by a Proof of Service. Although it's a matter of style, briefs should be broken down into the following four parts:

a.   Statement of Facts

This is a two or three-paragraph summary of the facts surrounding the conduct of the case, insofar as they're relevant to your ground(s) of appeal. You should not introduce any factual matters that aren't mentioned in the record, or Settled Statement. Refer to pages and line numbers in the Settled Statement, if possible.

b.   Questions or Issues Presented

These are one-sentence statements (usually in the form of questions) succinctly listing each separate legal issue you intend to argue. There should be at least one, and perhaps several, issues for each ground of appeal.

c.   Summary of Argument

This is a several-paragraph summary of your detailed legal argument. It's optional, but useful, since it helps the appeals judge figure out what you're saying in the next part.

d.   Argument

This is the "body" of the brief, and is written in the same way as the arguments in the Points and Authorities examples you saw in Chapter 10. Each distinct point must be listed under an appropriate heading, with sub-headings as desired. A short sample brief follows.

Roadsigns

meridian strip

---

[12]The Appellate Department of the Superior Court, by the way, is always located at the county seat.

[13]California Rules of Court 105, 15(d), 9(b).

mph speed zone on Milvia Street in Berkeley. Appellant objected to this testimony on the ground that the foundation for introduction of such testimony had not been established. That foundation requires proof of an engineering and traffic survey justifying the speed limit on that portion of Milvia Street. The court, Hon. T.M. Handimafine presiding, overruled appellant's objection, satisfying himself with a statement by Officer Smith that such a study had been made.

On cross-examination, Officer Smith admitted that he had not participated in conducting the alleged traffic study, and also admitted that he had refused appellant's request to cite him to the municipal court at the county seat. At the conclusion of this cross-examination, appellant testified as to his own vehicle's speed, and to the road, weather, and traffic conditions at the time he had been driving.

The court then found appellant guilty as charged.

DAVID W. BROWN
950 Parker St.
Berkeley, CA 94710
(415) 555-1234

Defendant and Appellant in Pro Per

IN THE SUPERIOR COURT OF CALIFORNIA, COUNTY OF ALAMEDA

APPELLATE DEPARTMENT

THE PEOPLE OF THE STATE)   No. CR - 1234
OF CALIFORNIA   )
)   APPELLANT'S OPENING BRIEF
        Plaintiff and Respondent,)
)
vs.   )
)
DAVID W. BROWN,   )
)
        Defendant and Appellant.)

SUMMARY OF FACTS

Appellant was cited on July 8, 199_ for an infraction violation of Vehicle Code § 22350, the "Basic Speed Law." At the time he was cited, he requested that the citing officer specify, on the Notice to Appear, the court at the county seat as the place for his appearance, pursuant to Vehicle Code § 40502(b). The officer refused to comply with this request, and directed him to appear instead at the municipal court for the Berkeley-Albany district.

At his arraignment on September 5, 199_ appellant appeared in the said municipal court at Berkeley and moved for a change of venue to the municipal court at the county seat, namely Oakland, a city that was also defendant's principal place of business. The motion was based on a previously filed Notice of Motion, Declaration, and Points and Authorities, a part of the record herein. The court, Hon. T.M. Handimafine presiding, denied the motion and set trial for October 10, 199_ in Department 3 of the Berkeley court.

At trial, the citing officer, Officer John Smith of the Berkeley Police Department, testified that, using a hand-held radar unit, he measured the speed of appellant's vehicle as 48 mph in a posted 35-

of justice, ordered dismissed by the appellate court, rather than be sent back to the trial court for retrial. (People v. Kriss (1979) 96 Cal.App.3d 913; People v. Binghinatti (1975) Cal.App.3d Supp. 5.)

ARGUMENT

I. THE TRIAL COURT WAS WITHOUT JURISDICTION TO TRY APPELLANT FOLLOWING HIS REQUEST AT ARRAIGNMENT THAT THE MATTER BE TRANSFERRED TO THE MUNICIPAL COURT AT THE COUNTY SEAT.

A. WHEN A PERSON CITED FOR A TRAFFIC VIOLATION SO REQUESTS, THE MATTER MUST BE COMMENCED IN THE MUNICIPAL OR JUSTICE COURT AT THE COUNTY SEAT.

[Note: Rather than repeat why this is so, we simply refer you back to Chapter 10, Section D(2)(a). The format and style of writing should be the same as in the motion papers for a motion requesting a transfer to the county seat.]

B. THE TRIAL COURT WAS WITHOUT JURISDICTION TO TRY THE MATTER FOLLOWING APPELLANT'S MOTION FOR TRANSFER TO THE COURT AT THE COUNTY SEAT.

Penal Code Section 1462.2 states that "Except as provided by the Vehicle Code," the proper court for trial of a misdemeanor (also infraction—see Penal Code § 19d) is the court in the county in which the offense is alleged to have been committed. The explicit reference to the Vehicle Code indicates that venue for Vehicle Code offenses may be different. In the instant case, appellant invoked Vehicle Code § 40502(b) to make the court at the county seat the only proper court for trial.

Section 1462.2 goes on to state that when the action is commenced in a court other than the proper one, it may nevertheless be tried there, "unless the defendant, at the time he pleads, requests an order transferring the action or proceeding to the proper court." The statement concludes:

If after such request it appears that the action or proceeding was not commenced in the proper court, the court shall order the action or proceeding transferred to the proper court."

QUESTIONS PRESENTED

I. WHETHER THE TRIAL COURT WAS WITHOUT JURISDICTION TO TRY APPELLANT FOLLOWING HIS REQUEST AT ARRAIGNMENT THAT THE ACTION BE TRANSFERRED TO THE MUNICIPAL COURT AT THE COUNTY SEAT FOR TRIAL.

II. WHETHER THE COURT WAS WITHOUT JURISDICTION TO FIND APPELLANT GUILTY WHEN, OVER APPELLANT'S OBJECTION, THE COURT ADMITTED TESTIMONY BASED ON THE USE OF SPEED-DETECTION RADAR EVEN THOUGH NO ENGINEERING AND TRAFFIC STUDY HAD BEEN INTRODUCED INTO EVIDENCE.

SUMMARY OF ARGUMENT

The Berkeley-Albany Judicial District was without jurisdiction to try appellant, given appellant's timely request to be tried in Oakland under Vehicle Code § 40502(b), and Penal Code § 1462.2, which, upon defendant's motion, require the court to transfer the case to such district.

In addition, even assuming the matter had been commenced in the proper court, the court nevertheless lacked jurisdiction to enter a judgment of conviction based upon a "speed trap" (Vehicle Code §§ 40801-40805), where accompanying evidence of a "traffic and engineering survey" justifying the posted speed limit was not also introduced, as required by Section 40803(b). People v. Halopoff (1976) 60 Cal.App.3d Supp. 1. A certified copy of the original study must be introduced into evidence. People v. Sterritt (1976) 65 Cal.App.3d Supp. 1. If the prosecution fails to do this, and the court nevertheless allows radar-based testimony, it is without jurisdiction to convict the defendant.

The prosecution's failure to establish this essential element of the case bars retrial, since the constitutional bar against double jeopardy forbids a second criminal trial where the prosecution failed to present sufficient evidence the first time. (Burks v. United States (1977) 437 U.S. 1.)

In any event, recent case law indicates that convictions for minor traffic infractions, when reversed, should be, in the interests

In _Smith v. Municipal Court_ (1959) 167 Cal.App.2d 534, 334 P.2d 931, the court held that it was the duty of a non-county-seat court to transfer the action, on defendant's request, to the county-seat court in which it would have been commenced had the citing officer abided by the dictates of Penal Code § 1462.2, now § 40502(b) of the Vehicle Code, stating:

The Municipal Court for the Los Angeles Judicial District being the proper place for the trial of the action against petitioner, § 1462.2 of the Penal Code made it the duty of the respondent court [Glendale Judicial District] to transfer the case to the municipal court for the Los Angeles Judicial District. [167 Cal.App.2d, at 541.]

Accordingly, the trial court in the instant case was without jurisdiction to try appellant. While _Smith_ was a mandamus action, language therein noted that even following trial, this type of error "might be reviewed upon an appeal from the final judgment" (167 Cal.App.2d, at 541).

II. THE COURT WAS WITHOUT JURISDICTION TO FIND APPELLANT GUILTY AFTER HAVING ADMITTED OVER APPELLANT'S OBJECTION TESTIMONY BASED ON THE USE OF RADAR, WHEN NO TRAFFIC AND ENGINEERING STUDY HAD BEEN INTRODUCED INTO EVIDENCE.

Section 40802 of the Vehicle Code defines a "speed trap" as follows:

(b) A particular section of a highway with a prima facie speed limit..which speed limit is not justified by an engineering and traffic survey conducted within five years prior to the date of the alleged violation, and where enforcement involves the use of radar...

The ramifications of such a definition of a speed trap are listed in §§ 40803, 40804(a), and 40805. The latter section states that any court that admits evidence based on the use of a speed trap

"shall be without jurisdiction to enter a judgment of conviction... for a violation of this code involving the speed of a vehicle." Section 40804(a) states that no such evidence shall be admitted. Finally, subdivision (b) of that section states:

(b) In any prosecution under this code of a charge involving the speed of a vehicle, where enforcement involves the use of radar..the prosecution shall establish, as part of its prima facie case, that the evidence or testimony presented is not based upon a speed trap as defined in subdivision (b) of § 40802. Evidence that an engineering and traffic survey has been conducted within five years of the date of the alleged violation or evidence that the offense was committed on a local street or road as defined in subdivision (b) of § 40802 shall constitute a prima facie case that the evidence or testimony is not based upon a speed trap...

In summary, the prosecution, in order to introduce radar-based testimony in a speed violation case, must introduce into evidence an engineering and traffic survey justifying the prima facie speed limit within the past five years. If it fails to do so, a "speed trap" involving radar must be presumed. In that event, the officer testifying as to his measurement of the defendant's vehicle's speed by radar is "incompetent as a witness" and the court may not receive such evidence. And in the event it does receive such evidence, it is "without jurisdiction" to convict the defendant of a speed violation (VC § 40805).

The provisions of subdivision (b) of Vehicle Code § 40803, recently added by the Legislature, are a codification of the law as set forth in _People v. Halopoff_ (1976) 60 Cal.App.3d Supp. 1, 131 Cal.Rptr. 531, where §§ 40801 through 40805 were construed. In

Halopoff, the court reversed a conviction of a defendant for violation of § 22350, where the trial court overruled defendant's objection to the introduction of radar-based testimony without direct evidence of the existence of an engineering and traffic survey. In speaking of the policy requiring the People to disclose material evidence favorable to the accused (In re Ferguson (1971) 5 Cal.3d 525, 532), the court held that the prosecution has the burden of proving the existence of such a survey as a prerequisite to the use of radar-based testimony, stating:

It is consonant with this policy to require the People to disclose without request that radar was used and to produce the engineering and traffic survey or declare their inability to do so. The prosecution will always know when radar has been used to apprehend a speeder. The defendant and the court may not be aware of that fact. Simple fairness, and ease of procedure, dictate that the prosecution make that fact known.

* * * * *

If the burden is placed on the defendant to establish the existence of a speed trap, he is required to prove a negative—the absence of the requisite survey. This is an onerous task which militates against the policy of the legislation. If it is far more easy and realistic in this connection to place the burden on the People...[60 Cal.App.3d Supp., at 6-7.]

In the instant case, no engineering and traffic survey was introduced into evidence by the prosecution. The officer merely testified that he knew of the existence of such a survey. This is not sufficient. When an officer who did not participate in conducting such a survey merely states that it exists, but does not produce it, any speed violation conviction based on the use of radar must be reversed. (People v. Sterritt (1976) 65 Cal.App.3d Supp. 1, 135 Cal.Rptr. 522.) The prosecution has failed to meet its burden of proving that the officer's use of radar did not constitute a speed trap. Therefore, the officer was incompetent as a witness, and his testimony should not have been admitted. In any event, the court was without jurisdiction to convict appellant after having admitted such evidence.

CONCLUSION

For the reasons set forth above, appellant's conviction should be reversed. In addition, the trial court should be ordered to dismiss the matter rather than retry appellant. The People's failure to introduce the survey into evidence constituted a failure of proof of an essential element expressly required by Vehicle Code Section 40803(b). In other words, the evidence was insufficient to support a conviction. Retrial is therefore barred by the Double Jeopardy clause. (Burks v. United States (1977) 437 U.S. 1.) Reversal would also advance the interests of justice. In People v. Kriss, supra, the court reversed traffic violation convictions for ten defendants in a consolidated appeal, and ordered them dismissed, stating:

Given the relatively minor nature of the infractions involved and the fines imposed, and the necessity for retrials that an unqualified reversal would require, we conclude that in these instances it would not be in the interest of justice to prolong these matters. Accordingly, the judgments are reversed with directions to dismiss the complaints. [96 Cal.App.3d, at 921.]

DATED: November 1, 199_   Respectfully submitted,

DAVID W. BROWN, Appellant in Pro Per

PROOF OF DEPOSIT WITH TRIAL COURT

I, RICHARD MILLER, declare:

On November 20, 199_ I caused a copy of the within Appellant's Opening Brief to be deposited with the trial court below by personally delivering a true copy thereof to a deputy clerk of the said court for delivery to the Hon. T.M. Handimafine, the judge who presided below at the trial in this action.

I declare under penalty of perjury under the laws of the State of California that the foregoing is true and correct.

DATED: November 2, 199_

                                    RICHARD MILLER

PROOF OF SERVICE

I, RICHARD MILLER, declare:

I am over the age of eighteen and not a party to the within action.

My business address is 123 Galvez Street, Oakland, California, in the county within which the within-mentioned mailing occurred.

On November 2, 199_ I served the within Appellant's Opening Brief on Respondent by placing a true copy thereof in a separate sealed envelope, with the postage thereon fully prepaid, in the United States Postal Service mailbox at Oakland, County of Alameda, California, the envelope being addressed as follows:

Office of the District Attorney

County of Alameda

1225 Fallon Street

Oakland, California 94612

I declare under penalty of perjury under the laws of the State of California that the foregoing is true and correct.

DATED: November 2 199_

                                    RICHARD MILLER

8.   The "Responding Brief"

If there is a hell to which incompetent, naughty, or just plain inexperienced deputy prosecutors are relegated, it is handling traffic appeals by pro per defendants. Doing an appeal may be interesting for you, but it's boring for them, and this often shows in the poor quality of their briefs. Also, they have many cases to work on, but you have just your own. If you do a good job of researching, writing, and preparing your brief, it will probably be a lot better than the prosecution's and you might even favorably impress the appellate judges. The prosecution also has 20 days to file this brief, and must mail you a copy.

9.   The Optional "Reply Brief"

You may file a "reply brief" in response to the prosecution's responding brief within 10 days after the prosecution has filed its brief. (This may work out to only a few days after you receive a copy in the mail.) Although you are not required to file a reply brief, it is a very good idea. Some judges regard the failure to file a reply brief as an admission that everything said in the prosecution's responding brief is true. The scope of your reply brief should be limited to new questions or arguments raised by the prosecution. The format of the Reply Brief is the same as the Opening Brief, except without a Statement of Facts.

Three copies and the original of the Reply Brief and Proof of Service must be filed in the Appellate Department of the Superior Court, after respective service and "deposit" of copies on the prosecution and trial court clerk.

10.   The Hearing

You will be notified of a hearing date, usually several months after the record has been transferred from the municipal or justice court to the superior court. This hearing is where you and the prosecutor present your arguments and/or respond to questions from the judges. There are usually three judges. Unlike the trial, this hearing is usually not the most important part of your appeal. The briefs are the most important, and most appeals judges will have tentatively decided whether to "affirm", or "reverse" after reading them. The judges may question you about some points of your legal theory. You should not be defensive in answering such questions. The fact that they're asking them is a good sign. Do not make the mistake of reiterating everything in your brief. If you must summarize the points raised in your brief, make that summary very short. The judges will have already read your argument.

After you and the prosecutor have made your statements, the judges may give their decision, usually by saying "affirmed" or "reversed." Sometimes they will take it under advisement; unlike in traffic court, there's no requirement that they tell you their decision right away.

11.   The "Remittitur"

Some time after the appeal has been decided, the court will mail you a copy of the written decision, usually just a one-sentence reversal or affirmance. It will also send a similar notice to the trial court (called a "Remittitur"). If it's affirmed, you will have to comply with whatever part of the original sentence that was postponed or "stayed" while the appeal was pending, unless the appeals court has ordered otherwise in its decision.

√ CHECKLIST FOR FILING AN APPEAL

(Follow *all* steps.)

1. _____ Type a Notice of Appeal stating that you are appealing from a finding of guilty rendered on a certain date. This must be filed with the clerk of the municipal or justice court at which you were found guilty within 30 days of the date you were found guilty. Keep a file-stamped photocopy for your records as proof that you filed it on time.

2. _____ Type a Proposed Statement on Appeal listing your grounds on appeal and a statement of the proceedings relevant to those grounds. Make two copies of this and have a friend mail one copy to the prosecutor. Your friend should fill out a Proof of Service on the last page of the original. This can be filed with the Notice of Appeal, or up to 15 days later. Keep a stamped copy for your records.

3. _____ You will be notified of a date for a hearing, before the judge who found you guilty, to "settle" your Statement on Appeal. If you received a Proposed Statement from the prosecution, read it carefully before you go to the hearing. Be prepared to counter anything the prosecution suggests that would hurt your case. Don't let the judge bully you. After the hearing, the judge will ask you to prepare an Engrossed Statement on Appeal. You must type this, make two copies, and have a friend mail a copy to the prosecutor and fill out the Proof of Service, present it to the judge to sign, and file it with the trial court within five days. Keep a file-stamped photocopy. Start researching and writing your brief.

4. _____ The trial court clerks then send the Notice of Appeal, Engrossed Statement and other papers to the appeals court. The appeals court will notify you when it has received them.

5. _____ You have 20 days from the time the appeals court receives the case file (not from the time the clerk sent out or you received the notice) to submit your opening brief. You should make six photocopies of your brief. Have a friend mail one copy to the prosecutor's office and deliver another to a traffic court clerk (with instructions to give it to the trial judge). Your friend then fills out a Proof of Service on the last page of the original brief. Three copies and the one original are filed with the appeals court clerk. The remaining copy is yours. Have the clerk file-stamp it.

6. _____ You will receive the prosecution's brief in the mail. Read it immediately and decide whether you should answer any of the points made in a Reply Brief. You have only a few days to file it.

7. _____ If you wish to file a Reply Brief, do so within 10 days of the date the prosecution filed its brief. The Reply Brief is prepared, served and filed in the same manner as an Opening Brief.

8. _____ Go to the appeals court hearing. Be prepared to argue your case and answer any questions you can anticipate.

If the trial court's decision is reversed with nothing else said, a new trial will have to be held before a judge other than the one who presided at your first trial. If it's reversed with orders to dismiss, you've won. Any fine you may have paid is refunded to you by the trial court. In either case, if the trial court clerks notified the DMV of your conviction, they will send an amended note telling the DMV to remove it from your driving record.[14]

12. A Final Word

For further information on traffic court appeals, read Rules 181 through 190 of California Rules of Court and any cases citing those rules. The procedure for filing, settling, and arguing motions in the appeals court when something goes wrong with the appeal, is covered in Rule 104. A good source of summary information on criminal procedure is found in Witkin, *Criminal Procedure*.

An appeal beyond the Superior Court is very complex and probably should be handled by an attorney. The right to go to a higher court isn't automatic; it depends upon whether that court wants to take the case. They will only grant a hearing if it is an exceptional situation.

---

[14]Of course, if you're convicted after a new trial, the court clerks will notify the DMV again, and the offense will go back on your record.

17

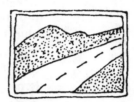

STAYING OUT OF TROUBLE

IF YOU'RE LIKE MOST readers of this book, you bought it to help you fight a ticket you have already received. Well, now that we've shown you how to fight your ticket, here are some tips on how you can avoid tickets in the future, and be better prepared if you are pulled over.

A. Avoiding the Traffic Officer

THE BEST WAY, OF COURSE, to minimize your chance of receiving a ticket is not to drive. Short of that, though, the next best way is to scrupulously obey all traffic laws. Unfortunately, however, police officers do stop and cite innocent drivers. Also, it's quite easy for a conservative and safe driver to be cited for a technical violation that defies common sense and endangers no one.

The purpose of this section is not to suggest ways for you to break the law and drive unsafely with impunity. Rather, it is written with the recognition that even a conscientious and safe driver may be unjustly cited by a police officer whose primary interest is in meeting his quota rather than encouraging safety. We don't advise you to "fight back" by breaking the law. But, knowing that you, and many others will do just that—while driving perfectly safely—we note a few ways for you to keep your contacts with traffic officers to a minimum.

1. On the Freeway

Speeding is by far the most common traffic offense for which people are cited. And most of these involve exceeding the 55-65 mph speed limit on freeways, and a stop by the CHP. Here are a few suggestions for avoiding a ticket in this situation:

First, make sure your car's equipped with decent mirrors that give you an unobstructed view. To this end, periodically clean your mirrors and rear window, do not put stickers on your rear window

unless you have to, and keep objects off the back ledge that may block your view.

If your rearview mirror vibrates at freeway speeds—as unfortunately many do—try to correct the problem. A mirror that vibrates only a little will blur the subtle features that often give away a following patrol car or motorcycle. (You can notice the difference a non-vibrating mirror makes by temporarily damping the vibration, i.e., holding the mirror tightly between your right thumb and forefinger.) Try tightening or slightly loosening any screws on the mirror mounting; if that doesn't help, remove the screws to add fiber, hard rubber, or even home-made cardboard or paper washers or shims to the mounting. Sometimes, you can reduce mirror vibration by having your front wheels balanced — usually for no more than $20.

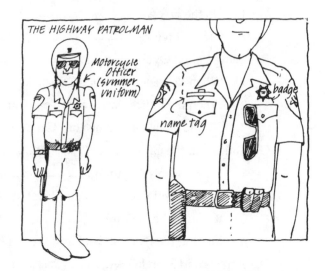

THE HIGHWAY PATROLMAN
Motorcycle Officer (summer uniform)
badge
name tag

With a little practice, you can learn to recognize a CHP car's front in your side or rearview mirrors. Most CHP cars are manned by one driver and no passenger. They are either white, or black and white in color. The roof is always white (in order to reduce heat from the beating sun). The fronts of CHP cars usually don't have much chrome, and often have black bumpers. One tell-tale sign of a CHP car behind you is the shotgun mounted vertically on a rack in the front of the car. From your rearview mirror, the shotgun on its rack seems to divide the police car windshield in two.

The CHP is beginning to experiment with smaller semi-compact cars, which are much harder to distinguish as patrol vehicles. While many larger CHP cars have conspicuous red-and-blue roof-rack lights, the smaller cars (and even some of the larger ones) use internally-mounted red lights that become noticeable only when they're turned on and it's too late. Even so, many of these smaller cars still have the shotgun conspicuously mounted in the front-windshield rack.

Black-and-white CHP vehicles can also be noticed by their all-white doors, which become visible in your rearview mirror as you enter a slight curve. Another feature is that they have very large and powerful engines that allow them to accelerate very quickly. Adopting a regular habit of glancing at your rearview mirror every five or ten seconds will help you to distinguish any quickly-accelerating cars whose distant image on your mirror seems to grow too fast.

You may also notice a CHP vehicle ahead of you, and slow down to 55. If you then see the officer pull off onto an exit ramp, resist the temptation to speed up right away. CHP officers regularly do this, only to re-enter the freeway from a nearby on-ramp a few seconds later. With your false sense of security at having seen the officer exit the freeway, the officer will be far enough behind so that you won't notice, but still close enough to begin "pacing" your car. Whenever you see the officer ahead of you get off the freeway, watch your mirrors to try and see what else she does. Even if you don't see the car re-enter the freeway, take a heightened interest in your rearview mirror for the next few miles.

Also, CHP officers will often park very near on-ramps, to allow them to quickly get onto the freeway to chase or pace a car they think is going too fast. It isn't a bad idea to glance about the area as you approach an on-ramp. After all, your heightened awareness will not only help you avoid a traffic officer, but will also help you be a better and safer driver!

Another trick CHP officers use is to "pace" you from a parallel frontage road. Watch out for this, too.

Keep in mind that another maneuver CHP officers can perform with amazing skill is a high-speed U-turn. You aren't safe from a CHP officer just because he's traveling in the opposite direction and thus can't "pace" your car. Officers are very good at judging the speed of oncoming vehicles, and, if an officer thinks yours is too high, he may well execute a movie-grade high speed U-turn to chase you. Even freeways have frequent spots where this can be done, and an officer who regularly patrols a particular section of road knows where such spots are. And with the high-powered equipment on CHP cars, he'll catch up with you in no time.

And in your search for CHP cars that might pull you over, don't forget that the CHP uses motorcycles as well. A CHP motorcycle can usually be recognized by its large size, radio antenna, emergency kit, red light in front, and uniformed driver. There are times during which the CHP does not use motorcycles—at night or when it rains.

Patrol cars and motorcycles aren't your only worry. As we discuss in Chapter 4, Section E, the CHP makes extensive use of aircraft to catch speeders on freeways. Not all freeways are appropriate for aircraft patrols, however. Freeways which are not straight over long distances, which are near the flight paths of major airports, or which are simply too far from a local airport or airstrip, are less than ideal for the use of aircraft patrols. Straight freeways in rural areas are preferred. In fact, freeways patrolled by CHP aircraft usually have signs that warn "patrolled by aircraft," and have white mile-markers (about a foot wide, by six or seven feet long) painted on the side of the freeway every mile. Even so, this doesn't mean that aircraft is used every hour of the day. Such aircraft are never flown at night for this purpose, and are flown during the day only when weather conditions permit. Ideal weather for this type of flying is a clear day with little or no wind.

We don't suggest that you stick your head out the window to look for CHP aircraft, or point your side-view mirror upward. Still, if you can do so safely, there's nothing wrong with being alert for any small Cessna-type airplane flying parallel to the freeway, either ahead of you in your direction or coming toward you from the other direction, especially on freeways with mile markers.

The best way to avoid speeding tickets on freeways is to remain as inconspicuous as possible. If you feel you must exceed the speed limit, try to stay within 10 miles of it—the speed at which most CHP officers begin to write tickets. A CHP officer who sees you doing 62 mph in the center lane (of three lanes in your direction) where the speed limit is 55, is likely to be going too fast to slow down and bother with you anyway—as he's chasing the other cars doing 65 and 70+ mph. Avoid the far-left lane if possible, since that's where officers usually look for the faster drivers. Also, try to avoid anything unusual that calls attention to your car—such as racing stripes, bumper or travel stickers on the back, jacked-up front and/or rear wheels, or high performance sports cars, especially ones that are red, yellow, or orange. (It really is true that officers are attracted to red Porsches and Corvettes.)

2. Off the Freeway

The two most common traffic violations for which people are cited while not driving on a freeway are speeding and rolling stops.

a. Speeding

After speeding on the freeway—in violation of the Maximum Speed Law—the next most common violation is—you guessed it—speeding off the freeway, usually in town, in violation of the Basic Speed Law.

Don't get us wrong. It's a lot more dangerous to exceed the speed limit in a city than it is to do 62 mph on the freeways built for safety at 70 and posted at 55. We do not suggest speeding in the city under any circumstances. However, there are times when a perfectly safe driver will exceed a posted speed limit and invite a ticket—from a city police officer whose job is partly to provide needed revenue for the city. Here are a few tips on how such a driver can avoid tickets under these circumstances.

When you first drive through a city or town, take a close look at the police cars. (You may see one stopped at a red light and have time to look it over thoroughly.) You will see mostly large American cars painted white or black-and-white (with the top always white). Often a large number of the cars are the same make and/or model, since cities purchase them in quantity from dealers or manufacturers. Unlike the CHP, city police departments are not moving rapidly toward purchasing small cars with hidden lights. Most are large and have roof-rack (or "bar") lights.

All police vehicles (except undercover ones, which can't be used for routine traffic enforcement) have front and rear license plates which contain as their first character a small letter "E" inside a diamond or hexagon. Knowing this can come in handy at times even though the "E" is often too small to notice at a distance, and other features are usually more noticeable anyway. For example, when you're stopped at a stop light and suddenly notice the lower part of the front of a car in your rearview mirror, seeing this feature of the front license plate can help you identify the car right behind you as a possible police car.

Unfortunately, city police rely much more on radar to catch speeders than do CHP officers, and much less on techniques like pacing that render patrol cars or motorcycles visible. We refer you to Chapter 4, Section F, for a discussion of where radar is most often used, and on the features and fallacies of radar detectors. Also, city police use motorcycles, particularly for radar enforcement.

One thing that will lessen your chances of being pulled over by an officer using radar is to drive in the left lane. True, the "fast" lane is where more speeders can be found. However, driving in the left lane will increase the angle between your car and a radar beam directed backward from a patrol car parked on the road shoulder in your direction of travel. The higher this angle, the lower the apparent speed on the radar unit, since this "cosine angle factor" error works in your favor. (See Chapter 4, Section F.)

b. Rolling Stops

The second most commonly cited violation off the freeway is for running a stop sign in what's called a "rolling stop." Sadly, this is also one of the most harmless violations, at least where the driver is carefully looking out for cross traffic. If you must do this (it seems almost instinctual, actually), you might as well get in the habit of thinking about hidden police cars. Glance in your rearview mirror (as you should anyway, for safety reasons), just before coming to the stop sign. Then be prepared to come to a complete stop if you encounter any cross traffic or see any police cars parked on either side of the cross street or the other side of the intersection. If you see an officer, come to a complete stop even if you've already crossed the limit line. Under these circumstances, an officer is still less likely to ticket you than if you roll through. Then wait at least a full three seconds before proceeding.

B. Being Pulled Over

IN THIS SECTION and the next two, you'll learn what you should and shouldn't do in that initial encounter with a police officer who pulls you over. Being observant of weather and road conditions,

getting the officer's name and identification number, asking the officer the right questions, and making specific requests of the officer at this early stage, can put you in a much better position to fight your ticket later on. Also, if you've been drinking (or smoking), there are certain things you can do to minimize the problems that can result from your encounter with the authorities.

1. When You See the Police Car

Your battle to beat the ticket begins the instant you realize you're being pulled over by a police officer. If a police car is following you with its siren blaring or emergency lights flashing, pull over to the right quickly (but safely) and come to a complete stop in a safe place. Do not be one of those people who nonchalantly continues to drive and pretends to be amazed at having been pulled over. This tactic just irritates the cops, and gives them ammunition to claim at trial that you were inattentive and therefore likely to have violated a traffic law.

Pulling over right away is not an admission of guilt. It just means that you were very alert to everything that was happening around you. Also, by stopping as soon as you can, you'll have a better chance of figuring out exactly where the officer says you drove too fast, made an illegal U-turn, didn't signal, etc. This information can be useful in preparing your defense. (See Section D, below.)

2. When the Police Can Search Your Car

A police officer who stops you for a traffic violation is normally not allowed to search your vehicle. However, there are several exceptions to this. An officer who observes you trying to either hide something under the seat or throw something out the window may legally search your car. Once the cop is on your rear bumper with his spotlight silhouetting your every move, he's watching for any sort of "furtive movement." A sudden lowering of one or both shoulders will tip him off that you're attempting to hide something under the seat. This gives him legal cause to search a car, and he'll know exactly what to look for and where. Police have had more experience watching people try to hide things then you've had trying to hide them.

Also, once you are stopped, a police officer may seize any illegal objects in your car that are in "plain view" (like open beer or wine bottles,[1] joints or roach clips). Once they see the object, they can open the car door to reach in and get it. Once they do, they may come across other objects that are in plain view and shouldn't be in your car, and they can seize these too. (If you are pulled over at night, there is somewhat less risk of plain-view observations if the car is not parked under a bright street lamp. However, an officer can still shine his flashlight into the car.[2])

Finally, your car may be searched if any occupant in it—passenger or driver—is physically arrested.[3] Also, if you're arrested and your car is towed, the police may make a supposed "inventory search" afterward, even if they have no reason to suspect there is anything illegal inside.[4]

3. Should You Get Out of Your Car?

It's usually better to get out of the car. It will make it easier for you to check road conditions, the weather, the place the violation supposedly occurred and, in radar-detected speeding violations, perhaps even the read-out on the officer's radar detector. (Don't forget your vehicle registration card in case the officer asks for it.)

However, if the officer orders you to stay in the car, you should cooperate. If you get out of the car against the officer's orders, don't be surprised to see a gun pointing at you. Cops are trained to expect the worst, so when you get out of your car they may assume you're about to pull a weapon or attempt to flee. So, don't panic, and make it apparent to the officer that you intend no harm.

If an officer does have any reason to believe that you might be dangerous, she has a right to conduct a quick "pat-down" search of your outer clothing while she is standing next to you, to make sure you don't have a concealed knife or gun that you could pull on her.[5] If the officer feels any weapon-sized object during the pat-down search, she can reach in and get it. Also, the officer's good faith belief that you may be dangerous justifies a search of the passenger compartment of your car for weapons.

For more on car searches, read Section D(2) below.

C. Talking to the Officer

MANY PEOPLE STOPPED by an officer make the mistake of saying the wrong thing to him or her, and fail to say the right things. As we see below, a case can be won or lost depending on what you say—or don't say—to the officer.

1. Don't Admit Anything

Many drivers who are pulled over destroy any chance they might have had to successfully contest a violation in court, because they mistakenly believe they can talk their way out of it. Nothing could be further from the truth.

---

[1]Thousands of people get busted every year for having an "open container" in their vehicle, even when they hadn't been drinking. (See Chapter 5, Section D.) Never open any alcoholic beverages, or allow passengers to, in your car. It will help give the police legal cause to arrest you for driving under the influence. (See Chapter 8, Section A.) Conviction of "open container," possession of marijuana (or liquor if under 21), or driving under the influence, is likely to raise the rates on your insurance or cause it to be cancelled.

[2]Under a recent law passed in 1988, you have the right to pull over in a safe, well-lighted place. This is especially important if you're a woman driving alone. Rapes and murders committed by police officers or persons who are impersonating police officers on unsuspecting female motorists have occurred.

[3]*New York v. Belton* (1981) 453 U.S. 454, 101 S.Ct. 2860; *People v. Hunt* (1990) 225 Cal.App.3d 498, 275 Cal.Rptr. 367.

[4]*South Dakota v. Opperman* (1976) 428 U.S. 364.

[5]*Terry v. Ohio* (1968) 392 U.S. 1, 88 S.Ct. 1868.

One of the first things traffic cops learn in the police academy is to decide, before getting out of their cars, or off their motorcycles, whether they're going to give a ticket or just a warning. They may act as though they still haven't made up their minds and are going to let you off if only you'll "cooperate." Don't fall for this. The hesitating officer is often just trying to appear open-minded in order to extract admissions out of you, to use them against you in court if necessary.[6] The strategy is to try to get you to admit either that you committed a violation, or that you were so careless, inattentive, or negligent that you don't know whether you did or not.[7] One way this is commonly done is for the officer to act friendly. If you learn nothing else from this book, learn that a police officer with a ticket book in his hand is not your friend.

---

[6]Your admissions can be used against you even though the officer doesn't give you a "Miranda" warning of your right to remain silent. See *Berkemer v. McCarty* (1984) 468 U.S. 420, 104 S.Ct. 3138. You still have the right to remain silent, but a traffic officer doesn't have to tell you.

[7]It may even happen that a cop who knows he doesn't have enough evidence to ticket you will do so after you admit something. But it rarely works the other way—if she plans to give you a ticket, your telling her of even a legitimate legal defense will probably not change her mind.

Don't speak first. Let the officer start talking. He will probably ask you the sort of question whose lack of a definite answer would imply guilt, like "Do you know why I stopped you?" (Suppress the impulse to reply, "Gee, no, officer, I thought *you* would know why you stopped me!") Or, he might ask, "Do you know how fast you were going?" Your answers, if any, should be non-committal and brief, like a simple "No" to the first question or a very confident, "Yes, I do," to the second. If he then tells you how fast he thinks you were going or what he thinks you did, don't argue. Either give a noncommittal answer, like "I see," or no answer at all. Silence is not an admission of guilt and cannot be used against you in court.

If the officer persists, tell him that you have nothing more to say or that you prefer not to answer any questions. And don't fall for the inevitable, "Got something to hide?" If he says this, just tell him, "I have nothing more to say. Please just write the ticket and we can both be on our way."

2. Remain Quiet or Ask a Few Questions?

Traffic officers issue many citations each day. By the time your case goes to trial, the officer who stopped and cited you may have issued dozens or even hundreds of tickets since. That being so, chances are good that he won't recall the events pertaining to your ticket very well by the time he has to come to court to testify against you, unless you've either committed an unusually outrageous offense or done something to focus his attention. If you're cited for a routine moving violation, you may be better off saying nothing or very little in order to increase the chance that the officer won't recall a rather uneventful encounter and the circumstances of the alleged violation later on. (Needless to say, an officer is more likely to remember you, and the events leading up to his citing you, if you are rude or offensive, so you should be polite, in any case.) Of course, being unobtrusive and otherwise acting like a "routine" motorist stopped for a traffic violation means not engaging in a great deal of conversation with the officer. Thus, if you ask the officer a lot of questions, even politely, you may give him a better chance to remember you. On the other hand, you may wish to ask the officer a few polite questions, even at the cost of fixing you better in his memory, in the hope that he will give you information which may prove helpful.

If you do want to ask the officer a few questions, you may want to try to get him to commit himself to where he was when he saw you, how far he followed you, and to similar facts noted below. If you're able to write this information down while it's fresh in your memory, you may be able to use it in court later on, especially if he gives conflicting information. If you have a witness in your car, so much the better. While some officers will refuse to answer more than a few direct questions, others will very happily answer most questions, if only to convince you that you haven't got a chance if you take it to court. So, if you get a chance, ask the officer any of the following questions:

- "Where were you when you say you saw the violation?" (If he tells you, you can go back to that spot later to check what he was able to see. Any obstructions to the view might show that he may have missed an essential element of the alleged violation, and that could be helpful.) Never ask a question that also contains an admission, like "Where were you hiding when I ran the red light?"

- If the officer was parked: "Was your engine running?" (If it was, it might suggest he was just a little too eager to race out and nab someone. There is some implication that he may have formulated a violation he wanted to observe before he caught anyone doing it.)

- If parked at night: "Were your headlights on or off?" (If off, it might also suggest too much zeal in lurking in wait for a violation already formulated in his mind.)

- If the charge is speeding: "How did you determine my speed?" (He will probably tell you this without your having to ask, particularly if he used radar. He may even show you a speed

reading. Most people mistakenly assume that radar is infallible and will give up all hope of fighting a ticket if they see a radar reading.)

- If he did not use radar: "How far did you follow me?" (If he followed you for just a short distance prior to charging you with speeding, you can later argue in court that he rapidly closed the distance between his car and yours, but wrongly attributed that speed to you. For example, if he says he followed you for one-quarter mile (1320 feet) and he actually started out a block (440 feet) behind you but wound up on your rear bumper, his speedometer reading of 45 mph really only means you were going 30 mph! [See Chapter 4, Section C(1), on speed violations to see how this calculation is done.]

- If he used radar to determine your speed: "May I see the speed reading on the radar unit?" (Often the officer will be happy to show it to you in order to convince you that you don't stand a chance of successfully fighting the ticket. This is called "selling the ticket" to you, and is such standard practice that if the officer *refuses* to show you his radar reading of your speed, it suggests that he may be lying and may not have clocked you on radar at all. If the speed is a suspicious multiple of 5 or 10, or if a dial is set on "calibrate," you'll want to make a mental note of that. [See Chapter 4, Section F(5).]

If you have been stopped by a particularly talkative officer, you may also want to ask one or more of the following questions (some are pretty technical, but can be very useful, as we pointed out in Chapter 4, Section F):

"Where were you located when you took the reading?"

"Where did you see my car when you took the reading?"

"When did you last calibrate this radar unit?"

"Do you use a tuning fork to calibrate it? May I see it, please?"

"Do you know the angle of the spread of the beam? (the beam width angle) How many degrees?"

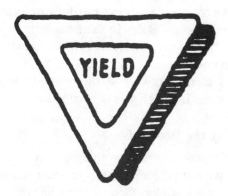

3. If You've Been Drinking

If you've had anything substantial to drink, it's best not to engage the officer in any conversation beyond brief, noncommittal answers. No use letting him hear your speech or giving him extra chances to closely study your eyes. Probably he'll ask the inevitable, "How much have you had to drink?" Many people will admit to "just a glass of wine" or "just two beers" in the hope that the officer will believe them and let them go. Rather, the officer will assume that you've had much more, and such an admission will do you no good. In addition, your statement that you have been drinking can be used against you in court.

The best answer to questions about whether or how much you've been drinking is: "I prefer to remain silent."

Which brings us to a minor point. Did you ever wonder why the cops always shine their flashlights right into your eyes at night? It's not necessarily because they're mildly sadistic (though some are). Rather, it's to see whether your eyes are watery or bloodshot, and also to see how fast the pupils of your eyes contract upon sudden exposure to the light. A slow contraction of the pupils, or none at all, suggests you're under the influence of alcohol or drugs (including legitimate prescription drugs[8]). Therefore, it's wise to avoid looking directly into the flashlight or the officer's eyes if you've had any alcohol, drugs, or even prescription medication (particularly tranquilizers). Try to look down at the ground or at your wallet or purse as you remove your driver's license. It's also helpful to look directly into a lighted street lamp for a moment to contract your pupils before the officer gets a chance to shine the light into your eyes.

4. Making the Place of Trial Inconvenient for the Officer

If your residence *or* workplace is located closer to the "county seat" than to the local court for the judicial district in which you're pulled over, then you have a right to insist that the officer send the ticket to the county seat. This little-known provision of the Vehicle Code[9] can often work to your advantage, as we discuss below.

a. *The County Seat*

Your right to request the county seat as the place of your trial requires some explanation. Every county has a "county seat," which is a sort of "capital" of the county and is usually the largest city in it. (See chart later in this section.) Most California counties are also divided into several "judicial districts." Each district has a court in which all non-felony criminal cases (including traffic cases) are heard. Some districts have one or more additional "branch" courts. The courts in the more populous areas are called "municipal courts," while sparsely-populated areas (under 40,000 population) have "justice courts." There is always a municipal or justice court at the county seat.

At the bottom of a traffic ticket, there is a space to list the "place to appear." Normally it will be the

_____

[8]It's just as illegal to drive under the influence of prescription drugs as it is to drive under the influence of alcohol or marijuana. VC § 23201. See Chapter 8.

courthouse closest to where the cop pulled you over, usually within 10 miles. This court will most likely be close to the officer's home base. But if the court at the county seat is different,[10] as it commonly is, it may be quite a distance from the officer's base.[11] *You must make the county seat demand before the officer finishes filling out the ticket.* See next section.

> **Example:** If you're stopped and cited in El Monte, in Los Angeles County, the officer would note on the ticket that you should appear at the local court there. But, since you work in Santa Monica, which is a lot closer to the county seat (Los Angeles city), you can insist that the court at which the ticket directs you to appear be the one at the county seat—Los Angeles.

Making such a demand will result in the following advantages to you:

- The officer is less likely to show up at a court miles away from his usual place of duty; if he doesn't show up for trial, your case will almost surely be dismissed. (See Chapter 10.)

- The police officer will most likely be a total stranger to the judge. This puts him on a more equal footing with you. In his hometown court, there is a good chance that the officer knows the judge, having often appeared before her. Going to the county seat evens your odds a little.

- The ticket might get lost. Sending a ticket to the county seat court goes against the usual procedure, and a confused clerk faced with the problem of properly routing your ticket may misplace it. Even if it turns up much later, you

may be able to get the charge dismissed on the grounds that you have been denied the right to a speedy trial. [See Chapter 10, Section E(2).]

Note: Of course, you may have been stopped in a city that is a county seat, or in a nearby area located in the same judicial district. In this situation, requesting the county seat won't help. (You may wish to review the tables set out later in this section and make a mental note of the county seat locations for the counties in which you normally drive.)

b. Making the Demand

Note: In order to preserve your right to have the county-seat court hear your case, you *must* demand the county seat *when the officer starts writing the ticket.*

There are two ways to make your county seat demand. One is to simply say, "I want this citation tried in the municipal or judicial court at the county seat. Please specify that court as the place to appear." Be prepared to give the officer your residence address—if different from that on your driver's license—or your business address, to establish that one or the other is closer to the county seat than to the local court.

The other way to make the county seat demand (for those of you who really believe in preparation) is to keep a copy of the following notice in your wallet and hand it to the officer with your license. If he refuses to do as you request, you can later show the judge the original (or another copy) of the card at your motion for change of venue (see Chapter 10), stating that you gave such a copy to the officer.

---

[9]VC § 40502(b). Also, see the case of *Smith v. Municipal Court* (1959) 167 Cal.App.2d 534, 334 P.2d 931.

[10]In counties having only one central court for the entire county, and no other municipal or justice courts, the ticket will always be tried in the county seat. This is true in the following counties: San Francisco, Alpine, Amador, Calaveras, Colusa, Del Norte, Lassen, Mariposa, Modoc, Stanislaus, and Sutter. (See the detailed list below.)

[11]The most extreme example of this is in huge San Bernardino County. A person stopped on Interstate 10 or 40 just inside the California line may be able to demand trial in the county seat of San Bernardino (provided you live or work nearer to there than to the local court), over 150 miles away!

TO: CITING POLICE OFFICER

If it is your intent to issue a Notice to Appear for a Vehicle Code violation, please specify the place to appear, pursuant to VC § 40502(b), as the municipal or justice court at the *county seat.* See *Smith v. Municipal Court* (1959) 167 Cal.App.2d 534.

Be prepared—the officer may try to talk you out of your county seat request. If he does, be firm. If he asks you why you want the county seat, you have no obligation to answer.[12] However, you should give the officer your residence or business address, emphasizing, if true, that this address is closer to the county seat than to the local court. If you want to, however, you can tell him you think the local traffic judges are prejudiced and always side with police officers.[13] The officer may try to tell you that you have no right to demand the county seat, or that if you wish to do so, your request must be made to the clerk or judge of the local court. Many cops believe this, but they're wrong. In an appeals court case known as *Smith v. Municipal Court*[14] an appeals court ruled that VC § 40502(b) says the choice of the county seat is entirely up to the person cited and that the officer must comply with the request. (Since the case was decided, the law was amended to require such compliance only if your business or residence address is closer to the county seat court.) This applies to *all* Vehicle Code violations, even jay-walking and littering, for which you're issued a Notice to Appear ticket. (See Chapter 3.)

Note: Some judges (and police) in certain counties, most notably Santa Clara, think the county-seat law doesn't apply when all the county's judicial districts have been consolidated into one "unified" county-wide district. This is based on a belief that the term "county seat" has no meaning when applied to such counties. This is false. "County seat"

refers to the city in which the county's Board of Supervisors meets.[15]

c. If the Demand is Refused

If the officer refuses to specify the court at the county seat as the place to appear, you should do one of the following :

- Sign the ticket, but protest loudly in the presence of any passengers so they can be witnesses.

- Sign the ticket, but add the notation, "County seat requested and refused" in small capital letters next to your name.[16] That way, you'll have indisputable proof on the citation that you made the demand. This will help you get the case transferred later. (See Chapter 10.)

- If it's not at night or a weekend (so you won't have to languish in jail) and you're willing to risk being physically arrested, you might want to consider refusing to sign the ticket until the officer gets the court right. This may cause the officer to arrest you for supposedly refusing to sign at all. Or, the officer might detain you while he calls in to headquarters for instructions.

---

[12]It may also hit him that you intend to fight the ticket and drag him down to the county seat; in borderline cases, this might be enough to discourage him from citing you, but don't count on it. Incidentally, Highway Patrol officers are more likely to know about this county seat law than are city police or sheriff's deputies.

[13]If for some reason you wind up in the hometown court anyway, and the officer testifies that you said this, you will have grounds for a mistrial based on the officer's trying to prejudice the judge.

[14]167 Cal.App.2d 534, 334 P.2d 931(1959).

---

[15]See *People v. Beltran* (1981) 124 Cal.App.3d 335, 177 Cal.Rptr. 262 and Government Code § 23600. Santa Clara County has already lost on this issue in *Fajardo v. Municipal Court*, Case No. P-38249, Sept. 5, 1980, but continues to ignore the law.

[16]A particularly belligerent cop might arrest you for doing this on some phony charge of "defacing a citation." If this happens, you should see an attorney about suing the cop for false arrest or malicious prosecution.

d. Table of County Seats and Judicial Districts

The county seats of the various California counties are as follows:

COUNTY	COUNTY SEAT
Alameda	Oakland
*Alpine	Markleeville
*Amador	Jackson
Butte	Oroville
*Calaveras	San Andreas
*Colusa	Williams
Contra Costa	Martinez
*Del Norte	Crescent City
El Dorado	Placerville
Fresno	Fresno
Glenn	Willows
Humboldt	Eureka
Imperial	El Centro
Inyo	Independence
Kern	Bakersfield
Kings	Hanford
Lake	Lakeport
*Lassen	Susanville
Los Angeles	Los Angeles
Marin	San Rafael
*Mariposa	Mariposa
Mendocino	Ukiah
Merced	Merced
*Modoc	Alturas
Mono	Bridgeport
Monterey	Salinas
Napa	Napa
Nevada	Nevada City
Orange	Santa Ana

COUNTY	COUNTY SEAT
Placer	Auburn
Plumas	Quincy
Riverside	Riverside
Sacramento	Sacramento
San Benito	Hollister
San Bernardino	San Bernardino
San Diego	San Diego
*San Francisco	San Francisco
San Joaquin	Stockton
San Luis Obispo	San Luis Obispo
San Mateo	Redwood City
Santa Barbara	Santa Barbara
Santa Clara	San Jose
Santa Cruz	Santa Cruz
Shasta	Redding
Sierra	Downieville
Siskiyou	Yreka
Solano	Fairfield
Sonoma	Santa Rosa
*Stanislaus	Modesto
*Sutter	Yuba City
Tehama	Red Bluff
Trinity	Weaverville
Tulare	Visalia
Tuolumne	Sonora
Ventura	Ventura
Yolo	Woodland
Yuba	Marysville

*In counties marked with an asterisk (*), the county seat has the *only* municipal or justice court in the county. All tickets will be tried there whether demanded or not.

Note: As you can see, the county seat is often the city with the same name as the county, yet the cities of Alameda, Marin, Monterey, San Mateo, Santa Clara and Sonoma are not county seats of their respectively-named counties.

The six largest counties and their various judicial district and branch court locations are listed below:

COUNTY	COUNTY SEAT
Los Angeles	Alhambra
	Antelope (Lancaster)
	Beverly Hills
	Burbank
	Citrus (W. Covina)
	Compton
	Culver (Culver City)
	Downey
	E. Los Angeles
	Glendale
	Inglewood
	Long Beach
	*Los Angeles
	Los Cerritos (Bellflower)
	Malibu
	Newhall (Valencia)
	Pasadena
	Pomona
	Rio Hondo (El Monte)
	Santa Anita (Monrovia)
	Santa Monica
	South Bay (Torrance)
	Southeast (Huntington Park)
	*Van Nuys Branch of L.A.
	Whittier
	•Catalina (Avalon)
Orange	*Central Orange County (Santa Ana)
	North Orange County (Fullerton)
	Orange County Harbor (Newport Beach)
	South Orange County (Laguna Niguel)
	West Orange County (Westminster)

COUNTY	COUNTY SEAT
San Diego	El Cajon
	Escondido Branch of N. County
	North County (Vista)
	*San Diego
	South Bay (Chula Vista)
Santa Clara (All courts are branches of a county-wide district. In dual-city court districts, court is located in the underlined city.)	Gilroy
	Los Gatos
	Morgan Hill
	Palo Alto/Mtn. View
	*San Jose/Milpitas
	Santa Clara
	Sunnyvale/Cupertino
Alameda	Alameda
	Berkeley/Albany
	Fremont/Newark/Union City
	Livermore/Pleasanton
	*Oakland/Piedmont/Emeryville
	San Leandro/Hayward
Sacramento	•Elk Grove/Galt
	*Fair Oaks Branch of Sacramento
	•Galt Branch of Elk Grove/Galt
	*Sacramento

*Indicates district containing county seat court.
•Indicates justice court; all other courts are municipal.

D. Arrests and Searches

The laws governing arrest, search and seizure are constantly changing. In this section we provide a general overview of the subject in the traffic stop context. But if you need a definitive opinion on a specific set of facts, see a criminal defense attorney.

1. Arrests

If you are stopped for one of the more serious traffic offenses (like driving under the influence or reckless driving), you may be arrested[17] and taken to jail. The officer has some discretion, but he is required to arrest you in the following situations:[18]

a. He has "probable cause" to believe you committed a felony [see Chapter 3, Section A(1)];

b. You are charged with driving under the influence of alcohol or drugs (see Chapter 8);

c. You don't have a driver's license or any other "satisfactory identification";

d. You refuse to sign the ticket (thereby refusing to promise to appear in court); or

e. He discovers there's a warrant out for your arrest.[19]

The officer might also arrest you in any of the following instances:

a. You're charged with reckless driving, engaging in a "speed contest" (drag racing), or "exhibition of speed";

b. You tried to outrun the patrol car;

c. You refused to honor the officer's request to test whether your lights or brakes work;

d. You're involved in a "hit-and-run" accident involving property damage (when there's personal injury, it's a felony and arrest is mandatory); or

e. You're caught driving while your license is suspended or revoked.

To state the obvious, it's not wise to resist an arrest even if it is in illegal one. Whether an arrest is legal is beyond the scope of this book. We suggest you check with a lawyer.

2. Searches

It used to be the case that, if you had anything in the car you'd rather have the officer not see, you could protect your rights by getting out of your car and walking away from it. But the law about searching cars is rapidly changing, and your privacy rights have been whittled away by recent federal and state court rulings.

Whether or not you are in your car, it is always perfectly legal for the officer to walk around the car and peer through the windows and shine a flashlight inside. The officer may seize anything illegal that is in "plain view" (e.g., marijuana in an open ash tray, an open alcoholic beverage container on the floor, the butt of a weapon protruding from under the seat). They don't need any excuse to do this.

The police may open the door of your car and search it, regardless of whether you are in it, in a wide range of circumstances. The basic rules are that an officer may search your car if he has:

a. your permission;

b. a reasonable belief that there may be weapons in your car;

c. probable cause to believe that there is something illegal in your car;

d. reason to place you or a passenger under arrest; or

---

[17]Technically you are under arrest the moment you are stopped. See *People v. Superior Court* (1972) 7 Cal.3d 186, 200; but here we're using the word "arrest" as meaning when you're taken to jail.

[18]VC § 40302.

[19]Police may no longer take five to ten minutes to routinely radio in to headquarters to see whether the person they've just stopped is wanted on an outstanding warrant. They need "probable cause." *People v. McGaughran* (1979) 25 Cal.3d 577, 159 Cal.Rptr. 191. (You will give them probable cause if you admit to outstanding warrants.) Even so, today's modern computer technology allows police officers to do warrant checks in a minute or two, so this rule has little practical application today.

e. a reason to have your car towed.

Interestingly, most automobile searches are conducted not because an officer has probable cause to search, or sees something in plain view, but rather because the driver gives the officer permission. Estimates are that permission is given for about 90% of all traffic stop searches! You're probably wondering why anyone would agree to a search of their car. This is because the driver is at her unprepared worst, and the officer is at his prepared and experienced best. He is just as adept at conning and cajoling you ("Got something to hide?") into agreeing to a search as he is in getting admissions from you. Even experienced attorneys with several ounces of marijuana in the glove compartment or trunk have been known to agree to an auto search because, in the excitement, they forgot it was in the car!

If you're absolutely sure that you have nothing to hide, consenting to a search may make the officer more accommodating toward you. (When was the last time you cleaned the inside of your car? Are you sure there are no partially-empty beer cans from a picnic several months ago, or no marijuana debris from the last five years still sitting in the ash tray, on the floor, or wedged in a crack in the seat cushions?) Consenting to a search might make the officer a little less likely to cite such a "cooperative" person—but don't count on it. At this point, the officer's purpose is to get evidence to convict you of a crime. Don't let his friendly smile disarm you.

If the officer has legal grounds to search your car, he doesn't need your consent. If he asks to do so (and you don't want him to), simply tell him, "I do not consent to a search." He'll probably go ahead and search anyway, even without your consent. If that happens, there's a chance that anything the officer finds won't be admissible evidence in court. But if you consent to the search, you'll never be able

to "exclude" any evidence that he finds from use against you at trial.[20]

If you're with a friend, try to arrange things so that he can hear the conversation between you and the officer. Either stand just outside the rolled-down window on your friend's side or ask your friend to join you outside. If the officer tries to separate the two of you, inform her that you are exercising your right to have a witness present. Your friend should just listen and say as little as possible. Some people keep a tape recorder or dictaphone in their car for a variety of reasons. If you have one, you may want to exercise your right to use it while conversing with the officer.

If there's noisy traffic or pouring-down rain, and if you're not worried about what the officer might see in your car, it's better to stay seated and let the cop approach you. A friend in the car can then easily hear the conversation between you and the officer.

Note: Keep in mind that you don't have to—and shouldn't—appear hostile or menacing in order to protect your rights. An obnoxious attitude toward a cop won't help you a bit, and may irritate him enough to cite you for additional violations he'd

---

[20]Getting "illegally seized" evidence excluded from trial is usually a complicated procedure—you should confer with a lawyer about this.

otherwise overlook. He may even find sufficient cause to arrest you if you give him a hard enough time. Just be polite but firm when you refuse permission to search.

Currently, the police can conduct a search without your consent if they have any reason to think you are a threat to their safety. In this situation, the search must be limited to a search for weapons in the passenger compartment.[21]

They can also search your car if they have probable cause to believe you have something illegal inside it (the odor of pot would give them cause to suspect that you have more inside). In this situation they can search the *entire car*—including in the trunk, under the seat, in the glove box, and in the ash tray—and they can open any containers found in the vehicle, such as purses, paper bags, suitcases, or crumpled cigarette packages.[22] The police can seize anything illegal they find (like an open beer can or liquor bottle, or marijuana) or anything dangerous (like a weapon), and use it as evidence against you.

If the police have legal cause to physically arrest you[23] (see Section 1, above), they can search you, and every inch of your car, as well as its contents.[24]

Finally, if your vehicle is towed away, the police can thoroughly search it in order to take an "inventory" of its contents—all for your "protection," of course.

If none of these circumstances are present, the officer does not have legal grounds to search your car.

E. Preparing for Your Trial—Notes and Pictures

As soon as you or the officer leaves the scene, you should find a safe and legal parking place and pull out that little note pad you've been keeping in your glove compartment. Write down what happened, what the officer said, and what you said in response. The facts surrounding the ticket will probably never be clearer in your mind than those first few minutes after you were cited. For this reason, your immediate handwritten recollections of your version of the incident can be used as important evidence later on. There is nothing, of course, to prevent you from putting more emphasis on the evidence which would tend to help you while paying less attention to evidence that might convict you.[25]

Example: Many speeding tickets can be beaten if the driver shows that his speed, even though slightly over the speed limit, was nevertheless safe. If the speed limit was 30 and you know you were doing a pretty safe 35 on a clear, dry day

---

[21]*Michigan v. Long* (1983) 463 U.S. 1032.

[22]*United States v. Ross* (1982) 456 U.S. 798.

[23]Possession of an ounce or less of marijuana found in plain view won't give the officer cause to arrest you, since the law says that he can only cite you for that offense —unless, of course, it appears that you were recently smoking it and therefore driving "under the influence."

[24]*New York v. Belton* (1981) 453 U.S. 454.

---

[25]But don't write down outright lies—if you do, you'll be committing perjury when you use the notes as evidence.

while just keeping up with the flow of traffic, you will want to write down all the evidence indicating that such a speed was safe, without admitting you were doing 35. [See Chapter 4, Section A(1), for more information on this defense.]

If you think it might help refresh your memory, go back to the "scene of the crime" (after the officer leaves) and take a thorough look around. Try to remember exactly what you did when the officer supposedly observed you. If you have a camera, pull over to a safe spot and take pictures from several different angles. You can later pick out the one or two most favorable to your case. Judges are often very impressed by people who come to their courts properly prepared, with original notes and pictures, to credibly testify against an unprepared officer who has numerous other tickets to think about.

F.   Accident Citations

AN OFFICER CALLED TO the scene of an accident will sometimes issue a "Notice of Violation"[26] to a person whom the officer believes contributed to the accident by disobeying the law. For example, the driver whose car rammed into the other vehicle may be cited for a speed violation or failure to yield the right of way by an officer who never saw the violation take place. If you were involved in an accident and receive such a Notice of Violation, you should never plead guilty or pay the fine to the clerk. Your doing so could be used against you in a lawsuit by other people involved in the accident. Also, since the officer didn't personally observe the violation, he can't testify against you (unless you admit things to him), and thus beating the ticket will be a lot easier. [See Chapter 2, Section D(2).]

---

[26]VC § 40600-40604.

18

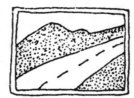

WHERE DO WE GO FROM HERE?

MUCH OF THIS BOOK was written on the assumption that you will get a fair hearing in traffic court. To a person wrongly accused of a traffic violation she knows she didn't commit, a fair hearing is obviously very important. Unfortunately, most folks accused of traffic violations experience a sham and corrupt system that mocks justice, not a fair process. Most judges presume a person who has gotten a ticket is guilty, will too often believe the word of a police officer over an individual accused of a violation, and will turn off their minds when it's the defendant's turn to tell her side of the story.

Okay, big deal. Traffic court is designed primarily to find people guilty as efficiently as possible. But let's step back for a moment and ask just how important a fair shake in traffic court is, as part of the whole picture. I believe it's very important. Traffic court is the place where the greatest number of Americans come into contact with the American justice system. Even serving on a jury is a distant second in terms of bringing ordinary folks to experience first hand and participate in the court system.

What people see when they're called to court affects how they see the entire system. If they see an even-handed system presided over by a neutral judge who seriously considers testimony and arguments, they are more likely to feel that our justice system is a good one—just like we were all told in our high-school civics classes.[1] Even where the judge (or commissioner, or referee) wrongly finds a person guilty, the trial may still have been fair, with the judge using the full force of his impartiality, fairness, and intelligence. Obviously no system of justice based on the perceptions of humans—on the road or in the courtroom—can ever be perfect. But if the basic system is perceived to be fair, everyone wins.

Of course, the reality is otherwise. All too often, what we see when we fight our tickets is an impersonal assembly-line court system presided over by a bored judge who assumes you're guilty and that police officers never lie or make mistakes. Not all traffic court judges are this way, but most are. Fair

---

[1] In the Foreword to "The Law on Speeding and Radar" (by A.S. Manraj and P.D. Haines—Butterworths 1985, 112 p.), R. Roy McMurtry, the former attorney general of the Canadian province of Ontario, states, "Most persons who come into contact with the justice system do so in response to the alleged infraction of the laws governing the use of motor vehicles. The fairness and justice they find in the courts dealing with these matters will color their perception of the entire justice system. It is accordingly very important that the courts which administer these laws....demonstrate a rigorous respect for, and a deep commitment to the even-handed administration of justice."

The idea that members of the motoring public haled into traffic court should be treated fairly is not an exclusively American one. In light of our 200-year-old Constitution and the Bill of Rights, shouldn't we be able to do at least as well in our own court system?

and impartial judges seem to be vastly outnumbered by those who regard traffic infraction trials as an annoying obstacle to the raising of revenue. The result is often that people emerge from traffic court disillusioned with the whole system of justice— wondering what went wrong in the years since they learned in civics classes that the American system of justice was the best in the world.

Am I exaggerating the defects of traffic court? Ask anyone who's contested a ticket for a moving violation. One reader says this:

The officer's testimony is apparently accepted as the one/only/total truth and the defendant is listened to grudgingly, as only a show of compliance with the forms of the law. I watched several cases before mine. The verdict was invariably guilty, even when the defendant had witnesses and documentation, which the judge did not look at. In my case, the judge seemed to have prejudged me. He seemed to barely listen to me, preferring to listen to a conversation between the officer and the prosecuting attorney, and he seemed to be communicating with them by means of signals. The judge refused to accept or even look at documents I wished to present as evidence. I presented various motions for dismissal, but the judge summarily dismissed them, sometimes cutting me off before I had finished the first sentence.

Many folks report similar experiences of feeling like the judge only grudgingly and half-heartedly gave the appearance of letting them say what they wanted before finding them guilty. Others have noted the smug and nonchalant attitudes of police officers in court, who seem to know they won't lose. One Los Angeles County judge routinely admitted that he always believes the word of a police officer over that of someone defending himself in traffic court. This judge's "defense" was that only he had the courage to say openly what in fact almost all judges believe and practice in their own courtrooms every day.[2]

As with Israeli lawyers in the West Bank, who refuse to prostitute themselves by representing defendants in rubber-stamp military courts, many California attorneys refuse to defend people accused of traffic violations, because the result is almost always an inevitable guilty verdict if the officer shows up to testify. There is very little an attorney can do to make any difference if the officer does show and the judge has his mind made up beforehand. For these lawyers, it's simply demoralizing to lose all the time, as well as dishonest to take the client's money without being able to increase the chances of an acquittal.

Why is traffic court so poorly run? Surely being appointed a judge or commissioner doesn't instantly convert a lawyer into a rubber-stamp for police and prosecutors. But as a judge settles into office, he begins to realize just how dependent he is on police officers' groups for both financial and public support, come re-election time. Police officers who appear before traffic-court judges all the time are generally part of an efficient political organization— you and the countless other ordinary folks haled

[2]The Supreme Court did remove the judge, former Judge Robert H. Furey of the Catalina Judicial District in Los Angeles County, from office, though primarily for other reasons. *Furey v. Commission on Judicial Performance* (1987) 43 Cal.3d 1297, 240 Cal.Rptr. 859. To complain about obnoxious judges, write to the Commission on Judicial Performances, 1390 Market St., Suite 304, San Francisco, CA 94102. [See Chapter 12, Section C(13).] To complain about obnoxious commissioners and traffic referees, you should write to the presiding judge of the appropriate municipal court.

into traffic court are not. A judge who frequently rules against police officers is likely to wake up next election to find police-organization support—and money—going to his opponent, probably an ambitious deputy prosecutor ready to accuse the judge of being "soft on crime."[3] And although appointed traffic "commissioners" don't have to stand for election, many, if not most of them hope some day to get promoted to the more-prestigious and higher-paying office of judge—extremely difficult without police support.

Another part of the problem is the role that tickets play in generating revenue for all sorts of purposes unrelated to promoting traffic safety. Over the years, this factor has assumed a greater importance than the quite legitimate concept of ticketing— and hopefully deterring—people who drive dangerously. If you figure that, on the average, a $40 fine is collected for each of the five million traffic citations handed out in California each year, the total fines would generate approximately $200 million—a very big business indeed. This amounts to an average of approximately $15 for every licensed driver during the year, or $10 for every car on the road.

The money collected from moving-violation ticket fines initially goes to the county treasury. After the county takes its share, the remaining revenue is returned to the various cities that produced it. Cities sometimes receive an amount as high as 75% of the fines collected. The county's share goes into a "road fund," and the city's share goes to a "Traffic Safety Fund" to be used to purchase "equipment and supplies for traffic law enforcement"—more radar equipment, to catch more "speeders," to get more money.[4] The fund cannot be used directly to pay police officer's salaries, but the effect is the same; if no money came in from the

fines, the cities would have to look elsewhere for money to maintain and buy "traffic safety" equipment, and might just be a little short of funds to pay police salaries.

In more recent years, the practice of adding onto each fine an ever-increasing "penalty assessment" (a sort of tax added to generate revenue for a specific stated purpose), has at least shown up the traffic-enforcement system for what it primarily is—a source of government revenue. As of this writing, the "penalty assessments" added to fines have skyrocketed to 160% of the fine itself. Thus, a $100 fine becomes $260, and a $50 fine becomes $130. Money generated from these penalty assessments goes to:

- a "peace officer's training fund";
- a "correction training fund";
- a jail construction fund in each county; and
- dearest to the hearts of judges, a courthouse construction fund in each county. [5]

Thus, a judge who consistently applies the "reasonable-doubt" rule, and who too frequently fails to find people guilty and impose fines, is considered by the system to be shortchanging the county of revenue needed to replace overcrowded and deteriorating courthouses and jails in the county. Is it any wonder that judges find traffic-court defendants guilty 90% of the time in cases where the officer does appear?

And then there are police-officer ticket quotas to make sure that enough tickets are issued to keep the flow of money coming in. If you've ever angrily asked an officer writing you a ticket something like, "Got to make this month's quota, eh?" you most likely got an emotionless, canned response like, "No, quotas were abolished by the Legislature in 1977."[6] Don't be fooled. Although public pressure has forced police departments to abandon formal numerical quotas, every police department in the

---

[3]Persons summoned as jurors, of course, suffer no such pressures. This is why conviction rates are much higher for judge trials than for jury trials.

[4]PC § 1463, VC §§ 42201, 42200. In the spring of 1987, for example, Alameda County purchased $27,500 of radar equipment for use by the CHP within the county, which will produce, according to county officials, an additional $200,000 a year in ticket revenues.

---

[5]PC §§ 1464 and 1465, VC § 42006, Government Code §§ 76011-76580.

[6]VC §§ 41600-41603.

state still uses an unwritten quota system. One way this works is the system of police officers' "performance evaluations." If a cop turns up short in the ticket race, her chances for promotion decline. In some cases, officers are suspended or even fired for "inefficiency" when they fail to produce enough tickets.

As a result of performance evaluations, each officer tries hard to write at least slightly more than the average number of department tickets per month. With everyone trying to beat the average, it doesn't take a mathematical genius to see that the average is likely to increase over time, and thus, average-beating becomes an important contributing factor to the rise in the number of tickets issued each year.

Ticket fighters are also faced with the systematic effort to remove from traffic court any constitutional protections that stand in the way of a more "efficient" production of revenue. Every important right mentioned in the Bill of Rights—whose purpose is to protect the people from oppression by government —adds a financial cost to the system. Jury trials cost money. So, starting in 1968, California politicians began a quiet campaign to gradually eliminate all procedural rights that interfered with the revenue-raising aspects of the traffic-enforcement system. The Legislature did this by creating a new category of crime known as the "infraction." Before that, offenses were either felonies or misdemeanors.

Anyone charged with either could, and often did, demand a trial by jury. The "infraction" was a new type of category for which no jury trial was allowed, even if demanded by the accused. As a trade-off, the law provided that no one could be imprisoned for conviction of an infraction.[7]

At first, only parking violations were classified as infractions. Then, when no one objected (or even noticed), running a stoplight was also defined as an infraction. No one objected to that either. Finally, the right to a jury trial was taken away from a whole list of common traffic offenses.[8] Indeed, all but a few of the most serious traffic offenses (e.g., drunk or reckless driving, drag racing) were classified as infractions. Again, few people complained; apparently, most never realized that they had lost a valuable right.[9] The right of an indigent person to the free services of a court-appointed attorney to defend against an infraction was also taken away. Then, the Legislature passed a law that allowed lower-paid non-judges to hear traffic cases. Appeals courts quickly rubber-stamped it.[10]

---

[7]PC § 19.6. In practice, only repeat offenders ever went to jail anyway, when all traffic offenses were misdemeanors. Repeat offenders can still go to jail today, since Vehicle Code section 40000.28 allows a person accused of a fourth infraction in a year to have a traffic offense charged as a misdemeanor. Thus, nothing has really changed, and the system's supposed trade-off of taking away the right to jury trial, in exchange for a guarantee of not going to jail, is a pretense.

[8]See PC § 19.6, whose removal of trial by jury was rubber-stamped by the appellate courts in *People v. Oppenheimer* (1974) 42 Cal.App.3d Supp. 4.

[9]The right to a trial by an impartial jury is more important than you might think. Judges, prosecutors, and even many defense attorneys often assume that the accused person is really guilty. Their years of experience dealing with criminals often sours them into thinking that nearly everyone must be guilty, or else why would they have been arrested? Although some people selected as jurors also have this attitude, it tends to be more widespread among people in the legal profession. ["The purpose of trial by jury is to prevent oppression by the Government by providing a safeguard ... against the compliant, biased, or eccentric judge." *Apodaca v. Oregon* (1972) 406 U.S. 404, 406.] Furthermore, the possibility that an accused defendant may opt for a jury trial in the face of a known "hanging judge," may itself serve as a check on such judges.

[10]*People v. Lucas* (1978) 82 Cal.App.3d 47. Similarly, appointed non-judges (who don't even have to be lawyers) may hear juvenile traffic cases despite any objections. *In re Kathy C.* (1979) 25 Cal.3d 91.

Even rights that don't cost the system very much have been ruled inapplicable to traffic matters. Appeals courts have ruled that the double-jeopardy clause of the Constitution, and a state law prohibiting multiple prosecutions for the same act, don't apply to infractions.[11] Neither does the right against self-incrimination. No police officer who stops you is required to tell you that you have a right to refuse to answer his questions, and can use any of your admissions against you. Hardened criminals get the benefit of "Miranda" warnings, but you the law-abiding citizen, are undeserving of such niceties.[12] This is true even though California law defines a traffic stop as an "arrest."[13]. Finally, the California Supreme Court, picking up where the politicians left off, decreed that the state doesn't even have to pay prosecuting attorneys to appear in traffic cases.[14] Since facing a prosecutor in traffic court is certainly no fun, even fewer people objected, failing to realize that the mere presence of a prosecutor reminds the judge that he or she is the neutral party whose job is to evenhandedly apply justice. Without prosecutors, traffic judges—in what is often a misguided desire to be helpful to the police— frequently help officers who neglect to testify to all the necessary elements of the offense. For example, the judge will ask (remind) the officer to testify that he was driving a marked patrol car and wearing his uniform, or that an engineering and traffic survey allowing the use of radar speed enforcement on a particular road has been conducted. In this way, the judge in a very real sense becomes prosecutor as well. With prosecuting attorneys gone from traffic court, many judges have indeed assumed the prosecutorial roles themselves—a concept completely foreign to the Anglo-American legal tradition, and

[11]*In re Dennis B.* (1976) 18 Cal.3d 687; *People v. Battle* (1975) 50 Cal.App.3d Supp. 1.

[12]*Berkemer v. McCarty* (1984) 468 U.S. 420, 104 S.Ct. 3138.

[13]VC §§ 40500-40502, 40504; *People v. Superior Court* (1972) 7 Cal.3d 186, 200.

[14]*People v. Carlucci* (1979) 23 Cal.3d 249 and *People v. Daggett* (1988) 206 Cal.App.3d Supp. 1. And, in *People v. Municipal Court* (1990) __ Cal.App.3d __, __ Cal.Rptr. __, an appeals court ruled that a traffic court judge may not insist that a prosecutor assigned to the court handle traffic cases.

actually more in line with the role of the Iranian mullahs and Russian commissars who run their respective kangaroo courts.

Most of us have been led to believe that any excesses of the system can be corrected by an appeal if you lose. Unfortunately, this is almost always a false hope. Appeals courts will only reverse cases on technicalities, and never on the basis that the judge should have believed you and your witnesses rather than an untruthful police officer. Appeals court judges will always rubber-stamp traffic-court judges' "findings of fact," on the basis that the trial judge, who observed the defendant, police officer, and other witnesses testify, was best able to tell who was telling the truth. (This will happen no matter how many believable witnesses supported your version of events, or how evasive and self-contradictory the officer was.) The rule that allows appeals courts to do this (called the "substantial evidence standard"), was originally adopted to prevent elitist English-trained judges from overturning common-sense verdicts of juries. Today, though, where the right to trial by jury has been taken away, it makes little sense, and simply shields dishonest judges from any meaningful scrutiny.

What it boils down to, is that appeals courts won't second-guess traffic court judges, who in turn don't want to think of themselves as second-guessing the police officer who writes you a ticket. Only you, the driver, get your driving conduct second-guessed—by the officer, the judge, and the appeals court.

The point is, that over the years, it's become too convenient for those in power to "economize" and "streamline" a system that generates a lot of money and deals with a lot of people. Mostly over the last 20 years, your rights have been whittled away, one at a time, as if the Bill of Rights had been repealed. (These days, procedural rights and due process seem to be reserved for murderers and rapists.) What started out as a legitimate offshoot from the criminal justice system, designed to correct the behavior of errant motorists and to deter dangerous drivers, has unfortunately degenerated in the past two decades into an assembly-line that grinds up your constitutional rights and spits out money into government coffers, at little overhead cost. Today, your rights consist mostly of hoping your case will be dismissed if the officer doesn't show up for trial. If he does, you have the right to present your case to a judge who more than likely wants you to hurry up and speak your piece so he can find you guilty, have the clerk collect your fine, call the next case, and finish up in court—perhaps in time for his luncheon speech to the local peace officers' association—before whom he can kneel and beg for endorsements and campaign contributions in the upcoming election.

In the case of *People v. Daggett* (1988) 206 Cal. App.3d Supp. 1, two out of three judges predictably ruled that in traffic cases, no prosecutor need be present, and that the judge can assist in presenting the government's case. The third judge stated this leads to "the inescapable conclusion that the court is, or at least appears to be, both the prosecutor and the court, rather than being impartial." He continued, "The people of this country have fought hard against a police state. Their success should not be erased by elimination of an adversary trial. Actually, traffic court is one of our most important venues. To a large part of our population, this will be their only contact with the justice system. They are certainly going to wonder what happened to the impartial, blind Miss Justice and the doctrine of separation of powers."

This "police state" reference is no exaggeration. One woman who did nothing more than refuse to enter a plea in traffic court was ordered by the judge to submit to examination by two psychiatrists. She went through 17 hearings and was forced to hire a third psychiatrist herself before she was declared competent.[15] The judge should have simply entered a not-guilty plea on her behalf and set her case for trial. (Not too different from the Stalinist practice of declaring political dissidents "insane" and locking them in psychiatric hospitals.) As was shown most

dramatically in Romania, and somewhat less dramatically in East Germany and Czechoslovakia, it is not so much a nation's military that is to be feared in a nation, but rather the nation's police. Today our traffic courts are more an instrument of the police than a bulwark between the police and the citizenry.

How would a fair traffic violation scheme work? A good start would be to instruct the police to hand out citations only where there was a clear violation of the law that either resulted in rudeness to another driver (or bicyclist or pedestrian) or caused a dangerous situation. Officers now hiding behind bushes with radar guns could be instructed to look for drunk drivers instead.

A traffic-enforcement system can serve a valid purpose. We all know of people who drive carelessly or dangerously, who legitimately deserve to be deterred before they injure or kill someone. Unfortunately, our current system utterly fails to distinguish between this sort of individual, and one who innocently violates a rule in a book without creating any danger to himself or others.

To achieve a better system in this regard, we almost surely must start by having money collected from fines go some place other than to the government entities—cities and counties—which must raise the money to pay the police and maintain the courts. As long as everyone knows that more fines mean more police cars, radar units, and more luxurious courthouses, the unholy alliance of politicians, judges, and police officers going after your fine money will never abate.

Another measure of fairness would be allow for jury trials, at least for those violations that are reported to the Department of Motor Vehicles and can be used as a basis for suspending your license. (Not parking or equipment violations.) How would this work? Why not the same way it does with traffic cases in some Eastern and New England states? A person accused of a moving traffic violation would first have a non-jury trial. If he lost and was dissatisfied with the way he was treated, he could "appeal" for a new trial, in superior court, where he could request a jury.

[15]See *Furey v. Commission on Judicial Performance* (1987) 43 Cal.3d 1297, 240 Cal.Rptr. 859.

But wouldn't this hopelessly tie up the courts? I don't think so. Jury trials are time-consuming and difficult; it is for this very reason that even before 1968, when everyone accused of a traffic violation was allowed the option of a jury trial at the outset, few people actually opted for one. Even so, the possibility that a traffic defendant treated unfairly by a traffic judge may appeal for a new trial—by jury—may keep judges a little more honest. In fact, judges could be evaluated based on the number of appeals they generated; a consistently arbitrary judge whose unfair decisions provoke an unusually high number of such appeals for trials by jury, could be given a different assignment—or perhaps tossed out of office.

While we're on the subject of new trials, you may recall that we noted earlier that the law allows traffic courts to hear cases in writing, by written declarations. If you lose a trial by declaration, you have the right to a regular trial. The problem is, very few courts have adopted this optional procedure. Most courts, it seems, would rather put you through the inconvenience of going to the courthouse several times—perhaps also driving hundreds of miles in the process if you were cited well away from home—as a price for fighting a ticket. Is this really necessary? Why not amend the law to require all courts to provide this trial-by-mail option?

Another reform would be to allow a defendant to opt between a "formal" hearing—at which a prosecuting attorney (or even a volunteer law student) would prosecute the case, to keep the judicial and prosecutorial functions separate, and an "informal" hearing that would be handled much as traffic cases are now. This idea isn't new; in license-suspension proceedings, the Department of Motor Vehicles always offers the driver the choice between "formal" and "informal" hearings. Let the defendant choose between a prosecutorless forum where the judge might be more inclined to assist the officer, and a more formal one with a prosecutor which, although perhaps more intimidating, at least keeps the prosecution and judicial roles separate.

Finally, how about an appeals court system that honestly looks at whether the defendant was really guilty, and not one that blindly rubber-stamps convictions based on the weakest of evidence? Let's have a system of appeals courts that thrives not just on technicalities, on arguments akin to the number of angels that can dance on the head of a pin. Appeals court judges should have the guts to decide cases on the real issues.[16]

In other words, as we celebrate the 200th anniversary of the Bill of Rights (adopted in 1791 as the first 10 amendments to the U.S. Constitution), let's resolve to bring the fairness and justice envisioned in it, back into the traffic court process. Let's work for the recall and election defeat of judges who think the Constitution is just for vicious criminals, but not for law-abiding folks who wind up in traffic court once in awhile. And above all, let's fight that ticket vigorously at every stage, putting on the best case we can while noting all along how the basic unfairness and corruption of the System works against us. If a majority of people charged with moving violations (not to mention parking violations) believed that they were unfairly singled out, and so fought their tickets—demanding in the process even the few rights that remain—the present system would collapse, and good riddance. It's probably only by completely getting rid of the travesty we now call a traffic court system that drastic changes can be made.

Have I rambled for a long time? I guess I have. But now it's your turn. If you have any ideas and comments on how you would like to see traffic laws and court procedures changed, let me know. You can write down your thoughts and mail them to me at 1201 Ninth Street, Monterey, California 93940.

---

[16]Under CCP § 909, appellate courts have full authority to reverse factual findings of trial judges in non-jury cases. Unfortunately, few appeals judges care (or even know) about this.

CODE SECTION INDEX

Vehicle Code

Code	Section
235	5/5
275	5/10
360	4/2, 5/3
365	2/4
440	2/4
515	2/4, 5/5
627	4/4, 11/13
1803	3/3, 3/12, 5/16, 5/17, 6/9, 10/5, 16/7
1803.3	16/7
1803.5	10/5
1807	3/3
1808	3/3
1808.7	10/5
4000-9982	3/14-3/15
4760	15/11
5602	15/11
11357	7/2
12500	7/4, 10/15, 10/28
12500-15028	3/14-3/15
12807	14/3, 15/10, 15/11
12808	7/10, 15/11
12810	3/3, 15/2
12810.2	6/10
12810.5	3/3, 15/2
13200	7/4, 7/6
13202	5/17
13202-13202.5	3/14-3/15
13202.5	5/7, 5/17
13350	7/4, 15/7, 15/8
13351	15/8
13352	7/6, 8/8-8/10, 8/11, 15/7, 15/8
13352.5	8/8-8/10, 15/8
13353	8/15, 8/22, 8/24, 15/6
13354	8/22
13355	15/8
13358	8/22
13360	15/2
13361	15/2

Code	Section
13363	15/2
13365	7/10, 15/10
13555	7/3
13800	15/2
13950	15/2, 15/3
13952	15/3
14100	15/2, 15/3
14101	15/2, 15/3
14103	15/2
14105.5	15/4
14104	15/3
14250	15/4
14250.5	15/4
14401	15/5
14601	7/3
14601-14601.2	7/10
14601.1	7/11, 10/28
14601.2	7/11, 14/4
15000	3/12
15022	3/12
15023	3/12
16000	15/9
16000-16560	3/14-3/15
16002	15/9
16004	15/9
16028	5/18, 15/10
16029	5/18, 15/10
16030	5/18, 15/10
16034	5/18
16050.5	5/19, 15/9
16052-16056	15/10
16070	15/9
16072	15/9
16075	5/19, 15/10
16076-16078	15/9
16250-16381	15/11
20001	3/3
20002	15/2
21200	6/9
21212	6/9
21000-23336	3/14-3/15
21451	5/8
21452	5/3

Code	Section
21453	5/3, 5/8, 11/22, 11/25
21460	5/5
21654	2/4, 5/10
21650	6/9
21650.1	6/9
21655.5-21655.8	5/14
21656	5/12
21658	5/13
21703	5/12
21750	5/14
21751	5/14
21752	5/14
21754	5/14
21755	5/14
21800	5/8
21801	5/9
21802	5/9, 16/5
21803	5/9
21950	5/10, 6/8
21951	5/10
21952	5/10
21953	6/8
21954	6/8
21955	6/8
22100	5/4
22100-22106	5/3, 11/23, 11/25-11/26
22100.5	5/5
22101	4/4, 5/4
22102	5/5
22102-22105	5/5
22103	2/3, 5/5
22105	5/5
22106	5/6
22107	5/6
22108	5/6
22109	5/6
22110	5/6
22348	3/8
22348-22413	3/14
22349	4/13, 11/16, 11/24

Code	Section
22350	4/2, 4/13, 10/13, 11/16, 11/24-11/25, 12/4, 16/8
22351	4/2, 4/3
22352	4/2, 4/5
22356	4/13
22400	5/11, 5/12
22405	4/12
22450	5/2, 11/22-11/23, 11/25
22651	6/2
22651.7	6/2
23103	7/3-7/4, 10/15, 15/2
23103-23109	3/14-3/15
23103.5	8/5, 8/9, 8/25
23104	7/3, 7/4
23109	7/3, 7/5-7/6
23140	5/17
23141-23144	5/17
23151-23229	3/14-3/15
23152	8/3, 8/5-8/7, 8/8, 8/9, 8/14, 8/20, 8/23
23153	3/2, 8/7, 8/9, 8/20
23155	8/5, 8/14
23157	8/15, 8/16, 15/6
23157.5	8/17, 15/6
23158	8/17, 8/19
23159	8/16, 8/24
23160	8/8
23161	8/8
23165	8/9, 14/4
23166	8/9
23167	8/9
23170	8/9
23171	8/9
23175	8/7, 8/9
23176	8/9
23180	8/7, 8/10
23181	8/10
23185	8/7, 8/10
23186	8/10
23190	8/7, 8/11

23194	8/10
23195	8/8, 8/9
23196	8/8, 8/10
23198	8/9
23201	8/5, 17/9
23208	8/10
23212	8/25
23220	5/16, 5,17
23220-23240	3/14
23221	5/17
23222	5/15-5/17
23223	5/17
23224	5/17
23225	5/16, 5/17
23226	5/15, 5/17
23229	5/17
24000-28085	3/14-3/15
24002	3/9, 6/5
24004	3/9
24250	3/9
24409	3/9
24604	3/9
24800	3/9
25103	3/9
26707	3/9
27151	3/9
27315	3/9, 6/10
27360	3/9, 6/10
27800	3/9
27801	3/9
40000.28	6/8, 7/11-7/12, 10/29
40200	6/2
40200.1-40200.6	6/3
40202	6/2
40206.5	6/3, 6/4
40207	6/3
40208-40210	15/11
40215	6/3, 6/4
40221	6/4
40225	6/7
40230	6/4
40300.5	2/6
40302	2/5, 2/6, 17/14
40303	17/14
40303.5	6/5, 6/6

40305	3/12
40309	6/4
40500	2/5, 10/20
40500-40502	10/24, 18/5
40501	2/5
40502	10/29, 10/32, 16/4, 17/10-17/11
40503	2/3
40504	18/5
40507	4/7
40508	7/6-7/10, 10/15, 10/28, 13/2, 13/13, 14/3
40508-40509	3/12-3/13
40509	7/10, 14/3, 15/10, 15/11
40513	2/6, 10/18, 10/19
40519	6/3, 10/10, 10/11
40522	6/5, 6/6, 6/8
40600	2/6, 10/19
40600-40604	10/21, 17/17
40601	2/6, 16/4
40603	2/6, 10/18
40604	2/6
40610	5/7, 6/5, 6/7
40616	6/7
40801	4/4
40801-40805	16/4
40802	4/3, 4/5-4/7, 4/14, 11/20
40802-40805	4/13
40803	4/5, 6/12, 11/13, 12/7, 12/8, 16/4
40804	4/5, 11/14
40805	4/5, 11/13
40834	9/3
40902	6/3, 10/3, 10/7, 10/9
40908	10/10
41102	6/2, 6/4, 15/11
41600-41603	18/3
42001	6/8
42001.11	5/14
42002	6/3, 7/3, 14/2
42003	7/3, 14/3
42004	14/2, 16/6
42004.5	14/5

42005	10/5, 14/4
42006	6/8, 6/9, 18/3
42200	18/3
42201	18/3

Penal Code

16	2/4, 4/11
17	7/7, 7/8, 7/11, 10/28, 13/3
19.6	9/9, 12/5, 18/4
19.7	4/11, 10/14, 12/5, 16/6
19.8	7/7, 7/8, 7/11, 13.3
20	2/4, 4/11
148	7/4
192	15/2
594	5/17
647	5/17
654	4/13
664	8/7
825	13/3
834	2/5
849.5	2/5
949	10/18
990	13/3
1003	10/19, 10/24, 10/28
1006	10/19, 10/24, 10/28
1192.7	8/25
1202	14/2
1203.4	7/3
1203.4a	7/3
1328	11/5, 11/8
1382	10/16, 10/30, 10/46, 16/4
1449	12/11, 14/1, 14/5, 14/6, 16/6
1462.2	10/11, 10/29, 10/32, 10/36, 16/15
1463	18/3
1464	3/4, 6/9, 18/3
1465	3/4, 6/9, 18/3
1466	16/8
1538.5	8/27, 10/30

Business & Professions Code

25662	5/17

Code of Civil Procedure

117.24	15/11
170.1	16/5
170.3	10/37
170.6	10/36, 16/34
223	13/6
909	18/7
1013	16/13
1094.5	15/5

Evidence Code

607	4/3
720	16/5

Goverment Code

23600	16/4, 17/11
76011	3/5
76011-76580	6/9, 18/3
76012	3/5
76013	3/5
76020-76580	3/5

Health & Safety Code

11357	5/17, 7/2

California Rules of Court

9	16/14
15	16/14
104	16/22
105	16/14
182	16/7, 16/8
184	16/9
185	16/13
187	16/13
187.5	16/9, 16/13
980	16/9

United States Code & Federal Regulations

18 U.S.C. § 13	6/11
36 C.F.R. § 4	6/11

INDEX

ESTATE PLANNING & PROBATE

Plan Your Estate With a Living Trust
Attorney Denis Clifford
National 1st Edition
This book covers every significant aspect of estate planning and gives detailed specific, instructions for preparing a living trust, a document that lets your family avoid expensive and lengthy probate court proceedings after your death. *Plan Your Estate* includes all the tear-out forms and step-by-step instructions to let you prepare an estate plan designed for your special needs.
$19.95/NEST

Nolo's Simple Will Book
Attorney Denis Clifford
National 2nd Edition
It's easy to write a legally valid will using this book. The instructions and forms enable people to draft a will for all needs, including naming a personal guardian for minor children, leaving property to minor children or young adults and updating a will when necessary. Good in all states except Louisiana.
$17.95/SWIL

The Power of Attorney Book
Attorney Denis Clifford
National 3rd Edition
Who will take care of your affairs, and make your financial and medical decisions if you can't? With this book you can appoint someone you trust to carry out your wishes and stipulate exactly what kind of care you want or don't want. Includes Durable Power of Attorney and Living Will Forms.
$19.95/POA

How to Probate an Estate
Julia Nissley
California 5th Edition
If you find yourself responsible for winding up the legal and financial affairs of a deceased family member or friend, you can often save costly attorneys' fees by handling the probate process yourself. This book shows you the simple procedures you can use to transfer assets that don't require probate, including property held in joint tenancy or living trusts or as community property.
$29.95/PAE

The Conservatorship Book
Lisa Goldoftas & Attorney Carolyn Farren
California 1st Edition
When a family member or close relative becomes incapacitated due to illness or age, it may be necessary to name a conservator for taking charge of their medical and financial affairs. *The Conservatorship Book* will help you determine when and what kind of conservatorship is necessary. The book comes with complete instructions and all the forms necessary to file conservatorship documents, appear in court, be appointed conservator and end a conservatorship when it is no longer necessary.
$24.95/CNSV

GOING TO COURT

Everybody's Guide to Small Claims Court
Attorney Ralph Warner
National 4th Edition
California 9th Edition
These books will help you decide if you should sue in small claims court, show you how to file and serve papers, tell you what to bring to court and how to collect a judgment.
National $14.95/NSCC
California $14.95/ CSCC

Dog Law
Attorney Mary Randolph
National 1st Edition
Dog Law is a practical guide to the laws that affect dog owners and their neighbors. You'll find answers to common questions on such topics as biting, barking, veterinarians and more.
$12.95/DOG

Fight Your Ticket
Attorney David Brown
California 4th Edition
This book shows you how to fight an unfair traffic ticket—when you're stopped, at arraignment, at trial and on appeal.
$17.95/FYT

Collect Your Court Judgment
Gini Graham Scott, Attorney Stephen Elias & Lisa Goldoftas
California 1st Edition
This book contains step-by-step instructions and all the forms you need to collect a court judgment from the debtor's bank accounts, wages, business receipts, real estate or other assets.
$24.95/JUDG

How to Change Your Name
Attorneys David Loeb & David Brown
California 5th Edition
This book explains how to change your name legally and provides all the necessary court forms with detailed instructions on how to fill them out.
$19.95/NAME

The Criminal Records Book
Attorney Warren Siegel
California 3rd Edition
This book shows you step-by-step how to seal criminal records, dismiss convictions, destroy marijuana records and reduce felony convictions.
$19.95/CRIM

MONEY MATTERS

Money Troubles: Legal Strategies to Cope With Your Debts

Attorney Robin Leonard
National 1st Edition

Are you behind on your credit card bills or loan payments? If you are, then *Money Troubles* is exactly what you need. Covering everything from knowing what your rights are—and asserting them to helping you evaluate your individual situation, this practical, straightforward book is for anyone who needs help understanding and dealing with the complex and often scary topic of debts.
$16.95/MT

How to File for Bankruptcy

Attorneys Stephen Elias, Albin Renauer & Robin Leonard
National 2nd Edition

Trying to decide whether or not filing for bankruptcy makes sense? *How to File for Bankruptcy* contains an overview of the process and all the forms plus step-by-step instructions on the procedures to follow.
$24.95/HFB

Simple Contracts for Personal Use

Attorney Stephen Elias
National 2nd Edition

This book contains clearly written legal form contracts to buy and sell property, borrow and lend money, store and lend personal property, release others from personal liability, or pay a contractor to do home repairs. Includes agreements to arrange child care and contract with caterers, photographers and other service providers for special events.
$16.95/CONT

FAMILY MATTERS

The Living Together Kit

Attorneys Toni Ihara & Ralph Warner
National 6th Edition

The Living Together Kit is a detailed guide designed to help the increasing number of unmarried couples living together understand the laws that affect them. Sample agreements and instructions are included.
$17.95/LTK

A Legal Guide for Lesbian and Gay Couples

Attorneys Hayden Curry & Denis Clifford
National 5th Edition

Laws designed to regulate and protect unmarried couples don't apply to lesbian and gay couples. This book shows you step-by-step how to write a living-together contract, plan for medical emergencies, and plan your estates. Includes forms, sample agreements and lists of both national lesbian and gay legal organizations, and AIDS organizations.
$17.95/LG

The Guardianship Book

Lisa Goldoftas & Attorney David Brown
California 1st Edition

The Guardianship Book provides step-by-step instructions and the forms needed to obtain a legal guardianship without a lawyer.
$19.95/GB

How to Do Your Own Divorce

Attorney Charles Sherman
(Texas Ed. by Sherman & Simons)
California 16th Edition & Texas 2nd Edition

These books contain all the forms and instructions you need to do your divorce without a lawyer.
California $18.95/CDIV
Texas $14.95/TDIV

Practical Divorce Solutions

Attorney Charles Sherman
California 2nd Edition

This book is a valuable guide to the emotional aspects of divorce as well as an overview of the legal and financial decisions that must be made.
$12.95/PDS

How to Adopt Your Stepchild in California

Frank Zagone & Attorney Mary Randolph
California 3rd Edition

There are many emotional, financial and legal reasons to adopt a stepchild, but among the most pressing legal reasons is the need to avoid confusion over inheritance or guardianship. This book provides sample forms and step-by-step instructions for completing a simple uncontested adoption by a stepparent
$19.95/ADOP

California Marriage & Divorce Law

Attorneys Ralph Warner, Toni Ihara & Stephen Elias
California 10th Edition

This book explains community property, pre-nuptial contracts, foreign marriages, buying a house, getting a divorce, dividing property, and more.
$17.95/MARR

OLDER AMERICANS

Elder Care: Choosing & Financing Long-Term Care

Attorney Joseph Matthews
National 1st Edition

This book will guide you in choosing and paying for long-term care, alerting you to practical concerns and explaining laws that may affect your decisions.
$16.95/ELD

Social Security, Medicare & Pensions
Attorney Joseph Matthews with Dorothy Matthews Berman
National 5th Edition
This book contains invaluable guidance through the current maze of rights and benefits for those 55 and over, including Medicare, Medicaid and Social Security retirement and disability benefits and age discrimination protections.
$15.95/SOA

BUSINESS

How to Write a Business Plan
Mike McKeever
National 3rd Edition
If you're thinking of starting a business or raising money to expand an existing one, this book will show you how to write the business plan and loan package necessary to finance your business and make it work.
$17.95/SBS

Marketing Without Advertising
Michael Phillips & Salli Rasberry
National 1st Edition
This book outlines practical steps for building and expanding a small business without spending a lot of money on advertising.
$14.00/MWA

The Partnership Book
Attorneys Denis Clifford & Ralph Warner
National 4th Edition
This book shows you step-by-step how to write a solid partnership agreement that meets your needs. It covers initial contributions to the business, wages, profit-sharing, buy-outs, death or retirement of a partner and disputes.
$24.95/PART

How to Form Your Own Nonprofit Corporation
Attorney Anthony Mancuso
National 1st Edition
This book explains the legal formalities involved and provides detailed information on the differences in the law among 50 states. It also contains forms for the Articles, Bylaws and Minutes you need, along with complete instructions for obtaining federal 501 (c) (3) tax exemptions and qualifying for public charity status.
$24.95/NNP

The California Nonprofit Corporation Handbook
Attorney Anthony Mancuso
California 5th Edition
This book shows you step-by-step how to form and operate a nonprofit corporation in California. It includes the latest corporate and tax law changes, and the forms for the Articles, Bylaws and Minutes.
$29.95/NON

How to Form Your Own Corporation
Attorney Anthony Mancuso
California 7th Edition
New York 2nd Edition
Florida 3rd Edition
These books contain the forms, instructions and tax information you need to incorporate a small business yourself and save hundreds of dollars in lawyers' fees.
California $29.95/CCOR
New York $24.95/NYCO
Florida $24.95/FLCO

The California Professional Corporation Handbook
Attorney Anthony Mancuso
California 4th Edition
Health care professionals, lawyers, accountants and members of certain other professions must fulfill special requirements when forming a corporation in California. This book contains up-to-date tax information plus all the forms and instructions necessary to form a California professional corporation.
$34.95/PROF

The Independent Paralegal's Handbook
Attorney Ralph Warner
National 2nd Edition
The Independent Paralegal's Handbook provides legal and business guidelines for those who want to take routine legal work out of the law office and offer it for a reasonable fee in an independent business.
$19.95/PARA

Getting Started as an Independent Paralegal
(Two Audio Tapes)
Attorney Ralph Warner
National 1st Edition
Approximately three hours in all, these tapes are a carefully edited version of a seminar given by *Nolo Press* founder Ralph Warner. They are designed to be used with *The Independent Paralegal's Handbook.*
$24.95/GSIP

PATENT, COPYRIGHT & TRADEMARK

Patent It Yourself
Attorney David Pressman
National 2nd Edition
From the patent search to the actual application, this book covers everything from use and licensing, successful marketing and how to deal with infringement.
$29.95/PAT

The Inventor's Notebook
Fred Grissom & Attorney David Pressman
National 1st Edition
This book helps you document the process of successful independent inventing by providing forms, instructions, references to relevant areas of patent law, a bibliography of legal and non-legal aids and more.
$19.95/INOT

How to Copyright Software
Attorney M.J. Salone
National 3rd Edition
This book tells you how to register your copyright for maximum protection and discusses who owns a copyright on software developed by more than one person.
$39.95/COPY

RESEARCH & REFERENCE

Legal Research
Attorney Stephen Elias
National 2nd Edition
A valuable tool on its own or as a companion to just about every other Nolo book. This book gives easy-to-use, step-by-step instructions on how to find legal information.
$14.95/LRES

Family Law Dictionary
Attorneys Robin Leonard & Stephen Elias
National 2nd Edition
Finally, a legal dictionary that's written in plain English, not "legalese"! *The Family Law Dictionary* is designed to help the nonlawyer who has a question or problem involving family law—marriage, divorce, adoption or living together.
$13.95/FLD

Patent, Copyright & Trademark: The Intellectual Property Law Dictionary
Attorney Stephen Elias
National 1st Edition
This book explains the terms associated with trade secrets, copyrights, trademarks, patents and contracts.
$19.95/IPLD

Legal Research Made Easy: A Roadmap Through the Law Library Maze
2-1/2 hr. videotape and 40-page manual
Nolo Press/Legal Star Communications
If you're a law student, paralegal or librarian—or just want to look up the law for yourself—this video is for you. University of California law professor Bob Berring explains how to use all the basic legal research tools in your local law library with an easy-to-follow six-step research plan and a sense of humor.
$89.95/LRME

HOMEOWNERS

How to Buy a House in California
Attorney Ralph Warner, Ira Serkes & George Devine
California 1st Edition
This book shows you how to find a house, work with a real estate agent, make an offer and negotiate intelligently. Includes information on all types of mortgages as well as private financing options.
$18.95/BHC

For Sale By Owner
George Devine
California 1st Edition
For Sale By Owner provides essential information about pricing your house, marketing it, writing a contract and going through escrow.
$24.95/FSBO

The Deeds Book
Attorney Mary Randolph
California 1st Edition
If you own real estate, you'll need to sign a new deed when you transfer the property or put it in trust as part of your estate planning. This book shows you how to find the right kind of deed, complete the tear-out forms and record them in the county recorder's public records.
$15.95/DEED

Homestead Your House
Attorneys Ralph Warner, Charles Sherman & Toni Ihara
California 7th Edition
This book shows you how to file a Declaration of Homestead and includes complete instructions and tear-out forms.
$9.95/HOME

LANDLORDS & TENANTS

The Landlord's Law Book: Rights & Responsibilities
Attorneys David Brown & Ralph Warner
California 3rd Edition
This book contains information on deposits, leases and rental agreements, inspections (tenant's privacy rights), habitability (rent withholding), ending a tenancy, liability and rent control.
$29.95/LBRT

The Landlord's Law Book: Evictions
Attorney David Brown
California 3rd Edition
Updated for 1991, this book will show you step-by-step how to go to court and get an eviction for a tenant who won't pay rent—and won't leave. Contains all the tear-out forms and necessary instructions.
$29.95/LBEV

Tenant's Rights
Attorneys Myron Moskovitz & Ralph Warner
California 10th Edition
This book explains the best way to handle your relationship both your landlord and your legal rights when you find yourself in disagreement. A special section on rent control cities is included.
$15.95/CTEN

LEGAL REFORM

Legal Breakdown: 40 Ways to Fix Our Legal System
Nolo Press Editors and Staff
National 1st Edition
Legal Breakdown presents 40 common sense proposals to make our legal system fairer, faster, cheaper and more accessible. It explains such things as why we should abolish probate, take divorce out of court, treat jurors better and give them more power, and make a host of other fundamental changes.
$8.95/LEG

CONSUMER MATTERS

Barbara Kaufman's Consumer Action Guide

Barbara Kaufman
California 1st Edition
This practical "how-go" handbook overflows with useful information on hundreds of topics. Barbara Kaufman, the Bay Area's award-winning host and producer of KCBS Radio's *Call for Action,* gives California consumers access to their legal rights, providing addresses and phone numbers of where to complain when things go wrong and recommending other resources if more help is necessary.
$14.95/CAG

SOFTWARE

WillMaker

Nolo Press/Legisoft
National 4th Edition
This easy-to-use software program lets you prepare and update a legal will—safely, privately and without the expense of a lawyer. Leading you step-by-step in a question-and-answer format, *WillMaker* builds a will around your answers, taking into account your state of residence. *WillMaker* comes with a 200-page legal manual which provides the legal background necessary to make sound choices. Good in all states except Louisiana.
IBM PC
(3-1/2 & 5-1/4 disks included) $69.95/WI4
MACINTOSH $69.95/WM4

For the Record

Carol Pladsen & Attorney Ralph Warner
National 2nd Edition
For the Record program provides a single place to keep a complete inventory of all your important legal, financial, personal and family records. It can compute your net worth and also create inventories of all insured property to protect your assets in the event of fire or theft. Includes a 200-page manual filled with practical and legal advice.
IBM PC
(3-1/2 & 5-1/4 disks included) $59.95/FRI2
MACINTOSH $59.95/FRM2

California Incorporator

Attorney Anthony Mancuso/Legisoft
California 1st Edition
Answer the questions on the screen and this software program will print out the 35-40 pages of documents you need to make your California corporation legal. Comes with a 200-page manual which explains the incorporation process.
IBM PC
(3-1/2 & 5-1/4 disks included)
$129.00/INCI

How to Form Your Own New York Corporation & How to Form Your Own Texas Corporation

Computer Editions
Attorney Anthony Mancuso
These book/software packages contain the instructions and tax information and forms you need to incorporate a small business and save hundreds of dollars in lawyers' fees. All organizational forms are on disk. Both come with a 250-page manual.
New York 1st Edition
IBM PC 5-1/4 $69.95/ NYCI
IBM PC 3-1/2 $69.95/ NYC3I
MACINTOSH $69.95/ NYCM
Texas 1st Edition
IBM PC 5-1/4 $69.95/ TCI
IBM PC 3-1/2 $69.95/ TC3I
MACINTOSH $69.95/ TCM

The California Nonprofit Corporation Handbook

(computer edition)
Attorney Anthony Mancuso
California 1st Edition
This book/software package shows you step-by-step how to form and operate a nonprofit corporation in California. Included on disk are the forms for the Articles, Bylaws and Minutes.
IBM PC 5-1/4 $69.95/ NPI
IBM PC 3-1/2 $69.95/ NP3I
MACINTOSH $69.95/ NPM

JUST FOR FUN

29 Reasons Not to Go to Law School

Attorneys Ralph Warner & Toni Ihara
National 3rd Edition
Filled with humor and piercing observations, this book can save you three years, $70,000 and your sanity.
$9.95/29R

Devil's Advocates: The Unnatural History of Lawyers

by Andrew & Jonathan Roth
National 1st Edition
This book is a painless and hilarious education, tracing the legal profession. Careful attention is given to the world's worst lawyers, most preposterous cases and most ludicrous courtroom strategies.
$12.95/DA

Poetic Justice: The Funniest, Meanest Things Ever Said About Lawyers

Edited by Jonathan & Andrew Roth
National 1st Edition
A great gift for anyone in the legal profession who has managed to maintain a sense of humor.
$8.95/PJ

VISIT OUR STORE

If you live in the Bay Area, be sure to visit the Nolo Press Bookstore on the corner of 9th & Parker Streets in West Berkeley. You'll find our complete line of books and software—new and "damaged"—all at a discount. We also have t-shirts, posters and a selection of business and legal self-help books from other publishers.

THE NOLO PRESS BOOKSTORE
950 Parker Street, Berkeley, California

Monday to Friday	10 a.m. to 5 p.m.
Thursdays	Until 6 p.m
Saturdays	10 a.m. to 4:30 p.m.
Sundays	10 a.m. to 3 p.m.

ORDER FORM

Name

Address (UPS to street address, Priority Mail to P.O. boxes)

Catalog Code	Quantity	Item	Unit price	Total
		Subtotal		
		Sales tax (California residents only)		
		Shipping & handling		
		2nd day UPS		
		TOTAL		
		PRICES SUBJECT TO CHANGE		

SALES TAX
California residents add your local tax:
6%, 6-1/2% or 7%

SHIPPING & HANDLING
$4.00   1 item
$5.00   2-3 items
+$.50   each additional item
Allow 2-3 weeks for delivery

IN A HURRY?
UPS 2nd day delivery is available:
Add $5.00 (contiguous states) or
$8.00 (Alaska & Hawaii) to your regular shipping and handling charges

FOR FASTER SERVICE, USE YOUR CREDIT CARD AND OUR TOLL-FREE NUMBERS:
Monday-Friday, 7 a.m. to 5 p.m. Pacific Time

US	1 (800) 992-6656
CA (outside 415 area code)	1 (800) 640-6656
(inside 415 area code)	549-1976
General Information	1 (415) 549-1976
Fax us your order	1 (415) 548-5902

METHOD OF PAYMENT
☐ Check enclosed
☐ VISA   ☐ Mastercard   ☐ Discover Card

Account #   Expiration Date

Signature

Phone

CCOR

N O L O   P R E S S   /   9 5 0   P A R K E R   S T R E E T   /   B E R K E L E Y   C A   9 4 7 1 0